MEMOIRS OF WILLIAM HICKEY

Vol. II

(1775-1782)

Joseph Hickey

From the picture by Angelica Kauffmann
in the National Portrait Gallery, Dublin.

MEMOIRS OF WILLIAM HICKEY

EDITED BY

ALFRED SPENCER

Vol. II

(1775–1782)

WITH THREE PHOTOGRAVURE PORTRAITS

EIGHTH EDITION

LONDON

HURST & BLACKETT, LTD.

PATERNOSTER HOUSE, E.C.

Printed in Great Britain at
The Mayflower Press, Plymouth.   William Brendon & Son, Ltd.

EDITOR'S NOTE

THE Editor regrets that the publication of this second instalment of the Memoirs of William Hickey has been so much delayed by the abnormal conditions occasioned by the War. He feels sure, however, that the great interest shown in the first portion already published will be revived by the present volume ; for in it Hickey covers an important period of his life, viz. from his twenty-sixth to his thirty-third year, and relates some of his most interesting and instructive experiences. There is sufficient material still remaining unpublished for a concluding volume, which the Editor expects to have ready shortly.

Those readers who have expressed a desire for information regarding the history of William Hickey's MS. may be interested to know that its ownership can be traced for a considerable number of years. It was as far back as 1880 that the MS. was first shown to the present owner by a very old friend who had received it with other effects on the death of a relative some fifteen years before that date. How this relative became possessed of the MS. is unknown, but quite possibly he obtained it from Hickey himself. It was given to the present owner by the executors of his friend, so its uninterrupted possession for at all events between fifty and sixty years is well established.

The references in the first volume to portraits of William Hickey and other members of the family were instrumental in bringing to light three portraits, two of them by Reynolds, both described as "Miss Hickey," but without any distinguishing Christian name ; they are apparently of an elder and a younger sister of William. There are indications, particularly in the dressing of the hair, that one of these paintings was executed much earlier than the other. Permission to reproduce them is gratefully acknowledged to the respective owners, the Right Hon. Frederick Leverton-Harris, M.P., and Mrs. Malkin ; also to Messrs. Thomas Agnew and Sons, the publishers of a mezzotint engraving of Mr. Leverton-Harris's picture. Although no portrait has as yet come to light of the author of these Memoirs, the Editor is able to include an interesting portrait of the author's father, Joseph Hickey, the friend of Burke and Goldsmith, from an oil painting by Angelica Kauffmann in the National Portrait Gallery, Dublin.

CONTENTS

ix

all the inns of Deal are wretched in comparison with those of every part of the Kentish road.

We had only twenty-four hours in the Downs when a light air from the northward tempted the fleet to weigh, seeing which I went off to the *New Shoreham* and found her just making sail. The whole fleet then stood down Channel.

The following morning the wind increased considerably, and before dark blew a gale, so that Captain Surman was afraid to venture carrying sail, and we lay to. At daylight not more than ten ships were in sight out of the great number that had left the Downs with us, and of those few three had signals of distress flying.

Before noon we discovered the French coast directly to leeward, it by that time blowing extremely hard. As an old cutter sailor, I knew our situation to be critical and dangerous, and evidently our Commander was seriously alarmed, as he declared the necessity of setting some sail as our only chance of clearing the land, and gave orders accordingly ; but so weakly were we manned, our crew consisting of no more than twenty-two, of whom half were landsmen, that some hours elapsed before we could effect close reefing and setting the topsails.

The gale continuing with unabated violence, we made little headway, driving bodily to leeward ; the sea ran dreadfully high, making the vessel labour and strain greatly. In this alarming situation we remained three days and nights.

On the fourth morning, being the 9th of the month, the French coast was seen trenching away as far forward as the lee bow, and at the same time the main topsail sheet giving way, the sail in a few seconds blew to pieces, where-upon Captain Surman exclaimed it was all over with us, and that within three hours we must be on shore. He was him-self as perfect a seaman as ever walked a deck, nor were his officers inferior in knowledge of their duty. These three persons, aided by the boatswain, whose name was Jerry Griffin, performed wonders. By their extraordinary exertions and spirited example a reefed mainsail was set, which happily stood, proving of more service than the topsail had been, so that we evidently made less leeway.

Griffin, the boatswain, was an uncommonly athletic and powerful man, upwards of six feet two inches high, of almost Herculean form, yet active as a deer. I early discovered him to be a strange and uncommon character.

We passed another anxious and miserable night. At daylight the land was still visible, though as far distant as the preceding day ; that is, about four leagues. At noon, in a severe gust, the mainsail and fore topsail both gave way in the same instant, the former blowing to atoms, but the latter, being a new sail, was saved, and soon reset.

Towards night in a very hard squall, the wind suddenly shifted to the south-west, whereupon Captain Surman determined to bear away for the Downs, in order to repair the serious damage sustained in the storm, particularly by the longboat, which a tremendous sea that broke on board had stove in. When running before the wind the ship rolled so deep that almost everything fetched way, and a dismal night I passed ; my spirits were, however, exhilarated at, just as the day broke, hearing the anchor let go, when leaving my cabin I went up on deck, and had the satisfaction to see the clouds had dispersed and that it was a fine morning.

As the sun rose the wind moderated and the sea decreased. My fellow-passenger, Mr. Byers, who had been so tortured by sea-sickness as to render him indifferent to all that was going on, now made his appearance, pale as death. I congratulated him upon our escape from shipwreck on the French coast, adding, " I suppose you will go on shore at Deal." To which, with some surprise, he answered, " Dear me, Sir, do you think of doing so ? I should be very glad could I venture." I replied, " Venture ! Why not, what's the risk ? I am determined to go by the first boat that arrives." " Then, so will I," said Byers.

Captain Surman, who had heard this conversation, addressing me, said, " Indeed, Mr. Hickey, it will, in my opinion, be very imprudent in either of you to leave the ship. From the present appearance of the weather I have little doubt but the first breeze that comes (for it was then nearly calm) will be from the eastward, in which case I shall be away before you will be able to reach the ship, so far out as we lay." I replied that I was obliged to him for his prudent advice, which I was conscious was given from friendly motives, but that I was so exhausted from want of sleep and anxiety, that let the consequences be what they might, on shore I would go if only for a few hours.

A boat just then running by, the man at the helm called out, "Does any one want to go on shore, hoa?" I immediately answered "yes," and they came alongside, when, putting a few shirts, &c., into a portmanteau, I asked Mr. Byers if he was ready, but the wary Scotch lad had been so deeply impressed by what the Captain said, that he was afraid to venture and declined leaving the ship; I therefore departed alone.

At this time (about half-past seven in the morning) there was scarce a cloud to be seen, but a light air blowing from the south-south-west freshened while we were running towards Deal, and the boatmen observed to each other that it looked as if another gale was blowing. In about an hour we reached the beach, and a few minutes more placed me before a fire in a comfortable room in the Hoop and Griffin, looking towards the sea, with a good breakfast upon the table, of which having partaken heartily, and thereby feeling greatly recruited, I sallied forth to make my observations. There were then upwards of a hundred ships of the fleet that had sailed with us at anchor in the Downs, and by noon upwards of seventy more came in, most of them having sustained damage, some materially, by loss of topmasts, or lower yards. The pilots conjectured that, upon the shift of wind to the westward, the remainder had made a push for Portsmouth, or that possibly some might be at anchor upon the flats off Dungeness.

The weather continued clear and beautifully fine until one o'clock, when I went into the house to dinner. Whilst at my meal a dismal alteration took place: the clouds suddenly collected, and it became squally, looking, as seafaring people phrase it, "exceedingly dirty." By three it blew strong, with severe gusts, and at times rain. I nevertheless walked out to the water-side to collect the different opinions, and found all agreed that a tempest was approaching, and they were right. Before five it blew an absolute hurricane ; the ships in every direction were seen driving from their anchors, although topmasts and yards were lowered, and every other possible precaution taken.

An immensely high and short sea rose, which occasioned so heavy a surf that not a boat would venture to encounter it, or go to the assistance of many vessels that were making signals of distress. Some in the commencement of the gale did attempt it, but being swamped discouraged the rest.

In spite of wind and rain, I remained at the seaside, and, seeing the pilot that brought us from the river, I asked his opinion about the *New Shoreham*. He told me that hard as the wind blew he did not think it was yet at the worst. "However," continued he, "your vessel is in the very best berth in the Downs."

Scarce were those words out of his mouth when it appeared to me that the *New Shoreham* moved, and I said : "Surely she now is drifting." The pilot, taking his glass, exclaimed, "By God, she is, and will certainly be foul of the frigate," the *Arethusa*, to which she was so close, "or compel them to cut." We, however, perceived that she passed without touching.

The wind now veered about between south and west, accompanied by loud peals of thunder and at times heavy rain.

At half-past five nine ships that had parted from their anchors drove on shore between Deal and Sandwich, a distance of only eight miles ; others, having drifted foul of each other, were obliged to cut away rigging and masts to prevent the dire alternative of going to the bottom together ; two were seen actually to founder. A more horrid spectacle I never beheld, yet so interested did I feel on account of the unhappy people on board the different vessels that neither wet nor cold nor want of rest could induce me to quit the beach whilst a ray of light remained.

At seven in the evening, no object being any longer discernible, I returned to my inn, where I drank tea. While at table, hearing the people in the kitchen talk to some one just landed, I went out and found it was a pilot who left the *Arethusa* at half-past six to endeavour to procure another spare anchor. He told me he left only ten ships at anchor, four of which were men-of-war. Upon my enquiring whether he knew anything of the *New Shoreham*, he answered, " She, with the rest, has drifted towards the North Sea, where in all probability every one of them will be lost upon some of the many shoals they must run upon."

At eight o'clock I followed the advice of the hostess by drinking some excellent hot punch, and going directly afterwards to bed, where, although anxiety for the sufferings of the many poor drowning wretches kept me awake some time, fatigue at last got the better, and I fell into a profound and deep sleep, which continued uninterrupted for full twelve hours.

Upon entering the room where breakfast was laid out for me and going to the window, a sad scene of desolation and ruin presented itself to my view. Of the numerous fleet that but twenty-four hours before had been proudly riding at anchor in the Downs no more than eight now remained, and three of those were totally dismasted. The *Arethusa* alone was in the spot where she had brought to, all the others having drifted several miles, but she was one of the finest frigates in the Navy with a noble ship's crew. The weather, though not quite so bad as the preceding day, still continued very boisterous, but the clouds had dispersed and there was no rain. Having breakfasted, I walked towards Sandwich. The beach was covered with pieces of wreck, dead bodies of the unfortunate persons that had perished, and hundreds of sheep and hogs from the Government transports. To describe the dreadful scene that presented itself is impossible; it was horrible in the extreme

I entered the town of Sandwich, enquiring of several sea-faring people if they knew anything of the *New Shoreham*, but could gain no tidings of her further than that a West Indiaman was seen the evening before driving past Rams-gate, close in with the land, with a signal of distress out—made in vain, as the weather was too violent for any boat to attempt going off to the numerous ships that drove by, all with the same signals of distress flying.

After being on my legs from ten o'clock until past four, I returned to the inn much fatigued, but a good dinner re-cruited me. Whilst ruminating upon what I should do, and determining, if I heard nothing of my ship in the course of the following day, to return to London, it occurred to me that my St. George's Fields acquaintance of the 10th of May, 1768 (Mr. Baker), was an inhabitant of Deal, and the land-lord of the Hoop and Griffin telling me he had seen him pass on horseback about two hours before, I immediately went to his house, where, enquiring for him, the servant showed me into a parlour, and I found Mr. Baker with two London friends who were upon a visit to him, sitting over their bottle. He instantly recognised me, and received me with infinite kindness. Upon my telling him I had been two days at Deal he upbraided me for not having sooner called. After a few glasses of wine he conducted us into another room, where Mrs. Baker was preparing tea. She was a well-looking, smart woman, with two fine boys, her sons leaning upon her chair. Both of them, I believe, after-wards became Post-Captains in the Navy.

Being most favourably introduced by Mr. Baker, his wife's reception was equally kind with his own. He lamented that he had not a bed to offer, the three spare rooms being then all occupied, two by the gentlemen present, the third by a female friend confined from a bad sprained ankle. This agreeable and hospitable family not only kept me to supper that night, but insisted upon my making their house my home at all meals during my stay.

The next day, being the 13th of the month, the tempest still raged with fury. After breakfast Mr. Baker asked me to accompany him in his phaeton, his two friends being out with the hounds. He drove along the coast, stopping occasionally to speak to persons he knew, who were engaged in endeavouring to save something from the different vessels that lay stranded, all of which (with the exception of one, which was a large Straitsman) were transports bound to America. This occasioned Mr. Baker very justly to observe what strange infatuation it had been in those who had the management to think of putting the livestock on board in the river Thames, thereby making them liable to all the risks of going down Channel, instead of shipping them from Ireland, or at least our most western ports, as surely ought to have been done, and would by any reasonable people. The unfortunate event, too, fatally proved the egregious mistake that was committed. Upon a calculation made it was clearly ascertained that every pound of fresh meat; that is, mutton and pork, thus conveyed to America, and which was there delivered out to the Army and Navy, stood the British Government in the enormous and almost incredible sum of eight shillings and sixpence.

On driving into Ramsgate we there learnt that several ships which had been blown out of the Downs were riding at anchor close in with the land, the jetty of the pier protecting them from the violent break of the sea. One of them was supposed to be the *New Shoreham*, yet, even sheltered as they were, they laboured so much as to be in momentary danger of parting, and every one of them had signals of distress flying. We were also informed that a number of vessels which had lost every anchor were driven into the North Sea, and their fate consequently very dubious. A few did manage to get into Margate roads, where assistance could be afforded them from the land.

During the 13th ten more ships entered the Downs from the westward, supposed to be transports, all being in a shattered condition and bearing signals of distress.

At three in the afternoon we returned to Deal, and, after spending the rest of the day very agreeably at Mr. Baker's, I went to my inn to sleep.

Upon rising the next morning, the 14th, I rejoiced to see the gale had abated, although it still blew strong. All the large boats were employed carrying off anchors, cables, and other stores to the ships. In the forenoon I mounted one of Mr. Baker's horses, when he, myself, and his two London guests rode to Margate, distant sixteen miles, where we also received dismal accounts of the mischief done during the hurricane.

On our return to dinner a boatman called at Mr. Baker's to let him know the *New Shoreham* was safe and then working into the Downs, which she reached by four o'clock, and once more anchored.

In the evening the wind died away, it becoming almost calm. At midnight I went to bed, and at four in the morning, hearing a great bustle amongst the boats, I rose, dressed myself, and going into the front room saw a black bank towards the horizon, in the east. Descending to the bar, I found a number of lodgers calling for their bills, as the wind was again fair. I did the same, and having by a little after five discharged it, and got my portmanteau ready, I sallied forth, a boatman immediately announcing a fine breeze from the north-east and asking if I wanted to go off. I answered yes, I did, to the *New Shoreham*. "She lays the very outermost ship," replied the extortioner. "However, I'll put you on board for ten guineas." Alarmed at the exorbitancy of the demand, which, by the by, exceeded my whole remaining stock of cash, I remonstrated, expressing a hope that he would take half the sum. This he absolutely refused, saying, "I'll be damned if I do, or if you find a boatman upon this beach who will take you on board for five guineas. It is now blowing fresh and will increase."

In this dilemma I began to apprehend I must lose my passage, and in great fright ran down to Mr. Baker's, who I had heard say he should ride at five to go out with the hounds. I met him mounting his horse, when, mentioning what had just happened and the state of my finances, he instantly said, "Oh, never fear, Hickey, I'll be bound for it I get you off, and in one of the best boats, too, or, if I am

disappointed, you shall have my own." He then sent a
servant to call a pilot of his acquaintance, who within five
minutes made his appearance, when Mr. Baker said,
" Charles, here is a most particular friend of mine who is
going to the West Indies in the *New Shoreham*, and, not
being very flush of cash, you must get him on board that
ship for a guinea." " Lord love your honour, to be sure I
will," said Charles, " for nothing, and with all my soul.
They are now launching the *Lovely Susan* (his boat's name),
to go off to the Commodore with fresh beef, so your friend is
kindly welcome to a passage." Then, turning to me, he
continued, " So step along, my master, we have no time
to lose." This was delightful language to my ears, and,
cordially thanking Mr. Baker for all his attentions I bid
him adieu, but he insisted upon seeing me embark, sent a
man for my portmanteau, and did not quit the shore until
I was seated in the stern-sheets of the *Lovely Susan*, and
fairly through the surf.

A little before seven I was alongside the *New Shoreham*,
completely drenched from the spray of the sea every instant breaking over us. I presented the boatmen with a
couple of guineas, which greatly pleased them, they not expecting a sixpence, their master having ordered them to
take me off without any charge whatever.

I found the *New Shoreham* with her anchor apeak, and
within a quarter of an hour after I reached her she was running seven knots an hour right before the wind. Thus I did
but just save my distance. Captain Surman congratulated
me on having, although contrary to his advice, gone on
shore, thereby avoiding the misery and distress they had
encountered. He said that when he perceived the ship
began to drive with three anchors ahead, he gave everything up and would not have given a single sixpence for
vessel and cargo. He further told me they had driven so
close to the *Arethusa* that their yard-arms touched, he
being obliged, in order to prevent falling on board her, to
cut from two of the anchors he was dragging, and within an
hour afterwards the third cable snapped close to her bows.

Being well acquainted with the whole coast of Kent, his intention was to run her on shore a little to the northward of Ramsgate, where he knew there was a soft chalk, whereby he hoped to save the lives of his crew and himself, but whilst carrying that resolution into effect he perceived that the sea became comparatively smooth from the pier of Ramsgate, in some measure sheltering them, and this induced him to let go the only remaining anchor they had, though he had scarce a hope it could hold her, it being smaller than either of the three that they had parted from. Fortunately however, it did, and to the agreeable surprise of every person on board she thus rode out the remainder of the gale, being within half a mile of the shore. She was also the means of saving several other ships, which, from seeing her thus riding, also let go anchors, with equal success. Three, however, less sheltered by the pier, parted, and, driving on shore, were wrecked.

Mr. Byers lamented that he had not followed my example by going on shore at Deal. He said what I beheld from the land could give no idea of the actual horror of the scene, the wind roaring with such superlative force that it became quite impossible to hear each other's voices, while the ship every instant was nearly overwhelmed by the seas that broke over her, so much so that all on board expected to go to the bottom ; they saw several vessels actually do so, close to them, whilst others driving foul tore away masts, yards, and rigging. He was certain that nothing enabled him to bear the terrors of the last three days but the immense quantities of gin he swallowed, which ran down his throat like the simple element water, not creating the least sensation in his stomach, nor passing into it, like spirits, and this was the more extraordinary from Mr. Byers never having thentofore drank anything stronger than small beer, his customary beverage being water.

Dreadful as was the above-mentioned storm, it was my fate to encounter and suffer under one still more violent, of which I shall hereafter state the particulars.

CHAPTER II

THE VOYAGE OUT

WE ran down Channel in what, had we not been right before the wind, would have been deemed a hard gale. During the first three days we had many ships in sight; the fourth morning we were, by reckoning, several leagues to the westward of Scilly, the weather becoming from thick and hazy to bright, clear sunshine. We ran on, entirely alone. By this time I had quite got the better of sea-sickness, and was able to walk the deck, which gave me an opportunity of observing the ignorance of the crew. There were only three that could take the helm at all, and these yawed the ship about sadly, nor did they seem conversant with a single point of seamanship. So very deficient were they in every respect that I often wondered at the ship ever reaching the West Indies. Happily for us the weather continued generally fine, there being nothing more than a few squalls, in some of which we were compelled to carry more sail than prudence could authorize from no other reason than inability to take it in quick enough. In those cases, the risk being over, Captain Surman used laughingly to observe to me, "I find some benefit arises from a badly manned ship, for had my ship been properly provided with hands I should, from the threatening appearance of the sky an hour ago, have now been under double or close reefed topsails, thereby losing time and distance, whereas here we are with everything set, and fine weather." This sort of argument, however, I did not approve of, and always felt uneasy upon the approach of a squall.

Our table was very differently provided from what I had been used to in the *Plassey*, but in this Captain Surman was not to blame, for he had an abundant stock of poultry,

sheep, and hogs at the time we first sailed out of the Downs,
the greater part of which was lost in the gale, and he had
afterwards no opportunity of procuring a sufficient supply,
all he could obtain being two or three dozen of fowls and
a few ducks, which were received while the ship was weigh-
ing anchor the last time. The salt provisions were excellent of their kind, and Mr. Scott, the chief mate, being
a capital fisherman, the table was almost daily furnished
with an albacore, boneta, or dolphin, and not unfrequently
with all three. Either of these fish, especially the dolphin,
when dressed in the American manner ; that is, cut in
slices, with layers of pork and vegetables, and well stewed,
is admirably good, and might meet the approbation of a fat
Common Council man of the City of London. We had
plenty of port wine and Lisbon, which, with uninterrupted
good humour, made the hours glide rapidly away.

Our mess consisted of five, the Captain, the chief and
second mates, Mr. Byers, and myself, and I can confidently
affirm that nothing like an angry word passed in the little
party during the voyage, which was made in the usual time,
the Island of Barbadoes being seen early in the morning of
the 18th of October. When within three miles this land presents to the eye one of the richest views that can be, one
side being covered with the most luxuriant verdure, handsome buildings belonging to the planters, and windmills
innumerable, the canes being ground by that machine. It
did not appear to me that there was a single foot of uncultivated land upon the whole Island.

The *New Shoreham's* first destination was Grenada, but
Captain Surman, wishing to gain information, ran close in
to Bridgetown, the capital of Barbadoes, and there hove to.
A boat, with only Caffres in her, having fruit to sell, came
off, and we purchased pines, oranges, plantains, guavas,
star apples, &c., all of which were highly acceptable. These
people, upon hearing we were bound to Grenada, said, " Oh,
Grenada all gone, no Grenada now." This inducing further
enquiry, we learnt that the chief town, called St. George's,
had recently been entirely destroyed by fire. After stopping

an hour we again made sail, passing St. Vincent's and two other small islands.

After the common run we saw Grenada, the appearance of which was very unlike that of Barbadoes, being entirely covered by forests of wood, and not a sign of cultivation or habitation until, rounding a point of land, the ruins of the town were seen, and sad havoc the conflagration had made. In the valley not a single house was left standing, and only a few upon the rising ground. A Government canoe that came alongside directed Captain Surman to stand on, and bring his ship to an anchor in the Carenage, situate on the south end of the Island. Here we found a neat little town, consisting of about fifty houses, all constructed of wood, whereas those of the capital were of masonry, mostly stone. There is a strong fort, standing upon an eminence, garrisoned, when we were there, by two regiments of Infantry, one of them Highlanders, and two companies of Artillery. The Carenage is separated from St. George's by a lofty hill.

The accident of the fire had happened a fortnight previous to our arrival, having commenced at ten o'clock at night in a large store, or magazine, in which unfortunately were a number of casks of rosin, pitch, and tar, which burnt with irresistible fury. The town, which had occupied an extent of nearly two miles along the seaside, was in twenty-four hours reduced to a pile of ruins and ashes. The miserable inhabitants, many of whom lost all they possessed in the world, were obliged to seek shelter in the Carenage, which consequently became so crowded that half a dozen families were put together in a small house until tents and temporary habitations could be erected for their accommodation. There was only one tavern in the place, to which I accompanied Captain Surman as soon as the ship was moored, and got a tolerable dinner.

Mr. Richard Burke, who was Collector of the Customs for this Island, had given me a letter to Mr. Irwin, an intimate friend of his. Enquiring for this gentleman, I was told he had that minute entered the house, and, being shown to the room where he was, I delivered my letter, which procured me the warmest possible reception, he expressing the greatest regard for Mr. Burke, about whom he made many earnest enquiries.

Mr. Irwin was a gentlemanlike man, advanced in years, and an old inhabitant of Grenada. His residence being in the Carenage he had not suffered from the late disaster. In the evening he took me to his house, insisting upon my living with him during my stay. His mansion was entirely of wood, a melancholy dirty concern, but pleasantly situated, being within five yards of the sea and commanding the circuit of the bay, in which three ships and a number of small craft were at anchor. He told me that four-fifths of the houses in the town were his property. Having sent to the tavern to request Captain Surman's company, he gave us a bottle of admirable madeira.

After a cheerful evening and good supper, Captain Surman went on board his ship to sleep, and I was shown to a large, dark, shocking looking chamber, the contents of which forcibly brought to my mind the first night I passed at Mr. Dawson's garden, near Madras, in the year 1769. The thing upon which it was intended I should rest, dignified with the improper title of bed, was a crazy old wooden frame, with planks at the bottom, upon which was laid a kind of rug, not of sufficient substance to preserve my bones from the hardness of the boards. The rest of the furniture was of a similar description. I, who had never before been lodged in so wretched a place, for it was infinitely worse than Mr. Dawson's, which was at least airy and open, was struck with surprize and disgust upon entering it. Mr. Irwin seemed unconscious of its demerits, and, having himself shown me into the dog hole, cordially shook me by the hand, wishing me a good night, a wish I felt utterly impossible to be accomplished. Low in spirits I sat myself down, contemplating the misery that surrounded me, and, dreadfully bit and stung by insects, watched until the few inches of candle left with me burnt out. My ruminations were then continued in the dark, until, beginning to think daylight would never arrive, I determined to endeavour to get into the open air. I began groping about the room, but for the life of me could not find the door, tumbling over different things half a dozen times. I was completely lost, so that at last in absolute despair I sat myself down upon the floor, where a host of fleas, in addition to the other annoyances, assailed me. The heat, too, was intense, keeping me in profuse perspiration ; a more miserable night I never passed.

Truly rejoiced was I when the first ray of light appeared through the small casement. The instant I could discern the door I issued forth from my *den*, walking about the town for an hour, when I saw a boat coming from the *New Shoreham*, in which was Captain Surman, who, the moment he saw the woeful plight I was in, said, " I was afraid such would be the case, and had thoughts of advising you to go with me and sleep in your own cabin, but was afraid of giving Mr. Irwin offence. I see you have not had your clothes off ; you had better therefore step into the boat, go to the ship, and lay down for a couple of hours." I accordingly did so, slept soundly, and got up refreshed, when I cleaned myself, and returned to Mr. Irwin, who seemed amazed at my account of the way in which I had passed the night, declaring he did not know there was an insect in the house, as they never molested him. He ordered breakfast for me, and I made a hearty meal, enjoying the new bread and fresh butter. Mr. Irwin then took me to visit Mr. Young, the Lieutenant-Governor, and other of the principal gentlemen of the settlement, most of whom were unhoused by the late fire, the occasion of which disaster still remained undiscovered. Mr. Young was one of the lucky few who lived constantly at a country house about a mile up one of the mountains with which the Island abounds, thereby escaping the effects of that dire calamity.

Grenada was also labouring under another heavy misfortune, many parts being overrun with ants. Such were the ravages these little animals committed that some of the finest and most productive plantations were entirely ruined by their eating the roots of the sugar cane, thereby destroying the plant and preventing its growth or produce of juice. Had I not myself seen what I am now going to mention, I could not have believed it; that is, the earth covered with small red ants heaped in a mass so as themselves to form a body *eleven inches* in depth! They made their appearance about sunset, continuing above ground all night, and soon after sunrise retreated into the earth again, so that at noon there was not one to be seen. Various attempts had been made to destroy them, but none effectual. Rewards to the amount of thirty thousand pounds had been offered to any person or persons who should succeed in clearing the land from this distressing visitation, the largeness of which sum had brought two enterprising Frenchmen from Martinique, who spoke confidently of themselves, and that they had no doubt a few months would entitle them to claim the promised gratuity. They were at work all the time I was at Grenada, but whether they ultimately succeeded or not I never heard. They gave out that exactly the same ant had for three following years been at Martinique, where they so entirely destroyed the canes that the proprietors of the finest plantations were compelled to give up sugar and cultivate the far less advantageous articles, coffee and cotton, and that they (these two persons) had effectually cleared the earth of them by the same process they were pursuing at Grenada.

The sixth day after our arrival, hearing that Mr. Byers was ill at the tavern, I called and found him, as I conceived, very seriously indisposed, having a considerable degree of fever. I recommended his sending for medical assistance, but he would not listen to such advice, saying nothing material ailed him, and that a double dose of sea-water (of which he had daily drank two pints during the voyage from England) would set him to rights. Eight hours after I left him he breathed his last! This very sudden death of my young shipmate greatly increased the insuper able dislike I had taken to Grenada, and made me anxious to leave it, but of doing so Captain Surman gave me no hopes for ten days, as he had a large quantity of heavy ironwork to deliver, which Messrs. Nesbitt's agent was not ready to receive, having no secure place in which he could deposit it.

Some days later I was taken ill, being attacked by violent headache and vomiting. Medicine being immediately administered relieved, but did not cure me, the doctor declaring I had lurking symptoms of fever. This made me still more anxious to leave the Island, which Mr. Irwin seeing, he offered me a passage in a small schooner of his that would sail the following day for Antigua, where I might stay until the *New Shoreham*, which was to stop there, should take me up again. This offer I gladly accepted upon Captain Surman's approval and assurance that he would touch at Antigua, and carry me on to Jamaica.

That night I went on board the schooner, a dirty vessel, abounding with vermin. I, however, felt happy in the idea of getting away from Grenada, the only place I ever left, after no matter how short a residence, without a particle of regret. Mr. Irwin favoured me with a letter to his correspondent at Antigua, who, in consequence thereof, received me into his house, where, in a very agreeable family named Mathison, I spent ten pleasant days, having quite recovered my health during the short voyage.

In the evening of the tenth day the *New Shoreham* arrived, and the next night we sailed from Antigua, having two gentlemen of that Island, who requested a passage to Jamaica. The day after we left Antigua the weather being delightfully fine, I was walking the quarter-deck with Mr. Scott, the chief mate, the people being down below at dinner, when Mr. Scott, observing the flying boom of the lower studding sail had got foul of a flue of the anchor, went forward himself to clear it, in doing which he missed his hold of a rope and fell overboard. As I saw the accident I told the man at the helm to heave the ship to, and opened the cabin door to call the Captain, who came out at the moment the sails were backing, and causing the ship to lay down so much that I thought she must overset. Every soul was instantly upon deck, the topsails were lowered

and she righted. The boatswain exerted himself amazingly ;
a boat was quickly out, into which he and four men got,
rowing in the direction in which Mr. Scott had fallen, the
sea being so high that we could see nothing of him.

Captain Surman, looking out with his spying glass, soon
called out, to our great joy, that they had got him, and in
about half an hour more the boat was alongside. The body,
for he was apparently dead, was immediately hoisted in, the
boatswain saying that he was in the act of sinking just as
they reached him, although he was an excellent swimmer.
Probably he had exhausted his strength by too great exertion at first. The means practised in those days for recovery of drowned persons were then resorted to, one of
which was bleeding (which has since been ascertained to
be very prejudicial). The arm being tied up, Captain
Surman paused from apprehension, as he had never blooded
any person, that he might open an artery instead of a vein,
a scruple of conscience that struck me as highly ill-timed
and absurd, and I could not help expressing my opinion,
remarking that, if left alone, clearly death, if it had not
already taken effect, must be the consequence, and all risks
ought therefore to be run. An incision was therefore made,
but no blood followed.

The other means, such as friction, the application of salt
and strong volatiles were continued two hours without the
smallest symptom of returning animation. At the end of
that time the blood suddenly spouted out from the arm,
copiously for a few seconds, then as suddenly stopped, in
ten minutes after which the limbs became stiff, the colour
of the skin changed, and life had evidently fled for ever.
In the evening the corpse was committed to the deep. This
fatal occurrence threw a damp upon our spirits the remainder
of the passage, Mr. Scott being deservedly esteemed by every
individual. He was of mild, unassuming manners, a sweet
temper, well informed, and a perfect master of his profession.

The day after Mr. Scott's death we made St. Domingo,
or, as it was then more generally called, Hispaniola, along
which we ran, the next land that appeared being our destina-

tion, Jamaica, an island then considered as one of the most unhealthy in the West Indies, or in the world. This had often been the topic during the voyage, Captain Surman relating many anecdotes respecting it, and saying that several of his best friends had been carried off after only an hour's illness. With respect to himself he observed he had no reason to complain, as during his numerous visits to that place he had always been blessed with uninterrupted good health.

Whilst turning up from Port Royal to Kingston, Captain Surman desired I would take notice of a dapper little man, dressed in black, with a spruce curled bob wig, who, upon my landing, would shake me by the hand, wishing me health and long life upon the Island, but watch him closely, said he, and you will perceive that whilst bowing and paying his compliments to you he is, with a small ruler, measuring your height. " And pray what is that for ? " enquired I. " In order to have a coffin for you, which he, being the principal undertaker, will immediately get ready, hoping to bury you to-morrow ! " said the Captain.

I felt monstrously provoked at hearing this, but kept it to myself, fully resolving, however, the instant " the dapper little man in black " addressed me to give him a kicking. I therefore kept a sharp look out for my little undertaker, but no such description of person did I see, and, mentioning the circumstance afterwards, I discovered this to be an old joke of Captain Surman's, which he practised upon all his youthful passengers on their approaching Jamaica.

On the 27th of November, 1775, we anchored within a cable's length of the shore, at the town of Kingston, the capital seaport of the Island, where Captain Surman took me on shore, conducting me to a famous lodging-house situate in the High Street, kept and admirably well managed by an elderly widow lady. Here he recommended me to fix my board, there being an excellent ordinary daily at two o'clock, at which I might dine or not as I pleased. I accordingly engaged a handsome bed-chamber with a small dressing-room adjoining

At a little before two the Captain accompanied me to an immense hall, where a table was laid for thirty, having silver forks and spoons before each plate, beautifully white cloth and napkins, with every other corresponding requisite. I was introduced to several gentlemen as they entered. Precisely at two o'clock, twenty-five of us sat down to a plentifully supplied board, having turtle in a variety of ways. The wines were madeira, hock, and port, little of the latter being drunk. I was surprized to see the rooms precisely like those in England, windows sashed, glazed, and no larger than in Europe. The heat consequently was intense, even to oppression, as may be conceived in such a description of apartment with a load of hot victuals upon the table, and twenty-five guests, besides servants. So profuse a perspiration for two hours I never underwent. The attendants were black—a man, named George, two young lads, and two females, Eve and Catalina. The noxious exhalations outdid all the offensive smells that ever met a nose. I was obliged to fortify myself with several glasses of madeira ere I could touch a morsel of victuals. No other person seemed to be at all annoyed. Such is the force of habit !

At four the party broke up, the gentlemen retiring to take their afternoon's nap according to the custom of the country. As neither Captain Surman nor I ever indulged in that way he proposed an excursion in a *kittareen*, or one-horse chaise, and showing me the skirts of the town. In a quarter of an hour we set off, driving through the whole of Kingston, which I found truly superb, abounding with noble public and private buildings, but, as I have already observed, they all appeared to me too much in the European style, and ill-calculated for such a climate as Jamaica. We then proceeded about four miles from the town, towards the foot of the Leganee Mountains, my conductor pointing out several beautiful *penns*, or farm-yards, at some of which we called.

After a pleasant drive we returned to tea, and in the evening I went visiting with Captain Surman, he having previously appointed ten o'clock the following day to go with me to those gentlemen for whom I had brought letters from England. Our first call (in the evening) was at the most celebrated tavern in the place, which Captain Surman told me was kept by a strange, eccentric fellow named Baggs, brother to the sporting and well-known Major Baggs. He had on a former residence in ten years acquired a fortune of upwards of twenty-five thousand pounds, as proprietor of a tavern in Kingston, with which sum in his pocket he returned to England, where he burst forth upon the public in all the splendour of dress, equipage, and establishment. His object seemed to be to outshine in folly and dissipation all the puppies of the day, and he succeeded so completely that at the end of four years he had not a single guinea left ; whereupon, with the utmost composure, he prepared to embark once more for Jamaica, saying he was able to make a second fortune as he had done the first, and left it not in the power of any man in Great Britain to say he had acted dishonourably, or owed a shilling to gentle or simple. At the time of my arrival at Jamaica this Mr. Baggs had been eight months returned after having squandered away his fortune, and had resumed his occupation with extraordinary success, being in a fair way of making as rapid and large a fortune as before.

My conductor and I entered an elegant hall, brilliantly lighted with wax candles, several waiters being busily employed attending the guests in different rooms. Enquiring of a servant if Mr. Baggs was at home, he answered, " Yes, over the way," pointing to a door on the opposite side of the street. Thither we went, and found the person we sought with three gentlemen just rising from the dinner-table. Mr. Baggs and his friends received Captain Surman very cordially, he being well known to them all. Upon my being introduced, Mr. Baggs asked whether I was related to Mr. Hickey of St. Albans Street. Being told I was his son come to settle upon the Island in the profession of the Law, he expressed much pleasure at seeing me, saying how happy he should be to assist me and promote my views by every means within his power, " and give me leave to add, Sir," said he, " I possess some little interest and influence upon this Island." He then insisted upon his guests resuming their seats, and that they and we should taste a fresh batch of *Mrs. Allen*, which he had just broached and which his friends pronounced choice stuff. Captain Surman pleaded that we had drunk tea, but it did not signify ; taste his claret we must and should, and certainly he produced some delicious wine.

Mrs. Allen was the widow of a long established London wine merchant who had for many years supplied Jamaica with Vin de Bourdeaux, and so partial were the inhabitants to his wine they would drink no other. Upon his death Mrs. Allen continued the business, keeping up the reputation her deceased husband had acquired.

Mr. Baggs told me he had for many years been acquainted with and highly respected my father, that he had been first introduced by his brother, the Major, who acknowledged himself under extraordinary obligations to him both professional and pecuniary.

After drinking half a dozen bumper toasts from enormous glasses we with difficulty were permitted to depart, Mr. Baggs saying to me, " Believe me, Mr. Hickey, I shall be happy to return to you some of those kindnesses my brother and self have received from your father. Let me request, whenever you are not otherwise engaged, that you will, *sans cérémonie*, consider this your home. Three times a week, at least, you will find a select little party, like this of to-day, always consisting of gentlemen of the first rank on the Island, with as good a dinner as Kingston affords, and there is no better in the universe. My wines will speak for themselves, and I promise you a cordial welcome. Here, Sir, I am *Squire Baggs*, upon a footing with the Governor or any other man—on the opposite side of the street the case is different. There I am *Jack Baggs*, the tavern keeper, where I know my distance and keep it, never using a freedom with any customers."

This I found was by no means an exaggerated account of

himself. In very many parties, whereof I made one, at his tavern he constantly accompanied the waiters, carrying in the dinner, directing them how to place it upon the table, remained in the room until the guests were seated, when, bowing respectfully, he withdrew. He was a good classical scholar, and well acquainted with mankind, but extremely tenacious of his own opinions, violent upon some topics, and so loud and incessant a talker as sometimes to become disagreeable, if not disgusting. During his former residence in Jamaica he had fought two duels, gaining credit upon both occasions for the propriety and spirit of his conduct. This eccentric body was disappointed in his expectation of again returning with affluence to England. About three years after I left Jamaica a fever carried him off. He had acquired more than eight thousand pounds, the whole of which he bequeathed to a natural son.

The morning after our visit to Baggs, Captain Surman took me in his *kittareen* to the Chief Justice, to Mr. Harrison, Mr. Welch, Mr. Baker, and others for whom I had letters, as well as to several of his own friends, of whom he had many. We finished a busy morning by calling upon Mr. Robert Richards, who resided a short distance from my lodgings. He received me with a hearty welcome, but observed, " a son of Joe Hickey, and a protégé of the Burkes, ought to have been with me the moment he set foot on shore. However," continued he, " as you have taken a lodging for a month, and I am going away soon, you may as well retain it. At the same time, that shall be quite optional," and, taking me to three neat rooms upon the second floor, he said, " These are exclusively yours ; use them as you please. You will find everything you want. To-day you and Captain Surman must dine with me, and you will meet some of the principal men of the place."

As Captain Surman had told me he was sure Mr. Richards would wish us to dine with him he had declined the various invitations we received during our morning visits, and we accepted Mr. Richards's. The party consisted of Mr. Webley, the Chief Justice, Mr. Harrison, Mr. Welch, and at least a dozen others, also a Colonel in the French service, who had recently arrived from St. Domingo (where he held a lucrative situation) on a visit to Sir Basil Keith, the Governor, but had found him so much indisposed that he could not leave his chamber. Sir Basil had therefore requested Mr. Richards and three other gentlemen to act for him, and escort the Colonel to all that deserved the inspection of a stranger. The four thus deputed resolved to make the circuit of the Island, and show their dignified visitor all the principal estates and romantic scenes with which Jamaica peculiarly abounds. This foreigner, whose name I have forgotten, seemed to be quite a man of fashion, of easy and elegant address.

The following day Mr. Richards took me to Messrs. Lyon and Ridge, eminent Attorneys, and old friends of both Mr. Edmund and Mr. Richard Burke, from whom I had letters to them. In fact, I fully expected to be received into their office as a prelude to my admission to practise in the Court. What then was my mortification and disappointment upon their immediately declaring the absolute impossibility of my having a chance of being put upon the roll of Attorneys for several years to come, nor did they think I should be able to procure any employment worthy acceptance or such as ought to induce me to wait an opening. At that time they told me every Attorney's office was overstocked with Articled Clerks, all of whom were waiting in hopes of admission upon the expiration of their indentures.

The Judges, finding the practitioners multiply so fast, had made a rule, intended for the benefit of the profession in general, by which the number was limited, so that it was impossible to be admitted except when a vacancy occurred. Of this Mr. Richards, who had himself been at the Bar and filled the high office of Attorney-General, expressed some fear when he first read the letters I delivered to him, and, that fear being realized by what Messrs. Lyon and Ridge said, these three gentlemen coincided in thinking there was nothing to encourage my remaining at Jamaica. Messrs.

Lyon and Ridge nevertheless observed that if I preferred waiting until I could be admitted they would readily give me a seat at one of their desks. Upon this I begged of a day to consider of their offer.

On my way home I asked Mr. Richards whether he thought I ought to accept or not. He answered, " Certainly not, for the highest salary they could give you would not half defray your unavoidable expences, and you will be obliged to draw upon your father for at least one hundred pounds a year." He desired before I gave a decisive answer that I would consult Mr. Welch, as he would Mr. Paxton, Mr. Coleborne, and some others of the Court. This being done, they all concurred in advising my return to England. Mr. Welch in particular said, " My dear Sir, when you first did me the honour of a visit and your letters announced the purpose for which you came to the West, nothing but the presence of some strangers prevented my instantly, and unasked, offering my sentiments upon the fruitless voyage you had made, and my advice that you should go back or adopt some other line of life. The law seems to me entirely out of the question. All I can say is, should you determine to stay and embark in mercantile concerns or otherwise, and money be required, my purse will always be open and at your command." This handsome and liberal speech I communicated to Mr. Richards, who thereupon enquired if I knew anything of commerce, to which I replied most truly, " Nothing whatever." " Then," continued he, " I see no alternative. You must go back."

Thus ended my Jamaica expectations, and although in this instance I could attach no blame to myself, I felt greatly distressed at again disappointing my father, nor could I venture a conjecture of what was to be my future lot. I had been obliged to take twenty pounds from Mr. Irwin to defray my expences at Grenada, and where I now was, money would be required every month.

CHAPTER III

AT KINGSTON, JAMAICA

MR. RICHARDS, the morning after my determination to return, suggested that I must want cash while at Jamaica. He therefore desired I would at my leisure draw for one hundred pounds, which amount he presented me with. My conscience smote me for thus trespassing upon the indulgent kindness of a fond father, yet what could I do ? I had no other human creature to draw upon.

Mr. Richards then observed that as all my views were frustrated my presence could no longer be necessary at Kingston, and he therefore hoped I would fix my abode at his house as well as accompany him on his journeys to his different estates. He further proposed my going the next day to Spanish Town, the seat of Government, where he would introduce me to Sir Basil Keith, &c. I accordingly attended him in his chariot and four over a better road than I ever saw in England. We were set down at a house of his own, fully equal in every respect to that at Kingston. After dressing, he took me to the Governor's, to whom I was presented. He looked dreadfully ill and emaciated.

Mr. Richards having briefly mentioned the circumstance of my hopes being blasted, Sir Basil very politely expressed his concern at my disappointment. He then conversed with Mr. Richards relative to the intended excursion with the French officer, and, after hearing the outlines of the journey, said, " I hope you intend your friend, Mr. Hickey, to be of the party, as it will be a good opportunity to let him see some of the beauties of our Island." Mr. Richards replied he meant to propose it to me. Sir Basil invited us to an entertainment that was to be given the next evening in compliment to Colonel Dalling, the Lieutenant-Governor,

27

on his arrival from Europe, adding, "My want of health will not allow of my doing the honours of my house in person, and I must therefore rely upon my staff to receive my guests."

The next evening we went to a splendid ball, at which all the principal people of the town, and several from Kingston, were present. My attention was much attracted by several groups of as lovely young women as ever I beheld, standing together in different parts of the sides of the room, looking at the dancers. These I learnt were the natural children of Europeans, originally descended from Caffres, but, being two or three removes, were nearly as fair as any British damsels. Girls of this description are frequently to be procured, though at a monstrous expence, far exceeding what frail ones in London cost.

Whilst contemplating the different bevies of beauties, I was highly pleased at seeing Captain Surman enter the ball-room accompanied by an elegant-looking young man, dressed in a full suit of azure blue silk, richly ornamented with spangled silver lace, his head covered with a profusion of curls inimitably well arranged. I concluded that he was a foreigner of distinction, but was not long left to conjecture, for Captain Surman, bringing his companion up to me, introduced him by the name of Bonynge, saying to us at the same time, " I am sure it will be enough to make you known to each other for you to become sincerely attached, for you are much alike in disposition and propensities, and are exactly of the same kidney." My new acquaintance smiled at the speech and was pleased to pay me a compliment, which it would be vanity in me to record. Captain Surman, however, had formed a just opinion of us. We soon became sworn friends. He informed me that he was the only child of Doctor Bonynge, whom he described as the most *outré* and extraordinary old quiz that ever lived. "This," said he, " you will consider not very respectful for a son to say of his father, but it is the veritable fact."

Bonynge further related of himself that he had been the pet and darling of his mother until he was ten years of age, when he had the misfortune to lose her. So partial was she to him that she would not allow of his being thwarted in any way whatever, a mistaken kindness that rendered him a completely spoiled child. During his infancy his father had practised as a physician in Jamaica, whereby he had amassed considerable wealth, besides which he inherited a large property from an elder brother. His father's avocations engaging him much abroad, little attention was paid to the son, and after the death of his mother no one seemed to care about him ; his education was never thought of, he spending the whole of his time in idleness.

"Thus," continued he, "passed two more years of my life. At twelve I was, I have often been told, a handsome boy, remarkably clever and sharp. My father, with whom I had never been a favourite, now took the most unaccountable dislike to me, amounting almost to aversion, so that whenever he saw me by accident, for he never desired to do so, he always abused me, using the most scurrilous epithets. This unnatural conduct sometimes surprized but did not hurt or distress me, for as I felt conscious I did not deserve such treatment, and that I was a favourite with everyone else, I in my own mind set my father down for a monster unworthy my notice, much less my affection. Being extremely volatile, with an uncommon flow of spirits, I generally laughed and ridiculed his wanton passions. Some of his warmest friends at length remonstrated against the injustice of his conduct towards me—that it was unpardonable in a parent to neglect a child as he had done, leaving me so ignorant as not even to know the alphabet. To which representations he always answered, ' I will have nothing to say to the cursed brat. I hate the sight of him, and will have nothing to do about education or otherwise. Take him amongst ye who are so damned fond of the odious animal and do with him what you please. If you want money call for it and you may have as much as you desire ; in other respects do, I beseech you, let me alone and judge for myself. I suppose I am arrived at the years of discretion and am capable of forming an opinion without these *friendly interferences.*'

" Immediately after this unsuccessful effort to awaken parental feelings in my father's breast, a brother-in-law of his took charge of me, and in a few weeks dispatched me to England, consigning me to his agent in London, who was my father's also, with a request that he would superintend my education and not spare any expence to render me perfectly accomplished. This agent having been brought up in a foreign University conceived no other mode of education so likely to make me what my friends wished. After spending a few months therefore very agreeably in his family and being shown all the curiosities of the British capital, he took me to Paris, placing me in a fashionable academy, where I was to be properly grounded in every point, and fitted for the University of Switzerland.

" At this French seminary I remained four years, making a proficiency at which my instructors were equally pleased and surprized. At the end of the fourth year the London agent again visited me, and upon examination of the progress I had made he expressed his high approbation at my improved state, both in mind and person. After a month allowed me for recreation in Paris my zealous friend conveyed me to the most celebrated college of Geneva, where three more years finished the important business of sending forth the *all-accomplished fellow*, the *garçon de bord* that now has the honour and happiness to stand before you."

This little abstract history of his youth he delivered with great ease and peculiar pleasantry. I afterwards became too well convinced the account he gave of his father's neglect of him in his infancy was in no way exaggerated. That this should have ever occurred or that the dislike should be continued to manhood was altogether unaccountable, for a more interesting or engaging young man I never saw. The greatest blemish in his character was excessive coxcombry in dress, and at times a little also in manner. But of this he was aware and always ready to admit the folly, and to join in a laugh though at his own expence.

Bonynge had only been three months returned to Jamaica

when I became acquainted with him. Upon my asking him how the Doctor now behaved towards him, he replied, " Oh, worse than ever. I really begin to think I cannot be a child of his, but I must not (changing his lively manner at once to the most determined gravity) even sportively traduce, or dare to injure the good fame of my revered mother—the best of wives and the best of parents !—but, Sir, you will scarcely believe what I am now about to tell you. Upon my arrival and my uncle's taking me to my father's study and announcing who I was, without a single syllable of kindness or common civility, the old gentleman eyed me, as he sat, with apparent astonishment, I thought disgust, after which, rising from his chair, he deliberately placéd his spectacles upon his nose and, walking close up to me, eyed me from head to foot, then rudely taking me by the shoulder turned me round and round, exclaiming, ' By God, I never saw the like ! Damn me if he does not put me in mind of the monkey that had seen the world, he wants nothing but the tail to complete it,' and, turning me round again, ejaculated, ' O tempora! O mores ! Pha ! how the animal dances about' (though I stirred not a foot). ' Oh, thou essence-essence, damn me, thou quintessence of cox-combs, if ever I beheld the like, so pray take yourself off ere I'm quite sick, for, damn me, if you don't stink worse than a legion of polecats ! ' I stayed to hear no more, but instantly left the room, and now, what think you of such a reception of a son—and such a son !—after an absence of near eight years ? "

I shall hereafter mention some more of the Doctor's whimsicalities to which I was an eyewitness.

From the first evening of our acquaintance young Bonynge and I were constantly together, except when my country excursions with Mr. Richards interfered. My young companion hearing of the party formed to escort the French Colonel upon the short circuit of the Island offered himself as a volunteer, facetiously remarking he could act as a capital master of the ceremonies, besides which he was competent to *shew the lions?* His proffered services were gladly accepted, the gentlemen knowing he would prove a great acquisition to their party.

Notwithstanding the uncommon dislike Dr. Bonynge seemed to have for his son, he was liberal in his pecuniary allowances, even to excess, and had always honoured his draughts, which were very frequent and for considerable sums, with the utmost regularity. Young Bonynge told me that he kept a phaeton, a stylish Tim Whiskey, and half a dozen blood horses, all or any of which would always be at my service. "Apropos," said he, "we must go to town (Kingston) to-morrow, for there is a famous play performed in the evening at the theatre, being the first this season. They have a passable set of actors, besides which all the beauties we boast of will be present, to some of whom I will introduce you."

At breakfast the following morning I told Mr. Richards I was going to Kingston and the reason for so doing, to which he replied, "By all means go. I am myself a constant frequenter of the theatre when open and would accompany you had I not last night accepted an invitation to dine with Colonel Dalling, where I also promised to take you. However, I will make your apology by fairly telling him that his burgundy, superior as it is, stood no chance when put in competition with a playhouse, and a parcel of fine girls. Bear in your recollection, nevertheless, that you and Bonynge must both be back by three o'clock the day after to-morrow as the travelling party are all to dine with me finally to settle our route, and the morning after we start."

At ten o'clock Bonynge came in his phaeton to Mr. Richards's door and we drove off, stopping at the half-way house to bait the horses and refresh ourselves with excellent cold ham and the finest shell-fish I ever saw, which we washed down with weak *punch* made of fresh limes, a beverage the European inhabitants of Jamaica daily drink large quantities of, commencing immediately after the clock strikes ten, prior to which it is never offered. This custom, I understand, has for several years past entirely ceased, from the use of it having been found prejudicial to health.

When within four miles of Kingston we were met by four Caffre servants leading my companion's saddle horses, two of which we mounted and cantered that distance, Bonynge undertaking to provide a dinner, and to call upon me at three o'clock, desiring me to dress in the interim. At the appointed hour he conducted me to Baggs's tavern, where we sat down to a most admirable dinner, during which Baggs himself made his appearance with a bottle of champagne in his hand, of which he desired our opinion, observing, " You, Mr. Bonynge, are from the land of champagne, consequently a judge." It was by us both, and I flattered myself I knew something of the matter, pronounced delicious.

Bonynge invited Baggs to take a seat with us at table, which he declined, saying, " No, no, young gentlemen. In this house I am Jack Baggs, the tavern keeper. I never have since the duel I was involved in joined my customers, nor will I ever do so again. But over the way, where I consider myself *out of office*, I am your man whenever you please to honour me, and the oftener the better. There you shall have the same fare, the same wine, the same attendants, and *no bill*." Then taking a bumper of the wine standing he pronounced a panegyric upon it and upon our judgment and, making his bow, retired.

After a moderate proportion of claret we adjourned to the theatre, which was commodious, neatly fitted up, and had a more than tolerable set of actors then recently arrived from New York, in America, which city they had quitted in consequence of the popular commotions and probability of hostilities commencing with the Mother Country. The manager was a Mr. Hallam, brother to Mrs. Mattocks of one of the London theatres. After being very well entertained at the play, where Bonynge had collected five as pretty girls as a man would wish to look at, we seven went to a tavern in the neighbourhood of the theatre, supped, and passed a jovial night.

The next day Bonynge " shewed me the Lions " as he

called it, that is, the few things worthy inspection at Kingston, after which we dined at the Harmonic, a very inferior house in every respect to Baggs's, where I met a party of gay young friends of Bonynge's and committed a debauch, continuing at the bottle until one o'clock in the morning, the consequence of which was that when called at five, the time appointed for going to Spanish Town, I had so excruciating a headache that rising was out of my power. Bonynge, finding me so ill, recommended strong coffee and a couple or three hours more sleep, which he had no doubt would restore me, and he would come again. His prescription completely succeeded; at nine I awoke tolerably well, dressed, repeated the dose of coffee, and at ten stepped into his post-chaise, which he had considerately brought as best adapted for an aching head, having sent his phaeton on halfway. By this double conveyance we reached Mr. Richards's in good time for dinner. The party consisted of the French Colonel, with three officers of his staff, the three gentlemen appointed to escort them, Captain Stair Douglas, one of his Lieutenants, four civilians, Bonynge, and myself. Our host entertained us sumptuously, and with abundance of *Mrs. Allen!* In the evening the arrangements were made for the route to be taken.

saw in Jamaica, abounding with fruits, tropical and European, vegetables the same, and an infinite variety of sweet-scented flowers. Being fatigued with our exercise, we took an early supper and, retiring to our beds, slept like English farmers.

I arose before the sun, walked forth, struck by the rich and beautiful scenery that appeared around, nor could I but contemplate with wonder and gratitude the beneficence of an all-ruling Providence that had thus furnished mankind with so useful a plant as the sugar cane, not an atom of which is lost. The green, or leafy part, affords excellent sustenance to the cattle, the juice drawn from the stem yields both sugar and spirit (rum), the dry cane after the juice is thus expressed becoming fuel for boiling it in the coppers.

The third day we proceeded into Savanna La Mar, visiting two noble estates, one belonging to the Forrest family, the other to Mr. Thellasso.

In Jamaica, and all over the West Indies, it is customary for all travellers to stop for refreshment and rest at gentlemen's plantations, there being scarcely an inn, or house of public reception, in a distance of a hundred miles. Whether the proprietor be present or not is never considered, for, if absent, the head overseer or manager does the honours of the mansion with equal hospitality as the owner.

The fourth day whilst we were viewing a remarkable cascade a quarter of a mile out of the road, a man on horseback came up who delivered a letter to our foreign companion, which, upon reading, he told us forced him to leave the party and return as fast as possible to Kingston, where a special messenger from his Government impatiently waited for him to attend him back to St. Domingo, an unpleasant circumstance having occurred which made his presence necessary. A sloop of war therefore waited to convey him to St. Domingo. This unexpected event, of course, put an end to our progress ; the Colonel and his suite, also Mr. Hall, as the youngest and most active of the managers, set

out on horseback in half an hour after he received the letter whilst the rest of us proceeded leisurely.

Young Bonynge observed that a good opportunity now offered for my visiting his father and passing some time at Bushy Park. I could have no objection, and, upon arriving at the road that led to it, we took leave of Mr. Richards and Mr. Harrison, bending our course to Bushy Park. On our way thither my companion said, " Although I have in some measure prepared you for the whimsicalities of my father, still it is impossible for you to have formed a just idea of the extent they are carried to. I think he will prove a fund of entertainment, only let me caution you to keep your countenance, for should his eccentricities excite your laughter in the commencement of the acquaintance he will take as great a dislike to you as he has to your humble servant, whom he abhors. Everything I say or do offends him. You must not be surprised at his calling me by all sorts of opprobrious names, damning my blood, or giving me the lie direct (you know, being my father, *I cannot kick him*). I firmly believe were I merely to observe how bright the sun shone he would instantly swear I lied—that there was no sun to be seen."

In a little more than an hour we entered the enclosed part of the grounds, which in point of natural beauties even excelled Mr. Kirkman's. It appeared to abound with timber trees of immense magnitude. As we approached the house, which had the grandeur about it of a palace, he pointed out to me his father, sitting in a noble portico at the head of a large flight of stone steps that led to the principal entrance, up which two negroes were leading a third, apparently so ill he could not support himself.

Dismounting from our horses, we ascended, the Doctor taking not the least notice of either of us, his sole attention being turned to the three negroes, whom with much vehemence and anger he addressed thus, " Well now, God damn your bloods, you infernal rascals, what do you want with that impostor, that sneaking, snivelling, shamming scoundrel lolling upon you. What do you want ? Damn your souls !

why don't you answer me ? " though from the rapidity
with which he spoke it was impossible for them to do so.
The moment he paused one of the men said, " Cato got
bad fever, Massa." " Fever ! " replied the Doctor, " you
lie, you scoundrel ! " Then turning to the invalid he violently exclaimed, " God damn you, you scoundrel ! How
dare you say you have a fever. I'll have you severely
flogged this minute. Call the driver." The sick person
answered not, but looked most piteously. The Doctor continued to thunder out, " God damn you ! Come here, you
scoundrel, put out your tongue, give me your hand," at the
same time applying his fingers to the wrist to feel the pulse,
which having done for a few seconds, he suddenly altered
his tone of voice and in the mildest accent and gentlest
manner said, " Get the Sedan and carry him softly to the
hospital. I'll send some medicine directly."

Then turning to me as if I had been an old friend, he
observed, " The poor wretch is dreadfully ill indeed, but
these cursed fellows plague my life out, for ever pretending
indisposition for the purpose of skulking from labour. The
whole world, I think, have united to torment me and reduce
me to beggary."

The son here, with a significant smile, said, " You are
speaking thus freely, Sir, to a stranger, a gentleman you
never saw before." " And who the devil told you so, Mr.
Jackanapes ? " said the Doctor, and, again addressing me,
enquired, " Pray where did you pick up this prince of
puppies ? " I replied, " Captain Surman had been good
enough to introduce me." " Surman ! " said the old man,
" what ! Paul Surman, my old crony Paul—he is as worthy
a fellow as lives. I have been intimately acquainted with
him these thirty years, nevertheless my back is up somewhat
just now. Why has not Paul found his way to Bushy ere
this time of day ? He never was so long in doing it before,
but he, too, supposes I am on the trot down hill, going the
way of all flesh and so to be forsaken."

The son, finding a pause, said, " That, Sir, is Mr. Hickey.
He was a passenger of Captain Surman's, and is come to

pass a week with you." "Sir," said the Doctor, taking me by the hand, which he shook heartily, "I am glad to see you with all my heart, and the longer you make your visit the more you will gratify me. I only fear you will not be able to endure that Frenchified puppy and his fopperies. Sir, he is the damnedest ass in existence." To this I observed he must forgive my doubting his sincerity when he spoke in such terms of his son, from whose acquaintance I had already derived much gratification, and should be proud to cultivate the regard of both father and son. "Sir," replied the Doctor, "you do us honour, and I hope the young man will exert himself to repay your kind partiality by showing every attention in his power. So go, Sir (to his son), and see that apartments are properly prepared for Mr. Hickey."

At dinner the Doctor was cheerful, perfectly correct in his behaviour, and did not use any offensive word to his son. There was only one other guest, Mr. Armstrong, an Irish gentleman, who lived within four miles, being the Doctor's nearest neighbour, and they lived upon terms of intimacy.

Mr. Armstrong was an unobtrusive, placid man who had been brought up at a provincial school in a pretty town in the North of Ireland, where little attention had been bestowed upon his education, a natural indolence of disposition tending to increase the evil. The consequence naturally was his being deficient in every point of learning, his knowledge extending no further than reading and writing, both moderately well. At the age of twenty he was sent for by his father to Jamaica, who, dying in five years, the son succeeded to a pretty fortune of between fifteen hundred and two thousand a year, from which time he had never been off the Island, and not often absent from his estate. At the time I first saw him he was sixty years of age, a strong, hale man, and notwithstanding so long a period had elapsed since he left his native country he still retained the "brogue" in a great degree. Doctor Bonynge was nearly of the same age, but looking more; thin in person, with plain features. He likewise was from Ireland, nearly related to the noble family of Belvidere.

The Doctor possessed three different estates, which together yielded him full twelve thousand pounds annually, and, according to the opinions of those conversant in such property, under any other management than his would have cleared at least sixteen thousand. The Doctor seemed determined to act unlike everybody else. A great schemer, he was for ever at some new experiment, none of which succeeded, on the contrary they materially deteriorated his property. Yet he obstinately and pertinaciously adhered to his own peculiar modes, constantly taxing Providence with dealing unjustly towards him and being sometimes exceedingly profane in his language upon that head.

Mr. Armstrong having invited us to spend the following day with him, we went accordingly. His house, which was small but comfortable, abounding with conveniences, stood upon an eminence commanding a delightful view of the adjacent country with a distant sight of the ocean. During this visit I was sorry to see a disposition in young Bonynge to turn Mr. Armstrong into ridicule by making him the object of his wit. Upon the impropriety of so doing I remarked to him aside, and he promised to cease, but still fell into the same error.

During my stay at Bushy Mr. Armstrong dined there several times, on one of which days he told us he had that morning received letters from England which mentioned that a disorder had raged in London during six weeks and had proved fatal to a great number of elderly people. After considering some time and endeavouring to recollect the name by which the malady was distinguished, he in a hesitating, doubting manner repeated the word, " Ama—Ama— Amanu—*Amanuensis!* Yes, I think that is the name." Whereupon young Bonynge burst into a violent roar of laughter, which induced the poor gentleman to enquire whether there was not such a disorder. " No, Sir, certainly not," said the young man. " An amanuensis, Sir, is a secretary, a person employed to write for another." The

Doctor on hearing this with much impetuosity cried out, "You lie, you puppy, you lie by God," and, turning to his friend, continued, "You are right, Armstrong, there is such a disorder." A stronger proof of the father's determination to contradict whatever the son asserted than this need not be given. The absurdity of both the elders only served to increase the mirth of the junior. I happily, though with some difficulty, preserved the gravity of my countenance.

Eight days having elapsed I mentioned my intention of returning to town, upon which occasion both father and son, for once in their lives, at least, were of the same way of thinking, uniting in their entreaties that I would lengthen my visit, and as I had no real business to call me away I willingly acceded, for which they both expressed their acknowledgments in very civil and friendly terms, the Doctor more especially, whose character I had seen a good deal into and clearly discovered that with all his oddities he possessed much philanthropy and benevolence, being ever ready to alleviate by every means in his power misery or distress ; but this was always done in his own peculiar and strange manner, as if he was ashamed it should be known he had done a generous or kind action. One of his greatest foibles was dealing in the marvellous, frequently relating the most incredible anecdotes, of which, too, himself was generally the hero. By patiently listening to these "poetical" effusions and never expressing a doubt of their authenticity, I completely gained his heart and became an uncommon favorite, he often declaring he had a greater regard for me than any man he was acquainted with. Occasionally he used to wonder that I could endure the extravagant and offensive coxcombry of "young Bonynge" (whom he never called "son").

The day after the time of my stay had been increased young Bonynge and I were walking in the portico when an exceedingly heavy shower of rain fell, and we observed at the distance of nearly two miles the Doctor galloping as fast as his horse could carry him to get out of it by sheltering himself under a shed erected for the cattle to feed in. As I had heard him arraign Providence with injustice by sending rain in every direction except upon his estate, I observed to my companion that his father would probably come to dinner in better spirits than usual from the abundant supply of water that was continuing to descend, when he said in answer, " Only congratulate him thereon and I'll bet ten to one he will say, nay swear, he has not had a single drop." This I deemed absolutely impossible.

During this conversation one of the under Europeans came into the house in great haste, and, being asked what he wanted, replied, " Clothes for the Doctor, Sir, he being wet through." " Now then," said I to the son, " I think you would certainly have lost your wager had I taken you up." " Not a bit," replied he, " I'll still lay the same wager." Two hours after this we met at dinner. I took an early opportunity of congratulating the Doctor upon the glorious shower that had fallen. " Shower, what shower, where, when ? " " All round, Sir," said I, " and very heavily, about two hours ago." " Yes," observed the son, " and I think you must have been wetted by it, Sir." " Wetted by what, you puppy ? " " Rain, Sir ! rain which made you put Dumpling (his horse's name) to his utmost speed." " You lie, you puppy, you lie, by God ! " and turning to me he continued, " There might possibly have been rain in the neighbourhood, but I give you my word, Mr. Hickey, not a single drop fell upon any cane piece belonging to me." I was confounded at this deliberate falsehood, whilst the son screeched with laughter, thereby exciting the Doctor's wrath, who abused him most grossly.

At the end of another week Bonynge, junior, conveyed me to town, which we reached on the 30th of December. Mr. Richards received me with much cordiality, saying he was glad I was come because a very pleasant party were to dine at his house on New Year's Day at an early hour, after which they were all to adjourn to Mr. Thomas Walling's, a few miles from Kingston, with which place he thought I should be greatly pleased.

On the 1st of January, 1776, after a light meal at one

o'clock we set off, myself and most of the party on horse-back. We ascended the Grand Leganee Mountain full four miles, and when at the perpendicular height of a mile and a half (as they told me) above the level of the sea, suddenly came upon one of the most romantic and beautiful spots I ever beheld, where stood an admirable mansion consisting of fifteen spacious apartments, from every one of which the magnificent city of Kingston, with the shipping, Port Royal, and intervening rich and fertile country met the eye ; a spectacle so sublime and magnificent I certainly never did see. The temperature of the air was delicious, forming a wonderful contrast to the extreme and burning heat we had been in only one hour before. At the back of the house rose the majestic and awfully grand mountain towering above the clouds in which its summit was completely en-veloped.

While partaking of a sumptuous supper Mr. Richards laughingly said to me, " I hope you have provided yourself with blankets, for I assure you they will be requisite at night." This I could scarcely credit, but found it very true, sleeping most comfortably under two, upon a nice, soft bed exactly as if in England. Indeed, the moment the sun dis-appeared the air became so sharp and keen we were glad to have all the doors and windows shut. Upon entering my bed-chamber I was agreeably surprized at seeing a fine, cheerful coal fire.

The next morning I arose at daylight, going to the window in the hope of seeing the effect of a clear sun rising, instead of which there was so thick a fog I could not see a yard before me. Much disappointed I dressed myself and went down to the breakfast-room, where most of the gentlemen were already assembled sitting by an excellent fire. On my lamenting the thickness of the weather, Mr. Richards said, " Oh, never mind the weather. Come and warm yourself," pointing to a chair next to his. I obeyed and was placed with my back to the windows. After chatting about half an hour Mr. Walling desired me to look whether it was clearer or not. Upon going to the window for that purpose

I found as bright a morning as ever shone, when Mr. Walling told me what I had imagined to be fog was an actual cloud passing slowly by us, both above and below, as was generally the case a short time before sunrise.

This truly charming place was called, "Cold Spring," taking that name from a remarkably cold and beautifully clear spring of water that issued from a fissure in the rock, supplying the family with the best water I ever tasted. To the touch it was like ice itself. Captain Surman was to have been of this party, but was prevented by a slight indisposition. Mr. Walling spoke of him with much respect and regard as being one of the best men he ever knew.

After spending three days as merrily and happily as any of my life we returned to Kingston. Here the journal of one day furnishes the history of all. I arose about seven; at eight breakfasted, after which I either rode out on horseback or walked down to the wharfs by the seaside to look at the busy scene of shipping or landing goods, &c. At ten commenced the round of coffee houses and taverns, reading the newspapers and conversing on the general topics. This usually occupied about two hours. From thence, either accompanied by Bonynge or other young friends, we lounged amongst the different *stores* (shops or warehouses where trade is carried on), or I attended Mr. Richards in his morning visits to families of his acquaintance until towards two in the afternoon, when we went home to dress for dinner, which meal, whether at home or abroad, filled up the space until it became time to attend the theatre, assembly, concert, or private party, as previous engagement or inclination led, retiring to sleep, in common, about midnight.

This sort of life necessarily required cash. The heaviest expence, I felt, was clothes, the inhabitants of the Island being fond of finery in dress, and as I had not such a stock in my possession as upon my eastern voyage, I was obliged to apply to a Jamaica tailor, a set of men who know how to make out a bill quite as well as the most fashionable fellow of St. James's Street. A second application to Mr.

Richards therefore became necessary, who advanced another hundred pounds.

I had written to my father a few days after I landed at Jamaica, truly stating all that had occurred, and the serious disappointment I had met with, as well as the kind reception I had had from his old friend, Mr. Richards. This gentleman, about fourteen years prior to the time of my acquaintance with him, had married a widow lady possessed of large property. In two years after their being united she died, leaving all she had to her husband, part of which was a noble estate in the parish of St. Ann's, on the north side of the Island, yielding upwards of three thousand pounds per annum. In eighteen months after this lady's death another widow of equal affluence with the former became enamoured of Mr. Richards. Courtship and wedlock ensued; ten years of uninterrupted felicity was enjoyed by both, when she also was carried off and an accumulation of wealth followed to the survivor, to whom she left a fine plantation in St. Mary's, almost at the eastern extremity of the Island, of at least six thousand pounds a year. Thus with his own private fortune he possessed property to an amount of between eleven and twelve thousand per annum. He was considered as one of the best planters in Jamaica, and being particularly fond of the business never spoke of returning to Europe.

When at Kingston I constantly attended Divine Service on Sunday, there being a large and commodious church. Mr. Richards's pew, in which I sat, was directly under the monument erected to the memory of the gallant Admiral Benbow, whose history and untimely death are recorded in a celebrated ditty, known to and in the mouth of every old British tar.

CHAPTER V

SUGAR ESTATES—THE NEGROES

AT the end of January Mr. Richards told me he intended visiting his estate in St. Mary's, and hoped I would accompany him. On the 3rd of February, immediately after breakfast, we set out in an open phaeton, but as I had not lost my Eastern fears of the sun, I carried an umbrella to defend my head from the influence of its piercing heat, a precaution my host treated with some contempt, observing that the rays of that useful luminary never injured anyone, an opinion clearly erroneous, but which Mr. Richards persisted in, protesting that nothing but indolence, or pride, made people dread the sun, or decline going out whilst it shone. Notwithstanding this prejudice of my friend I continued the use of an umbrella, and have no doubt I escaped many a severe headache, if not something worse by so doing.

In a part of our journey, which was close at the edge of the sea, Mr. Richards got out of the carriage. After walking a few yards he picked up a shell, in form very like the English periwinkle, only larger. This he gave to me, desiring I would take off my glove and hold the shell in the palm of my hand when the *curious* inhabitant would soon make his appearance. I did as he desired, and while he drove on attentively watched it for a few minutes. Nothing coming forth I had almost forgot I held the shell and was conversing with Mr. Richards when, feeling something tickle my hand, I looked and saw a hideous, large, black spider, whose long legs spread over my entire palm. In a monstrous fright I shook my hand violently and so got rid of my disagreeable visitor. Mr. Richards then informed me that this odious insect bred in a particular vegetable substance that grew on the sandy beach. At a certain age it

47

crawled forth in search of the fish to which the shell I had seen belonged, which, having killed, he left until the sun completely dried it up, when he took possession of the shell, using it as an habitation, from which strange circumstance it was distinguished by the name of "the soldier!"

Having gone a distance of about eighteen miles, we stopped at a gentleman's house to dine, after which we mounted two horses to finish our journey. Proceeding in that manner nearly as many more miles, I perceived upon a hill a large body of negroes apparently running with great swiftness towards us. I knew not what to make of this, and had I not observed my companion was perfectly tranquil, should have felt alarmed from an apprehension they might be maroons (runaway slaves) coming to rob and perhaps murder us. As these people approached I asked Mr. Richards the meaning of it, who answered, "Have a little patience and you will see." Scarcely had he said this when the whole posse of men set up a general shout, danced, played a thousand antics, and seemed to be elated with joy, several calling out, "God bless Massa! Good Massa, poor negro glad Massa come, good Massa!" In this manner they attended us, running by the side of our horses full two miles, when we reached the mansion house and I first learnt they were the plantation slaves, really rejoiced and happy at the presence of their owner, a circumstance that surprized me, as most of those I had seen upon other estates appeared dejected and miserable. Mr. Richards's, on the contrary, were the most cheerful and contented creatures that could be, nor did I ever visit either of his plantations without being a witness to the same expressions of joy on his arrival and concern at his departure.

Mr. Richards told me that from the day he became proprietor of an estate he had made it a rule to treat his slaves with kindness, and to show them every indulgence within reason, that he never allowed his overseers to work them beyond their ability or at unseasonable hours, Sunday being always set apart for their own benefit. On that day they never went to the cane pieces, but employed themselves in cultivating small pieces of land allotted to each, whereon they grew fruits and vegetables not only sufficient for their own consumption but to sell a considerable quantity, which they took to the public markets, the produce being considered their own absolute property.

The consequence of this humane and sensible plan was, as Mr. Richards said, not only gratifying to his own feelings, but proved very advantageous, for his slaves, instead of considering him a tyrant and oppressor, looked upon him as their friend and protector, and were always willing to labour to the utmost extent of their strength, even much more than ever was required. Such is the effect of kind treatment, of which that long-oppressed race were as susceptible as men could be. Mr. Richards likewise encouraged them to marry, by which means his estates were amply stocked without making any new purchases of slaves (he assured me he had not bought twenty during the last ten years). When any of them became infirm or incapable of work, from age or otherwise, they were taken care of and comfortably provided with habitation, food, and all the common comforts of life.

Mr. Richards's house was all upon one floor, delightfully situated upon the side of one of the most lofty mountains in that part of the Island, commanding an extensive and luxuriant prospect. Towards the east and south the ocean presented itself, and in every direction on the land were beautiful buildings, where different gentlemen planters resided. During my stay at this paradise, as I may call it, I had opportunities innumerable of seeing the affectionate attachment of the house slaves, and of noticing the extraordinary cleverness of the men.

I one day heard Mr. Richards directing a male negro to carry a message of considerable length and very complimentary to a family that resided a mile off. As soon as he set out I observed to Mr. Richards, " You cannot suppose that man will recollect one-third part of what you told him to say, I presume." " Indeed I can," replied my friend ; " he will not only deliver every word I bid him, but will

embellish from his own head." And this was actually the
case. He also showed me another instance of their sagacity
by ordering a man to go to a lady in the neighbourhood with
a message which, although in plausible language, amounted
to nothing. The slave, who listened with the utmost attention, the moment Mr. Richards ceased speaking, with a smile
upon his countenance, said, " Cin Massa, you give me basket
for fetch water," than which nothing could be more expressive.

Our style of living was very different from that of Kingston
or Spanish Town. Instead of the splendidly covered table of
those places our daily fare was fish, a single joint of meat,
and a pudding, sometimes poultry instead of meat, but all
being of the best I thought such dinners far preferable to
the perpetual round of many courses. The only thing
that annoyed me was the bread, which I observed was
full of black specks, and upon more minutely examining the
cause ascertained those specks to be insects that were baked
in the loaves and rolls. I therefore picked out as many as
I could, laying them by the side of my plate, which drew
Mr. Richards's attention, and he said, " What do you do
that for ? it is only *weevils* " (an insect that breeds in
flour or bread long kept in hot countries, with which sea
biscuit frequently abounds). I answered, " That might be,
but I could not bring myself to swallow them ! "

As we kept early hours at night we generally arose with
the sun, riding to some one of the neighbours to breakfast,
after which five hours were occupied in the cane pieces,
the curing house and distillery, so that I might soon have
completely qualified myself for the *enviable* office of a
negro driver, as the inferior overseers are called, but
I happened not to have any turn that way, and although at first much amused by inspecting the processes of
sugar and rum making and hearing learned dissertations
upon every branch of a planter's business I soon tired of it,
leaving my host to proceed alone to his daily avocation,
whilst I contented myself riding about the most romantic
country in the world, or amusing myself in observing the

gambols of a variety of game, which were so familiar as to come close to me.

Whilst at this charming place an opportunity was afforded me of seeing the effect of the current in the ocean, which along the whole coast of Jamaica, as well as the other Islands, sets with more or less force to the westward. Sitting one day at dinner with Mr. Richards we saw a ship, close hauled, standing in from sea direct for the land, which by his telescope he knew to be the *Augustus Cæsar*, one of the finest vessels in the West India trade. She was commanded by Captain Duffell, a friend of Mr. Richards's, and was endeavouring to work up from Kingston to Port Morant at the east end, where she was to receive cargo for England. When within half a mile of the shore she tacked and stood out to sea again, by dusk being out of sight. The next day at the same hour we observed her coming in, putting about when near the shore as on the preceding afternoon. This continued eight successive days without her gaining a single mile, but on the ninth the wind went a couple of points more favourably and she gained her destination, from which she was not more than three leagues distant when we first saw her, the current operating so powerfully against her she could not get to the eastward at all ; it was all the time blowing so strong she could only carry double-reefed topsails.

At the end of eighteen days we took our departure from St. Mary's, with which I had been greatly delighted, the slaves accompanying us running by the side of the phaeton, but without any of the expressions of joy they had shown on our approach. When we had gone about two miles Mr. Richards stopped, and, bidding them " Good-bye," desired them to return home, which order they instantly obeyed, many of them crying out in their broken English, " Good-bye, Massa ! God save Massa and send him soon again to poor negro man."

Having driven the longest half, or about one and twenty miles, we stopped at a pretty penn to breakfast, where the owner gave us some well-made *Johnny* cakes, supposed to be an adulteration of *Journey* cakes from their being prepared in a few minutes. We then mounted our nags, reaching Kingston to a late dinner. I there resumed my former mode of living, passing my time very pleasantly in the society of agreeable persons of both sexes.

Captain Surman, on my return to town, called upon me to say he hoped if I remained at Jamaica until the *New Shoreham* should depart on her return to Europe that I would occupy my old cabin on board, which, and with truth, I assured him I should be happy to do. He at the same time gave me an invitation to Old Harbour (about thirty-five miles from Kingston), where his ship was receiving her cargo of sugar, for the 17th of March, St. Patrick's Day, when he was to have several friends to dine on board the *New Shoreham*, and celebrate the nativity of their tutelar saint.

On the 15th young Bonynge conveyed Captain Surman and myself to his father's, which was in the road to Old Harbour and only six miles from it. Here we were to remain until St. Patrick's Day, and on that morning proceed on board. Three other gentlemen who were to be of the party were likewise at Dr. Bonynge's.

Early in the morning of the 17th the party assembled on board the *New Shoreham*, where due honour was paid to the memory of St. Paddy. The old Doctor (Bonynge) was particularly gay and elated, protesting he would not quit the ship until an equal sacrifice at the shrine of Bacchus had been offered to Shela, Paddy's wife, according to the laudable custom observed in Old Ireland. "And by my faith and troth we will celebrate her as she deserves." This jolly proposal was carried by acclamation. The whole party slept on board, and the following day "took a hair of the same dog," after which we went back to Bushy Park and from thence to Kingston, where I found Mr. Richards within an hour of departure for Spanish Town, to which he insisted upon my accompanying him, as he intended to proceed from thence to the north side, which I must see, as he was clear I should be as much pleased with the beauties of that part as I had been with St. Mary's.

After a few merry days with his friends at Spanish Town we set out for his estate in St. Ann's on horseback. After riding about eight miles we reached a part of the country more magnificently and awfully grand than I had ever before seen, which drew from me expressions of rapturous surprize, with which Mr. Richards seemed highly pleased. He told me it was called sixteen-mile walk, and was undoubtedly the masterpiece of nature. He said he had forborne to say a syllable about its beauties in order to let them burst upon me without any previous notice or raising my expectation respecting it.

The road is admirably good, passing between prodigious rocks and mountains, so lofty and so close to each other in many parts as to obscure the sun and render it almost like twilight, the sides of both mountains and rocks being entirely covered by a variety of beautiful trees, some of immense size. At intervals, through openings at the summit, large bodies of water came foaming and dashing down from point to point, making a noise equal to thunder, at the bottom forming a clear and transparent spring that runs with great velocity close to the edge of the road. At no time is it possible to see more than half a mile before you, the road going by a very acute angle round a bluff and perpendicular rock of tremendous height. Now and then a small chasm affords for a moment a more distant view, which increases the novelty of the scene.

When at the end of this terrestrial paradise we began to ascend a prodigious mountain, one of a range that runs directly across the centre of the Island. Upon reaching the top the prospect was beautiful and grand beyond imagination in every direction, especially towards another range of stupendous mountains extending from the northeast to the south-west called the Blue Mountains, from constantly bearing a tinge of that colour.

In all my travels through the four quarters of the world I have never beheld any scenes equal to those in this altogether beautiful Island, and in my opinion no time could be better or more pleasantly employed than in making a voyage to Jamaica for the sole purpose of viewing and admiring its various and incomparable natural beauties.

In order to indulge me with every new view, Mr. Richards made many halts for half an hour at a time, from which cause the day was far advanced when we got to the bottom of the mountain to an inn, the only one I saw out of Kingston or Spanish Town. Here we procured a tolerable dinner, and being both somewhat fatigued from the journey and remaining so long exposed to the fierce rays of a burning sun, Mr. Richards resolved to stay the night.

At daylight the following morning we got into the phaeton and reached his house to a late breakfast. This mansion was very superior to the one at the east end, being of the best masonry, built in the modern style of architecture, and had the advantage of two stories. The furniture was neat and handsome. Mr. Richards told me it had been planned and erected under the particular direction of his first lady, who, from her partiality to the spot, resided there the greater part of the year. In other respects, too, it differed from St. Mary's by standing low, at the very edge of the surf which broke upon a gradually sloping beach of fine hard sand.

From the rooms in which we breakfasted and dined we could see the people catching the fish of many sorts, all excellent, with which the table was supplied. The windows of my bed-chamber, which was on the upper floor, looked inland over a delightful plain several miles in extent, the whole covered with the richest verdure and many fine cane plantations. Adjoining the house was a spacious and admirable garden, both kitchen and pleasure, so well laid out that it would not have disgraced a gentleman's seat in England. There not being any other resident within a dozen miles we had no society, notwithstanding which time never hung heavily. The mornings were spent rambling amongst the fields and the works, occasionally hunting and shooting. During dinner we drank three or four glasses of Madeira and, after it, a bottle of claret between us, then walked in the garden or amused ourselves at a capital billiard-table until tea. Picquet or books occupied us from that to supper, and at ten o'clock we retired to bed.

Although the slaves had not, like those of St. Mary's, run out to meet us, they appeared equally attached to their master and happy at seeing him. Five hundred were assembled in the court-yard to greet his arrival, which they did in as barbarous a noise as I ever heard, but with unaffected joy in their faces and manner. They all looked fat and sleek, seeming as contented a set of mortals as could be. Upon expressing the pleasure it afforded me to find this race so differently treated from what I expected and so opposite to the opinions entertained by the generality of people in England, Mr. Richards observed that, independent of common humanity, which ought to influence the minds and conduct of superiors to those placed under them, their own interest should induce lenient, if not kind, treatment, and he was convinced by his own experience that more was to be effected by moderation and gentleness than ever was accomplished by the whip or punishments of any sort. " Of this fact," continued he, " to-morrow will, I lament to say, afford you a melancholy proof, for I propose driving, or riding, over to an estate of my brother Fitzherbert's, nine miles hence, one of the finest upon the Island, abounding with the important article of water, as well as every other natural advantage. The annual produce until the last five years was five hundred hogsheads of the very best sugar and four hundred puncheons of rum, whereas it now yields not one-third of either, and is every year becoming worse, the mortality amongst the slaves being unparalleled, and all this owing to a system of the most dreadful tyranny and severity practised by a scoundrel overseer, whose mismanagement and brutality I have over and over again represented by letter to my brother in Ireland, beseeching him to get rid of the villain, but all in vain. He seems infatuated and has rejected my offer to take the management of the estate into my hands."

We accordingly mounted our horses at break of day and rode over, where a sad reverse did present itself. At the instant of our arrival the most melancholy and piercing cries met our ears, sounding like that of a female. Upon advancing to the inner yard we beheld a wretched girl, apparently not more than sixteen years of age, tied by her wrists to a stake whilst a stout negro man was flogging her with such severity that every lash tore away the flesh from the back of the miserable victim. An ill-looking savage of a European was looking on, desiring the man to strike harder. My blood boiled with indignation at the sight, and I would gladly have put the fellow to death upon the spot.

Mr. Richards instantly ordered the flogger to cease and the girl to be released, an order no negro would venture to execute, but, another European coming up, did as Mr. Richards desired. My companion then in glowing language reproached the overseer with his brutality, asking what offence the wretched child could have committed to call for such inhuman butchery. The scoundrel, with a contemptuous sneer, replied it was no matter what the offence was, that he was the best judge how his slaves were to be managed. Mr. Richards then addressed the other European, a young man about two and twenty, asking if he knew the crime that had occasioned such murderous conduct, whereupon the overseer insolently said, " If you presume to answer a single question, or say one word without my permission, Charles, I'll make it the worst job of your life. You know me, Charles, and, believe me, you shall bitterly, most bitterly, repent it."

This was too much for even the mild temper of Mr. Richards to submit to. With far more warmth than I had ever seen him assume, he said to the overseer, " You horrid scoundrel, who are a disgrace to the name of man. I am determined from this moment your tyranny shall cease, nor shall you remain another day upon this plantation." " Shan't I ? " impertinently retorted the fellow, " and are you the man to displace me ? Pray, Mr. *Champion*, by what authority ? " " By my own as a magistrate," said Mr. Richards, " and I now tell you that if in two hours

you are to be found I will send you off to Spanish Town in
irons."

The villain, finding Mr. Richards thus determined,
lowered his tone. He observed that all the accounts of the
estate were unsettled and no person but himself competent
to arrange them properly, besides which he alone was responsible to his employer for every guinea disbursed or
received. To this Mr. Richards said he cared not about
responsibility—there he should not remain let the consequence be what it might, adding, " My brother has already
suffered too much by placing confidence in so infamous a
fellow as you are. As to your accounts, I will, after they
have undergone the most scrupulous examination by me,
settle them, for which purpose I desire you will attend with
all the papers and vouchers at my house at Spanish Town
this day week, when I shall be there." The man then for
a short time became as abject and submissive as he had
previously been insolent and haughty, but finding his
servility was not likely to operate in his favour, and that
Mr. Richards continued inflexible and firm in his determination, he resumed his natural character, once more became
excessively impertinent, using the most scurrilous language,
and swearing and blaspheming in a manner I never before
heard, vowing he would have full revenge. He finished by
threatening Mr. Richards with a variety of prosecutions,
that he had property of his own upon the premises to the
amount in value of at least five thousand pounds, for every
shilling of which he would attack him, and having recovered
his money he would next have his heart's blood. From the
appearance and conduct of the fellow I really began to
apprehend he would proceed to some personal violence.

By this time the other Europeans employed, four in number, were all assembled around us, and as I concluded they
would support their leader as head overseer and manager I
thought our situation critical and alarming. Upon that
head, however, my mind was soon set at ease by the young
man we had first seen saying to Mr. Richards, " Indeed,
Sir, it is high time the tyranny and ferocity of this man

should be put a stop to. If it is not I am sure within three months there will not be a single slave left alive." The moment these words were uttered, the overseer became mad with rage. He flew upon the young man like a tiger, seized him by the throat and would soon have strangled him. Seeing the danger I made a blow at him with the butt end of a heavy horse whip which I had in my hand. Fortunately, it took place upon the side of his head, which gushed out with blood, and he fell, apparently dead as a stone. I certainly thought I had put an end to his mortal career. The standers-by, both black and white, seeing him down, immediately bound him hand and foot, running a pole between the cords with which he was pinioned, exactly as I have seen practised for carrying hogs, and thus they bore him off to his house.

One of the Europeans returning soon after to us, I feared he was come to announce the man's death, and asked the question, to which I was answered, "Dead, Sir! Lord love you no, not he. No, no, the rascal is not so easily killed, or he would have met the fate he deserves over and over again. A bit of plaster will soon set his damned skull to rights. In an hour or two he will be as ripe for mischief as ever." I was not sorry to find I was not doomed to be his executioner.

Mr. Richards then dispatched a messenger to summon a party of the military who are stationed all over the Island, at about four leagues apart. Luckily, one of the posts was within two miles of his house. We then went up to the unhappy object who had been so barbarously treated, whom we found in so languid a state as to apprehend that her life was in danger. Mr. Richards caused her to be immediately conveyed to the house and there laid upon a couch. A cordial draught somewhat restored her, when her cruelly lacerated back and other parts of her body were dressed, and we left her to repose. We were informed by the other Europeans that the only cause of such punishment was her refusing to gratify the lustful wishes of the overseer, whose conduct was rendered still more reprehensible from his knowing that the poor creature was suffering under a violent fever at the time he inflicted the whipping.

At two in the afternoon a party of the military arrived, into whose charge the brute was delivered, the corporal commanding being directed to conduct him to Kingston and there deposit him in prison, for which purpose Mr. Richards gave his warrant as a magistrate. We subsequently learnt that the villain in the commencement of his march was so obstreperous they were obliged to handcuff him and bind his arms back with cords, when he had nothing left for it but abuse, which he dealt out most abundantly.

On the second night of his journey he made a desperate attempt to escape, which cost him his life. The party having stopped for the night, all but one, who stood to watch the prisoner, lay down to sleep. The fellow himself also pretended to be asleep, making a noise in imitation of snoring. His plan so far succeeded that the sentry, having no suspicion of his intention, laid his musket down, seating himself upon the side of the bank under which the rest were sleeping, where he soon began to nod. The prisoner perceived this, and softly raising himself from the ground made a blow at the soldier with his irons, so effectual that the cross-bar fractured the poor man's skull. The noise of his fall, however, awakened his comrades, who, jumping up and seeing the prisoner running off, they all as fast as they could presented their pieces and fired. Two of the shots took effect, one striking the backbone, of which wound the horrible villain languished for three weeks and then died, thus cheating the gallows of its due. The wounded soldier happily recovered.

The same hour that this wretch was sent off the estate innumerable complaints of his atrocities were made, whereupon Mr. Richards issued a proclamation assuring the slaves that they would no more be treated with severity. On the contrary, that they should meet with every encouragement and indulgence, recommending them therefore to leave off *dirt eating*.

It is no less singular than true that the miserable Africans employed to cultivate our West India Islands were driven by despair, more especially from harsh and cruel treatment to destroy themselves by eating the earth, a small quantity of which they swallow daily. This gradually reduces them, finally causing death as certainly as the most potent poison. I saw several so weak and ill from this practice they could scarcely drag one leg after the other, with countenances inexpressibly melancholy and ghastly. We found that upwards of two hundred of the unhappy men belonging to Mr. Fitzherbert Richards had thus destroyed themselves, to the enormous loss of six thousand pounds.

Mr. Richards having settled all matters for the future good management of his brother's estate, and sent for a new overseer, in whose integrity and abilities he could confide, we, on the 24th of March, left St. Ann's on our return to Spanish Town, retracing the same enchanting ground we had before passed. Upon arriving at Mr. Richards's I found a letter from my father in answer to the one I had written him, positively prohibiting me from returning to England, insisting upon my getting employment in an Attorney's office, the salary from which must support me, and to wait with patience until I could get admitted to practise for myself ; that should I, in defiance of his strict injunctions to the contrary, quit Jamaica as I had done the East Indies I might provide for myself, as he would have nothing more to say or do with or about me.

My pride could ill brook the idea of settling down as a hackney writer in a place where from the day of my arrival I had lived in splendour, keeping company with all the first people of the Island, nay, I pronounced it utterly impossible so to do. I mentioned the purport of this letter to Mr. Richards, at the same time observing I had made up my mind on the subject. He expressed his surprize that my father should desire me to stay after the communication that had been made to him, giving it as his decided opinion that were I to comply it would cost him (my father) at least two hundred a year to maintain me. He therefore thought me right in my determination to return.

I went to Kingston the beginning of April, where I passed a week of dissipation with young Bonynge and his gay associates. Captain Surman called upon me to say he hoped his ship would be quite ready in a fortnight, for which purpose he was labouring hard, and hoped to sail under convoy, report saying the Americans had a number of privateers out to intercept our West Indiamen. He requested I would be at Old Harbour by the 17th at the latest.

On the 4th I once more accompanied Mr. Richards to St. Mary's, where we remained only two days and then returned to Kingston. On the 7th Captain Surman came to take leave of Mr. Richards, intending to leave town finally that afternoon.

Young Bonynge insisted upon my passing the last few days with his father and him, fixing upon the 12th to convey me to Bushy Park. The interval was occupied in paying my respects to the many families and individuals both in Kingston and Spanish Town, from whom I had received the utmost hospitality and kindness. My name with a notice of my intention to embark for England in the *New Shoreham* had, according to the custom of the place, been stuck up for eight days at the Town Hall, Court House, and Church, without which ceremony and a certificate from the Provost Marshal, no Commander can receive a passenger on board his ship. This practice was adopted to prevent persons clandestinely leaving Jamaica after having run in debt with everybody who would trust them, and taken up goods from the merchants, as had often been done to the ruin of many industrious, honest men.

The day previous to that fixed for my departure I was agreeably surprized by a visit from my young Streatham companion, Lewis, who only arrived the preceding evening. We spent the remainder of the day together very pleasantly, talking over old scenes and past times.

After a cordial farewell to Mr. Richards, on the 10th of

April, 1776, I got into Bonynge's phaeton, who drove me down to his father's, which we reached just in time for dinner. The Doctor expressed himself with uncommon civility, and, as his son observed, seemed really glad to see me, which was not often the case with his guests. I remained with him till the evening of the 16th, when I proceeded to Old Harbour, where I stopped at a miserable hole of a house, although dignified with the name of "Inn," where I found my Commander and a Captain Dobbins, who was going passenger with him. Captain Surman said he hoped to sail the following day as he only waited for thirty hogsheads of sugar from Savanna, which he expected every moment. Having been introduced to Captain Dobbins, he told me he had been upwards of sixteen years in the West Indies, the greater part of which he was in the 36th Regiment of Foot and latterly had a company in that fine corps.

The next morning I arose before the sun, but found Captain Dobbins already up. We amused ourselves in gathering shaddocks fresh from the trees to send on board for the voyage, also in preparing eggs by dipping them in melted fat and placing them in kegs of flour, both which processes he seemed quite *au fait* with, and they did him credit, keeping admirably well the whole voyage. He appeared to be a good-humoured, cheerful man, but as I soon discovered had a great propensity to the marvellous. In the evening of the 17th we sailed, and off the west end of the Island joined two other homeward-bound ships, both of which, being better goers than we were, left us in a few hours.

CHAPTER VI

HOMEWARD BOUND

I LEFT Jamaica with considerable regret, for independent of its being the finest country I ever beheld, the extraordinary civilities and acts of kindness I experienced from many of its inhabitants claimed my warmest gratitude. The climate agreed with me perfectly. During a residence of near five months I lived extremely free in point of wine and kept late hours, exposed myself to the heats and damps and all the sudden changes prevalent there, yet never had the slightest attack of fever or any malady whatever beyond headache, which pain I was subject to in every climate. I am therefore bound to speak well of Jamaica.

When off the Island of Cuba I expressed a wish to see the famous fortress at the Havannah, against which our Navy and Army had been so successful several years before, whereupon Captain Surman good-naturedly hauled in for the land and ran so near that several shot were fired at us from the different batteries we passed. Fortunately none struck us, though within a few yards of doing so. Whilst running along this coast, canoes came off to us with turtle, different fruits, and turtles' eggs, made up in the form of Bologna sausages with spices, &c. They were highly smoked and proved an excellent relish.

There were no other passengers on board the *New Shoreham* than Captain Dobbins and myself, except a fine little boy of about nine years of age, son of a gentleman of large fortune, who was going to England to be educated. This little fellow had a voracious appetite, eating more than two of us at table. Captain Dobbins took delight in cramming him until he could not swallow another morsel. At

63

one of these superabundant meals, his friend continuing to supply his plate, the boy was obliged to give out, saying in the true Creolian style and language, " No ! me no can yam more, maw Billy have so full, if my yam any more me shall pop ! "

Having entered the Gulf of Florida, we experienced a current so rapid as to set us from fifty to seventy-five miles to the northward every twenty-four hours, which appeared the more extraordinary as the wind blew strong from the north, thereby raising a high, short, and disagreeable sea, which tumbled us about sadly. We had scarcely cleared the gulf when a violent storm arose, in the commencement of which we saw at a distance the two ships that had run from us off the west end of Jamaica. The gale increased so much at night we were obliged to lay to under bare poles, and the wind blowing dead on shore, we began to be under some apprehensions. At daylight the other two ships that had been to leeward had made so much better weather of it than we did that they were four miles to windward of us. This increased our alarm.

The third morning the ship suddenly sprung so dangerous a leak as to make it necessary to keep the pumps constantly going, and even then the water gained so fast that Captain Surman told us there was no alternative or chance of preservation but by bearing up and endeavouring to make the port of Charles Town in South Carolina, which, by reckoning, was directly under our lee. We accordingly set our foresail, running for the land, which we saw close to us at three in the afternoon, before sunset got a pilot on board, and by dark came to an anchor off the town.

Several armed boats came alongside, the officers from which told us our ship would certainly be made a prize of, as war was declared and they had many frigates out. Captain Surman, upon hearing this, immediately addressed a memorial to the Governor, stating that an act of Providence had sent him into port for the preservation of the lives of those on board ; he therefore trusted he should be allowed to refit and depart. This document Captain Surman read to me for my opinion previous to sending it, observing at the same time I must make up my mind to becoming a prisoner, as he was convinced no advantage would arise from his statement, the Americans in general, especially those of the southern provinces, being the basest and most unprincipled people under the sun. Upon this occasion, however, he did them injustice, the answer to his memorial being extremely liberal. It stated that Americans warred not with Providence, that the elements having forced the *New Shoreham* into their harbour they scorned to increase our misfortune by using a right they were entitled to, and therefore every relief and assistance within their power should be afforded, and permission to depart when repaired to a distance of twenty leagues from their coast without molestation.

In consequence of this handsome determination carpenters and other artificers were sent on board, the leak found and stopped. In three days the ship was reported fit to proceed, and an order was forthwith sent on board for us to put to sea within twelve hours, a pilot attending to conduct us out. Neither Captain Dobbins nor myself were permitted to go on shore during our short stay, but we daily received an ample supply of fresh provisions, fruits, vegetables, and bread from the town. Having passed the bar we stood away with a fine fresh breeze. We afterwards heard that the two ships that sailed with us from Jamaica were both captured by an American privateer that fell in with them a few hours after we saw them in the gale.

Before we had been a week at sea the leak broke out afresh, not much to the credit of the Carolina workmen, and bad weather coming on it increased so quickly as to keep one pump at work night and day. The rain made things extremely disagreeable as owing to the necessity of keeping everything close shut the steam from the sugar in the hold turned every article in our cabins of the colour of lead, and caused, too, a most offensive smell; but notwithstanding this state of the ship a branch of an Arabian jessamine that was tied up to the deck between the beams in the great cabin continued blossoming and bursting into beautiful flower the whole voyage, and arrived at London in the most perfect vigour and condition. This is a very extraordinary plant, the produce of Jamaica for many years back, but said to have come originally from Arabia. Its height when full grown is from forty to fifty feet, with a great spread of branches. The flower, which is a bright red, is uncommonly rich, yielding a strong aromatic scent, and is in full beauty before a single leaf makes its appearance. It is a hardy plant ; the piece I am speaking of I saw Captain Surman tear off the tree, chuck it into the boat and send it off to the ship just as if it had been to burn, without the least care or attention, nor was anything done to it during the passage, yet no part of it seemed at all dry or decayed.

Captain Dobbins, who was a strong, robust man, proved a useful hand at the pump, where every soul on board, including even the Commander, took his spell in turn, except that we passengers were not summoned to it during the night. Jerry Griffin one morning finding more time elapse ere the water came than he thought ought to be, exclaimed, " Damn my eyes ! if this pump does not put me in mind of my grandmother." " How so, boatswain ? " enquired Captain Surman, who was standing by. " Why, too old to suck," replied Jerry.

It continued to blow hard, but, fortunately, from the north-west, which was nearly right aft. Not a day passed without something giving way, such as tacks, sheets, halliards or braces, which made the demand for cordage so frequent that at last we had not a single fathom left. On the banks of Newfoundland the weather was horribly bad, and, notwithstanding a severe gale of wind, there was so thick a fog we could not see the length of the ship. This I was told is peculiar to that part of the world.

On the 12th of June at daylight a large fleet was seen right ahead, laying to, which, as we approached, were ascertained to be men-of-war and transports. At eight one of the frigates spoke us, saying they were bound to America with troops and stores, had been eight days from Cork, for five of which they had laid to in the same gale that was then blowing. They also gave us the bearings of Cape Clear, distant as they supposed forty-five leagues. As this corresponded exactly with our ship's reckoning, Captain Surman stood on with confidence, knowing that one hundred and thirty-five miles would allow us a fair run for thirty hours. It had always been a practice of his, when wind and weather permitted, to run up mid-Channel until abreast of the Isle of Wight, which was the first land he made, unless he happened to see Guernsey, which he told us we most likely should have a view of by noon the following day.

From the time of Mr. Scott's death, as already stated, Jerry Griffin, the boatswain, had taken the command of a watch in his stead. The night of the day on which the frigate spoke us he relieved the second mate at midnight, when he observed to him there was a great change in the sea, which was become much smoother although the wind had not decreased. He therefore supposed we must be well up Channel. This the mate did not think possible. Jerry commenced his usual walk, keeping a good look out. We were then running before the wind under double-reefed top-sails, the top-gallant masts and yards being down upon deck. He soon observed a black object upon the horizon, which at first he imagined to be a cloud, but seeing it stationary he then supposed it a ship. In about an hour it had so much increased in size that he became alarmed and called the mate, who could not discern anything. But as the men upon deck all saw it and pronounced it land, he went to the Captain's cabin and awakened him, telling him we were near some land, whereupon Captain Surman jumped up, and so did I, having heard him called.

The moment the Captain got upon deck, he cried out, "Zounds! it is the Island of Guernsey. Here's the Casket lights within half a mile of us, and we shall certainly be upon the rocks." All hands were instantly summoned, the yards braced up and the ship brought upon a wind. In less than an hour the day broke, when to our surprize and terror we beheld the black and terrific stony side of Guernsey, with a most tremendous sea breaking over the rocks almost around us, some of them being within a few hundred yards. I thought nothing could save us! Providence, however, preserved us from destruction and we cleared every danger, passing so close to one set of breakers that I could have jumped upon them. It was a truly terrific and awful scene. By five in the morning we were well out to sea again, and the wind fell considerably. We therefore once more stood our course up Channel; by noon it became quite moderate and turned to a beautiful summer day.

At sunset we saw the Isle of Wight, and a number of ships standing in different directions; at daylight of the 14th saw the South Foreland, and at half-past five anchored in the Downs; fine, clear sky, not a cloud appearing. Captain Dobbins having proposed that we should travel together to London, we took leave of our good-tempered Commander, went on shore, and I once more entered the Hoop and Griffin Inn, where I ordered breakfast. Whilst it was preparing we went out to stroll about the town, and my companion in passing the larder observed a prodigious fine rump of beef hanging up, upon which he exclaimed, " Oh ! what a glorious sight. How heartily I could eat from that charming joint." The landlord happening to hear him, said, " Sir, the cook shall cut and dress a steak for you directly, if you please," which offer was eagerly accepted. We then sallied forth for a quarter of an hour and returning, I sat me down to tea and coffee, but the admirably well-looking steak being brought in with fine oyster sauce, I could not resist the temptation, joined my messmate, and made a delicious meal, the slip slops going away untouched.

After this old English breakfast I went to my old friend, Mr. Baker's, where a servant told me he and family were all at Brighthelmstone. At eleven we got into a post-chaise, and between four and five reached Rochester, putting up at the Crown, where Dobbins proposed staying the night. We made dinner and supper, walked to Chatham in the evening, and the next morning proceeded to London.

As black was a cheap and good travelling dress I had put on a suit of mourning. Having no intention of going to my father's after the letter I received from him at Jamaica until I had first felt my way a little, I advised Captain Dobbins, instead of going to a noisy inn, as he had intended, to let me introduce him to Lowe's Hotel as far preferable in every respect. He agreed and we there dined together, after which he went in search of his agent and I to take a sly peep at St. Albans Street. Calling at Davies's mineral water warehouse, which was only three doors from my father's, I was informed that all my family were in town, and that an account had just arrived of the death of my brother Henry at Madras, whose loss I sincerely deplored.

Not knowing what was to become of me, or how I should act, it, after much cogitation, occurred to me that I had better consult my steady and attached friend, William Cane, upon the subject. I therefore immediately bent my steps to his house in Berners Street, but found he was at a country house at Erith in Kent. The following day, with a clean shirt in my pocket, I set out for Erith, intending to walk the road until some return chaise overtook me. Thus I marched to Shooter's Hill, when I reflected that should Mr. Cane's house be full of company, my going there uninvited and unexpected might not be prudent. I therefore resolved to alter my plan by going to Gravesend, and from thence to address a letter to my friend, stating the disagreeable situation I was in, and asking his advice. I stopped at Dartford, where I dined, drank a bottle of port, which gave me new vigour, and then continued my pedestrian journey, reaching Gravesend at seven in the evening. This was the longest walk I had ever taken, being full five and twenty miles, and I felt fatigued by it.

The next morning I wrote and sent my letter, and in the evening received the kindest answer, desiring me directly to come to his house, where a cordial welcome awaited me, and that he would talk over the state of my affairs and see what plan would be best to adopt in future. To Erith I accordingly went, the family then consisting of Mr. and Mrs. Cane,

Mrs. Johnston, her mother, and one child, a beautiful boy four years old. The house, although upon a small scale, was neat and convenient, delightfully situated upon the edge of the Thames, down to which his garden went, his famous cutter which I have already spoken of, laying at moorings within a few yards of his steps, forming a very pretty object.

Mr. Cane's establishment was rather splendid than otherwise. He had an excellent town house in Berners Street, six male-servants within doors—that is, his own man, two in livery, coachman, postilion, and groom, besides which there were two gardeners, a helper in the stable, and four hands in the cutter. He had five beautiful carriage horses, with three for the saddle, a coach, post-chaise, and phaeton ; being somewhat of an epicure, his table was always well furnished, and he took special care to have the best of wines. He had estates of his own which yielded rather above two thousand pounds per annum. Mrs. Cane's fortune was thirty thousand pounds, but the match being disapproved by her trustees though they could not prevent it as she was of age, they shackled the husband to the utmost of their power, positively refusing to advance a single guinea. This occasioned him a temporary embarrassment, for as he had always lived up to the extent of his income, perhaps some years a little beyond, he found a difficulty in raising sufficient cash to purchase equipage, plate, furniture, and the numerous et ceteras indispensably requisite upon commencing housekeeper with a wife and family.

Mrs. Cane was the youngest of three daughters, their father leaving to each twenty-five thousand pounds, but as Mrs. Cane was an infant when he died her fortune accumulated to more than thirty thousand. One of her sisters married Sir William Beauchamp Proctor, many years one of the Members for Middlesex. The other wedded the famous Charles Yorke (brother to Lord Hardwicke), who for a few days was Lord Chancellor, which high office he had been induced to accept by the particular and earnest request of the King, and that contrary to a promise made his brother that he would resist all importunities and that nothing should induce him to accept the Seals under the then administration. He, however, had not fortitude enough to withstand His Majesty's personal entreaties and yielded. Going from Court to Lord Hardwicke's to endeavour to make his peace, his Lordship, who was rather apprehensive of the consequence of his visit to Saint James's, when he saw his brother's carriage drive up, went to the head of the stairs to meet him, but the servants at that moment announcing Mr. Yorke as Chancellor, his Lordship hastily returned to his apartment, dashing the door in his brother's face and indignantly refusing to admit him. Mr. Yorke instantly went home and cut his throat, of which wound he died two days after, tearing the dressings off when he understood there was a probability of his recovery. At the time of his death a patent of peerage for him had been made out, and only awaited the affixing of the Great Seal thereto.

At Erith I was surrounded with every elegance, and treated with respect and kindness by each individual of the family. We spent the first day very cheerfully, Mr. Cane forbidding anything relative to business. The next day he told me that from the disposition he understood my father to be in respecting me I must not expect much, or that he would even see me, adding, " But don't be cast down by what I have said ; we shall be able to strike out something for you without his assistance, upon which point we shall have sufficient time and opportunities to consult together during a voyage I am going upon in a few days with some friends, and which party you shall join." He then ordered his phaeton, and I accompanied him therein to London, ordered my trunk from Lowe's Hotel to Berners Street, and after purchasing a supply of readymade linen from Blunts' warehouse at Charing Cross, returned in the same carriage to Erith.

On the 20th (of June) the company that were to go upon the cruise assembled at Mr. Cane's, consisting of Lord George Gordon (who afterwards engaged so much of the public attention and was the primary cause of the dreadful riots of

1780). He was then a gay, volatile and elegant young man, of the most affable and engaging manners ; George Dempster, Esq., a Member of Parliament, and secretary to the Order of the Thistle, the badge of which he wore suspended to a broad green silk ribbon round his neck ; Sir Charles Bingham, afterwards created Earl of Lucan ; Mr. Stephenson, who had made a large fortune in the East India Company's service at Bombay ; Mr. Cane and myself, making six in number. The gentlemen above specified were all men of superior talents, and being of exactly the same political way of thinking, condemning the folly and injustice of the Government in endeavouring to dragoon the Americans into unconditional submission, we were in no danger of arguments or difference of opinion upon that head.

Upon Mrs. Cane and her mother leaving the table after dinner, our host desired each guest to fill a bumper of champagne, which being complied with, he gave, "Success to the Americans," a toast that was applauded by all present with enthusiasm, and which we daily did due honour to during the time we were out. At night we went on board the *Henrietta*, the cutter being so named in compliment to Mrs. Cane, where we retired to our respective cots. Before break of day the crew got under weigh (having four additional hands, besides a Channel pilot, for the voyage), standing down the river with a fine breeze at north-west. At seven we passed Gravesend.

It having been previously resolved to keep early hours, we assembled to breakfast precisely at eight o'clock, dined at two, and supped at nine. Lord George Gordon, hearing I had recently been in the West Indies, asked me a variety of questions relative to the state of the British Islands. He seemed extremely pleased with the account I gave of the reception we had experienced at Charles Town, saying the Ministry ought to make a public acknowledgment of the liberality of the Americans upon that occasion. He then observed that he had two days before met at his father, the Duke of Gordon's, a gentleman just come from America, who had given them a most entertaining and interesting account of the ingenious manœuvres by which he had saved the ship in which he was a passenger from being captured. This account was that in the commencement of the voyage he had amused himself by painting upon pasteboard the mouths of canon, one of which he fixed into the different ports, being eight in number, and so well were they executed that any one at the outside must be deceived and take them for guns. After being ten days at sea a strange sail hove in sight, which upon nearing them was discovered to be an American privateer mounting thirty guns and full of men. While the enemy was in chase he dressed a dozen of the crew in old regimental coats, and made them, thus equipped, exhibit themselves in the most conspicuous parts of the quarter-deck. He also ordered two four-pounders that were placed upon the forecastle (to use as signals) to be discharged, and put on every appearance of being determined to resist. The stratagem succeeded, the privateer after hovering near the vessel for a couple of hours, firing now and then a random shot, having sheered off. Upon presenting her stern they read on the taffrail, *The Washington of Charles Town.* His Lordship then asked me if I had heard of that ship whilst at Charles Town, which I answered I had not.

In the afternoon, off the Island of Shippey, we lay to, sending a boat to Sheerness for a supply of vegetables and bread, which having procured we made sail again. The next morning early we saw three ships working up, one of which from her rigging I knew to be my old ship, where-upon I observed, " Here comes the *New Shoreham.*" Lord George, hearing this, earnestly exclaimed, " The *New Shoreham !* That's the very ship I alluded to." " Then, my Lord," said I, laughing, " the ingenious contriver of her escape must have been Captain Dobbins, for we had no other passenger." " Assuredly it was," said his Lordship, " and it is odd you did not notice the circumstance when I mentioned the privateer's name." " It would have been still more extraordinary if I had," was my reply, " not having seen or heard of any such privateer until spoken of by your Lordship." " You astonish me," said he. " What in God's name could have led the man to tell so strange and so wanton a falsehood, or to humbug my father and me with his idle invention?" The only way I could at all account for it was "his propensity to fiction," but in justice to my poor shipmate's good nature I thought it right to add, that "not one of the many marvellous anecdotes he had favoured me with ever tended to the injury of any human creature. In all he was 'himself the hero of each little tale.'" "Upon my word," observed Lord George, "this is the most ridiculous circumstance I ever heard of, and pray did nothing occur to give him the idea of such a story?" "Nothing," said I. "We saw no privateer, nor any sail whatever until near England, neither had the *New Shoreham* a single port, as you may perceive, or the sign of a gun on board, nor do I believe Captain Dobbins had a second regimental coat in his wardrobe." We then had a hearty laugh at the man's folly, Mr. Dempster remarking how very singular the discovery of it had been! Lord George could talk of nothing else for some time, protesting he would inform the Duke of the propensity his friend had.

In the evening we entered Margate pier, where we landed, attended the Rooms, supped, and returned on board to sleep, the people directly warping out and bending their course towards Boulogne, off which port we found ourselves upon rising in the morning. The tide being out we came to an anchor, stepping into our yawl to row on shore, but when within thirty yards of the harbour she grounded. A dozen flat-bottomed boats then approached, from whence issued a parcel of Amazonian fish women with their petticoats rolled close up, their whole thighs being bare. These masculine creatures seized hold of us, lifting us, whether we would or not, out of the yawl, and carried us in their arms to the land, a smart contest, in which several of them lay sprawling in the sea, taking place who should secure the prey.

Upon reaching *terra firma* we immediately proceeded to the house of Messrs. Meriton and Smith, eminent English wine merchants, who carried on a prodigious trade in that town. Mr. Smith, who was well acquainted with Mr. Cane and Mr. Dempster, received us with true hospitality. After having sacrificed freely at the shrine of Bacchus, Lord George Gordon proposed a dash off to Paris for a couple of days, which being agreed to three *voitures* were sent for to be at the door at daybreak the next morning, when the whole party set off, and early on the third day entered the French capital, driving to a handsome hotel in Rue St Sauveur.

The general appearance of the city by no means answered my expectation or the opinion I had formed of the far-famed Paris. It, however, certainly contains a number of magnificent public edifices.

Mr. Cane and I went to visit Messieurs Panchaud, two brothers who carried on the business of bankers, and with whom I had become acquainted at my father's in London, where they generally went once a year. They invited our party to dinner the next day, giving us a very cheerful " Faire Fête." We there met several of the *noblesse*, most of whom accompanied us to the opera in the evening.

The following day we went to Versailles and saw the Royal Family at Chapel. Having viewed the Palace and Gardens we returned to Paris, again to dine with the Panchauds, one of the guests being Major Baggs, brother to the Jamaica hero. He was very civil and attentive to me, and at night took me to his box at the *Comédie*, where he introduced me to Mr. Taaffe, an Irish gentleman of fortune, who told me my father was one of the oldest friends he had. Mr. Taaffe and Major Baggs lived together. They insisted upon our party dining with them and gave an entertainment in princely magnificence, the wines being delicious, especially the burgundy, of which I took a large quantity.

Having made the most of our time and seen the rarities of Paris, we on the 28th (of June) commenced our journey back to Boulogne, arriving at Meriton and Smith's on the 1st of July, where we took another batch of his excellent wine, and prepared for sea, Mr. Cane sending on board the

Henrietta a plentiful supply of champagne and claret, the hampers containing the same half filling the cabin.

On the 2nd we sailed out of the harbour at high water with a fine fresh breeze from the south-west, which drove us on at a fine rate, bending our course across the Channel direct for Portsmouth. When we had been about seven hours at sea a Custom House cutter ranged up alongside, one of the officers coming on board to examine our vessel. The man was as civil as possible, paying vast respect to Mr. Dempster's ribbon and insignia of the Thistle. After enquiring from whence we came and whither bound, Mr. Cane invited him into the cabin, where, seeing the hampers arranged, he observed, "You have laid in a good stock of wine, Sir." Mr. Cane replied, "It is necessary as we mean to be out several weeks and are six in number. Besides, you know it would not do to stint ourselves." The officer good-humouredly agreed, saying, "Certainly, Sir, you are quite right to have enough. It is not to watch pleasure vessels like this that we are employed." Having eat some cold fowl and ham, with a tumbler of madeira, he returned to his cutter and stood up Channel.

After dinner our conversation turned upon the usual subject—America, when Lord George Gordon said to Mr. Cane, "I think in compliment to the worthy patriots of our injured Colonies upon the Continent you ought to call your cutter the *Congress* (the meeting of the people under that title having been then established). This observation was unanimously deemed a very proper one, and Mr. Cane determined forthwith to rechristen her. All hands instantly filling a bumper, we drank, "Success to the *Congress*." Johnson, the head man or master, being summoned, was told she was no longer the *Henrietta*, but was in future to be called the *Congress*, a bowl of punch being ordered for the crew thereupon.

On the 3rd we made the Isle of Wight and stood for Portsmouth Harbour with a pleasant light wind. At Spithead we passed close to an eighty-gun ship laying at anchor. All our party being upon deck, Johnson at the

helm, the Lieutenant on duty very civilly asked, " Pray,
my lad, whose cutter is that, and what's her name ? "
Johnson answered readily enough to the first part, " Squire
Cane's, Sir," after which he paused, and in a hesitating
manner added, " The *Congress*." In the very moment he
said so, we had shot ahead sufficiently for the Lieutenant
to see " *Henrietta* " upon her stern. He therefore, naturally
enough, conceived the man meant to be impertinent, and
angrily said, " Damn your blood, you impudent scoundrel,
I wish I had you here and I'd congress you. Your master
ought not to encourage such insolence."

Having entered the harbour we brought to alongside
a hulk and went ashore to view the dock, store-houses, and
other works worth attention, which occupied three hours
very pleasantly, after which we returned to our cutter, and,
dropping down with the tide, got out to sea again and made
sail. The 4th, after a fine run, we arrived at Weymouth.
This place had been fixed upon as the extent of our trip to
the westward, and we spent ten days at it most agreeably in
as good a tavern as any in England. Our whole party subscribed to the Rooms, but my chief amusement was the
theatre, where there were a set of very tolerable actors.
We dined one day with Mr. Sturt, at his elegant villa a few
miles from the town, and another with Mr. Buxton, a great
Russian merchant, who resided upon the highest part of
Portland, commanding an extensive prospect of the ocean
with ships constantly passing and repassing, but the want
of trees made it, in my opinion, look dreary ; in winter it
must be dreadfully so.

The 15th we embarked in the *Congress*, reaching Portsmouth in the night of the 16th. In the morning we landed,
and in our walk upon the sea-line met my old friend, Gam-
bier, then an Admiral, commanding a fleet. He made us
stay to dine with him, and while over our wine told the
party how very ill I had behaved to him in the year 1756.
Upon hearing which Lord George Gordon exclaimed, " I
think Mr. Hickey was right, and acted prudently. There
is no encouragement nowadays in the navy to induce any

man to enter it ; it is all job and trick. This I know too well by woeful experience, having already been nine years a lieutenant without the least prospect of promotion." This, however, was not quite candid or fair in his lordship, for having constantly opposed Government in his place as a Member of Parliament, making violent speeches against all its measures, he could not reasonably expect that the administration would think themselves bound to give him rank in his profession.

CHAPTER VII

REST AT ERITH

WE left Portsmouth the 18th, early in the morning, and on the 20th our party landed at Erith in high health and spirits, finding Mrs. Cane and family perfectly well. The same evening Lord George Gordon and the other gentlemen left us. The following day Mr. Cane took me to town, where he said business would detain him some days. Calling at the Jerusalem coffee-house, I there heard that my old friend and shipmate, Mr. Jacob Rider, was returned to England with an ample fortune, residing in Upper Harley Street. I immediately went in search of him, and found him in a capital good house, splendidly furnished. He introduced me to his wife, whom he had married in Bengal, by whom he had one child, a fine little girl then four years of age. He received me with the most affectionate regard, said he had lately made many enquiries about me in St. Albans Street, and was sorry to see I was in disgrace with my father, who seemed greatly offended with me. "However," added he, "I, and the rest of your numerous friends and well-wishers, must exert our influence to bring about a reconciliation, and that once effected, away with you to Bengal as fast as you can. In the new Court established at Calcutta, I am certain you will succeed, nature having intended you for the profession of the Law."

Upon my return to Berners Street I told Mr. Cane what Rider had said, and he was of the same opinion, promising me he would directly apply to all his India connections respecting the obtaining leave for me to go out as an Attorney. The next day he took me to visit Mr. Gregory, who had resided for many years in India, where he had acquired an immense fortune, and was then a director, with whom he was upon the most intimate terms. This gentleman readily promised to give his interest towards promoting the object I had in view, observing that I ought not to think of going out until the spring, which would not only secure me a good passage, but make me arrive at Calcutta in the most pleasant and healthy season of the year. Having ascertained that my father was gone to Bath, I called in St. Albans Street to see my sisters, from whom I grieved to hear that he continued inexorable respecting me, and was resolved to interest himself no further about me. From my father's I went to Mrs. Forrest's, whom I found quite well, with all her lovely daughters about her. The whole family received me most kindly. Arthur was become an ensign in the Guards, leading a dissipated London life ; my favourite, Tom, was at sea.

After passing a week in town, I returned with Mr. Cane to the elegant and tranquil scenes of his retreat at Erith, where everything was so comfortable and so pleasing as to make time glide away imperceptibly. Our mornings were spent in either sailing, riding on horseback or driving in my host's phaeton to visit the numerous friends he had in the neighbourhood. The most intimate of these were : Mr. Wheatly, who possessed a fine estate about five miles from Erith ; Sir Sampson Gideon, nearly the same distance on an eminence between Greenwich and Woolwich ; Mr. Adair, father of the Recorder of London, who inhabited an old house in which Oliver Cromwell resided, within a mile of Mr. Cane's ; Alderman Kirkman, who had Calcraft's famous place at Norfleet ; Mr. Shuttleworth and Mr. Hussey, who lived together, also near Norfleet ; General Desaguliers and Lord Ferrers, who had cottages on the banks of the Thames. At all these houses we frequently dined in the pleasantest and most informal manner.

Frequently Mr. Cane and I, when sitting *tête à tête* over our bottle, have, upon observing a fresh westerly wind blowing, instantly gone on board the *Congress,* got under way, and in a few minutes been running nine or ten knots an hour on our way towards Boulogne. The cutter was kept in such a style that it was like moving from one splendid room into another equally so. Upon embarking the only difference was that instead of the handsome dining parlour of Erith we were in a neat cabin with the best wines upon a snug little table. Mr. Cane, observing that I was partial to champagne, always ordered a bottle to be brought during dinner, of which he usually drank a couple of glasses, and I finished it, after which we each took at least a bottle of claret, sometimes more.

I occasionally amused myself by making sketches of the beautiful landscapes that met the eye in every direction from my host's garden. I made two in particular, which I finished highly in water-colours, one being Mr. Cane's house and garden, &c., taken from on board the cutter, the other, the gunpowder magazines at Purfleet, three miles below Erith on the Essex shore. These drawings I presented to Mrs. Cane, who was so delighted with them that it induced in her a wish to acquire the art herself, and she expressed an earnest wish that I would become her instructor, an office I readily undertook knowing the docility and genius of my pupil. She entered upon the business with such zeal as very soon to make a considerable proficiency. The evenings (when only the family were present) we passed in playing at half-crown whist, or four-handed cribbage.

In the latter end of the month of July, a relation of Mr. Cane's, Mr. Peter Wybrants, a fine young man, came over from Dublin for the purpose of being entered at the Temple, being intended for the Bar. This young gentleman had chambers of his own, but spent much of his time in Mr. Cane's family, who were all sincerely attached to him. He therefore joined us on a party to Margate, where Mrs. Cane had been directed to go for the benefit of sea bathing. On the 31st Mrs. Cane (who never ventured upon the water) with her mother, Mrs. Johnson, departed for London, and from thence proceeded the following day by land to Margate. In the afternoon of the same day Mr. Cane, Mr. Wybrants, and myself, embarked in the *Congress* with a fresh south-west wind, reaching the place of our destination almost in the same moment that the ladies did. We immediately went to an excellent house that Mr. Cane had, by letter, engaged in Cecil Square, close to the new Rooms. After three days' sojourn Mr. Cane, Mr. Wybrants, Mr. Stephenson, whom I have already spoken of, and myself, set out on an expedition to Boulogne and down Channel.

As we did not intend to remain many hours at Boulogne, instead of entering the harbour, we came to an anchor outside the Bar, and went on shore in the boat, dined at Meriton and Smith's, returning at night to the *Congress* with an ample supply of wines for the voyage. We immediately made sail, steering direct for Beachy Head, intending to visit Brighthelmstone and stay there some days.

During our passage across the Channel it came on to blow strong from the south-west ; a high sea arose, which made Mr. Stephenson so violently sick we apprehended his bursting a blood-vessel. After a most boisterous night we the following day made the English coast and soon saw Beachy Head, distant about seven leagues, at which time it blew so hard we could scarcely carry a close-reefed mainsail and storm-jib, the sea making a fair breach over us every moment. The pilot assured us it would become much worse when off the pitch of the head, upon hearing which Mr. Stephenson begged most earnestly that he might be put on shore, he cared not where, for if he were obliged to remain on board another night he was sure he should die. Mr. Cane thereupon directed the pilot to stand close inshore in hopes of meeting with some fishing boat. We accordingly did run for the land, and the pilot soon informed us we were off the little village of Eastbourne. A small boat coming alongside, the people belonging to her said the gale would certainly increase, which induced Mr. Cane to resolve to stop a few hours to wait the result of the weather. Our whole party got into the boat and were landed through a tremendous surf, which completely drenched us.

Eastbourne, since become a fashionable place of resort, was then only an insignificant fishing town, consisting of about eight or ten scattered houses. The boatmen conducted us to the only public-house in the village, as miserable-looking a dwelling from the outside as I ever beheld, where, from its appearance, we expected neither victuals, drink, or any sort of comfortable refreshment. Upon entering, however, we were shown into a very clean room, where the landlady, in five minutes, made a cheerful and blazing fire. Whilst employed drying our clothes, Mr. Cane made enquiries whether we could have anything to eat. The hostess replied if we could put up with fish and poultry she could supply us, but she had no butcher's meat remaining. Being told we should be content with whatever she could produce she promised to do her best, and in half an hour we sat down to a beautifully white tablecloth, and she brought in as fine a dish of fish as ever was seen at Billingsgate, with excellent lobster and oyster sauces. This was followed by a pair of tender, well-dressed chickens, and we finished an ample repast with good old Cheshire cheese.

Concluding no wine was procurable in such a house, we washed down our food with tolerable ale, but one of the gentlemen asking if they ever sold wine of any sort, the landlady answered, " Yes, sometimes, but she could not expect such gentry as we would be able to drink it." A bottle was thereupon ordered, not with any intention of drinking it, but merely for the benefit of the mistress of the mansion who had furnished us with so admirable a meal. A bottle being opened, I poured out a glass, which smelling, I found to be claret, and tasting, pronounced it very fair wine. Mr. Cane thereupon took some, which he instantly declared to be as high flavoured claret as any in his own cellar. The consequence was a liberal potation, each of us drinking full two bottles.

Another matter of surprize awaited us, for upon calling for a bill, the landlady made a demand of eighteen-pence apiece, amounting to six shillings. " Six shillings, my good lady," said Mr. Cane, " is indeed a most moderate demand, but you must tell us what we are to pay for drink as well as eating." " Oh, dear gentlemen," replied the woman, " I can make no charge for that. You are heartily welcome to the wine, and I'm glad you were able to drink it. The case is, my poor boys now and then run over to Guernsey on little matters of business, and generally bring home with them a few dozen of wine, which I seldom find occasion to use, and as it costs me nothing, you are heartily welcome and much good may you do with it." By a few more questions we ascertained that her " poor boys " were neither more nor less than professed smugglers. With considerable difficulty we prevailed upon her to accept a guinea for as excellent a repast as ever four hungry fellows sat down to, and then began to talk of returning on board the *Congress* to proceed on to Brighthelmstone.

Mr. Stephenson thereupon declared that nothing should induce him ever to set foot on board a ship or vessel of any kind again, and as it still continued to blow hard he advised the whole party to send to Lewes for chaises and go across by land to Brighthelmstone, leaving the *Congress* to the management of her crew to convey her round by sea, orders to which effect were, in consequence, forthwith given to Johnson.

Having procured carriages from the nearest town, we reached Brighton in the course of two hours and a half. Here we anxiously looked out for the *Congress*, that we might change our clothes, having nothing with us except what was on our backs. The morning, however, appeared without any tidings of the cutter. We were therefore under the necessity of sending to a slop shop, each purchasing a shirt, &c.

After passing another anxious day at the principal inn and still hearing nothing of the *Congress*, the south-west gale continuing with unabated force, Mr. Cane determined to return to Eastbourne in search of her.

After breakfast the second morning, Cane, Wybrants, myself, and Tiger (an immense sized Newfoundland dog of Mr. Cane's), stepped into a post-chaise with four excellent horses, and set off for Eastbourne, where upon our arrival we learnt that the cutter had been seen about six o'clock that morning running by to the eastward, apparently in distress, having no jib-boom and the mainsail lowered down ; that while a boat was preparing to go off to her assistance she hoisted her cross-jack and topsail and run up Channel before the wind at a great rate.

Upon receiving this information we continued our journey along the coast, hoping she would stop at the first secure place. The wind was extremely high and blew in such violent gusts that at times we thought chaise, horses, and all would be driven bodily to leeward. The wind was from the sea, otherwise I should have felt very uncomfortable in running along the tops of exceedingly high hills and within a few feet of the edge of perpendicular precipices scores of fathoms deep.

After stopping at every town and fishing village on our route without getting any intelligence respecting the *Congress*, we, late in the evening, reached Dover, where we supped and slept. Early the following morning we walked down to the pier, making enquiries whether our runaway vessel had been seen, when the master of one of the Custom House schooners said he had observed a cutter of the description we mentioned pass the evening before at an immense rate, and stand round the Foreland into the Downs. We thereupon continued our journey to Margate, where we found the *Congress* very quietly laying at anchor.

Johnson lay the whole blame upon the pilot, who he spoke of as being frightened out of his wits when off Beachy Head from the sea breaking heavily on board every two or three minutes, so much so that the pilot insisted upon bearing away to prevent her foundering, notwithstanding he (Johnson) strongly objected, stating the necessity of getting to Brighthelmstone, as he knew neither his master or friends had a change of linen with them. The pilot, however, said he alone was responsible for the safety of the cutter, and bear up he would and did. Johnson further told us that when off Eastbourne he much wanted to stop there and land to ask about his master, but the pilot peremptorily refused, saying there was too much sea for any boat to venture landing in, and he must make the best of his way to find some shelter; that he (Johnson) being entirely ignorant of the navigation of the Channel, dared not venture to take the command from the pilot lest any accident should happen, and he therefore reluctantly yielded to his (the pilot's) orders.

As we were fatigued by our hurried journey along the coast of Hampshire, Sussex, and Kent, we complied with the wish of Mrs. Cane and her mother by staying at home the whole evening, determining to play a family rubber at whist, take an early supper, and retire to bed by ten o'clock. After playing one rubber I became so drowsy that I requested Mr. Wybrants to take my place at the card table, which he did, and I seated myself by the fireside, where I fell into a profound sleep, from which I awoke in the tortures of the damned, bouncing up, and screeching with a dreadful pain in my right foot. The whole party seemed to enjoy my distress, laughing immoderately, until the severity of the pain occasioned me to faint. All then were in the utmost distress on my account.

Upon recovering myself, I entreated that my boot might be cut off, which Mr. Wybrants instantly effected, and my foot was discovered to be in a dreadful state of inflammation. Oil and a variety of remedies recommended by the ladies were applied, but without procuring me the least relief. A surgeon was thereupon sent for, upon whose appearance I first learnt that the cause of my sufferings arose from a severe burn. Mr. Cane, not at all aware of the mischief he was about to do, observing me sitting cross-legged and fast asleep, twisted a piece of paper which he dipped in the wax of the candle, and lighting one end, lay it upon the top of my foot. I had on a pair of thick wax leather boots, and so deep and profound was my sleep that the entire paper was consumed before the anguish awakened me. So grievously had it operated that the upper part of the leather was burnt to a cinder.

The surgeon having examined and dressed my foot, ordered me to bed, there to remain until he saw me again. He then told Mr. Cane that he was apprehensive from the situation and appearance of the wound some of the large vessels were so materially hurt that I might be a cripple for life, upon hearing which my friend Cane was beyond measure distressed. He instantly dispatched an express to London to summon Mr. Robin Adair to come and attend me, but that gentleman happening to be at Bristol at the time, Mr. John Hunter, who had undertaken to act for him during his absence, instantly left town and came to me. After meeting the Margate surgeon and inspecting my foot he at once declared no ill consequence would arise, and that a few days' quiet, keeping my leg in a horizontal position, and frequently applying an embrocation which he ordered, would completely cure the hurt. And so it proved; in a week I was perfectly recovered, but during that period I was kept upon chicken broth, and not allowed a drop of wine, lest fever should ensue.

The whole family had attended me with the utmost assiduity and kindest attention, Mr. Cane or Mr. Wybrants being constantly in my room, reading or contriving some means to amuse me. The ladies, too, generally passed a couple of hours daily in my chamber. Mr. Cane was much hurt at the suffering he had occasioned me, declaring every hour his concern, adding that it would for the remainder of his life prevent his ever using, or permitting where he could prevent it, any practical jokes of the same kind.

After spending ten days in a sick room attending upon me, Mr. Wybrants left us to resume his studies at the Temple, though I believe much more of his time was sacrificed to Bacchus and Venus than to Coke upon Littleton.

On the 10th (August) I was so perfectly recovered as to be able to take a hard day's sail with Mr. Cane, and he then said if the wind continued in the same quarter, and equally fresh, he would the next day run over to Boulogne. Returning at six o'clock, completely drenched from the seas breaking over us every five minutes, we took a larger allowance than usual of claret, I having, as usual, previously dispatched a bottle of champagne. After receiving three or four different summonses to coffee, we, about ten o'clock, went upstairs to the ladies. I had my recollection perfectly, and I accomplished the getting to the drawing-room, where I seated myself as quickly as possible, but the heat of the fire brought on a sickness at my stomach which made it necessary for me to retreat rather precipitately, when I became so giddy that I thought it prudent to follow the advice of the housekeeper, and, instead of returning to the family, went to bed, where I immediately fell into a profound sleep, from which I did not awake until I perceived the sun shining brightly into my room, and, looking at my watch, found it was past nine. As we were to have started at five in the morning, I bounced out of bed, and, dressing myself with the utmost dispatch, went out to enquire the reason why I had not been called. Meeting Mr. Cane's valet, I asked the cause of his master's not having risen to embark for France, upon which he said, " Is it possible, Sir, you did not hear the confusion we were in for three hours last night ? My master fell downstairs and we all thought he was killed. My mistress was, from fright, thrown into hysterics, and screamed so violently I should have thought it must have awakened the soundest sleeper. In half an hour the house was filled with physicians and surgeons. The first report was that my poor master was dead, but I had soon the consolation to hear the surgeon reply, ' It may be so, but I'll answer for it he is only dead drunk.' " Luckily, he sustained no material injury in his fall, which was headlong down a flight of twenty steps. His escape was extraordinary, he being a very heavy man. I understood that after I left the drawing-room he got up to give some orders relative to our intended excursion the following morning, and in descending the stairs his foot slipped and he fell to the bottom, miserably bruised but without any fracture. Mrs. Cane privately, and with great gravity, the tears streaming down her cheeks, most earnestly entreated me to endeavour to discourage Mr. Cane from committing such excesses in wine, which she was sure must be prejudicial to his health. This I faithfully promised.

CHAPTER VIII

PREPARATIONS FOR EAST INDIA AGAIN

ON the morning of the 17th (August) we went to town to meet a large party dining with Mr. Cane in Berners Street, which consisted of Mr. John O'Neil, afterwards Lord O'Neil, Mr. Dawson, Mr. Martin, Lord Bellamont, Mr. Gregory, Mr. Dempster, General Armstrong, and Mr. Erskine, now Lord Erskine, who had just then commenced his study as a lawyer, intending to qualify himself for the Bar, where he subsequently made so conspicuous and brilliant a figure. At this dinner I first heard him recite his famous poem, called, "The Jeranium," a *jeu d'esprit* that showed more than common talents, with the most classical and elegant taste. After passing one of the pleasantest days of my life I looked at my watch, expecting to find it about ten o'clock. I, to my surprize, saw it was two, so rapidly had the time slipped away.

The following day my friend Cane took me to Mr. Roberts, an East India Director, to whom Mr. Gregory had spoken about me, and who, in consequence thereof, promised to obtain leave from the Court for me to proceed to Bengal in one of their ships. He received me with the utmost politeness, assuring me he should exert his interest in my behalf and, observing there would not be another Court for near a fortnight to come, desired I would call again upon him about that time. In the evening Mr. Cane returned to Erith, but I remained in London, being engaged to dine with my old *Plassey* shipmate, Mr. Jacob Rider, who had been some time returned from India, where I was most hospitably entertained. He told me he had spoken to General Richard Smith, Mr. Leicester, and others of his India connections, from all of whom he should get very powerful and useful recommendations for me.

89

Upon breaking up at Mr. Rider's I went to the Bedford Coffee House, where, meeting Major Nugent, Jack Tethrington, and some others of the old set, they made me promise to dine with them the next day at the Shakespear. I accordingly did so, and there once more fell in with the choice female spirits, Pris. Vincent, Newton, Sally Hudson, Kit Frederick, &c. The two first-named sang a number of delightful songs, and proved themselves in as fine voice as I had left them before my India voyage. The women all expressed great satisfaction at thus unexpectedly meeting me. This convivial party brought to my recollection many former scenes of dissipation, which, though highly gratifying at the time, ultimately occasioned me acute suffering and remorse.

On the 20th I returned to Erith, where I found Peter Wybrants just arrived before me. The following day we all went to dine with Mr. Wheatley, where we met General Desaguliers, and a pleasant party of both sexes.

On the 27th I went down in the *Congress* to Tilbury Fort, where I landed and walked to my friend, Colonel Cooper's, who had an excellent house about two miles inland, with whom I had promised to spend some days. On the 2nd of September I returned to Erith. The 3rd, Mr. Cane drove me to London and back in the evening, Mr. Wybrants accompanying us. The 5th, we sailed for Margate.

Upon my return to Erith I found a letter from Mr. Roberts, the Director, telling me there would not be a Court held for some weeks to come and desiring me to call upon him the first time I went to London. On the 18th (September) I therefore went to London for the express purpose of seeing him, when he said it would not be practicable to get me to Bengal in the capacity of a lawyer, the Directors having recently passed a resolution not to *let loose* any more Attorneys upon the public in Bengal; nevertheless he felt sure he should be able to get me out in some way or other with the sanction of the Court of Directors, of which he would inform me in the month of October.

On the 19th I went with Mr. Cane and his family to dine at Mr. Adair's, where, in the evening, I was set down to a half-guinea point party at whist. Bungler's luck attended me, for I won a rubber of three upon balance.

At Mr. Adair's I met a gentleman named Geoghagan who, upon hearing me called Hickey, enquired of what family I was. Being told in answer that I was a son of his old friend, Joe Hickey, "Impossible," replied he, "that is no more a child of his than of mine." Being again assured the fact was so, "Then, by God," said he, "his mother must have been either a mulatto or a Portuguese." This opinion was in some measure justified by my colour, which had become extremely dark from exposing myself so much to the sun whilst in Jamaica.

On the 21st Mr. Cane and I, notwithstanding the remonstrances of Mrs. Cane and her mother against our going to sea at the critical time of the Equinox, set off with a strong south-west wind for Boulogne, my host wishing to supply himself with his winter stock of champagne and burgundy. This voyage proved the roughest and most unpleasant we ever made.

At ten in the morning of the 1st of October we made fast to our buoy off Erith, and there learnt that Mrs. Cane had been extremely uneasy on account of the tempestuous weather. Upon our landing she expressed her joy at the approach of winter as that would put an end to the sailing parties. Mr. Cane afforded her infinite satisfaction by assuring her he would not cross the Channel any more until the next spring.

A week was passed very agreeably in visiting the different families round the neighbourhood, several of whom dined with Mr. Cane on the 8th. Whilst at our wine he was called out by his own servant who said a gentleman wished to speak to him in a carriage at the door. After being absent about five minutes, he sent for me. I found him conversing with a fashionable-looking man, to whom he introduced me, calling him Major Read. Mr. Cane then told me that business of the utmost importance required the Major's presence

as soon as possible in Paris, and as no mode of travelling
would convey him so rapidly as his cutter he had sent
to Johnson to get her ready forthwith, but that being himself
prevented accompanying his friend, from having a party
at his house, he should feel greatly obliged if I would go in
his stead, which I readily consented to do. Major Read then
took leave, saying he must go to Maidstone, but would be
back before midnight, and immediately embark.

Mr. Cane and I then returned to our company. Upon
their breaking up about twelve o'clock I went on board,
and, being tired, turned in, desiring I might be called upon
Major Read's arrival. He, however, came alongside so
quietly that I heard nothing of it, he positively forbidding
my being disturbed. I did not awake until past nine in the
morning, when looking out I found we were in the sea
reach. Dressing myself directly, I went upon deck and
there joined the Major, who said that not being used to a
swinging bed he had had no sleep and therefore rose at daybreak. He seemed to be an elegant man, well acquainted
with high life, had travelled much and spoke familiarly of
all the Courts of Europe.

There being a light breeze it was evening when we
reached Margate Roads. Johnson then asked me whether
I intended stopping for the night at Margate, or proceeding
immediately for France, to which I replied that Major Read
being most desirous to get to Paris he must stand on,
whereupon the Major observed that if I had no objection
he should prefer looking in for a few hours. We accordingly
entered the pier, dressed and went on shore to the Assembly
Rooms, where I found several acquaintances. I observed
my companion kept his pocket-handkerchief constantly
to his face, appearing solicitous to pass unnoticed by any
one, which I thought extraordinary.

At one in the morning we returned to the *Congress*,
immediately went to bed, and at daybreak left the pier,
steering for the French coast. At seven o'clock we perceived a boat following us, having every sail out that could
be used. Major Read became very uneasy when Johnson

declared she must be desirous of overtaking us from the signals she made, and that we had better heave to for a few minutes until she came up, to which I acceded, at the same time asking the Major if he had any objection. He eagerly answered, "Yes, he had, the greatest possible objection, everything dear to him in life depending upon his escaping." Whereupon Johnson instantly said, "Then never fear, Sir, I'll forfeit my life if ever she gets a foot nearer than she now is." Hauling up a couple of points closer to the wind, we ran from her as if at anchor, in little more than an hour losing sight of her entirely, and we resumed our proper course for Calais.

The Major expressed himself infinitely obliged by the successful exertions of Johnson and the cutter's crew in getting away from the chase. Observing my surprize at the earnestness with which he had spoken, and his anxiety while the boat continued in sight, he requested a few words with me in private. Retiring to the cabin, he there informed me that "Major Read" was an assumed name and title, his name being Bailley; that after many years' successful traffic as a merchant he suddenly became unlucky, some deep engagements he had entered into turning out so ill he was under a necessity of stopping payment, and found himself involved to an extent of nearly two hundred thousand pounds beyond his capital; that some of his largest creditors, conceiving (though wholly without foundation) he had not acted honourably, avowed their unalterable resolution of throwing him into jail, for which purpose they had issued writs, and he had too much reason to think sheriffs' officers were waiting at every seaport town along the coast to intercept him; that if one of them met with him his inevitable doom would be a prison for the remainder of his life. Thus circumstanced, he said, he had no alternative but becoming a fugitive, and greatly feared he never more should see his native land; that having in his prosperity been intimate with Mr. Cane, and knowing he kept a fine sailing vessel, it occurred to him as the most likely way to get off with safety, to effect which he disguised himself as a military man and was fortunate enough to make his escape from London.

Upon hearing this account, I asked how he could be so inconsiderate as to venture on shore and to go to the public Assembly Rooms at Margate. He admitted that it was imprudent, but he did not think the bailiffs would expect to find him there, adding, that when he saw the boat in chase of us he had given himself up, imagining a few hours would have placed him within a jail.

Some time after I discovered this gentleman to be the husband of the beautiful but frail woman rendered famous by her incontinence and amour with His Royal Highness the Duke of Cumberland. I also learnt that Mr. Bailley had not absconded empty-handed, having furnished himself with the means of living elegantly upon the Continent by secreting property to an amount of full thirty thousand pounds, the greater part of which was lodged in different foreign banks, and that a discovery of this dishonest conduct had justly irritated his creditors, inducing them to adopt harsh measures and to endeavour to secure his person.

On the 12th of October we reached Calais, putting up at the far-famed *Lion d'Argent*, of which hotel the voluble Monsieur Dessein was the proprietor.[1] After the usual salutations to *mi Lords anglais*, he told us they were in daily apprehension of a war breaking out between their nation and ours, owing to the decided part France had taken in aid of the American Colonies then engaged in a bloody contest with the Mother Country ; that a number of able and experienced officers had already actually sailed to give their assistance to the oppressed and ill-treated Americans.

Mr. Bailley rewarded Johnson and the crew most liberally ; he pressed me exceedingly to accompany him to Paris, where he would frank me as well as back to England. I had a

---

[1] Dessein's, the famous hostelry at Calais—now a thing of the past—was patronized by many notable Englishmen, including Sterne, who was there in October, 1765, and who mentions the hotel in his *Sentimental Journey*. Thackeray was also an *habitué* of Dessein's, and made it the scene of an imaginary conversation with Sterne in one of his *Roundabout Papers*.—ED.

great inclination to accept the invitation, but considering that I had to prepare for India, I did not think it prudent to absent myself, besides which I had for several days been considerably annoyed by a sore throat, which from its continuance created a considerable degree of uneasiness. I therefore resisted the temptation. After spending three days as agreeably as the state of my throat would allow I took leave of Mr. Bailley, who stepped into a cabriole to proceed towards Paris, whilst I, with an immense store of game, embarked in the *Congress* and sailed for the white cliffs of Albion.

The morning we separated Mr. Bailley presented me with a very handsome diamond ring, which he entreated my acceptance of, and that I would wear it as a token of his gratitude, and in remembrance of him.

I did not reach Margate until the 18th, having experienced much calm weather. Upon going on shore, Mitchiner immediately explained the cause of the boat that had given Bailley so much alarm following us. A gentleman, the nephew of Mr. Brown, the banker, was bound to France upon urgent business of his uncle's. He arrived at Margate just as we sailed, and hearing it was Squire Cane's cutter then leaving the pier to proceed to Calais he hired a small boat to convey him to her, meaning to request a passage. The boatmen ran foul of a collier, which carried away their rudder, delaying them half an hour ere they got another. During that time we had run so far they could not catch us, although they persevered in manner already mentioned.

After staying one day at Margate I sailed for the river, and in the morning of the 20th brought to at the moorings at Erith. Mr. Cane told me he began to be seriously alarmed at my long stay, fearing we had grounded upon some of the sands.

My pupil in drawing, Mrs. Cane, was delighted with the amusement and made a rapid progress. The day after my return I mentioned to Mr. Cane my having a bad sore

throat, whereupon he insisted upon my going instantly to
town to consult his surgeon, Mr. Robin Adair. I accordingly the next tide went in the *Congress* to Deptford, from
whence I took a coach. I had the disappointment to find
Mr. Adair had that morning departed for Ireland, and
would be absent at least a month. I next called at my old
operator's, Mr. Hayes, who had recently married one of the
Miss Basils, by whom he got a noble fortune. Here I was
equally unfortunate, he having just left town with his wife
and her sister for the German Spa. Near his residence I
accidentally met Jack Tethrington, to whom I mentioned
the object of my visit to London, asking if he could recommend me to a medical man. He instantly named Mr.
Howard, of Bow Street, as a man of superior skill in his
profession, being then Chief Surgeon to the Middlesex
Hospital. Tethrington kindly offered to go with me and
introduce me, which he did. After inspecting my throat,
Mr. Howard gave me a prescription for a gargle and for some
pills, desiring to see me again in a few days. I therefore
thought it prudent to remain in town, and as I had ascertained that my father was absent I called in St. Albans
Street to see my sisters. They, amongst a variety of other
particulars relative to old acquaintances, informed me that
Arthur Forrest had involved himself in debt so deeply as to
be obliged to leave the Guards and go into a regiment of the
line which formed part of the Garrison of Gibraltar, for
which place he had embarked. From St. Albans Street I
went to Mr. Roberts's, but he was not in town.

After continuing twelve days under the care of Mr.
Howard, I, on the 4th of November, returned to Erith,
chiefly because I knew that about that time the family
usually went to town for the winter. Both Mrs. Cane and
her mother were so attached to the spot and the agreeable
society of the neighbourhood that they thought with regret
of the change to the noise and dissipated scenes of the
metropolis.

The weather proving uncommonly pleasant, with fine
fresh winds which induced sailing almost daily, we re-

mained at Erith until the 1st of December, except that during the period I went twice to London to see Mr. Howard, who at my last visit pronounced me perfectly cured and well.

When settled in Berners Street I went at least twice a week to the India House and Jerusalem Coffee House, the latter being the general resort of all those who had anything to do with India. I there learnt that the early ships for Madras and China were to be dispatched in a few days ; I therefore immediately wrote to my favourite Bob Pott, to announce to him my intentions of proceeding to Bengal, in order to practise as an Attorney in the Supreme Court of Judicature there, and that he might expect to see me in a few months after that letter reached him.

I frequently dined with my *Plassey* shipmate, Jacob Rider, in Upper Harley Street, where I always met uncommonly gay and pleasant parties. He proved himself sincerely and zealously attached to my interest.

I often attended the theatre in the evening, went sometimes to the opera, and occasionally mixed with my former profligate associates of both sexes.

A few days before Christmas Mr. Roberts, with a number of Indians and others, dined with Mr. Cane, when that gentleman (Mr. Roberts) informed me he had obtained the permission of his brother Directors for my going out to Bengal, and that if I would call at the Secretary's office within the course of a week and make use of his name, Mr. Mitchel would do all that was requisite on my behalf.

On the 2nd of January, 1777, I went to Mr. Mitchel, who told me the necessary documents should all be prepared for me by the 6th, on which day I found they were so, but I was not a little surprized at receiving amongst them Free Merchant's indentures, because I had heard that it was nearly as difficult to obtain that mode of getting to India as the appointment of a writer. Mr. Gregory advised me to try to be on board the *Duke of Portland*, and gave me a letter of introduction to her Commander, Captain Sutton, who behaved with the greatest civility, but expressed his concern at the impossibility of taking me in his ship, the whole accommodation being engaged for Mr. Wheler, a member of the Supreme Council. He, however, suggested the probability of my getting a berth in the *Seahorse*, which would sail at the same time, and kindly offered to speak to Captain Arthur, the Commander, to receive me, and he requested I would meet him the following morning at the Jerusalem Coffee House, where both he and Captain Arthur would be at noon. I accordingly observed the appointment and was introduced to Captain Arthur, who lamented his ship's being so crowded he could not give me a cabin to myself, but if I would submit to be with three other gentlemen I might have a passage in the *Seahorse*. Circumstanced as I was I, without further hesitation, settled the business. Captain Arthur's purser thereupon told me I must forthwith send one hundred guineas for a seat at the Captain's table, which was double what I had paid to Captain Waddell in the year 1768.

A few days after I had engaged my passage, Mr. Howorth, a barrister and man of eminent talents, called upon me to introduce a brother of his, Humphry Howorth, who was going out to India as an assistant surgeon in the service of the Company, and wished to be in the same ship with me, a wish I could have no objection to, but I told Mr. Howorth I was afraid he would find a difficulty in procuring a passage for his brother in the *Seahorse* from her being already much crowded with passengers. To this he replied that Captain Arthur was a particular friend of his and would submit to any inconvenience to oblige him. He then asked me to dine with him on a future day and he would get the Captain to meet me. At the appointed day I went, and was made acquainted with his brother, in whom I recognized a constant frequenter of the different billiard-tables and tennis-courts, to whom I had lost many sixpences. I had never heard his name, and considered him to be one of the numerous herd of pettifogging little sharpers who were constantly upon the look out in the hope of fleecing some novice or unwary young man, nor do I believe I was much

mistaken in forming such an opinion of Mr. Humphry
Howorth at the time I so used to meet him. Upon entering
the room in the Temple where we dined, Mr. Howorth told
me his friend, Captain Arthur, had consented to take his
brother out to Bengal, and that his ship would probably
sail early in April.

The requisite cash for fitting me out and paying the
passage was furnished by my steady friend, Mr. Cane,
without whose aid I know not what I should have done.

Towards the end of the month (January, 1777) I was
attacked with the same sort of sore throat I had suffered
under in the preceding autumn. I became uneasy, mentioning the circumstance to Mr. Cane, who thereupon
immediately took me to Mr. Adair's. Mr. Cane told him that
as I was upon the eve of departing for the East Indies no time
was to be lost, and Mr. Adair engaged to restore me to as
good health as ever, to effect which I must go through the
very unpleasant process of salivation.

I took lodgings directly opposite my father's in St. Albans
Street, which I was induced to do that I might have the
use of his kitchen, of servants, &c., in supplying me with the
requisite broths and articles I should want during my
confinement. I took possession of my new abode on the
1st of February. My friends were all very kind, endeavouring by every means in their power to beguile my hours of
anguish. My sisters and brothers also came sometimes to
see me. Mr. Cane and Mr. Wybrants never missed a day,
the latter usually sitting two or three hours. With the
latter occasionally came a Mr. William Burroughs, a distant
relation of Mr. Cane's, and then at the Temple preparing
himself for the Bar.

I derived the greatest advantage from the situation of
my lodgings, especially when upon the recovery, by being
supplied with poultry, wines, and various good things from
my father's. Mr. Adair had been uncommonly attentive
during my confinement, and as his professional skill was
of the very first rate, I felt confident in a perfect cure. On
the 10th of March he pronounced me fit to embark for any

part of the world, but he recommended me to use the warm
bath and drink plentifully of sarsaparilla for a fortnight.
I therefore went to Nerot's famous baths in King Street,
St. James's Square, where my career had nearly terminated.
The heat of the bath brought on a fainting fit in a few
minutes after I got in. The waiter in attendance had just
then gone into another room for something he wanted;
he was greatly terrified on his return to find me entirely
under water, apparently dead. He roared out for assistance,
which instantly arriving I was taken from the bath, and by
the application of strong volatiles soon recovered. Had the
man remained absent a short time longer probably there
would have been an end of me. He got a very severe rebuke for quitting the bath at all.

The first day of my emancipation I paid my respects to
Captain Arthur, who told me that he and the other Commanders were to take leave of the Court of Directors on the
following Wednesday. He then advised me to be at Portsmouth by the 30th of the month. Whilst with him Mr.
Howorth came in, and we agreed to proceed together on
that day (the 30th). On the 14th (March) I returned to
Mr. Cane's, who desired me not to engage myself for the
following day, as he should have a pleasant party at his
house at dinner and wished me to be present. I accordingly
refused Mr. Rider and another friend who asked me, but
being detained at the India House the company had assembled and before I could change my dress had sat down
to table. Upon entering the room I was agreeably surprized
to see amongst the guests my father, who rose and received
me with the utmost affection. Messieurs Edmund and
Richard Burke were also present, who both kindly promised
to give me letters to different friends of theirs in India.

The day after this dinner I had the supreme felicity once
more openly to enter my father's house. He behaved with
his accustomed goodness, only remarking that as my own
judgment must bespeak the necessity of a steady and
decorous conduct in future, he would not distress me by
a word more upon the subject of what had passed. He then

presented me with fifty pounds, adding, too, his blessing and ardent prayers for my success. The carriage being prepared he took me to Mr. Wedderburn, afterwards created Lord Loughborough, and finally Earl of Rosslyn, who gave me a letter to Sir Robert Chambers, one of the Judges of the Supreme Court of Bengal. Our next visit was to Sir George Colebrooke, then to Mr. Dunning, afterwards Lord Ashburton, Mr. Dempster, Mr. Maclean, Mr. Potter, a Welsh Judge, and several others whose names I do not now recollect, who all gave me letters.

My father wrote to Sir Elijah Impey, the Chief Justice, with whom he had for many years been upon a familiar footing, also to Mr. Macpherson, a member of the Supreme Council. Mr. Cane likewise procured many letters for me addressed to persons of the highest rank in Bengal. The two Mr. Burkes wrote to Mr. Francis,[1] who had received favours of importance from them, and they therefore had a claim upon him. In short, I believe there never was a man better recommended than myself.

On the 30th of March I took leave of my invaluable friend, Mr. Cane, and his family, and of many others from whom I had received numberless acts of kindness and civility. On the 31st I embraced my revered and indulgent father as I verily believed for the last time of my life, little imagining I should ever more behold him or one of my relations. After an affectionate adieu to my sisters and brother, Mr. Howorth and I stepped into a post-chaise, and at four o'clock in the afternoon arrived at the George Inn at Portsmouth, where we found Captain Arthur, his wife, and two of her sisters, Miss Berties, who were going out to India in the *Seahorse* in search of husbands. Mrs. Arthur was a fine, showy woman, dressed in the highest style of fashion, the sisters rather plain in features but well accomplished. We immediately went through the ceremony of introduction to the whole party and soon became familiar and pleasant.

On the 1st of April Mr. Wheler with his lady and family

---

[1] Afterwards Sir Philip Francis, the reputed writer of the famous *Junius Letters.*—ED.

arrived at the same inn where Howorth and myself were lodged. Mr. Wheler's party consisted of himself, Mrs. Wheler, Miss Durnford (who upon the death of Mrs. Wheler a few months after her reaching Bengal supplied her place, the widower endeavouring to console himself for his domestic loss in her arms), Captain Richard Chichely Plowden (now a Director of the East India Company) and his wife ; Mr. Markham, eldest son of the Archbishop of York ; Mr. William Harding, Mr. John Buller, and Mr. John Melville, the four last named being writers appointed to Bengal.

The wind remaining fixed at south-west, with fine clear weather, we spent the time very agreeably in excursions round the neighbourhood during the mornings, returned to Portsmouth to dinner, finishing our evenings with the merry dance which, the ladies of the *York* Indiaman joining us, made a set of a dozen couples. In this manner three weeks slipped rapidly away.

On the 23rd a packet from Bengal came in, bringing an account of the death of the Honourable Colonel Monson, one of the members of the Supreme Government, which event occasioned Mr. Wheler's returning to London, for his appointment being to succeed to the first vacancy that should occur after his arrival at Calcutta it became an object of importance to him to get his situation altered by naming him as successor to Mr. Monson. Having previously got Captain Sutton's promise not to sail for eight and forty hours, Mr. Wheler set off post for the capital accompanied by Captain Plowden. In the morning of the 28th they once more reached Portsmouth, Mr. Wheler having effected his purpose and got his appointment to fill the vacancy made by Monson's death, a circumstance that afforded much satisfaction to all who knew him, he being a man of the utmost gentleness of manners and suavity of temper.

On the 30th, whilst taking our wine after dinner it was announced that the wind had gone to the eastward, whereupon preparations were immediately made for our embarkation. Several passengers went off to their respective ships that evening. Early the next morning Captain Sutton, of the *Duke of Portland*, gave Mr. Howorth and myself a passage off in his pinnace, together with Mrs. Wheler and her company. Exactly at noon the three Indiamen, that is, the *Duke of Portland*, *York*, and *Seahorse*, got under way.

At two o'clock we sat down to an excellent dinner, oui party consisting of Captain David Arthur, Commander of the ship ; the two Miss Berties ; a nephew of the Captain's, a fine boy of about fourteen, going his first voyage as a guinea - pig ; Lieutenant - Colonel Henry Watson, Chief Engineer in Bengal ; Major Lewis Mestayer, of the same corps ; Captain James Dickson, of the Infantry ; Mr. Jacob Blaquiere, superintendent of piece goods ; a son of his of thirteen, William Coats Blaquiere, a remarkably smart, clever lad ; Mr. Richard Tilghman, a barrister of the Supreme Court ; Mr. Robert Morse of the same ; Mr. George Dallas (now a Baronet), Mr. John Martin Playdell, and Mr. John Guichard Booth, all three writers for Bengal ; Mr. Cleveland, assistant surgeon ; my friend, Mr. Humphry Howorth, also an assistant surgeon ; and myself ; Mr. George Simson, chief mate ; Mr. Henry Warre, second ; Mr. James Laird, surgeon of the ship ; Mr. John Wingrove, purser ; and a Mr. John Cressy, being engaged in the service of Colonel Watson as head conductor of his intended works in Bengal. This Cressy was an extraordinary creature. Notwithstanding his being a superior mathematician and able mechanic, he was so deficient in point of education as to be unequal to penning a letter upon the most common subject other than in the lowest language void of everything like grammar.

The foregoing list made the number of the Captain's table twenty-two. The third mate's name was George Curtis (now an Elder Brother of Trinity House) ; the fourth, Archibald Anderson. At Mr. Curtis's mess, were Mr. MacCullock, now a Lieutenant-Colonel on the Bengal establishment ; Mr. Frederick Maitland Arnott, an uncommon fine young man going out as a cadet, whose untimely and melancholy end I shall take occasion hereaftei to mention ; Mr. James Agg, a modest and ingenious man, so superior to Cressy in address and manners as to cause great surprize to us all that Colonel Watson, in whose employ he also was, should have placed him at the third mate's mess, while the other vulgar fellow had a seat at the Captain's table. Mr. Agg was, some years after he arrived in Bengal, appointed an Engineer officer, in which corps he rose to the rank of Captain, when he quitted the service and returned to Europe with a handsome fortune. Soon after he reached England the Court of Directors offered him the situation of Lieutenant-Governor of Saint Helena, which he declined accepting.

CHAPTER IX

THE VOYAGE TO CALCUTTA

WE left Portsmouth on the 1st of May, 1777, and had a pleasant run down Channel. In the Bay of Biscay we experienced some boisterous weather, as frequently occurs in that part of the Atlantic Ocean. Fortunately the wind was fair, driving us on at an immense rate. We ate in the round house, where Captain Arthur and his nephew slept in swinging cots. Mr. Cressy's cot was hung in the cuddy, but taken down and stowed away every morning at seven o'clock, in order to leave a free passage to the round house, where we assembled to breakfast a little before eight.

Upon the coast of Spain we fell in with a squadron of large ships, which, on their first appearance, created great alarm from an apprehension of their being French, with whom hostilities had commenced although no actual declaration of war had been made at the time of our leaving Portsmouth, but it was daily expected. These ships were three English seventy-fours, one of which spoke us.

Drawing near the Cape of Good Hope, we heard that we were to stop at that delightful part of the world. On the 13th of July, Captain Sutton, of the *Duke of Portland*, spoke us to say he intended putting in, and hoped the *Seahorse* would do the same. Captain Arthur replied that he had no objection provided the *York* accompanied. We then ran close to that ship. Upon putting the question, Captain Blanshard answered, that having abundance of water and stock on board he should run on, but as we must at any rate separate in a few days, his intention being to go the inner passage as the shortest to Bombay, his standing on could make no difference to the other ships.

On the 15th soon after daylight we saw a large ship in the

south-east, it then blowing strong from the south-west. We could just distinguish her colours to be English ; she was therefore pronounced to be the Company's ship, *Bridgewater*, bound to Bencoolen. At noon the same day we made the land, at two in the afternoon were well in with the Table Mountain, and at six in the evening anchored in False Bay. We instantly were regaled with the most delicious fruits.

The next morning the passengers went on shore to the house of Mr. Brandt, the Dutch Chief of the place, who, like most of his countrymen, had no objection to exchange his poultry and other articles of provender, together with execrable stuff he called *wine* for British guineas. Upon landing we sent off a messenger to the Cape Town to bring us a sufficient number of carriages to convey us thither.

In the morning of the 19th we commenced our little journey, some in open caravans, something resembling an English waggon, some in a miserable kind of phaeton, and some on horseback. The caravans which, by the by, they thought proper to call coaches, were drawn by eight horses ; wretched-looking, half-starved animals. Two persons sat on the box, one holding the reins and guiding the horses, the other carrying a tremendously long whip, which he smacked loudly and managed with considerable dexterity. After passing over a rocky, abominable road, the ladies complaining of the dreadful jolting, we in four hours reached the half-way house, where Mr. Wheler and his party had arrived a few minutes before us. There being but one room, he invited us to join his mess, which all the *Seahorse* passengers did, eating heartily of new laid eggs and excellent bacon, though badly dressed. This dish, with cheese, made the whole of our fare. They gave us some stuff under the name of Constantia, which to my palate was more like treacle and water than a rich and generous wine. Keen appetites, however, reconciled us to the poverty of the meal.

Our horses being reported ready, we renewed our journey, in little more than three hours arriving at the end of it. The approach to the Cape Town is extremely beautiful and romantic. In one direction is Table Bay, where, during the summer months, which are the reverse of ours, the ships anchor. To the southward and eastward is a long range of stupendous mountains, amongst the nearest of which is the *Table Land,* so called from the top of it, for many miles in extent, being quite flat, and when seen from a distance appearing like a table.

We took up our abode in different lodging-houses where we could find apartments. Colonel Watson, Major Mestayer, Captain Dickson, Dallas, Booth, Howorth, Arnott, Cressy, Agg, and myself were in the same house, and, as we were informed, the best in the town. It was kept by Mrs. Vanrenen, a respectable and opulent widow lady. She had two daughters grown up, rather well looking, and three younger by several years. We slept in double-bedded rooms, my companion being Mr. Arnott, to whom during the voyage I became greatly attached. He was a fine young man, in figure quite equal to Bob Pott. Soon after we left England he told me he was a natural son of the Honourable Frederick Maitland, a post-captain in the Navy and son to the Earl of Lauderdale, by a native woman of Jamaica, on which Island he (Arnott) was born.

We spent our time pleasantly enough, visiting and admiring the curiosities of that part of the continent of Africa. In the mornings and evenings we walked in the Company's gardens, which are well stored with curious plants, the choicest fruits and vegetables. There is also the finest menagerie in the world, in which are collected the most extraordinary animals and birds of every quarter of the globe. During the heat of the day we played at billiards or other games within doors ; in the evening we visited or went to the public entertainments, and generally had a dance previous to retiring to rest.

Colonel Gordon, the second-in-command at the Cape, was very civil, showing us everything that was worth seeing. This gentleman's ancestors were Scotch, but his father as well as himself was born in Holland and had from infancy been in the Dutch military service. He was a very accomplished man, an excellent classical as well as general scholar, spoke English, and, indeed, all the languages of Europe fluently. Here we also met with another ingenious young man, Mr. Paterson, a great botanist, who had for several years been employed by that strange and eccentric woman, Lady Strathmore, to go into the interior of Africa for the purpose of collecting rare plants and natural curiosities of every description. Mr. Paterson published an account of his different excursions, a work that gained him some credit.

Colonel Gordon proposed our taking a view of the summit of the Table Mountain, premising that it would be attended with considerable fatigue. A party was immediately formed to take place when Colonel Gordon should fix, as it was requisite to attend to the state of the weather. The next morning he called to desire we would walk out with him, " the *tablecloth* being laid." Following him clear of the town, we observed upon the flat of the hill a thick white cloud entirely stationary, the sky above it and the land below being perfectly clear. This he told us was what the Cape people called the " tablecloth being laid." He said it was a certain indication of an approaching storm for two or three hours, but would ensure fine weather for at least three days after, and that our excursion should therefore take place the next morning. He then directed us to assemble half an hour before sunrise at the foot of the mountain, where he would be ready to receive and escort us up. Provisions in abundance were prepared and sent forward by Hottentots.

At four o'clock in the morning Colonel Gordon and Mr. Paterson were at our door, soon after which Colonel Watson, Major Mestayer, Messrs. Cleveland, Buller, Booth, Arnott, Cressy, Agg, and myself set out with them. Rather before five we had reached the foot of the mountain and began our ascent, which we found dreadfully steep and rugged ; the path being covered with loose stones rendered walking difficult and tiresome. Colonel Gordon consoled us by saying the road would improve as we ascended.

At eight we came to a cave or recess in the side of the huge mass of rock, forming a spacious apartment, and were very agreeably surprized at seeing a table spread with tea, coffee, cold ham, fowls, with other articles of food, all of the best kind. With keen appetites we fell to, doing complete justice to the stores thus unexpectedly supplied. The prospect from the mouth of our natural chamber was uncommonly grand and beautiful. We beheld beneath us both the Cape Town and that of False Bay, an immense tract of rich and fertile country, bounded by the ocean. Colonel Gordon had predicted truly respecting the weather, which was mild and pleasant without a single cloud in the sky.

Whilst contemplating the magnificence of the scene around, which in my own mind I was comparing with some of those I have (though very inadequately) attempted to describe in Jamaica, I thought we were suddenly got into enchanted ground, such celestial sounds burst upon our ears. It seemed to come from the air above us, and consisted of the sweetest harmony I ever heard. Our surprize was increased upon Colonel Gordon informing us that what we imagined came from a complete band of instrumental music proceeded from nothing more than two flutes played upon by his servants whom he had sent forward for the purpose, but that the peculiar sweetness and melody arose from the situation of the spot where they had performed which was surrounded by echoes innumerable.

Having finished the pleasantest breakfast I ever made, we proceeded, our kind conductor pointing out every object deserving attention, likewise showing us a variety of beautiful wild flowers and plants. Having ascended to the recess where the flutemen were sitting, we stopped some minutes to enjoy the delightful tones. After marching on for two hours more I became very tired; Colonel Watson also began to complain of being so fatigued he could go no further, and it was not without considerable difficulty that Colonel Gordon could persuade him to persevere, telling him too that a tent was pitched upon the flat of the mountain, wherein he might rest as long as he pleased. Thus urged we continued to mount the steep ascent and at last reached the summit. Here we found every kind of refreshment both as to eating and drinking spread ready for us, with comfortable camp stools to rest our wearied limbs upon, whilst a pair of excellent French horns yielded us increased pleasure.

Having recruited our strength by a plentiful meal, washed down by large draughts of delicious cool wine, Colonel Gordon observed that as it was then half-past eleven he should order dinner to be ready at half-past one, which two hours we could not occupy better than in accompanying him to look down upon the most luxuriant plantation of the Cape. After some little objection on the part of Colonel Watson, on account of increasing the fatigue, we all set out, and after walking about two miles on the plain came to an abrupt precipice of several hundred feet, at the bottom of which was a prodigious fine estate, which, from its peculiar beauties, was called Paradise, where grew the only grape from which the proper Constantia was made.

Whilst admiring the various beauties of this charming vineyard, Mr. Cleveland, who was fifty or sixty yards from us, called to Colonel Gordon to request he would come and tell him what reptile he was looking at, which was close to him and which he was just about to lay hold of, when the Colonel, seeing what it was, eagerly cried out desiring him for God's sake to desist and go further off, as the animal was the most destructive snake in the world, the slightest bite causing death in a few minutes, nor had any antidote ever been found. It was quite black, about ten inches in length, somewhat resembling a young grig. It is called the *Copra manille*, and is so seldom met with that some naturalists were of opinion there was no such snake. Colonel Gordon said that he had seen two or three of them in different parts of the world during his travels. Mr. Paterson had also seen more than one of them and had actually lost a servant from the bite of one, the unfortunate person being dead in twenty minutes after the injury received. This offensive and dangerous snake we caused to be put into a bottle with gin, and thus conveyed him to town. Although the *Copra manille* is not so frequently met with as many other kinds of snakes, yet it is well known throughout Asia and many parts of Africa.

Having satisfied our curiosity we returned to the tent at two o'clock and sat down to a capital dinner, which, notwithstanding our recent meal, we did ample justice to. While at our bottle I expressed my satisfaction at our journey home being all downhill, consequently comparatively easy to what the ascending had been, when Colonel Gordon said I laboured under a great mistake, and should find the descent even more fatiguing than the coming up, an assertion I could not give credit to.

At half-past four we commenced our march homeward. I had not gone more than two hundred yards downward when I was seized with so excruciating a pain in each thigh as to render me incapable of moving, and I was compelled to stop and seat myself on a piece of rock, actually imagining I must remain until people arrived to carry me, for no carriage could be used in such a road. Colonel Watson was as bad as myself. We were obliged to stop and rest every six or eight minutes, which made our progress extremely tedious and slow. At last, however, we reached the bottom of the mountain, and by half-past eleven at night arrived at Mrs. Vanrenen's house quite exhausted and worn out with fatigue. I instantly went to bed, swallowing by Colonel Gordon's advice a large draught of hot and strong brandy and water. This, however, did not procure me any sleep. After a restless and uncomfortable night I endeavoured to get up, but was unable ; my limbs refused their office and ached so intolerably I was obliged to remain in bed.

About nine in the morning our Surgeon, Mr. Laird, came to see me. He gave me some medicine that caused a profuse perspiration that relieved me materially. About noon I fell into a profound sleep which continued eight hours, at the end of which time I awoke, finding myself vastly better. I therefore rose, dressed myself, and made an attempt to go downstairs, but at the first step so acute a pain arose in my legs and thighs that had I not had hold of Arnott's arm, who supported me, I must have gone headlong to the bottom. Nor did I completely recover from the effects of this jaunt for five days. Every one of the party was affected more or less from the fatigue except the uncouth Cressy, who, notwithstanding he doubled the distance any other person went by bounding about like a deer in every direction from the straight path, did not appear to be in the least tired, and the next day walked to False Bay to get something he wanted from the ship and back again.

After a fortnight spent very agreeably at the Cape Town we returned to False Bay to be ready to re-embark. On the 5th of August we were summoned on board our respective ships, and by three in the afternoon were fairly out at sea. To our great surprize we found that the *Duke of Portland*, for whom between England and the Cape we were obliged to shorten the sail every four hours, now outran us. As it was presumed this change must have arisen from the stowage of the water, &c., taken in at the Cape, Captain Arthur immediately began to make various experiments and changes in the trim of the ship. Still, however, she beat us. Imagining therefore that they should shorten their passage by parting company they availed themselves of blowing weather that commenced the day after we quitted the Cape and a dark night to get away from the *Seahorse*. This manœuvre of the *Duke of Portland* did not answer, for in spite of her improved style of sailing we arrived in the River Hooghly fourteen days before her.

We reached the mouth of the Bay of Bengal about the 8th of October, which being too late in the season for us to venture upon the coast of Coromandel, where we should otherwise have stopped for a few hours, we stood down on the eastern side of the Bay, had an admirable good run for seven days, and then made the land, which was entered in the log-book as the Island of Cheduba, upon seeing which entry Colonel Watson said it was not Cheduba, but one of the

Islands on the coast of Aracan, considerably more to the northward.

Lunar observations were not then come into general use and none were ever taken on board the *Seahorse*. Colonel Watson, amongst his many accomplishments, was a perfect algebraist, thereby correcting his watch to such a nicety as to render it to all intents and purposes a complete time-piece. By his account thus kept he made the ship more to the northward and eastward than the reckonings of any of the officers, and during the voyage he had always been found right, especially with respect to the Cape of Good Hope, which we made within half an hour of the time he said we should, although by the ship's reckoning we were near three hundred miles from it.

The weather in the Bay had been thick, with frequent squalls and much rain for six days successively, during which we had no observation. At dinner the day the land had been seen, Colonel Watson said aloud the Island was not Cheduba, but one at least a degree and a half more to the eastward and northward. Of this remark Captain Arthur took no sort of notice, whereupon the Colonel, addressing himself to Mr. Simson, said, " I take upon my-self, though no seaman, to assert that if you stand on the same course you are now going, and at the same rate, by two o'clock in the morning you will run the ship ashore, and that very near the place where the *Falmouth* Indiaman was wrecked, owing to a similar mistake, when every soul on board perished." Mr. Simson replied he thought we were further down the Bay than the ship's reckoning gave, and Colonel Watson added he was clear the fact was so and equally certain that we were at that moment upon soundings, probably in fifty or sixty fathoms. Captain Arthur, bursting with rage, looked as red as a turkey cock, puffing and blowing with more than usual violence, but he uttered not a syllable.

We continued standing on the same course, running seven knots an hour under topsails and foresail, not feeling quite comfortable at what the Colonel had said, having,

too, a dark night of twelve hours fast approaching and a
strong gale blowing. At dusk all hands were called to reef
topsails, when most of the passengers, also Captain Arthur,
were upon the quarter-deck. Colonel Watson asked the
second officer, Mr. Warre, whether he had ascertained what
depth of water we had, to which Mr. Warre answered, " No,
Sir, the Captain does not consider it necessary." Colonel
Watson replied aloud, " Good God, what madness or infatuation is this ! Is it to be endured that a man should thus
wantonly court danger and risk the lives of all on board,
and to do so from sheer obstinacy ? " The Captain still
continued silent.

At eight o'clock when the first watch was called, Mr.
Simson went into the round-house to Captain Arthur to
say he thought they had better heave a cast of the lead,
but the Captain forbid it, observing it would be a pity to
lose the time sounding would require, especially as there
was no sort of occasion for it. At eleven I turned in, and
notwithstanding I felt uneasy at our precarious state I soon
fell asleep, from which I was suddenly aroused by a tremendous noise in the steerage. I jumped out of my cot and
went into the steerage, where I met Mr. Booth, who had
not been in bed. He immediately told me it was all over
with us, that we were surrounded by rocks with no possibility of escaping. He then violently threw open the door
of Messieurs Tilghman and Morse's cabin, crying out that
in a few moments we must be all drowned, and desiring
them to get up and help to save the ship. Mr. Tilghman,
raising his head from the pillow, enquired what was the
matter. " Matter ! " answered Booth, " why, we are in
three fathoms of water, and the moment the ship strikes
she must inevitably go to pieces." " That's not pleasant
intelligence," said Tilghman, and directly laid himself down
again in his cot. We went from thence into Mr. Cleveland's
cabin, where we found him in great agitation, Mr. Blaquiere
and Dickson being with him. Mr. Cleveland proposed that
we should go upon deck to see if we could be of any use,
but to that I objected, observing that we might increase the

confusion by being in the way of the seamen, but could render them no aid and had better remain where we were. We therefore did so. It was then just three o'clock in the morning, the ship upon a wind, carrying a press of sail which made her lay down very deep.

In about an hour Dr. Laird came down with the glad tidings that we were rather deepening our water, the danger consequently decreasing, and in another hour Mr. Simson assured us we should do very well, having run into thirty fathoms. From him we learned the following particulars : that Captain Arthur had remained upon deck until twelve o'clock, during which time he (Simson) had repeatedly expressed his wish to sound as a matter of prudence ; but the Captain, notwithstanding he was evidently uneasy, resisted it, saying, " To-morrow morning at daybreak will be early enough," and then retired to the round-house ; that at midnight when Mr. Warre, the second mate, came upon deck to take charge of the watch he (Simson) observed to him that he felt convinced Colonel Watson was right as to the situation of the ship, and he therefore requested Mr. Warre would have everything ready for a cast of the lead and keep a sharp look out. The weather had happily become much clearer, though it still blew strong, we continuing running right before it under double-reefed topsails. Mr. Warre upon Mr. Simson's leaving him immediately made the people pass the line forward, stationing men in each of the chains with coils ready to heave at a moment's notice. A little before two in the morning Colonel Watson went out of his cabin, and whilst walking the quarter-deck with Mr. Warre, said he thought there was an evident change in the water, it having become smoother. He therefore had no doubt we had shoaled materially. Mr. Warre being of the same opinion had resolved to heave the lead without saying anything to the Captain, and was in the act of ordering it when a man from the bowsprit end cried out, " Breakers right ahead and close aboard." In the same moment the leadsman hove the lead, and finding it directly take the ground, he in his fright called out, " There's only three fathom." The utmost confusion and dismay ensued. Captain Arthur ran out of his cabin almost frantic, crying like a child that he was ruined past redemption and had sacrificed his own life as well as that of all on board. In the most abject and pusillanimous manner he besought the crew and officers to exert themselves, if possible, to save the ship. In his fright he ordered and counterordered in the same breath, and was in such consternation he knew not what he said or did. Mr. Simson seeing him so incapable advised his going to his cabin.

Mr. Warre had, upon the first alarm, ordered the man at the wheel to put the helm up, braced the yards sharp up, and hauled his wind, heaving the lead as fast as it could be carried forward. The second cast we had ten fathoms, the third only seven, the fourth ten again, then several casts between seven and twelve fathom, after which it suddenly deepened to twenty-five fathom, when the risk was supposed to be over. Yet so irregular was the bottom that after having run at least a mile in twenty-five fathom we had two casts with no more than seven fathom.

At daylight the mainland of Aracan was distinctly seen from deck with breakers extending a great way out, over which the sea broke with immense fury. Our escape certainly was almost miraculous. Colonel Watson behaved with much moderation and propriety on the occasion, nor did he ever allude to the circumstance afterward when Captain Arthur was present, a delicacy and forbearance our Commander was scarcely deserving of, for his ignorance and obstinate stupidity had nearly cost us our lives.

Having cleared the coast we stood to the westward for the purpose of making Point Palmiras. On the 18th (October), the weather being then quite moderate and fine, we saw the land, the sea unruffled and smooth as glass. During the night it fell calm. At daylight of the 19th we were well in with the land; by observation at noon found we were embayed between the real and false points, a situation that Colonel Watson privately told us was big with evil, as, should it come on to blow from the eastward, which was likely to happen at that season, our prospect would become critical and alarming, as we might not be able to clear either of the points, and at any rate the current, which then set strongly to the southward and against us, would probably detain us a long time in the nook we had very improperly and unnecessarily got into. Here again he showed his superior judgment. We actually remained nine days land-locked, being obliged to bring the ship to an anchor to prevent her being carried away by the current, which upon trial they ascertained ran at the rate of three knots an hour.

On the 30th a light breeze from the south-west luckily sprang up, which carried us into Balasore Roads, where we came to an anchor. At daylight of the 31st we had the pleasure to see two schooners standing towards us with the Company's colours flying, from which they were known to be pilot vessels. By eight o'clock one of them put a pilot on board of us, who took charge of the ship, immediately getting her under way, and stood for the river. In about an hour the wind failed, and as the ebb tide began to make we again brought to.

CHAPTER X

ATTORNEY AND PROCTOR IN BENGAL

WE remained at anchor until four in the morning of the 1st of November, when we once more made sail, and at noon anchored off the Island of Sangor. Soon after having so done a Bengal boat, called a paunceway, came alongside, which Colonel Watson engaged to convey him to Calcutta. At two in the afternoon the Colonel, with his assistants, Cressy and Agg, Major Mestayer, Mr. Morse, and myself took our final leave of the *Seahorse*.

This mode of travelling did not exactly meet our approbation, paunceways being so constructed that you have not room to sit upright under the roof or covering of mat to protect those within from sun or rain, nor is there any place to let your legs hang down in, passengers sitting upon a platform like tailors on their shopboard. The novelty of the thing, however, and every mile we went bringing us nearer to our destination, reconciled us to the uneasy position. We proceeded in high glee. The boat was rowed by six black fellows, who were not sparing of their labour, so that we went at a good rate, and by six in the evening arrived off Culpee, where the Indiamen and other ships of heavy burthen then lay. Here we stopped to let the people rest and to wait for the next flood.

Going a quarter of a mile up a creek, we landed at a poor, shabby house called a *tavern*, the appearance of which both internal and external gave us new-comers a very unfavourable idea of a Bengal house of entertainment. It was in every respect uncomfortable and beastly dirty. It was the Colonel's intention that the party should sleep here, but not a single bed could be obtained. In about an hour and a half after our arrival we had served up some very excellent fish, tolerable fowls, with plenty of eggs and bacon, and, what was a prodigious luxury to me who had been so long without it, capitally good bread. Claret and Madeira we had plenty of in the same boat, so that altogether we made a hearty meal.

Having satisfied our appetites, we fixed upon a billiard-table as our resting-place, the Colonel, Major Mestayer, and myself taking our respective stations at full length upon it. Sleep was, however, entirely out of the question from the myriads of mosquitoes that assailed us. At the end of three hours' misery I arose and walked about the room, surprized at the hideous yells of jackals innumerable. Towards daybreak the troublesome insects quitted the apartment for the open air. I then lay down upon three chairs, and, being exhausted from want of rest, fell into a sound sleep, which continued upwards of two hours and refreshed me wonderfully.

At eight I arose, and did ample justice to the hot rolls, tea, and coffee. At ten, the tide suiting, we re-embarked in our unaccommodating vessel, taking with us a plentiful supply of cold fowls and other articles of food. Colonel Watson said he hoped we should reach his house by dark, but, owing to the wind coming to the north and impeding our progress, we were disappointed. Finding this to be the case and our boat's crew being quite tired from a severe day's work, it was decided that we should stop to let them refresh themselves at a small village called Woolburreah, where we all landed, Colonel Watson undertaking to procure curry and rice for us, for which purpose he began to speak Moors to the natives, which excited our mirth. We laughed heartily, not only at the language so new to our ears, but at the whole scene that presented itself and the many grotesque figures that appeared amongst the spectators.

The Colonel (absurdly as I conceived) took offence at our merriment, pettishly observing that if we chose to laugh at his exertions to get us a hot meal we might try for ourselves and see what we should make of it. We assured him very truly that our laugh was not at him, but at the ludicrous figures and postures the black people put themselves into, and which was so entirely new to us. Our apology was well received, he renewed his cookery, soon placing before us some smoking hot curry of fish and fowl, which we devoured voraciously, pronouncing them delicious, though I cannot say that I much admired them, nor did I ever become fond of Hindustani cookery. Having washed down our food with claret, we resumed our stations in the paunceway, rolling ourselves up in boat cloaks, and thus made it out for the night tolerably well.

Between two and three in the morning, the flood tide making, we got under way. At daybreak we all mounted upon the chopper of the boat, at five came in sight of Garden Reach, where I was greatly pleased by a rich and magnificent view of a number of splendid houses, the residences of gentlemen of the highest rank in the Company's service, who, with their families, usually left Calcutta in the hot season to enjoy the cooler and more refreshing air of these pleasant situations. Some of the occupants resided there throughout the year, going to town in the morning to transact their business and returning to the country in the evening. The verdure throughout on every side was beautiful beyond imagination, the whole of the landscape being more luxuriant than I had any expectation of seeing in the burning climate of Bengal.

In less than an hour we were at the upper part of the reach, where we went on shore to Colonel Watson's, the beauty of which my powers of description are utterly inadequate to do justice to. The mansion was within a few yards of the edge of the river upon an elevation or bank full thirty feet above the level of the water, commanding a noble view of Garden Reach with all its palaces downward, and upward Fort William with the magnificent city of Calcutta, a sheet of water more than nine miles in extent, nearly two in breadth, covered with innumerable ships of different sizes.

Colonel Watson had within a brick wall at least four hundred bogahs of land, of which the East India Company had executed a grant to him to construct docks, both wet and dry, build ships and establish a complete dockyard. An immense range of buildings was already erected intended for blacksmiths, carpenters, sailmakers, and all the different artificers employed in a dockyard. There was also another range of handsome, well-constructed warehouses, in which were deposited naval stores of every description, working tools of all sorts, besides anchors, cables, cordage, and canvas. Timber to a great value lay upon the premises in every direction. In short, there never was in any part of the world so stupendous and so expensive an undertaking attempted to be carried into effect by a single individual as this of Colonel Watson's, yet extensive and prodigious as it was he would beyond a doubt have effected his object had not a party started up to oppose and thwart him, which ultimately succeeded in its base plan, thereby stopping a work that would have done honour to the British name in Asia.

In this stupendous work Colonel Watson originally embarked with Major Archibald Campbell, then Chief Engineer in Bengal and afterwards created a Knight of the Bath and Governor of Madras. Those two gentlemen having arranged their plan at Raderpore, about three miles and a half from Calcutta, where they fixed on the ground required, they both proceeded to England to obtain the aid and sanction of the Company. The Court of Directors, on having the circumstances fully before them, were so satisfied of the extraordinary merit of the proposers as to determine at once to afford them every assistance they could expect or ask for. A grant, by regular deed, was immediately made out by their Law officers of the quantity of ground required, tonnage to a considerable extent being likewise allowed them in each of their ships to transport the necessary heavy stores from Europe free of tonnage and every other incidental expense except the prime cost of the different articles. The Directors likewise sent out orders to their Government in Bengal to support and promote the work by every means in their power.

In the beginning of the year 1777 Colonel Watson pur-

chased Campbell's interest in the concern, and became the
sole proprietor of the premises and immense stock that was
upon it. At the time I accompanied him to India he had
expended in the purchase money, in preparations for executing this stupendous work and collecting all kinds of
stores, no less a sum than one hundred and eighty thousand
pounds, an incredible amount for a private person to risk
upon any speculation.

Colonel Watson whilst at Portsmouth had showed me much
civility. In the course of the voyage our intimacy increased,
and he observed that he had little doubt he could have
it in his power to push me forward in my profession by
introducing me to some of the most opulent and respectable
natives. He also desired that upon our arrival in Bengal
I would make his house my home until I could establish
myself to my own satisfaction.

I was highly pleased in viewing the extensive works
which the Colonel took us over, explaining every part and
particular. A European manager of his also attended, of
whom the Colonel enquired what news there was in Calcutta.
The man answered he knew of none, but, recollecting himself, added, " Oh, I forgot to tell you we have lost two of
our great people, General Clavering, the Commander-in-
Chief, who has recently died, and Judge Le Maître, of the
Supreme Court, who departed this life only the day before
your arrival. I suppose you must have heard the minute
guns which were fired for his funeral at sunrise this morning from the ramparts of Fort William." The death of the
Judge was likely to be of importance to Mr. Morse and
myself, both of us having letters of recommendation to him.
Previous to our arrival Mr. Morse and I had agreed to
keep house together, and he undertook to look out for a
suitable habitation.

At eleven o'clock in the forenoon I was agreeably
surprized by seeing my young friend and companion,
Robert Pott, driving up the avenue in a very jemmy
equipage. Our joy at meeting was sincere and recip-
rocal. He said he had an excellent apartment fitted up

and ready for my sole use, which I must forthwith take possession of, and for that purpose accompany him in his phaeton into Calcutta. But this Colonel Watson, who overheard him, said could not be, nor would he part with me. He said he should be glad to see him (Pott) at all times at the docks, where he might have as much of my company as he pleased. He then invited him to dinner that day, which he accepted, observing that he must go back to town to tell Daniel Barwell, his chum, to entertain a large party that were engaged to dine with them. He insisted upon my accompanying him to Calcutta, which I did, finding it a pleasant ride of nearly four miles.

Although it was called the cold weather the sun appeared to me to have prodigious influence, and to strike hotter than I ever felt it in England at any season. Pott drove me to his residence, a noble mansion belonging to Richard Barwell, Esq., a member of the Supreme Council, who lent it to his younger brother, Daniel Barwell, and three friends, these being Pott, Mr. Cator, and Mr. Gosling. I was immediately introduced by Pott in the most affectionate manner to the other inmates, after which he conducted me into very spacious rooms, elegantly furnished, and having some valuable paintings in them. They consisted of three chambers opening into each other. Pott told me these were exclusively appropriated to my use. In one, where a bed was preparing for me, Pott took from a writing-desk a bundle of letters all under one envelope, addressed to me. These he had prepared in the event of his not being upon the spot when I arrived, to ensure me a kind and hospitable reception from several of his friends. He in these letters spoke of me as the dearest friend he had in the world. They were addressed to Captain William Palmer (now a General officer), Mr. John Shore (now Lord Teignmouth), Messieurs Montgomery, Kneller, Purling, Ducarel, Bird, Bristow, Graham, Hatch, Adair, Evelyn, and Mr. Justice Hyde.

As one o'clock was at that time the general hour of dining I was obliged to remind Robert, and hasten him. Having fleet horses we went back at a great rate, but found the

Colonel waiting for us. At dinner, Mr. Cleveland, who was likewise a guest of the Colonel's and had been to town that morning, gave us an account of his trip, which excited the Colonel's mirth. It having been his first exhibition in a palankeen he was highly disgusted with such a mode of conveyance, the poor creatures who carried him being dreadfully fatigued before he had done a mile, so much so that their groans distressed him beyond measure, and he called to them to stop, but could not make them understand. They therefore continued grunting on until he again called out, by signs making them understand he wanted them to rest, whereupon they set the palankeen down and immediately began to converse very cheerfully. He therefore concluded they were sufficiently recruited and made signs to them to proceed, which they did, but had not gone more than a hundred yards when they resumed their moanings, upon which he stopped, got out, said he would walk, and gave them a rupee by way of encouragement. He acknowledged that he was surprized to see that they laughed when he offered the money, as he thought they were suffering under too much pain to appear so cheerful. Colonel Watson told him it was a custom amongst bearers when carrying a palankeen to make that moaning noise, which did not at all indicate fatigue, and that the front bearer always noticed the sort of road they were passing over, pointing out any impediments, as " Here's a hole," " Here's a puddle of water," " Here's long grass," " Here's a parcel of bricks," &c.

The next day Colonel Watson took me to the Government House to introduce me to Mr. Hastings, the Governor-General ; General Stibbert, the Commander-in-Chief ; and Mr. Barwell. When at the house of the latter he observed to me in a whisper, " The owner is an infamous scoundrel, I feel a strong inclination, instead of paying him the compliment of a visit, to tell my opinion of him. However, I suspect he is aware of the sentiments I entertain respecting him, and that I visit the public station he fills, not the individual."

Mr. Francis, the other member of the Supreme Board, was then absent, being upon a visit at Chinsurah. Colonel Watson expressed great doubts as to the reception he should meet with from this gentleman from the following circumstance : Colonel Watson had commenced his military career as a subaltern in the corps of Engineers in His Majesty's service, in which he had served abroad, particularly at the famous siege of the Havannah in the West Indies, where, as a young officer, he had acquired much credit. Upon the capture of that fortress he was summoned to England in great haste. On his arrival in London he found a letter from Lord Clive, who patronised him, desiring him in case he reached London by a certain day therein specified, immediately to follow him (Lord Clive) to Portsmouth, as he proposed taking him with him to Bengal, where he should be able to provide for him, having already secured an appointment for him in the Company's Engineers at that Presidency. His lordship added that he had arranged everything respecting his leave of absence from His Majesty's service with Mr. Welbore Ellis, the Secretary at War.

In the same letter was enclosed a few lines of introduction to Mr. Ellis, which he (Watson) was desired to deliver in person, when every requisite document would directly be furnished. He accordingly waited upon the Secretary at War, who received him with the utmost politeness, giving him a line to the chief clerk in a particular department to supply the necessary papers. This clerk happened to be Mr. Philip Francis, a pompous, haughty coxcomb, who, very unlike Mr. Ellis, received Mr. Watson with much superciliousness of manners, by some described as " insolence of office." Being obliged to accept the Secretary's note he did so, but instantly laid it down upon his desk without perusal, whereupon Mr. Watson civilly requested his immediate attention to his business, every minute being of importance. Thus urged he did condescend to read Mr. Ellis's note, after which he coolly and deliberately referred to three or four large manuscript books, examined them in several different parts, then, turning to Watson, said :

"You are all wrong in applying here, your leave of absence must come from the Master-General of the Ordnance, not the Secretary at War."

"Upon my word, Sir," answered Watson, "I must think Mr. Ellis is well acquainted with the duties of his office and not likely to make the mistake you charge him with. However, be that as it may, I cannot lose my time in discussing matters of form with you," and seizing Mr. Ellis's note from the desk he instantly ran with it back to that gentleman, Mr. Francis calling after him not to be in such a hurry.

Watson having stated what had occurred, the Secretary rang his bell with some violence, desiring Mr. Francis might come to him, which he directly did, when Mr. Ellis said, "I sent this gentlemen with an order to you to fill up a permission for him to go to India without prejudice to his rank in the King's service, instead of doing which you have insolently and presumptuously opposed your opinion, thereby betraying your ignorance as well as impertinence, for which I am inclined to punish you as you deserve. Go along and do as you are ordered without comment, and be upon your guard in future, for should a similar behaviour occur you remain not another hour in the War Office."

The humbled and mortified clerk bowed and retired. He forthwith drew the paper, sulkily chucking it across his desk to Watson, and observing, "You were in a damned hurry." Mr. Watson merely replied, "True, I was, and am."

This circumstance the Colonel thought might have made too strong an impression upon Francis's mind ever to be forgotten, and now that they were about to meet, both in elevated stations, he apprehended Mr. Francis would show that he did recollect it by his treatment of him. Mr. Francis, however, if he did recognize his old War Office acquaintance, betrayed not the smallest sign of his so doing. He received him with the utmost respect, and was upon all occasions a strenuous supporter of the Colonel's plans.

Pott, who always complained if I addressed him by any other title than that of " Bob," having presented me with a buggy horse, I every morning drove into Calcutta directly after breakfast. Bob introduced me in the kindest manner to Judge Hyde and his family, saying to him with his usual familiar style, " My dear friend William must be taken care of, so pray mind you give him your support and interest whenever necessary," and, turning to Mrs. Hyde (then a very lovely woman), he continued, " And the more civilities and attentions you show to the friend of my heart, whom I sincerely love, the more I shall love you, my charming Mrs. Hyde." To do this couple justice they did invariably treat me with every possible degree of kind and hospitable attention.

Bob Pott likewise introduced me to Sir Elijah Impey, the Chief Justice, and to Mr. Chambers, afterwards Sir Robert, at both of whose houses I was always treated most kindly. Sir Robert Chambers made a point of my spending every Saturday and Sunday with him at his house about two miles from town. His family then consisted of Lady Chambers, at that time a beautiful creature not more than eighteen years of age, two lovely children, a boy and a girl ; Mrs. Chambers, mother of Sir Robert, a worthy and cheerful old lady ; Mr. William Johnson and Mr. William Smoult, both Attorneys, who went out in the same ship with the Judges, and under the immediate protection of Sir Robert. Mr. Johnson at the time I arrived was Clerk of the Crown and one of the Sworn Clerks in Equity ; Mr. Smoult was Sealer and Clerk to Sir Robert. These two young men are now both dead.

A few days after my arrival in Calcutta Mr. Morse called to say he had been informed by several persons competent to judge of the measure that it would be bad policy for us to live together, for that the natives, prone to mean suspicion, would conclude when we acted on different sides as Counsel and Attorney that the interests of our respective clients would be sacrificed to our private attachment to each other. Our intended junction as housekeepers was therefore given up and relinquished. This, however, made not the least alteration in our friendship or regard for each other, which continued unabated during our mutual residence in Bengal.

Mr. Morse one day observed that going about to deliver letters of introduction alone was a very unpleasant ceremony, to remedy which he proposed we should do it together. In those houses where he delivered a letter he would introduce me, and I should do the same with respect to him where I gave mine. This proposal I agreed to, and it was adopted.

Looking over the letters that remained from the persons to whom they were addressed being dead, or having left the country, Morse holding out one in particular and referring to his memorandum book to see who had given it to him, said, "This I should like to read because it contains, I have no doubt, a high panegyric upon me. Dining at an intimate friend of mine, Mr. Lee, in Berners Street, some weeks prior to my leaving London, I there met Mr. Potter, who, I was informed, was a Welsh Judge, a man of large fortune, living in the first company; his address was elegant and fashionable. Upon my introduction to him as a person just going to Bengal as a Barrister of the Supreme Court, he made a number of civil speeches. Soon after dinner, again coming up to me, he said Mr. Lee appeared so greatly interested in my success abroad that he (Potter) should request I would be the bearer of a letter to Mr. Le Maître, one of the Judges with whom he had been brought up from early infancy, and between whom the most cordial attachment subsisted, and who, he was sure, would take every opportunity of promoting my success in consequence of his desire. Now," continued Morse, "a letter thus, as I may say forced upon me, makes me solicitous to learn what an entire stranger like Mr. Potter can say of me in the complimentary way."

I told Morse that this Mr. Potter was an intimate ac-

quaintance of my father and sisters, that I also had several
letters from him to gentlemen in India, all of which were
given to me open, as was customary, and I could not help
thinking his to Mr. Le Maître being sealed made the contents a little suspicious, at least as far as he (Morse) was
concerned. "Then," said Morse, " by God, I'll ascertain
that fact," and he instantly broke open the letter in question. It contained two sheets of paper close written, the
first consisted of domestic circumstances with an account
of mutual friends, the second, politics, comments upon the
mode in which the Government of India was conducted
and severe strictures upon the conduct of the gentry in
Leadenhall Street. As I saw Morse had read almost to
the end of the letter without his name being once mentioned I observed to him, "Morse, this new and zealous
friend of yours seems slow in naming you to the Judge."
"Oh, never fear," replied Morse, "I shall appear when I
am brought forth with the higher colouring, and I conclude
something *fulsomely complimentary !* " He did appear ! in
the last two lines, and in these very extraordinary words !
"This will, I believe, be delivered to you by a Mr. Morse,
who the devil he is or what sort of a man I cannot tell,
never having seen him in my life ! "

Poor Morse looked quite confounded at this strange and
unexpected paragraph. After a pause he suddenly exclaimed, "Damn the fellow, what could he mean by this
infamous duplicity ! Had he been teased by one who had
little or no claim upon him for a letter of introduction, that
might have been some sort of excuse for so outrageous and
impudent a falsehood and such contemptuous terms relating to me, but crammed down my throat as his letter was
unsought and unwished for by me, renders his conduct base
and unaccountable."

I firmly believe there have been too many instances of
similar *kind* recommendations ; it would surely be more
fair and candid to refuse writing at all than to do as Mr.
Potter did. It was reported, and I fear truly, that Mr.
Laurence Sullivan, when Chairman of the Court of Directors,

made a private mark upon such letters as he wished should be attended to, a shameful and unjust practice.

On the 12th of November Sir Elijah Impey desired I would attend in Court the following morning, and I should be entered upon the Roll. I accordingly did so, took the usual oaths, and became Solicitor, Attorney, and Proctor of the Supreme Court, the latter branch being particularly productive, from the fees being nearly double in ecclesiastical business. My shipmates, Messieurs Tilghman and Morse, were the same morning admitted as Advocates.

In consequence of my numerous acquaintances I had many invitations to large dinner parties, which often led me into excess, it being the custom in those days to drink freely. Having landed in Bengal with my blood in a ferment from the intemperance committed on board ship, the evil was not lessened by daily superabundant potations of champagne and claret, the serious effects of which I began to experience by severe headaches and other feverish symptoms.

On the 13th (November) I had been in town and was returning to Colonel Watson's in my buggy about one o'clock when I met Mr. Justice Hyde in his palankeen, who stopped me to say I was guilty of great imprudence by daily exposing myself to the sun, thereby running the risk of laying myself up with a fever. He therefore recommended me to have recourse to medicine forthwith. I promised to follow his advice, but being engaged on the next day to a famous tavern dinner to be given by Captain William Palmer, I could not prevail on myself to forego the pleasure of joining the convivial set. I therefore went to the Harmonic, though suffering under an excruciating headache and pain in my back. My illness increased so much that before dinner was half over I was obliged to leave the table and house. Pott observing I turned very pale followed me out, insisting on attending me home to his house instead of going to Colonel Watson's, a desire I willingly complied with, as I was, upon moving, seized with a violent sickness at my stomach.

Being conveyed to Pott's, I was directly put to bed, my friend Bob only leaving me to procure the attendance of the doctors. He speedily returned, bringing with him James Laird and his elder brother John Laird, then high in the Company's service and eminent in his profession. I soon perceived from the language of the latter that he was alarmed about me. Notwithstanding various medicines were resorted to nothing would stop the vomiting, which continued the whole night, I expecting every moment to be my last. Towards morning a delirium came on, and for four days I was not conscious of anything that passed.

Upon recovering my senses I seemed to awake as if from a horrid dream, accompanied with sensations of agonies so complicated I cannot describe. I found my beloved friend Pott, with several servants, standing by my bedside, he with a countenance expressive of the deepest sorrow, nor did he appear gratified at my knowing him, the reason of which, as I afterwards learnt, was that the physicians had told him it was all over with me, not the smallest probability of recovery remaining, but that most likely the delirium would cease a few minutes before death. He therefore concluded the fatal time was arrived. A blister that entirely covered my breast annoyed me greatly, especially one corner that was loose. I asked for a pair of scissors to cut it off. This induced Pott to suppose me again wandering, and I was astonished at his saying, "No, no, my dear William, you shall have no scissors I assure you." I then explained what I wanted them for, when he instantly sent off for the doctors. Within half an hour I was surrounded by seven of them, that is, Dr. A. Campbell, Stark, Robertson, two Lairds, and my shipmates, Cleveland and Howorth. They all looked very dismal, and I saw clearly they expected my dissolution, yet I never gave myself up, nor felt any particular dread at the thoughts of dying.

I continued in this hopeless state ten days, the doctors in the morning thinking it impossible for me to survive until night, and the same from night to morning. In this forlorn condition I was allowed to drink as much claret as I pleased, and delicious it was to my palate. Equally grateful and refreshing were oranges which were given me several times a day.

In the heighth of the fever I had frequently been lifted out of bed and put into the warm bath, though without deriving any benefit until the 30th (November) about noon, when just as they were taking me out of the bath a rash suddenly appeared over my whole body, attended with a profuse perspiration. Dr. Campbell, who happened to be present, ordered the attendants instantly to cover me with shawls, observing the crisis was arrived, and an hour would decide the business. He sat down by the side of my bed to wait the issue, and soon told Pott he had hopes of saving me. A new medicine that was prescribed acted most favourably, so much so that at a consultation of the doctors in the evening I was pronounced in a fair way for recovery.

The following day, being the 1st of December, I had a slight return of fever, which soon yielded to medicine, and from that time I gradually came about, though I continued so weak I could scarcely turn myself as I lay on the bed, nor had I the least degree of appetite. The doctors teased me to eat, but obey I could not, until about the 7th of the month, when I fancied I should like a little dry toast, which being prepared and brought I with difficulty swallowed a morsel, soon after which Dr. Stark arrived. His first question was had I eat anything ? Upon my replying, " Yes, some dry toast," he said, " Well, I am glad you have begun at last, though I had rather you had eat anything else ; dry toast is not wholesome." In an hour after he left me, Dr. Campbell called, who likewise enquired as to eating, and, being told what I had done, said, " I am glad to hear it, you cannot eat a better thing. Take it frequently and as much of it as you please ! " So much for the difference of doctors' opinions ! I, however, have no doubt but Dr. Campbell was right. The toast certainly did me good.

I continued improving in health, but so slowly that it was the 17th before I could stir a step without assistance.

Dr. Campbell said that in all his practice he had never seen a person recover from such a state as I was in. I certainly owed my life to the unusual exertions and attendance of the physicians united to the indefatigable attention of Pott and his servants. Amongst the latter there was an old fellow who had been in the service of Lord Clive. He scarcely ever left my bedside, nor ever appeared to sleep. How he bore the fatigue was a matter of surprize to every person that came to me.

When the violence of the fever abated, languor and total want of appetite being the most dangerous symptoms that remained, this good body was for ever preparing something new in the way of nourishment to tempt me with, which finding me averse to eat of he would with the most persevering mildness endeavour to persuade me at least to taste, saying he was sure it would do me good, and that his old master, Lord Clive, always benefited by such things when ill. He used also, if he thought my spirits lower than in general, to try to raise them by roundly asserting I should be free from every attack of illness for at least seven years to come in consequence of the fever I had just escaped from, and that during his long life he had never seen it otherwise.

On the 24th, by Dr. Campbell's orders, being completely enveloped in shawls, I was put into a palankeen and once more conveyed to Colonel Watson's house at the docks, where, from the change of air, I recovered rapidly. In three days my appetite became so keen there was no satisfying me. On the 1st of January, 1778, the only traces of my illness were a very pale face and thin, emaciated body.

Soon after my return to Colonel Watson's he told me that my shipmate, Cleveland, had more than once expressed a wish that we should join and live together in a very good house he had taken, which from its vicinity to the Court House would suit me admirably. To this proposal I readily agreed, and as soon as I had sufficient strength to go to Calcutta, called upon him.

I found the house delightfully situated upon the Esplanade, open to the southward and eastward, and commanding an extensive view both up and down the river, to which it was close. It belonged to Mrs. Ogden, the widow of a pilot then recently dead, who had left her this house with other property. The only reasonable objection that could be made was its being *cutcha*, that is, built with mud instead of mortar. Formerly the greater part of the buildings in Bengal were of that description, whereas there is now hardly one to be seen throughout Calcutta, being replaced by well constructed solid masonry. For this house we agreed to pay three hundred sicca rupees, or thirty-seven pounds ten shillings a month. Pott exclaimed upon entering it at its unfurnished state, and undertook to get it put into a proper condition for us, which he did, but at an expense of nearly one thousand pounds. On the 6th of January we became joint householders.

The following day, being that on which the term commenced, Sir Elijah Impey, Chief Justice, Sir Robert Chambers, the officers of the Court, Barristers, and Attorneys assembled at nine o'clock in the morning at the house of Mr. Justice Hyde, who always gave them a breakfast the first of every term and sessions, the whole body afterwards proceeding in a line to the Court, attended by the Sheriff, Under-Sheriff, his servants and constables. At the door of the Court House, one of the Supreme Council joined the procession and took his seat upon the bench, which was then considered a proper compliment to His Majesty's Justices. For many years back that ceremony has ceased to be observed.

I had no want of clients, having within a week after I commenced business twelve actions and three equity suits to prosecute or defend. The difference in the practice from that pursued in Westminster Hall at first puzzled me a little, but the Advocates and Attorneys, showing the utmost readiness to give me information and assistance, I soon made myself master of the forms. Being invited to dine with Sir Elijah Impey after the Court broke up, I dressed and went there, where I met many of the principal gentlemen of the Settlement, being introduced to those I was not already acquainted with, and passed a cheerful, pleasant day.

On the 8th I went to Mr. Francis's public breakfast, it being the custom in those days for the Governor-General and members of Council to receive visits of compliments or strangers for introduction at breakfast, each having one morning a week for the purpose. Mr. Tilghman, who was related to Mr. Francis and resided at his house, seeing me enter, immediately rose from the table at which he with about thirty others were sitting, and conducted me to Mr. Francis at the head of it, to whom I delivered my letters, which to my great surprize he directly opened and read. He had, however, previously pointed to a chair near him on which I sat down. Having perused the first letter he opened, he looked me full in the face and burst into a hoarse laugh, for which in a few seconds he apologized by observing that it struck him as superlatively ridiculous for Mr. Burke to imagine he could be of the smallest use to an Attorney (placing a strong emphasis on the last word).

I felt extremely mortified at his impertinent manner especially before so large a company, and I believe my countenance showed that I was offended, for he suddenly altered his behaviour and made a great many civil speeches. He requested I would do him the honour to dine with him, lamented the very severe indisposition I had undergone, adding if I would follow his advice he would answer for it I never should be troubled with bile, his preventative being a glass of cold water as soon as I awoke in the morning, and another on retiring to rest at night. This, he said, a physician of eminence in London had recommended, and he had found it answer most completely.

At dinner I met Mr. Shee (now Sir George, a baronet), Sir John D'Oyley, Mr. Peter Moore, Mr. Leonard Collins, Mr. Edward Hay, Mr. George Hatch, Mr. Richard Johnson, and Mr. John Haldane, with all of whom I became very intimate and lived in habits of great kindness. I lament to say the five last named have been dead for several years. During dinner Mr. Francis, speaking to a gentleman near him, said, "When do you expect to get away, Captain Newte ? " and was answered, "I hope, sir, by this day month." Mr. Francis then addressing Pott, who sat next to me, asked him, "Are you ready to embark, Pott?" Robert replied, "I have not yet thought of a single article, but can provide myself fully in one week." This was the first I had heard of Pott's having any intention to leave India, and truly concerned was I at thus learning I was so soon to be deprived of the society of my much esteemed friend. Upon my upbraiding him for not telling me, he said he had daily meant to do so, but could not bring himself to speak upon a subject the very thought of which made him miserable, but family circumstances made his presence in England indispensable.

A succession of large and formal dinners followed Mr. Francis's, beginning with the Governor-General, Mr. Wheler, General Stibbert, Mr. Barwell, and in fact all the *Burra Sahibs* (great men) of Calcutta. The first really pleasant party I was at after my illness was given by Daniel Barwell, who, as I have before observed, kept house with Pott and others. The most highly dressed and splendid hookah was prepared for me. I tried, but did not like it. As after several trials I still found it disagreeable, I with much gravity requested to know whether it was indispensably necessary that I should become a smoker, which was answered with equal gravity, "Undoubtedly it is, for you might as well be out of the world as out of the fashion. Here everybody uses a hookah, and it is impossible to get on without." Mr. Gosling, less volatile and flighty than the rest of the party, immediately said, "Don't mind these rattling young men, Mr. Hickey, there is no sort of occasion for your doing what is unpleasant, and although hookahs are in pretty general use there are several gentlemen that never smoke them." I directly dismissed the hookah, never after tasting one. Often since have I rejoiced that I did not happen to like it, as I have seen the want of it, from servants misunderstanding where they were ordered to attend their masters, or some other accident, a source of absolute misery, and have frequently heard men declare they would much rather be deprived of their dinner than their hookah.

In this party I first saw the barbarous custom of pelleting each other, with little balls of bread made like pills, across the table, which was even practised by the fair sex. Some people could discharge them with such force as to cause considerable pain when struck in the face. Mr. Daniel Barwell was such a proficient that he could at the distance of three or four yards snuff a candle, and that several times successively.

This strange trick, fitter for savages than polished society, produced many quarrels, and at last entirely ceased from the following occurrence : A Captain Morrison had repeatedly expressed his abhorrence of pelleting, and said that if any person struck him with one he should consider it intended as an insult and resent it accordingly. In a few minutes after he had so said he received a smart blow in the face from one which, although discharged from a hand below the table, he could trace by the motion of the arm from whence it came, and saw that the pelleter was a very recent acquaintance. He therefore, without the least hesitation, took up a dish that stood before him and contained a leg of mutton, which he discharged with all his strength at the offender, and with such well-directed aim that it took place upon the head, knocking him off his chair and giving him a severe cut upon the temple. This produced a duel, in which the unfortunate pelleter was shot through the body, lay upon his bed many months, and never perfectly recovered. This put a complete stop to the absurd practice.

Having partaken of several entertainments given at the tavern by Captain Sutton and other gentlemen, I thought it incumbent upon me to return the compliment, and accordingly bespoke the handsomest dinner that could be provided for forty, at the Harmonic Tavern. On the day appointed thirty-nine sat down to table, all of whom did ample justice to the feast, and drank freely, some of my guests remaining till three in the morning, when they staggered home, well pleased with their fare and declaring I was an admirable host.

CHAPTER XI

COLONEL WATSON AND HIS BIG UNDERTAKING

AT the time I arrived in Bengal everybody dressed splendidly, being covered with lace, spangles, and foil. I, who always had a tendency to be a beau, gave in to the fashion with much good will, no person appearing in richer suits of velvet and lace than myself. I kept a handsome phaeton and beautiful pair of horses, and also had two noble Arabian saddle horses, my whole establishment being of the best and most expensive kind. I was soon distinguished in Calcutta by the title of "the Gentleman Attorney," in contradistinction to the blackguard practitioners, of which description I am sorry to say there were several. In fact, with the exception of Messrs. Tolfrey and Nailor, Foxcroft, Johnson, Jarrett (who was solicitor to the Company), and Smoult, I never met any attorneys in the company I kept, which always was the best. Once a week I had a party to dine with me, when we kept it up merrily, but my chum, Cleveland, was not to be led astray by bad example. A debauch he had unexpectedly fallen into at the Cape of Good Hope made so deep an impression upon his mind that nothing could efface it, or induce him to commit excess. He invariably left the table at an early hour in the evening, retiring to his own chamber.

Notwithstanding I lived so dissipated a life in point of drinking and late hours, no man laboured harder. I was always at my desk before seven in the morning, and with the break of half an hour for breakfast, never ceased work until dinner, after which, unless upon emergencies, I never took pen in hand. I had sufficient business to occupy myself and three native clerks : money consequently came in fast, so that I never bestowed a thought about the price of an article ; whatever I wanted was ordered home. I made it a rule, however, to discharge every demand upon me the first of each month.

Not a week ever passed without my visiting Colonel Watson, who stuck close to his dockyard. One day I happened to be with him looking at the workmen boring to ascertain the different kinds of soil, when at the depth of more than one hundred feet from the surface of the earth the augur met with a substance so hard it was with extreme difficulty they could force it on. Upon the different divisions of the borer being brought up and unscrewed, this resistance was found to have been occasioned by the augur coming against and going through a piece of perfectly sound timber of full three feet in thickness. This was considered as a most extraordinary event, nor could any of the ingenious men or naturalists of Asia in any manner account for it.

In the month of December (1778) my old friend and shipmate in the *Plassey*, Samuel Rogers, arrived in Bengal, having the command of the *Osterley* East Indiaman. I was sincerely glad to see this worthy man. He came out with the unfortunate *Grosvenor* which on her return to Europe crowded with passengers ran aground upon the coast of Africa considerably to the northward of the Cape, she having been grossly mistaken in her reckoning. Although it blew strong when the accident happened, which was in the middle of the night, most of the people and passengers reached the shore in safety, being assisted therein by the savage inhabitants of that part of the country. They were, however, many hundred miles from the Cape or the residence of any Europeans.

Amongst the hapless passengers were Mr. and Mrs. Hosea with two children (Mr. Hosea having acquired a handsome fortune in the Company's civil service at Bengal), the wife of the Chief Officer, and Charles Newman, Esq., Barrister of the Supreme Court, who had also made a fine fortune by his profession. These, with others whose names

I do not now recollect, were either murdered or carried prisoners into the interior of the country by the natives, a race of Caffres. Three persons only of the whole crew (seamen), after undergoing almost unequalled hardships, reached the Cape, none of the rest having ever since been heard of, notwithstanding the Dutch Governor dispatched several different parties in quest of them. Within the last five years it is said that one of the travellers into Africa at a great distance from the sea coast saw some young persons of a much fairer skin than the inhabitants in general. It has therefore been supposed that these may have been the offspring of the unfortunate ladies by the Caffres that made them prisoners. Lady Chambers lost one of her children that was on board this ill-fated ship.

In the middle of February my friend, Bob Pott, took leave of me and embarked in the *Ceres*, and towards the end of the same month Mr. Daniel Barwell also departed with Captain Rogers. Their voyage turned out disastrous and proved fatal to Mr. Barwell. When off the Mauritius they unfortunately fell in with a large French privateer, in which ship Mr. Whittall, then high in the Company's civil service at Madras, but much engaged in commercial concerns with the French, was said to be a part owner. Be that as it may, she attacked the *Osterley*, and, being a powerful vessel, full of men, after a short and unavailing conflict on the part of the *Osterley* the latter was obliged to strike her colours, and was carried a prize to the Isle of France, or Mauritius.

Mr. Barwell in a few weeks obtained permission to leave the island in an American vessel which was bound to the Cape of Good Hope, where having arrived in safety he engaged a passage to Europe on board a Dutch East Indiaman. This ship reached the coast of Holland off the port of Middleburgh, where she was to stop. An ignorant fellow went on board and took charge of her as pilot to conduct her in, who ran her upon a sand-bank, where she was totally lost. The brutal Dutchmen on shore made no effort to prevent the accident, which from the course she steered they saw for several hours must happen, nor did they when the disaster had actually occurred take any measures to save the lives of the unfortunate persons on board. They supposed, notwithstanding the vessel had Dutch colours flying, that she was English, and had hoisted the ensign of Holland to induce the people on shore to send off assistance, for they pronounced it impossible that any Dutch ship could betray such ignorance as this ship had done in running for the harbour.

Towards evening of the day on which she struck it began to blow strong, the sea consequently rose, which made those on board apprehend she must go to pieces before the morning.   Mr. Barwell, who was a remarkably good swimmer, therefore determined to leave the wreck and make for the nearest land, about three miles distant, another young man who had been a midshipman of the *Osterley* agreeing to accompany him.   They accordingly swam from the ship and both perished, whereas almost the whole of those that remained with the wreck were saved. By daybreak the people on shore had ascertained the ship in distress to be a Dutch homeward bound East Indiaman, whereupon a scene of general confusion ensued, each man in office upbraiding his neighbour with inattention and negligence in not sending off aid the day before.   A great number of boats were forthwith manned and dispatched to the wreck, but before they reached her she was nearly buried in the sand and completely filled with water so that no article of any kind could be saved.   The lives of the people on board, with the exception of six, were, however, preserved.   Had assistance been given when the ship first struck much of the cargo and probably the vessel itself might have been saved.

Mr. Barwell's corpse was found three days after by some fishermen ; was by them carried on shore and there buried in the church of Middleburgh.   Miss Mary Barwell, a maiden sister of Daniel's, an eccentric, odd woman, took it into her head that her brother had been basely murdered by the Dutchmen in order to possess themselves of an immense property in money and jewels which Mr. Barwell was well known to have had on board, of the truth of which suspicion she had formed her own belief so firmly that nothing could shake it. She became outrageously violent on the subject, addressing letters to the Court of Directors, also to the different Cabinet Ministers, in consequence of which the most rigid enquiry and examination took place. The result satisfied every unprejudiced person that there was not a shadow of foundation for the insinuations and charges made by Miss Barwell.

All the circumstances of the investigation were committed to writing and forwarded to that lady, who, instead of being satisfied thereby, wrote the most scurrilous and abusive letters to the Prime Minister of England, likewise to the Court of Directors, wherein she taxed them with sanctioning robbery and murder. She also addressed Sir Joseph Yorke, the British Ambassador at the Hague, calling upon him as the public representative of his country to exert himself in bringing the offenders to justice. Sir Joseph Yorke, anxious to convince the unhappy old gentlewoman that her suspicions were unfounded, procured affidavits of the captain, the officers, and every respectable person on board the unfortunate ship, stating the manner in which Mr. Barwell and the midshipman had, contrary to the opinions and advice of all on board, abandoned the wreck in order to swim on shore, and shewing that previous to so doing Mr. Barwell delivered the keys of his trunk and bureau to the captain, telling him that in the bureau all his papers of consequence were deposited. Miss Barwell, nevertheless, continued unsatisfied, again addressing Sir Joseph Yorke in writing, and charging him directly with countenancing and protecting *murderers*.

This last-mentioned letter, which was as scurrilous a production as I ever saw, Sir Joseph Yorke showed to me when I was subsequently at the Hague, nor could any arguments or any documents make the prejudiced woman change her opinion. To the day of her death she declared that her brother had been inhumanly murdered by the base

Dutchmen, who possessed themselves of his property to an immense amount.

In the *Ceres* Mr. Jarrett, Attorney to the Company, also embarked for Europe, whereupon Mr. Nailor, through the interest of Sir Elijah Impey, succeeded to that lucrative appointment.

My friend Colonel Watson now began his docks, and erected two large windmills. Being the first that had ever been built in Bengal, they excited much astonishment amongst the natives. The two mills were exactly alike, being one hundred and fourteen feet in height, consisting of five stories or floors, the upper ones for grinding grain of every description, the ground floor to saw timber by circular saws worked by the wind, an ingenious invention then recently found out.

It was one of my principal daily amusements to observe the progress of these works. The surprize of the native artificers was great beyond belief when told that the operation of the wind on the sails at the outside would affect every floor, grinding flour or grain of some sort upon each. Indeed, they pronounced such an event utterly impossible. Upon the first trial when the flyers were fixed it was set in motion at a time when there were upwards of one hundred workmen employed on the upper floors, who, seeing the immense upright timber in motion and the whole fabric considerably agitated, were greatly alarmed, conceiving nothing short of magic could have produced so extraordinary an effect. In their fright their first object was to escape from the building, and in their endeavours to effect that object they tumbled heels over head down the different flights of stairs. Such was their anxiety to get clear of what they considered the enchanted spot that several were seriously hurt. Altogether the scene was most strange " Wah, wah ! " (an exclamation of surprize) was heard from all quarters !

The Colonel had also commenced a mould loft of sufficient dimensions to lay down a first-rate ship, the outer walls of which being more than half up he found he should be deficient in teak timbers for laying the usual flat terrace. He therefore determined to make a pitched roof, a mode of building never practised in Asia, but, from the uncommon width of the loft, even to form a pitched roof, it became necessary to contract the upper part. The last ten layers of bricks were therefore carried in half an inch each layer for the purpose of lessening the width. Mr. Cressy gave it as his opinion that a wall so constructed could not stand, and would undoubtedly bulge, whilst, on the other hand, Colonel Watson and Mr. Agg were clear that it would answer, but at any rate the Colonel was resolved to make the trial.

I was one morning looking at the workmen, the Colonel being by, when he suddenly exclaimed, " That fellow Cressy is clearly right. This building won't do ; indeed, I always had great doubts about it. However, keep this to yourself, Hickey, for I will proceed with the work." The next day he brought Mr. Thomas Lyon, the architect, to inspect the building. This gentleman having ascertained every particular, also the number of square feet the roof would consist of, he calculated the weight of the whole terrace, which he found so immense that he at once declared it would not do, that the wall on one side or the other must inevitably bulge. Being asked what he meant by " bulge," he replied, " Give way outward and fall " ; but he observed that had the walls been continued to the top of the same thickness, and more slope given to the rafters, he had not the least doubt but that it would have fully answered the intended purpose.

At dinner Cressy, having heard that his judgment was supported by so able a mechanist as Mr. Lyon, was exceedingly proud, exultingly saying over and over again, " I knew it could not stand, there could be no doubt about it." " No doubt you are a foolish coxcomb," retorted the Colonel, " but stand or fall I am determined to proceed with the building and in my own way." " Then it will be down about your ears," said Cressy. " And I'll have it up again notwithstanding," said the Colonel. A few days after this discussion I went out to dine at the docks, when the Colonel exultingly said, " Well, Hickey, you see these wondrous clever fellows are egregiously wrong ; in spite of their predictions the walls stand and will, I doubt not, bear the weight of the terrace, more than half of which is already on." " It will be down within eight and forty hours," said Cressy. " I'll bet you one thousand guineas to one hundred it is not," said the Colonel. " Done, Sir," says Cressy, when the Colonel coolly observed, " You know very well that I never lay wagers." Whereupon Cressy pertly observed, " You are right not to do so upon this occasion as you would clearly lose both your building and your guineas."

Two days afterwards the Colonel called to take me in his buggy out to dinner. Upon the way to the docks he told me when he left home in the morning nearly the whole terrace was on, and he was in great hopes, after all, that the building would stand. When within half a mile of his gate we heard a tremendous crash. " Heh ! Heh ! Hickey," said the Colonel in his usual quick manner of speaking ; " heh ! what the devil is that, Hickey ? " " It sounds like thunder," replied I. " Heh, what ! thunder. Zounds ! I'm cursedly afraid, Hickey, Cressy will prove right. However," continued he, " it was a nice point."

Just at that moment we perceived an immense body of dust rising in the air, and a few minutes taking us to the entrance of his premises, we saw the fabric laying in ruins upon the ground. The Colonel, with extreme anxiety, enquired if any of the people were hurt, and was told the workmen had quitted the roof a few moments before to refresh themselves, only two young boys remaining, neither of whom had received the slightest injury. Had the accident occurred half an hour sooner or later in all probability many people would have lost their lives, there being upwards of two hundred men, women, and children employed in beating the terrace.

I have already observed that Colonel Watson was not upon good terms with Mr. Barwell, and conceiving he could carry on his scheme without his aid or assistance in Council he paid him no sort of attention. This, Barwell, who was a proud man and tenacious of the public situation he held, highly resented, and malignantly determined in consequence to throw every possible impediment in the way.

When the grant of land was first made by Government to Campbell he was directed, upon ousting the natives from their different spots of ground, to make each an adequate compensation, or an equivalent in ground elsewhere, but the natives of India, high and low, being superstitiously attached to the spot in which they were born and brought up, no consideration whatever will induce them to relinquish it, and this was strongly proved upon this occasion. Colonel Campbell could bring them to no terms. Miserable as the huts they resided in were, they were content and peremptorily refused to leave them. Force was therefore resorted to ; the Colonel sent a party of Sepoys, who turned the wretched creatures out of their habitations and then levelled them with the earth.

The persons thus treated went in a body to the Council House, where with their usual noise they cried out for justice. Colonel Campbell was thereupon asked the reason of such violence, to which he replied that he had always been ready to execute the orders of Government, had offered the proprietors five times the value of their land and buildings, or to give them a far greater quantity of ground in the neighbourhood, but that the parties complaining were so unreasonable as to refuse any terms, whereby the progress of the public works was impeded. Government then named four respectable gentlemen to determine upon the fair value of the spots of ground in question, which when done the proprietors should be compelled to accept. These gentlemen accordingly met many times during a period of ten months, when their opinions differed so widely as to the quantum of compensation that nothing decisive was ever done nor any report made by them. The inhabitants, however, were effectually excluded from their land, and a high brick wall built round the whole space. Immense ranges of workshops and godowns for stores were also erected.

Besides those expensive buildings Mr. Watson, who had then joined Campbell in the undertaking, built a range of barracks sufficiently spacious to accommodate three hundred persons, part of their scheme being to purchase slaves at Mozambique and Madagascar to carry on the laborious part of their undertaking.

Messieurs Campbell and Watson, who had already sunk a large sum and aware how much more it would take to complete so stupendous a work, were, of course, extremely anxious to secure themselves against any future obstructions by native claiments or otherwise, and after much consultation with their friends it was deemed prudent to solicit a legal grant of the land which, as mentioned, was prepared by the Company's law officers. This deed Colonel Watson conceived it impossible to shake or affect.

Gocul Gosaul, a man of opulence, was one of those who had been dispossessed of a certain quantity of land for which he had refused to receive any compensation, it being taken from him against his will. This Gocul Gosaul upon the Colonel's arrival paid him a visit, at which time I was present, and I was much struck by the elegance of his address and manners. In the best language he complimented the Colonel upon his return to Bengal, expressing the gratification it gave him to see him and to hear that he was authorized to carry into effect an undertaking that must do honour to India.

During this interview not an allusion was made by Gocul Gosaul to his parcel of land, or anything like a complaint, so far otherwise he was profuse in his offers of aiding the prosecution of the work by every means in his power, observing that he would readily advance at any time three or four lacs of rupees to promote the object in view, yet this very Gocul Gosaul was the man that in a few months subsequent to these voluntary offers and civil declarations became the Colonel's first and serious opponent. In this, however, he was encouraged by Mr. Barwell, at whose instigation he made a formal demand of the piece of ground of which he had been dispossessed, in answer to which application the Colonel referred him to the Governor-General and Council.

Gocul Gosaul replied he had nothing to do with Government, that Colonel Watson had tortiously ousted him from his property, and if it was not forthwith restored he should commence a prosecution against him in the Supreme Court by way of ejectment for the recovery thereof. Colonel Watson, alarmed at the threat, desired to see him. He repeatedly promised to call, but did not. The Colonel therefore determined to go to his house, and did so, I, at his particular desire, accompanying him. Gocaul Gosaul seemed much distressed, made a thousand apologies, and pleaded indisposition in excuse for not having waited upon the Colonel according to his promise. His confusion was increased by the Colonel coolly saying, "Illness did not prevent your doing as you ought to have done. You very well know you acted under the orders of a member of Government, Mr. Barwell." After remaining silent some minutes and looking extremely awkward, he observed, "Mr. Barwell was a great man and his protector, he was therefore bound to act in obedience to his wishes." The Colonel, in a rage, said, he (Gocul Gocaul) and his protector, Barwell, were a pair of infamous rascals, and instantly walked out of the house.

Three days after an action was commenced, whereupon Colonel Watson went to Mr. Hastings, the Governor-General, to Mr. Francis and Mr. Wheler, to inform them thereof, when they all reprobated the conduct of Mr. Barwell,[1] to whom Mr. Hastings said he would speak privately upon the business, and endeavour to stop the proceedings. He did

[1] Richard Barwell (1741-1804) was born in Calcutta. Francis, who had a contempt for him, wrote: "Mr. Barwell, I think, has all the bad qualities common to this climate and country, of which he is in every sense a native, but I do not affirm that there is no mixture whatsoever of good in his composition. He is rapacious without industry, and ambitious without exertion of his faculties or steady application to affairs. He would be Governor-General if money could make him so, and in that station he would soon engross the wealth of the country. He will do whatever can be done by bribery and intrigue. He has no other resource. His mind is strictly effeminate and unequal to any serious constant occupation except gaming in which alone he is indefatigable." (Busteed's *Echoes from Old Calcutta.*)—ED.

accordingly speak to the gentleman, who was mean enough
to deny his having at all interfered or influenced Gocul
Gosaul in what he had done. Thus circumstanced, Colonel
Watson had nothing left but to defend himself as well as
he could.

The land claimed by Gocul Gosaul was of the utmost
importance, being a narrow slip or footpath to the water-
side by which Gocul Gosaul and his family had formerly
gone to the river to perform their daily ablutions. According
to his pointing out of his claim, it went directly through the
centre of the newly finished windmill, interfering also with
both the projected wet and dry docks. In short, if he
succeeded in establishing his right to the land it completely
did away with the possibility of carrying the proposed plan
into execution.

The Attorney employed by Gocul Gosaul was Mr. North
Nailor, then the Company's Solicitor, and acting likewise
for Mr. Barwell in all legal business he had to do, by which
gentleman he had been recommended to Gocul Gosaul.
The Colonel having requested me to act on his part, I
entered an appearance. I also desired to see the grant from
the Company, which, upon reading, I found to be so strong
in the Colonel's favour that I immediately advised my
client to apply to Government to act in the defence, they
being bound to support their own acts. Colonel Watson
accordingly did so, when the question was referred to Sir
John Day, their Advocate-General, who without hesitation decided in the Colonel's favour. Mr. Nailor therefore
received orders from the Company's Secretary to undertake
the defence of the action, to which he answered that, having
in his private capacity of an Attorney commenced the suit
and thus become acquainted with every particular of the
plaintiff's case, it would be highly improper in him to be
concerned for the defendant. Thus awkwardly circumstanced he said he could have nothing more to do in the
cause, and he handed over the papers to another Attorney,
his own partner, Mr. Samuel Tolfrey !

Mr. James Pater Auriol, at that time principal Secretary,

then addressed a letter to me authorizing me to continue the defence on behalf of the Company, and directing me in the progress of the cause to apply to Mr. Isaac Bonigh, a Civil servant, then recently appointed to a new office called Commissioner of Law Suits, who would furnish me with every information I might require, and supply every necessary document from the Council House.

Gocul Gosaul, upon finding the matter thus seriously taken up by Government, became greatly alarmed, apprehending that should he persist in his demand he might incur the displeasure of the Governor-General, a circumstance in those days of much importance. Having expressed his fears to Mr. Barwell, that artful man encouraged him to go on, reminding him that the chief object of the British Legislature in constituting a Supreme Court in Bengal was to efface from men's minds a too prevalent idea that Europeans holding the most elevated rank might with impunity harass and oppress the natives of every description; that the duty of the Judges was to prevent such oppression or to punish the offenders when legally brought before them, to promote which object a pauper establishment of law officers were appointed and paid by Government to act for those who could not afford to apply for redress from their own private funds. Gocul Gosaul, however, notwithstanding the encouragement Mr. Barwell gave him, proceeded in the action with extreme reluctance.

The trial commenced at nine in the morning, and did not finish until eight at night, when Gocul Gosaul having sufficiently proved his right to a certain portion of the land from which he had been forcibly ejected, Sir Elijah Impey pronounced judgment for the Plaintiff in a very eloquent speech in which he feelingly lamented the agitation of such a question as was then before him, pretty plainly saying he thought the Government ought, from every motive, to have prevented it.

Thus a complete stop was put to the further progress of an undertaking that, if completed, would have been of the utmost national importance.

This may be a proper moment to say a word relative to Sir John Day, the Advocate-General who ought to have appeared as Counsel.

A short time before his leaving England he married Miss Ramus, whose father was an old and favourite servant of His Majesty's, upon which occasion, going to pay his compliments at St. James's, he received the honour of Knighthood, a circumstance that occasioned a witticism in the newspapers from it having occurred in the month of September. The facetious George Selwyn, seeing in the *Gazette* that Mr. Day was made a Knight, exclaimed, " By God, this is out-heroding Herod. I have long heard of the extraordinary power His Majesty exercised, but until this moment could not have believed that he could turn Day into KNIGHT, and make a Lady Day at Michaelmas."

Colonel Watson, being thus interrupted in his plan by the verdict pronounced, feeling also that he was liable to many similar attacks by persons who had been forcibly dispossessed of their ground and received no compensation, he did not think it prudent to proceed on his great work, but stopped short, serving a formal notice upon the Governor-General and Council, declaring that he should, in consequence of the legal interruption, look to the East India Company for remuneration for his losses, as also for damages for the injury he must unavoidably sustain by being thus impeded in the execution of a work commenced and proceeded into a ruinous extent as to his private fortune under the faith and security of a grant formally executed by the Court of Directors to him. He likewise transmitted orders to his Agents in London to serve a similar notice upon the Chairman and Deputy-Chairman in Leadenhall Street.

The situation of Chief Engineer, which Colonel Watson held, being at that time one of prodigious emolument, the Colonel did not choose to relinquish it, which must have been the case had he left India. He therefore resolved to remain in Bengal and endeavour to dispose of at least a part of the immense quantity of marine stores he possessed, or to turn the same to advantage by employing the ingenious artificers he had brought from England with him in building ships. He accordingly set them to work upon a part of the ground about which there was no contest, and within two years launched three as beautiful vessels as ever were constructed in any dockyard in Great Britain. The first was named the *Surprize*, the second the *Nonsuch*, and · the third the *Laurel*. The *Surprize*, of three hundred tons, was, previous to leaving the stocks, taken up by Government and sent to Europe as a packet, making a very excellent passage and proving a first-rate sailer. The *Nonsuch* and *Laurel* were both engaged in the China trade, but were afterwards also employed as packets to England, and were much admired for their strength and beauty by the London shipwrights.

CHAPTER XII

THE HASTINGS-CLAVERING DISPUTE AND THE GRAND-FRANCIS ACTION

IN the month of February the *Duke of Portland*, Captain Sutton, left Bengal on her return to Europe, and by her went passenger Mr. Farrer, the barrister, who, in little more than three years, acquired a fortune of eighty thousand pounds by his profession, a considerable proportion of which he made as Counsel for the much talked of Nundcomar, a Hindu Rajah and man of the first consequence from rank and wealth amongst the natives, who, being charged with forgery, was brought to trial for that offence, condemned, and, to the eternal disgrace of the British Government, executed under an *ex post facto* law. The fact is that this poor man, like the unfortunate Admiral Byng, fell a sacrifice to party.

The most violent animosity then prevailed between Mr. Hastings, as Governor, and General Clavering, first member of Council, and Commander-in-Chief. An account reached India that Mr. Hastings had on a certain day which was named, tendered his resignation to the Court of Directors by his Agent, Colonel Maclean. In consequence thereof General Clavering immediately caused himself to be proclaimed and assumed the Government, attempting at the same time to get possession of Fort William, but the friends of Mr. Hastings, who were always upon the alert, prevented it. Mr. Hastings was strenuously supported by Mr. Barwell, whilst General Clavering was equally so by Colonel Monson and Mr. Francis. At the most critical period of the dispute, Colonel Monson was taken ill and died, which gave Mr. Hastings a majority in Council by his own casting voice.

During the contest the partisans of each party were excessively violent, putting the Settlement into a state of the greatest anarchy. For several successive days a general insurrection was hourly expected, so much so that the competitors themselves were extremely alarmed for the consequences, when a sensible and considerate man of rank in the army, with a view to put an end to the dangerous controversy, proposed a reference to His Majesty's Judges of the Supreme Court, requesting them to decide the right, a proposal that was instantly agreed to by Mr. Hastings and General Clavering. A written statement was prepared, which, being acceded to by both parties, was presented to the Judges, who, after taking the same into their most serious and mature consideration, declared it to be their unanimous opinion that the Government ought to remain with Mr. Hastings, to which decision General Clavering yielded at once, thus ending a dispute that was near proving fatal to the very existence of the East India Company. As it was, the evils attending the discussion continued to operate for years, producing innumerable quarrels between the Advocates for each gentleman, and several duels, one of which occurred with two of the principals, Mr. Hastings and Mr. Francis.[1]

Another of the duels was between my friends, Robert Pott and James Grant, Pott being a staunch Hastingsite, while Grant was equally zealous on the part of Clavering. These young men had thentofore been intimate friends, but during the contest for the Government Pott charged Grant with duplicity and with acting the base part of an informer, divulging opinions that had been delivered in confidence and privacy. Grant thereupon challenged Pott. They met, when after exchanging several shots, Pott wounded his adversary in the leg, and the matter ended, but Grant was ever after distinguished from many of the same name by the title of "Informer Grant."

[1] Colonel Watson was Francis's second in this famous duel.—Ed

Rajah Nundcomar had been a warm supporter of General Clavering, from which many people thought he lost his life. There is no doubt but that in summing up the evidence and charging the Jury the Chief Justice, Sir Elijah Impey,[1] was as hostile to the prisoner as could be. The Jury, after being shut up many hours, and great difference of opinion prevailing amongst them, at last brought in a verdict of Guilty, but which several of them have since assured me they would sooner have starved than consented to had they entertained the most distant idea of execution following such a verdict, and most indignant were they upon finding the sentence carried into effect. Upon the day of the Rajah's execution every Hindu, high and low, at an early hour in the morning left Calcutta in the utmost despair.

Sir Robert Chambers, then the senior puisne Judge, differed from his brethren, declaring it to be his opinion not only that the Rajah ought not to suffer, but that the verdict was wrong, yet from his natural frivolity and want of firmness he allowed the influence the Chief Justice had over him to operate so far as to subscribe his name to the death warrant as with those of the other Judges.

Shortly after the above serious contest for the Government had taken place General Clavering was attacked by a malady of which he died, leaving a widow and three daughters of a former marriage. They were all remarkably fine young women, especially Caroline, the youngest, who was most bewitchingly attractive. She was volatile to the greatest degree and full of monkey tricks, nevertheless has since proved a most exemplary wife and mother. Shortly after her return to England she married Sir John Borlase Warren, a British Admiral of high reputation, to whom she has borne a number of children.

Mr. Cleveland and I continued joint housekeepers until the middle of April (1778), when, feeling ashamed of his

[1] Although Macaulay, in his essay on Warren Hastings, makes the gravest imputation against Impey for his sentence on Nundcomar, Impey had defended himself successfully against this and other charges at the Bar of the House of Commons. The injustice of Macaulay's strictures was, it is said, pointed out to him, but he never corrected them.—ED.

contributing one-half of the house expenses, especially the
serious article of wine, of which he scarcely ever took more
than two glasses daily, and rarely invited anyone to dinner,
whilst I with my frequent parties was taking large potations,
I determined upon dissolving our partnership, and took a
house for myself which was then finishing, and which I was
to enter upon on the 1st of May. The one Mr. Cleveland
and I inhabited was, as I have already observed, constructed of mud instead of chunam. The sun striking upon
the southern front made it intensely hot, to correct which I
sent for a native builder, directing him to put up a matted
verandah. My landlady, Mrs. Ogden, hearing this, came to
me in the utmost alarm, expressing her fears that I should
throw the house down, the walls not being sufficiently
strong to bear a verandah. Having purchased all the
requisite materials I did not like to give up my plan, though
staggered by what she said. I, however, consulted Mr.
Lyon, who pointed out some precautions, the adoption of
which he thought would do away with all risk. Pursuant to
Mr. Lyon's hints I built my verandah and found it of infinite advantage.

The months of March, April, and May in Bengal is the
season for wild and sudden tempests, called North-Westers.
Though tremendous in their appearance and effect they are
expected with pleasure from rendering the air cool and
delightful. The Saturdays and Sundays that I did not go
to Sir Robert Chambers's I generally spent at Captain
Thornhill's, the master attendant, who had a magnificent
country house upon the bank of the river at Cosspore, four
miles above Calcutta, where he received and entertained his
numerous friends with the greatest degree of hospitality
and good humour. Towards the end of April, while I was
at this gay mansion, there came on one of the most severe
north-westers that had been experienced for many years.
It commenced about six o'clock in the evening, blowing for
upwards of an hour an absolute hurricane, and, as was often
the case, after so doing from the north-west suddenly
shifted to the opposite point, north-east, returning with

even increased force. As my house stood openly exposed to the north-east I felt exceedingly uneasy about my newly erected verandah, expecting every instant to receive an account that the whole fabric was level with the earth. A little before twelve I got into my phaeton and drove to town in as great a funk as ever I was in when I entered Westminster School, knowing I was to be flogged. Upon turning the corner of a street close to which my house stood, I had the consolation to perceive at least that the body of the building still stood. Driving up to the door, however, I found my famous verandah entirely down and demolished, the wreck of it laying in the courtyard, yet I felt happy that it had not brought the crazy old building along with it.

During the period that Mr. Cleveland and I lived together a young Jewess of the name of Isaacs arrived in Calcutta to exercise the profession of miniature painting. Cleveland having known her family in England, interested himself to promote her success. He therefore observed to me that as he had heard me say I meant to send my picture to a favourite sister he should be obliged if I would sit to his friend. I accordingly did so. At the first sitting he was present, when he surprized me not a little by saying, "It has always been a matter of wonder to me how ugly fellows can ever bring themselves to sit for their pictures," to which I replied, "Upon my word, the remark comes with an ill grace from you who are the cause of my being in the situation that excites your wonder upon the present occasion." Miss Isaacs thereupon with much *naïveté* observed, "It was not kind in my friend to make such a speech, but," continued she, "were none but the handsome men of Calcutta to apply to me in my profession I should have very little occupation indeed." This lady, two years afterwards, married Mr. Higginson, a gentleman high in the Company's civil service and of large fortune.

I have already stated the strange reception I met with from Mr. Francis when I presented Mr. Burke's letter of introduction of me to him. Now, it so happened that this pompous gentleman who had so pointedly ridiculed the idea " of his ever having it in his power to be of use to an Attorney," was under the necessity of bestowing a considerable part of his fortune upon the members of a profession he seemed disposed to treat so contemptuously, and this arose from the following circumstance. A gentleman in the Company's civil service, named George Francis Grand, had married a pretty little French girl to whom Mr. Francis attached himself, and was supposed soon to have accomplished all he wished. He at least by his conduct laid himself open to be attacked by law. This occurred a few months after my arrival in Bengal, and Mr. Grand did me the honour to select me from the Corps of Attorneys to act on his behalf, but upon his calling at my office for the purpose of giving instructions for commencing the action I declined undertaking it, not from any particular attachment to Mr. Francis, but from motives of delicacy towards my respected friend, Mr. Burke, who had introduced me to him. Mr. Grand did not consider my reason sufficient to justify my refusal to act, and continued to press me upon the subject so that I had no other means of getting rid of his importunities than by leaving Calcutta. The same morning that I did so, Mr. Grand once more went to my office, where meeting a fine lad, Mr. Stackhouse Tolfrey, then a clerk of mine, he persuaded that young man to commence the action, which having done, Tolfrey directly announced it to me by letter, apologizing for taking such a step without my special orders, but pleaded the earnest solicitations of my friend, Mr. Grand. Though exceedingly vexed I could not be angry with Tolfrey, conscious that he had acted from the best motives. I, however, went to town and discontinued the action as having been commenced in my name without my authority. From the Prothonotary's office I proceeded to Mr. Grand's to express my displeasure at his having urged young Tolfrey to issue a writ contrary to my orders. He was very humble, made many apologies, paid me a number of compliments, and again entreated I would act as his Attorney, which I, of course, again refused.

He thereupon applied to another Attorney, by whom the action was commenced. Mr. Francis upon being served with a copy of the writ brought it to me, requesting I would defend on his part, but which I also refused, declaring I would have nothing to do on either side.

In the then ensuing term the cause came on for trial, wherein Mr. Shee (now Sir George) cut an awkward figure, the Chief Justice observing that his behaviour had been as reprehensible as it was derogatory to the character of a gentleman. The only material facts proved against Mr. Francis were his frequent visits at the house when Mr. Grand, the master, was from home, his being discovered, disguised in black, with a ladder upon his shoulder, which he was seen to place against the wall of Mr. Grand's house, and his being discovered at night in Mrs. Grand's bed-chamber by the servants. Yet upon that evidence, slight and unsatisfactory as it no doubt was, the plaintiff obtained a judgment. The defence was most ably conducted by Mr. Tilghman,[1] who insisted upon the impossibility of the plaintiff's succeeding upon such evidence, and he quoted a variety of modern cases in support of his opinion.

As the Judges differed each gave his separate opinion, Mr. Hyde, as junior, commencing, who commented upon the evidence, observing that, though slight, it satisfied his mind of the guilt of the defendant and justified a judgment for the plaintiff. Sir Robert Chambers spoke next. He said he had very maturely read over and weighed the depositions and sincerely lamented he was compelled to differ from his learned brethren by declaring he thought the plaintiff had totally failed to make out his case, and must be nonsuited, in support of which opinion he cited many late cases wherein the law had been clearly laid down by the ablest civilians of the present day, men who were equally an honour and an ornament to the British Bench.

---

[1] Tilghman was Francis's Philadelphian cousin, and after Mackrabier's death his greatest friend. His letters show that he was a most amusing, cheery fellow. It was conjectured that he supplied legal lore to juniors. He died on his voyage home from Bengal in January, 1786, aged 39. (See Busteed's *Echoes from Old Calcutta*.)— ED.

Sir Elijah Impey was evidently surprized and vexed at the depth of learning displayed by Sir Robert upon the occasion. He petulantly observed that he was not prepared to comment upon such a mass of learning in Ecclesiastical Law as had been, he thought unnecessarily and inapplicably, introduced by his brother Chambers, not a particle of which applied to the present case. He entirely concurred in opinion with Mr. Justice Hyde that the evidence entitled the plaintiff to a judgment, and that such judgment should be fifty thousand rupees ! Mr. Hyde, in a low voice, said " Siccas." " Aye, siccas, brother Hyde," added the Chief. This produced a roar of mirth from the auditors, at which Sir Elijah was greatly offended.

Within a week after the trial, Mr. Tilghman presented to the Court a petition of Appeal to His Majesty in Council against the judgment so given, and in the speech upon moving that the said petition be filed quoted the same cases Sir Robert had done, whereupon the Chief Justice angrily observed, " This is precisely the language and construction of the law used by Sir Robert Chambers on Saturday last." " True, my Lord," replied Mr. Tilghman, " and I am proud at having such respectable authority for using it to-day." At the moment he said this he received a note, which I, who was sitting next to him, saw was Mr. Francis's handwriting, consisting of only three lines. What the contents were I know not, but upon perusal Mr. Tilghman directly requested leave to withdraw the motion he had just before made, which being granted no more was ever heard about appealing. Various conjectures were made thereon, but the prevailing opinion was that Mr. Grand, who was embarrassed in his circumstances, had proposed a composition, and consented to take a part of the damages to put an end to the discussion, to which Mr. Francis readily acceded, thereby preventing the matters being brought forward in England to his disgrace as a married man. This business created much wit in Calcutta. Amongst a variety of *jeu d'esprits* the following by Colonel Ironside was handed about :

"Psha! what a Fuss, 'twixt SHEE, and 'twixt her!
  What abuse of a dear little creature,
A GRAND and a mighty affair to be sure,
  Just to give a light PHILIP (fillip) to nature.
How can you, ye prudes, blame a luscious young wench,
  Who so fond is of Love and romances,
Whose customs and manners are tout à fait French,
  For admiring whatever from FRANCE-IS!"

Soon after the decision of the cause the fair lady quitted India and went to Paris, where the famous Talleyrand saw her, was captivated by her beauty and married her.

At the expiration of the March term my shipmate, Mr. Morse, proposed an excursion for a week or ten days. We accordingly set out in his phaeton, driving to Barrackpore, distant fifteen miles from Calcutta. This is the place where the Sepoys and troops attached to the Presidency are cantoned, one battalion marching on the first day of each month to perform the duty in Fort William, relieving those who had preceded them.

After passing four and twenty hours at Barrackpore we went to Mr. John Prinsep's at Puttah (who is now an Alderman of London). He received and entertained us most hospitably at his manufactory for printing cottons, where after spending two pleasant days we proceeded to Ghyretty, a noble edifice, the country residence of the French Governor of Chandernagore. At the time of our visit it was inhabited by Monsieur Chevillard, of a noble French family.

Mr. Chevillard entertained us in a princely style. At the capture of Pondicherry, somewhere about the year 1759, Ghyretty House was made over to the late Sir Eyre Coote, then a Lieutenant-Colonel in the King's service and Commander of the British Forces. Upon the peace made in 1763, Colonel Coote having then returned to Europe, Chandernagore was restored to France, when Ghyretty House once more became the country residence of the French Governor, it being only five miles distant from Chandernagore and on the same side of the river. Coote's Agents generally once in each year served a notice upon the inhabitant that the premises belonged to their constituent, but neither he during his life, nor his representatives after his decease, ever derived a sixpence advantage from the ownership. The building has long been in a state of decay, and no one choosing to expend money in repairs, it must soon, if it has not already, fall to the ground.

From Ghyretty we went to Chandernagore and next to Chinsurah, the principal settlement of the Dutch in Bengal. The Governor of the latter place was Mr. Ross, who though himself born and bred in Holland was the son of a Scotchman. By him we were received with a degree of hospitality that quite equalled Mr. Chevillard's. Mr. Ross lived in a state of regal magnificence. When sitting in Council no man whatever his rank ever turned his back on the president, and in their awkward retreat towards the door stopped at every third or fourth step to make a profound bow. On the day of our arrival we assembled at one o'clock in a prodigious sized hall, where a table was laid with fifty covers upon it. Dinner being announced, a pair of folding doors were thrown open and Mr. Ross made his appearance, whereupon a band of martial instruments struck up and continued playing during the meal. In the evening we were shown the fort and public buildings. After spending three days very pleasantly we took our leave, returned to Mr. Prinsep's at Puttah, where we remained three more days, and then departed for our homes at Calcutta, much gratified by the jaunt.

Soon after my return to town I was elected a member of the Catch Club, one of the pleasantest societies I ever belonged to, but unpopular with the ladies, no female being admitted. It was originally established by some musical men, seceders from a meeting called the Harmonic, at which the younger people of both sexes being more pleased with their own rattling chatter and noise, paid no attention to the sweet strains of Corelli and other famous composers, and thereby gave great offence to the real lovers of music. A party thereupon resolved to establish a sort of club, where none of the profane should gain admittance

and women to be excluded altogether. This was the society
to which I was admitted, and a delightful thing it proved. I
was also a member of the old Harmonic, which, upon the
establishment of the new one, sunk into a mere dance. The
young women facetiously termed the new meeting, "The
He Harmonic." The latter commenced with a capital
concert, at which all the talents of the Settlement were
displayed. It commenced at seven and ended at half-past
nine. Precisely at ten we sat down to an excellent supper,
after which catches, glees, and single songs were kept up
until a late hour. Amongst the party were several uncommon fine voices, especially Mr. Platel, a member of
Lord Sandwich's celebrated Catch Club, Messrs. Golding,
Haynes, Messnick, and Playdell, all of whom sung with
extraordinary taste and execution. The Chair was taken
in rotation, the President being omnipotent. Upon its
coming to my turn to preside, I gave the master of the
house private directions as soon as the clock struck two
to introduce some kettles of burnt champagne, a measure
that was highly applauded by all, particularly by Mr.
Platel, who declared it was a glorious thought, and that
I deserved to have my name recorded in letters of gold.
We sat until an hour after sunrise. From that night it
became an established rule to have burnt champagne the
moment it was two o'clock. The number of members was
limited to twenty-five, and so popular did the club become
that there were seldom less than fifty candidates to fill up
any vacancy that occurred.

It being the general custom of Bengal in those days to
drink freely and to assemble in numerous parties at each
other's houses, I, who had always been disposed to con-
viviality, soon rendered myself conspicuous, and by the
splendour of my entertainments gained the reputation of
being the best host in Calcutta. The dining hour being
one o'clock, it was customary after that meal and about
sunset to take an airing, driving to the race-course, where
the carriages all drew up and a general chat took place.
I had one day given a dinner to a large party, one of whom

was an Irishman, Captain Richard Heffernan, as benevolent and good a creature as ever breathed, but quite a Paddy. I had filled them all so full of wine that by seven in the evening they had all slunk off, except Heffernan, and he positively refused to swallow another drop. I therefore proposed giving him a little exercise, to which he consenting, I ordered my phaeton, and off we set as hard as a pair of high-mettled horses could go. By the time we had been out half an hour it became quite dark, a matter of indifference to me whose head was overcharged with claret, and on I dashed pell-mell. My companion soon remarked from the violent jolts of the carriage that the way was cursed rough, and at last he asked whether I was sure I was in the right road, for so great a sea had got up he conceived it would be prudent either to shorten sail or bear up. I was obliged to confess I did not know where we had got to, and scarcely had I made that confession when away we went, phaeton, horses, and all, into a hole twelve or fourteen feet deep, which, as I afterwards ascertained, for eight months out of the twelve was filled with water, but at the time of our tumble was quite dry. Stunned by the violence of the fall, we lay for some moments insensible, when, somewhat recovering, I endeavoured to extricate myself from the pit in which amidst an almost impenetrable darkness we were enveloped. Whilst groping about, my companion, with his strong native accent, remarked, " Upon my conscience, this is a scurvy sort of a hole you have pop't me into, and the devil a chance do I percave of getting clear of it." In a few minutes I had scrambled up the side and reached the level. Having assisted my friend to do the same, I advised him to sit quietly there while I went to a light I saw at a distance to procure assistance and ascertain where we had got to and the state of my horses, both of whom I feared were killed. I therefore ran with all my speed towards the light, which having, as I conceived, nearly reached, my progress was interrupted by going heels over head into a deep ditch, the shock of which second fall totally unhinged me. seeming to dislocate every bone in my body. Fortunately, some natives were passing near the spot at the time, who, hearing my groans, came up, and, finding me incapable of personal exertion, said they would go to the hospital, close to which we were, and procure aid. They accordingly did so, and within a quarter of an hour a number of servants with palankeens and lights came to me, and I was conducted to the apartments of the head surgeon. Upon my representing to him the situation I had left my friend in, and that of my horses and carriage, he sent off in search of them, and in about an hour I had the pleasure to see Heffernan with my favourite horses, both having escaped without serious injury. For myself, I was miserably bruised, yet, all circumstances considered, escaped wonderfully. The greatest injury my friend Heffernan sustained was alarm from the first pitch we had into the hole, from which he had no other hurt than a slight sprain of one ankle. He, however, declared that in future he would cautiously avoid putting himself under charge of a drunken pilot. My phaeton and the horses' harness were totally demolished.

Soon after my return from the excursion with Mr. Morse I was invited to a splendid ball given by Lady Impey, at which all the fashionable people of the Settlement were present. At supper I was at the same table with Mr. Justice Hyde and a group of fine dashing lads, who, not supposing their observations were overheard by the Judge, amused themselves in commenting upon his quizzical dress, &c. At last one of them remarked what a glorious appetite he had and what a quantity he ate, finishing his speech by saying, "Damn me if I don't believe he loves the breast of turkey much better than he does his wife," whereupon, to his utter confusion, Mr. Hyde, though without taking his eyes from the plate before him or ceasing to eat, drily said, "No, I don't, young man, you are mistaken!" The youth bounced up from his seat, making a precipitate retreat.

I generally went once a week to very pleasant musical parties at Mr. Hyde's, his lady being much attached to music, playing admirably herself and possessing an uncommon fine voice.

CHAPTER XIII

A VAIN COMMODORE AND AN ENTERPRISING PRINTER

AT the time of my arrival in Bengal an expedition was fitting out, as was supposed, to go against the French Settlement of Pondicherry, and as Sir Edward Vernon, the British Admiral, had not a fleet sufficient to encounter that of Monsieur Trou Jolie, the French Commander, he had applied to the Government of India to supply a reinforcement of ships and men, in consequence of which the Governor-General directed the *Resolution* and *Royal Charlotte*, two very fine merchant vessels, to be engaged and equipped as vessels of war, and to be sent to the support of the Admiral at Madras. The command of these ships was given to Mr. Joseph Price, a gentleman who had formerly been in the sea service, but had quitted it and made a large fortune as a merchant, having always been patronised by Mr. Hastings. He had the title of Commodore given him, hoisting a broad pennant on board the *Resolution* and having a Captain on board under him.

Mr. Hastings, who had long been desirous of establishing a permanent marine in Calcutta upon a similar footing with that of Bombay, availed himself of Sir Edward Vernon's call for aid to set it on foot. He therefore proposed the measure in Council as likely to be most beneficial to the Company and to Great Britain, as thereby a force would always be at hand to scour the Bay of Bengal and rid the Indian seas of all French privateers, some of whom had committed dreadful depredations upon our country trade. The proposition being immediately sanctioned by the Council, was carried into effect. The *Britannia*, one of the Com-

pany's own ships, with two others of nearly the same
burthen and a small schooner, called the *Nancy*, were fitted
out as ships of war, a Mr. Richardson, also a protégé of
Mr. Hastings, and who was then Sheriff of Calcutta, being
appointed Commodore. Mr. Richardson was a Lieutenant
in the Royal Navy, but had been many years in India and
acquired a handsome independence.

This squadron was preparing at the same time with that
going to assist the Admiral, and upon the *Britannia* being
put into commission, Mr. Richardson hoisted a broad
pennant, upon which Price sent a boat on board with orders
that it should be struck, he being Commodore at Calcutta
and two pennants could not fly in the same port. Richardson answered he had a superior right to carry a broad
pennant, being at the head of the Bengal Marine, whereas
Price was merely engaged on a temporary service and had
no claim whatever to a distinguishing flag. The dispute
became so high between the rival Commodores, each
threatening to fire into the other, that it reached the ears
of the Governor-General, who forthwith ordered them
both to appear before him, when he expressed his displeasure
at their mutual folly and imprudence, and after the most
severe reprimand dismissed them with a caution to take
care what they were about, for that if they, like children,
were disposed to quarrel for their playthings, the toys
should be taken from both. This rebuke had its due effect,
and the two broad pennants flew unmolested. The lesson,
however, was in a degree lost upon Richardson, who,
previous to going with his squadron to sea, avowed his
determination to enforce the payment of all due respect to
his flag, and that he would compel every Company's ship
that he fell in with to strike their pennants while he continued in sight. He also said that being aware of the insolence of Captains of East Indiamen he should be the more
tenacious respecting them.

The command of the *Nancy* schooner was given to my
Irish friend, Heffernan, who, having been brought up in
the British Navy, was considered an expert seaman. This

little vessel was to be dispatched as an avant courier to the coast of Coromandel to communicate to the British Admiral the accession of strength he was soon to have. Previous to Captain Heffernan's departure he waited upon Richardson for final instructions, when the Commodore in the most peremptory language insisted upon his requiring the same respect from the Company's ship that a man-of-war would exact. "And pray, sir," asked Heffernan, "how am I to act in case of refusal?" "Enforce it," answered the Commodore. "How, sir, pray, considering the size of my vessel?" "Zounds, sir," furiously retorted Richardson, "fire into the vessel that dares persist in refusing to pay the required compliment. I have taken care, sir, to arm myself with authority to justify the orders I give you, and have the power of inflicting death by court martial," a power Mr. Hastings had most incautiously and inconsiderately given him, and which had he ever acted upon would have laid him open to be charged with murder! Fortunately, no instance occurred to bring the question into agitation. Captain Heffernan having had his audience of leave departed.

About the middle of April, 1778, Commodore Price and his squadron sailed for Madras, and proved of important service to the Admiral. Soon after the departure of the *Resolution* and *Royal Charlotte*, Commodore Richardson gave a splendid fête on board the *Britannia* to the whole gentry of Calcutta. The ship was fitted up for the occasion with the greatest taste, no expence being spared. The sole error committed was not having a fixed accommodation ladder, from the want of which the ladies were obliged to be hoisted in by the common coarse method of a chair. There was in Calcutta at that time a Mrs. Wood, wife to a gentleman of rank in the Company's service. This good lady was of a most unwieldy form, her size being immense. Being one of the guests invited, upon coming alongside the *Britannia* she was placed in the chair, and the four men stationed at the halliards directed to hoist away. They accordingly started, but making no progress imagined the

rope had jammed in the block. Finding upon examination
that not to be the case, the boatswain looked from the
deck into the boat, when seeing the enormous figure in the
chair he exclaimed, " Oh, damn my eyes, but I don't wonder,
my lads, you could not budge. There's a cargo nothing
short of all hands can move, so clap on, clap on, I say, my
lads," and he put half a dozen more men to the halliards,
when they set out with a loud huzza, actually running the
chair with Mrs. Wood in it almost up to the main yard-arm.
Although all who saw it felt the great impropriety and insolence of the act, the scene was so irresistibly ridiculous
as to excite a general laugh. The officers, of course, interfered and procured the lowering and release of the terrified
lady, whose husband was loud in his calls for having the
delinquents punished. For some minutes we feared this
untoward circumstance would have interrupted the harmony
of the day, but Mrs. Wood with great good nature inter-
ceded for the culprits, who were suffered to escape with a
severe reprimand from Captain Hicks, who was the next
officer to Commodore Richardson.

After a most magnificent dinner, at which were present
one hundred and fifty ladies and gentlemen, arranged
between decks, the bulkhead of the great cabin having been
removed so as to make a space sufficient for the tables, an
excellent band of martial music played a variety of favourite
tunes. The meal being finished, the ladies adjourned to the
quarter-deck and round-house, where after coffee, tea, and
all the usual accompaniments, dancing commenced under
a spacious awning, brilliantly illuminated by many hundred
coloured lamps, the effect of which was beautiful. A party
of men who preferred sacrificing at the shrine of Bacchus
to that of joining the damsels in the merry dance remained below, swilling burgundy, champagne, and claret,
all rendered most palatable by being cooled in ice.

At one in the morning a supper in every respect correspondent with the elegance of the dinner was served, to which
ample justice was done. A couple of hours were then agreeably occupied by delightful singing of catches and glees,

which being finished the lively girls resumed the sprightly dance, continuing thereat until six in the morning, when quite exhausted they were obliged to give over, and all departed for their respective homes much gratified with the entertainment.

Captain Heffernan having sailed from Calcutta, in four and twenty hours afterwards reached Culpee, where the East Indiamen of the season lay moored. Upon approaching the first he hailed, desiring they would strike their pennant. The commanding officer on board, who happened to be an intimate acquaintance of Heffernan's and knew the vessel, asked why he was to lower his pennant, to which Heffernan replied, "In compliment to one of the Bengal Marine." "Very well, Dickey," said the officer, "bring your man-of-war alongside and I'll hoist her in, and bear a hand as the soup is just coming aft." Heffernan brought the *Nancy* to an anchor, went to dine with his friend, and over a cheerful glass commented upon the vanity and folly of Commodore Richardson. This unfortunate *Nancy* upon the doing away of the Bengal marine scheme by orders for that purpose from the Court of Directors was sent from Bombay to Europe as a packet, under the command of Captain Haldane, whom the public prints too truly termed "the child of misfortune," he having been once cast away when mate of an Indiaman, losing everything he possessed. He afterwards got the command of the *Fairford*, a noble vessel of the Company's which upon her first voyage was destroyed by fire in the harbour of Bombay, he again losing all but life. Mr. Hornby, the Governor at the time, feeling for the heavy loss Captain Haldane thus sustained, with the humane intention of assisting him, fitted out the *Nancy* as a packet, giving him the command and also lending him a considerable sum of money to purchase an investment.

Captain Haldane had taken out in the *Fairford* the famous actress, Mrs. Cargill, who was greatly attached to him, so much so as to relinquish the stage on which she had attained much celebrity, to follow his fortunes. This beautiful and accomplished woman embarked with him in the *Nancy* for

England. After a remarkable fine passage they reached
the British soundings, when a tremendous tempest arose.
It being in the depth of winter, and they being (as was supposed) mistaken in their reckoning, ran ashore upon the
rocks off the Islands of Scilly, where every soul on board
perished. The corpse of Mrs. Cargill, with a child clasped in
her arms, was washed on shore upon one of the Islands
where both were buried.

Admiral Sir Edward Vernon, in consequence of his great
want of ships to act as transports and victuallers, had in
1778 detained at Madras two East Indiamen, the *Nassau*,
Captain Gore, and the *Southampton*, Captain Lenox, which
continued to act with the King's ships during the entire
siege of Pondicherry. Upon the surrender of that fortress,
the Admiral dismissed them with many compliments in his
public orders for their zeal and activity whilst acting with
his fleet. He also authorized them to carry the King's
pennant until they arrived at their moorings in the Bengal
River. The *Nassau* whilst on her passage from Madras to
Bengal fell in with Commodore Richardson and his squadron.
The Commodore ranged up alongside the *Nassau*, hailed and
desired his pennant might be struck. Upon which Captain
Gore, with much violence, answered that, having a greater
right to carry one than he (Richardson) had, he deemed
it the height of impertinence to presume to give an order
for its being lowered. To this the haughty Commodore
replied, if it was not instantly struck he would fire into the
ship. "Will you, by God ? then do so as soon as you please,
I am ready for you," at the same time ordering the boatswain to pipe all hands to quarters. In an instant the ports
fore and aft were up, guns run out, and matches lighted.
The Commodore, surprized at the promptness with which
the *Nassau* appeared in a state of formidable resistance,
cooled upon it and mildly said, "Why are you so hasty,
Sir ? " to which Gore answered, "Because your extraordinary
and unjustifiable conduct makes it necessary." "Will you
send a boat on board with an officer ? " demanded Richardson. "No," gruffly answered Gore. "My boats are all

caulking," said the Commodore, "and having information of importance to communicate I request you will send a boat." "Being civilly asked for I have no objection," said Gore, and he immediately dispatched his yawl with the third mate. The information alluded to being given in writing, the boat returned, and the ships parted without further intercourse.

My Irish friend Heffernan was fortunate enough while in the command of the *Nancy* to make some rich prizes by which he gained sufficient fortune to induce him to resign his situation and return to Europe, where, in the year 1781, he married a very beautiful young woman and lived happily for several years, when he departed this life.

On the 10th of May, 1778, I went into my new house, which belonged to Thomas Motte, Esq., then a respectable, and considered a very opulent, man. On the 1st of June following I invited a large party to dinner. Among the guests was my said landlord, Mr. Motte, whom I found a pleasant, well-informed man, also Mr. Shore (now Lord Teignmouth), Mr. Purling, Mr. Montgomery, and his brother, who commanded the *Besborough* Indiaman, Mr. Kneller, Colonel Watson, Major Mestayer, and some other of my *Seahorse* companions. I had likewise Captain John Durand, with whom I had been at school at Streatham. Although not then quite twenty-one years of age he had the command of the *Northington*, one of the Company's ships. He was the eldest son of the infamous scoundrel I have already mentioned in connection with his treatment of the worthy Captain Waddell, of the *Plassey*.

The morning had been very threatening, it blowing hard. By the time we sat down at table it increased to a violent gale with incessant heavy rain; so heavy it poured down that not one of my party chose to encounter it, and we therefore continued drinking until morning. Some of my guests being then convinced it was the setting in of the rains and might not cease for days, in spite of its fury set out for their own houses, but three remained with me until the morning of the 4th, when it suddenly cleared up, leaving the town completely deluged.

At that period the King's birthday was celebrated with much pomp, the Governor-General always giving a dinner to the gentlemen of the Settlement, and a ball and supper to the ladies at night, at which entertainments everybody, *malgré* the extreme heat, appeared in full dress, with bags and swords. I made up for the occasion a coat of pea-green, lined with white silk and richly ornamented with a spangled and foiled lace, waistcoat and breeches decorated in like manner being also of white silk. All the company appearing in splendid apparel made a very handsome show. The Governor-General presided at the dinner-table. Upon the cloth being removed, he gave as first toast, The King; then, The Queen and Royal Family; The East India Company; The Army and Navy; The Commander-in-Chief; Success to the British arms in India—each toast being followed by a salute of twenty-one guns, from cannon drawn up for the purpose in front of the Court House.

I had only been a few days in Calcutta when I received a letter from a Mr. James Augustus Hicky, then a prisoner for debt in the common jail, requesting I would have the goodness to call upon him. I did so and found a most eccentric creature apparently possessed of considerable natural talents, but entirely uncultivated. Never before had I beheld a mortal who so completely came up to what I had often heard described as "a wild Irishman!" He related a lamentable tale of the unmerited cruelty with which he had been persecuted by a few malignant Bengalis, who had kept him locked up in prison upwards of two years upon false debts, which, although supported by the oaths of different plaintiffs, were founded only in perjury. During several visits I made him on different days he showed me many written documents strongly corroborative of what he asserted. I therefore determined to give him all the aid in my power.

Upon enquiring particularly into the character and conduct of my namesake, I learnt that he was extremely violent, yielding so much to sudden gusts of passion and so grossly abusing whoever acted for him that at length not a professional man could be found to act for him, and he actually remained a prisoner from there not being an Attorney who would have anything to say to him. I early saw that this account was not an exaggerated one, yet I could not help feeling for the unfortunate man. After requiring from him the most sacred promise that if I became his Attorney he would leave the conduct of his business entirely to me and not, as I understood had thentofore been the case, bounce up in Court every five minutes to complain of his lawyers to the Judges, I would do all I could to assist him. Such promise being readily given, I read the papers in each of his causes.

After making myself master of the leading facts, I applied to, and prevailed upon, my friends, Tilghman and Morse, to be Hicky's Counsel. As we all thought it right he should be present at the trial of his causes, I applied for a writ of Habeas Corpus for that purpose. Upon the first trial, Mr. Tilghman having a witness under cross-examination, Hicky suddenly started from his seat like a maniac, swearing he (Tilghman) did not know how to probe the conscience of a rascally native of Bengal and he would question him himself. Mr. Tilghman instantly, with great indignation, threw up his brief, accusing me with breach of my word, inasmuch as I had ventured to say I could be answerable for the propriety of my client.

Enraged at Hicky's behaviour, I told him he was a lying vagabond scoundrel, who ought, and should for me, rot in jail. The poor devil burst into a violent flood of tears, threw himself upon his knees, entreating the Judges to plead for him with me, and that if I would forgive him and continue to manage his business he would leave the Court and in future be guided solely by me. The Chief Justice humanely desired I would comply, and I did so, prevailing also upon Mr. Tilghman to resume his brief. In this case we succeeded in getting a judgment for the defendant, whereby a pretended debt of twenty thousand rupees for which he had been arrested was completely done away, the Court expressing a wish that the plaintiff should be indicted for perjury.

Two days after this success another of Hicky's causes came on, when he was again present, and extremely agitated during the testimony given by the plaintiff's witnesses, frequently exclaiming, though in an under voice, and as it were to himself, " Auch, the thief ! The villain ! The perjured villain, how he lies ! Auch, Jasus, sweet Jasus, how am I persecuted and torn to paces (pieces)." In this case we also succeeded, and by the end of the term I got rid of all his roguish plaintiffs and procured his liberation, for which he was most truly grateful.

At the time I first saw Hicky he had been about seven years in India. During his confinement he met with a treatise upon printing, from which he collected sufficient information to commence printer, there never having been a press in Calcutta. By indefatigable attention and unremitting labour he succeeded in cutting a rough set of types which answered very well for hand-bills and common advertisements, and as he could afford to work cheap he met with considerable encouragement. Having scraped together by this means a few hundred rupees he sent to England for a regular and proper set of materials for printing. Resolving also to have two strings to his bow, he at the same time gave orders for a quantity of medicine, as he proposed to exercise the business of physician, surgeon, and apothecary, as well as that of printer.

Whilst patiently waiting the arrival of these articles, it occurred to Hicky that great benefit might arise from setting on foot a public newspaper, nothing of that kind ever having appeared. Upon his types, &c., therefore reaching him, he issued proposals for printing a weekly paper, which, meeting with extraordinary encouragement, he speedily issued his first work. As a novelty every person read it, and was delighted. Possessing a fund of low wit, his paper abounded with proof of that talent. He had also a happy knack at applying appropriate nicknames and relating satirical anecdotes.

There was at that time in the Settlement a gentleman named Tiretta, of considerable eminence as an architect. By birth he was an Italian, but had passed the early part of his life in France and Germany. Notwithstanding he had resided twenty years in a British Settlement, he had made no great proficiency in the English language, nor, in fact, did he shine in any other, it being perfectly ridiculous to hear the strange *mélange* he made when speaking, especially if ruffled, as was often the case, upon which occasions what he uttered was a compound of English, French, Portuguese, and Hindustani, interlarded with the most uncouth and *outré* oaths in each language. His figure was uncommonly good, and he was fond of exhibiting it in a minuet, his address and manners elegant, with an animated countenance and handsome in spite of an enormous nose.

The heat in Bengal in the month of June is extreme, notwithstanding which Mr. Tiretta always appeared on the 4th, being the King's birthday, at the ball given by the Governor, in a full-trimmed suit of rich velvet. Hicky, in giving an account of this entertainment in his newspaper, and the guests that were present, says of Tiretta, " Nosey Jargon danced his annual minuets, seasonably dressed in a full suit of crimson velvet ! " The title of " Nosey Jargon " from thenceforward stuck to Mr. Tiretta.

The emolument arising from Hicky's newspaper became immense, and with common prudence he would have made a large fortune, but suffering it to become the channel of personal invective and the most scurrilous abuse of individuals of all ranks, high and low, rich and poor, many were attacked in the most wanton and cruel manner. The consequence was that several prosecutions were instituted against Hicky as the printer and publisher of the paper in which these libels were. His utter ruin was the consequence.

During the hot months, and the rainy season, I made frequent visits to my shipmate, Major Mestayer, who commanded at Budge Budge, a fort about twenty miles below Calcutta, delightfully situated on the bank of the river.

Notwithstanding I lived much in the best society, passing every evening in parties, my mornings were dedicated to hard work at my desk, from which cash accumulated rapidly.

CHAPTER XIV

THE AGITATION FOR TRIAL BY JURY

IN the month of August, Mr. Cressy, also one of my *Sea-horse* shipmates, got into a dispute which occasioned infinite trouble to him. Two Bengali carpenters, in the employ of Colonel Watson, being detected in purloining a quantity of tools and other things, were carried before Cressy, as the Chief Superintendent, whereupon he, imprudently taking the law into his own hands, forthwith ordered the aggressors to be tied up and severely flogged, and then confined them in a godown for two days. The moment these men were released they found their way to an Attorney, who addressed a letter to Cressy, saying if he did not make ample compensation to the injured persons, actions would be commenced against him for assaults and false imprisonment. Cressy instead of endeavouring to settle or conciliate, treated the application with contempt, setting the humble instrument of the law at defiance. Two actions were in consequence immediately set on foot, the damages in each case being laid at five thousand sicca rupees.

Writs of summons being served upon Cressy, a consultation was held at Colonel Watson's, who wished the actions to be defended in the usual manner, but this Cressy would not hear of, declaring he wanted no assistance and would plead for himself, that being born and bred in Great Britain and then residing in a British Settlement, he should insist upon his birthright—Trial by Jury. In vain did I endeavour to convince him that the Court was established under the authority of Parliament, which empowered the Judges in all civil cases to act also as Jurors. He insisted that was contrary to the Constitution, and he would oppose it to his latest breath. Colonel Watson, finding him thus obstinate, requested I would point out the requisite steps to be taken. I accordingly did direct him how to enter an appearance with the Prothonotary and to obtain a copy of the plaint or declaration. I also drew a plea of the general issue, not guilty, substituting instead of the customary conclusion, " And of this he puts himself *upon the Court*," " And of this he puts himself *upon the Country*."

In doing this I informed Cressy that unless the plaintiff's Attorney was an egregious blockhead it could answer no purpose, for that the process so worded must be considered as no plea, and the cause would be set down *ex parte*. Cressy still persevered, and the plaintiff's Attorney neglecting to avail himself of the advantage he might have taken, filed a demurrer to the plea, which in due course being set down for hearing, Cressy determined to argue it in person.

A day being appointed for the argument of the demurrer, the Court by eight o'clock in the morning was crowded by the British inhabitants of Calcutta, both civil and military, but the Chief Justice being indisposed could not attend. The discussion was therefore postponed. This happened in the middle of the Mohammedan festival of the Mohurrem, during which the lower orders of Mussulman by swallowing large quantities of an intoxicating drug called Bang, work themselves up to a state of absolute madness and commit great excess. Their zeal was increased that year by the Nabob Sydaat Ali being in Calcutta.

Soon after Sir Robert Chambers and Mr. Justice Hyde had taken their seats upon the Bench and the common routine of business was entered upon, a prodigious mob assembled directly under the windows, when the beating of tom-toms (a small sort of drum in use all over Hindustan) and the shrill squeaking of their trumpets made such a horrible din, the Counsellors could not possibly make themselves heard by the Judges. Sir Robert therefore directed the constables in attendance to go down and disperse the

people. In a few minutes one of these constables, whose
name was Roop, an old German, ran into Court in great
agitation, without his wig, crying out that he had been
violently assailed by the mob, who had severely beaten him,
carried off his hat and wig, and upon his showing his staff
of office, requiring peace in His Majesty's name, two English
sailors who were amongst the crowd, seized his said staff,
and carried it off in triumph.

The tumult, instead of subsiding, seeming greatly to
increase, the Under Sheriff was ordered to interfere and do
his duty by forthwith dispersing the mob, which by that
time had increased to several thousands, showing strong
symptoms of riot. The moment Mr. Harry Stark (the
Under Sheriff) made his appearance in the street the leaders
of the band seized him, broke his wand, and were carrying
him bodily away, when he was rescued by some of the
Nabob's servants who happened to know him, but for which
he would probably have been murdered. The mob then
attacked and maltreated the bearers and Hircarrahs that
were in attendance waiting for their masters, demolishing
every palankeen they could lay hands on. Another party
assailed the Court House, discharging showers of brick-
bats through the windows, which were soon demolished, the
bricks flying through the Court-room in all directions, for
unluckily there was abundant *ammunition* from a part of
the building being under repair.

In about half an hour after the first grand attack had been
thus made, an alarm was given that the mob, armed with
tulwars (scimitars), had forced the sentries and were in a
vast body rushing up the principal staircase. A general
panic prevailed, the spectators running in all directions to
seek shelter. I was one who went with the stream, seeking
safety at the top of the Court-house, where was also Mr.
William Chambers, brother to Sir Robert, a gentleman well
acquainted with the dispositions of the natives, and who
seemed particularly uneasy at the situation we were in,
declaring our lives were in imminent danger and that most
likely every European would be put to death.

I own I felt considerable alarm at finding matters becoming so serious, but the champion for the privilege of a Briton (Cressy), upon hearing Mr. Chambers's speech, very spiritedly said, "If such be the case let us act like Englishmen and not run from a parcel of vagabond Indians. Let us resolutely face them and at least sell our lives dearly," at the same time seizing a pike from the hands of one of the Sheriff's péons, who happened to stand near him. He continued, "Now, let all who feel like me follow my example," and he boldly descended the staircase, followed by many who were encouraged by his behaviour.

The event justified Cressy's spirit; the mob instantly retreated, and a party of Invalids from the old fort arriving at that critical moment, the rioters went off after letting fly one terrible shower of bricks, Major Sturgeon, which was literally the name of the officer who commanded the Invalids, receiving a blow on his head which set the blood streaming down his face, in which condition he entered the Court, desiring the Judge to rest assured that he and his *brave fellows* would shed the last drop of their blood in defence of their Lordships! This part of the scene was most truly ridiculous, the more so from there being present nearly an hundred officers, all with their swords on, who had been drawn to the Court House in the hopes of entertainment from hearing Cressy abuse the Judges, but who seemed quite moonstruck when the riot commenced and more frightened than any other of the spectators! The mob, although they left the front of the Court House, still seemed disposed to mischief until a large body of Europeans marching from Fort William effectually dispersed them.

In this attack I was one amongst many other sufferers, having a palankeen which cost me three hundred rupees totally demolished. The infuriated Mussulmen also broke down several of the gates to the entrance of a range called the Writers' Buildings, demolishing the windows, lamps, and everything that came within their power, pelting and beating every European they met with.

So uncommon and extraordinary a breach of the peace

occurring in the British capital of India, and upon the Court itself, occasioned universal astonishment all over the provinces. A common opinion prevailed that Sydaat Ali had encouraged and promoted the riot with a view to a general massacre of the Europeans, which, coming to the Nabob's knowledge, he instantly published and distributed throughout Calcutta a strong and energetic disclaimer of his being directly or indirectly privy to the intentions of the mob or having anything to do with them. On the contrary, that himself and all his attendants had done their utmost to pacify the rioters and to quell the disturbance. He concluded a well-drawn address by offering a reward of five thousand rupees to any person or persons who would discover the principals, or any of those who had either directly or indirectly promoted or encouraged the riot.

In consequence of this outrageous tumult, Government issued an order that thenceforward no religious processions should be allowed to pass through the town of Calcutta during the celebration of the Mohurrem, which order has from that time been strictly adhered to.

Cressy's demurrer coming on for argument in a few days after the above extraordinary occurrence, the Court-room was once more crowded with auditors at an early hour. The business being called on, Cressy acquitted himself better than I thought possible, but in giving judgment the Chief Justice remarked that " although the plaintiff's Attorney inadvertently demurred to the plea, instead of setting down the cause *ex parte*, as he should have done, still the Judges upon reading the record ought to have rectified that inadvertency, and not have heard a syllable upon the occasion." He added that he should give a judgment for the plaintiff with four hundred sicca rupees damages and costs !

The other action against Cressy was not tried, his Counsel advising him to let a judgment go for the same damages as in the one determined, reserving a right of appeal. The agitation of this question created a great interest not only in Bengal, but all over the Company's provinces, Cressy receiving the most flattering and complimentary addresses from every direction as the staunch supporter of the rights and privileges of Englishmen. He was pronounced the Wilkes of India ! A subscription was instantly set on foot by which a large sum was raised and presented to him, to reimburse him the expense and trouble he had been put to.

Colonel Watson was extremely desirous of appealing from the judgment of the Court, a measure I could not sanction, because I saw no chance of success. I therefore said as much to the gentlemen of the committee, but recommended their being governed, not by what I said, but by the opinions of the Counsel concerned in the cause. To this they acceded. I therefore drew a case, stating every circumstance candidly and fairly, of which Colonel Watson approved. One copy was submitted to Mr. Newman, another to Mr. Lawrence, and a third to Mr. Tilghman, who all in the most decided language said no appeal could possibly succeed under such circumstances, nor did they believe a lawyer could be found who would affix his name to a petition of appeal in such a case. Colonel Watson, notwithstanding this opinion, resolved that the matter should not drop. He therefore got together a few leading men, to whom he proposed calling a meeting of the British inhabitants of Calcutta to deliberate on the steps most proper to be taken in order to bring the question before the Legislature of Great Britain. A summons was issued, and in January, 1779, a very numerous assembly met at the theatre, at which a petition to Parliament was unanimously voted, praying a repeal of the Act under which the Court was constituted, and that British subjects might in India, as they were in all other parts of His Majesty's dominions, be allowed a trial by jury !

A committee was chosen to prepare this petition, and to do all that was requisite to promote the success of the same. This committee consisted of Colonel Pearse, Colonel Watson, Mr. John Shore (now Lord Teignmouth), Messrs. John Petrie, Alexander Higginson, Henry Cotterell, John Eveling, Charles Purling, Francis Gladwin, and Giles Rooke, all men of considerable talents, who paid the utmost attention to the cause placed under their management. They met four times a week. In the progress of their task they found it necessary to apply to the prothonotary and other officers of the Court for copies of certain documents. These officers, feeling some doubt as to the propriety of giving the papers demanded, submitted the matter to the Chief Justice, who instantly prohibited any copies of the records of the Court being furnished to any persons except those properly authorized to ask them. They were consequently refused.

Colonel Watson, at the next meeting of the committee, after commenting upon the arbitrary and unconstitutional conduct of the judges, was pleased to pay me some high compliments for my honourable and independent behaviour upon all occasions, finishing his encomiums by recommending that I should be employed as the attorney of the committee. This proposal being carried without a dissenting voice, the secretary apprized me thereof by letter, and from that time I constantly received official notice of the meetings and attended them.

For my success in obtaining the required copies of documents I gained great credit with the committee, who had altogether despaired of obtaining what they wanted, and without some of the papers they could scarcely have accomplished their purpose. One of the members proposed that I, who had in several instances shown my zeal and anxiety for the success of the business they were engaged upon, should be sent to Europe as the agent for the petitioners. The motion was, however, deemed premature.

This it was that first led me to turn my thoughts towards my old companions in London, and made me desirous of revisiting them. I immediately began to calculate what my outstanding debts would amount to, also the probable emoluments arising from the business then going on in my office. Upon a rough sketch I found the sum-total at the lowest estimate would be between three and four thousand pounds. I did not, however, for some time afterwards throw out the slightest hint to anyone that I intended leaving India, but continued to labour assiduously at my profession and to assist the furtherance of the petition, whereby, although I gained popularity, I at the same time incurred the heavy displeasure of the judges, especially Sir Elijah Impey, who, when we met in society, ceased to speak or to take any sort of notice of me. Sir Robert Chambers and Mr. Hyde were less illiberal, behaving to me in public as usual. Sir Robert being near me one night at supper observed he was sorry to find I had turned a *traitor*, the more so as he was convinced I was acting contrary to my own interest, which undoubtedly proved to be the case.

Early in February, 1779, the committee had prepared the petition to His Majesty and to the Parliament of Great Britain, praying that the Act under which the Supreme Court was established might be amended, especially by granting His Majesty's subjects resident within the provinces of Bengal, Behar, and Orissa, their right of trial by jury in all cases, civil as well as criminal. A meeting of the British inhabitants was then convened to hear this petition read, which was unanimously approved and pronounced an eloquent and masterly performance. Of this document I should here have introduced a copy had I not lost the only one I had in a tremendous storm in the year 1782 (of which more hereafter). A further large sum was next raised by subscription to defray the expenses of carrying the object into effect, and now I first communicated to my friend, Colonel Watson, my wish to go to Europe for a couple of years and to be the bearer of the petition, &c. He gave the most decided opinion against my taking what he called so inconsiderate and imprudent a step, observing that I was in the fair and high road to fortune, universally respected, living in the first society ; in short, " *with the ball at my foot*," to relinquish which unnecessarily seemed to him to be absolute insanity. Notwithstanding I felt the truth and full force of the Colonel's remarks, yet the idea of revisiting old haunts having once got into my giddy brain I had neither prudence nor fortitude enough to resist.

Colonel Watson, finding me obstinately regardless of what he and all my real friends urged, and that nothing could dissuade me from the voyage, he most kindly endeavoured to render the trip as beneficial to me as possible. He, at the next meeting of the committee, mentioned my sudden determination to leave India, and proposed that the petition should be delivered into my charge to convey it to Europe, that my expences should be paid, and a further sum of two hundred pounds be allowed me annually for two years after my arrival in London. All which was agreed to by the committee, every member expressing himself happy at having an opportunity to comply with my wishes, though they lamented my thus early leaving Bengal. At a subsequent meeting it was resolved that the allowance should be increased to four, instead of two hundred pounds, and that I should be fully reimbursed the expences of my voyage home.

In March, 1779, I applied to Captain Arthur Gore, of the *Nassau*, for accommodation in his ship, which, together with the *Southampton*, Captain Lenox, was shortly to sail. These two ships, as I have already observed, had been assisting in Sir Edward Vernon's fleet for upwards of a twelvemonth. Captain Gore told me the whole of his roundhouse and great cabin were already disposed of, but that I might have a spacious cabin on the larboard side of the cuddy for five thousand sicca rupees. I therefore closed the business at once by consenting to take that accommodation upon the terms proposed. Mentioning this to Colonel Watson, he said he would make the committee forthwith advance me ten thousand rupees to pay Gore and other port charges during my voyage, but I said I had already more cash than was necessary for those purposes, and should prefer receiving the whole amount in England. The Colonel still urging me to take a part at least, I drew upon the committee for the sum I was to pay Captain Gore, and lucky would it have been for me had I taken all that was offered.

The time of my departure fast approaching, I desired my Banyan Durgachuru Muckerjee to prepare his accounts for settlement, which he promised but neglected to perform. My debts were soon ascertained, I having made it a rule to pay everything I owed at the end of each month, except my tailor, to whom I imagined I might be indebted from fifteen hundred to two thousand rupees, but to my utter astonishment received a bill for near five thousand. Certainly I had a great wardrobe of rich clothes.

Having got intimation that I must embark, I again pressed my Banyan for his accounts, but in vain—I could not procure them. I called to take leave of Sir Robert Chambers and Mr. Justice Hyde, both of whom were very civil and kind. Sir Elijah Impey had spoken with so much anger against me for the assistance I had afforded in the petition that I did not choose to pay him the compliment of a visit.

The 10th of April being fixed for our departure, Mr. Lacam offered me the use of a very commodious yacht of his to convey me to the ship, then laying at the Barrabulla, and Mr. Lacam being thoroughly acquainted with that difficult and dangerous channel I thought it prudent to accept his offer. As I always shunned the ceremony of leave-taking, I left Calcutta privately on the 15th, having that morning received my final instructions and dispatches from the committee, and went down to Mr. Lacam's house, where I remained three days.

In the evening of the 17th Captain Gore, accompanied by Major Webber, called at Mr. Lacam's, when the Major, who lived within half a mile, invited Mr. Lacam and me to take an early dinner with him the following day, as we were to embark at four o'clock. The Major also communicated to me a plan he had formed for alarming a Captain Bentley, of the Bengal army, who was going to Europe in the *Nassau*. This Bentley I had heard spoken of as little removed from an idiot, though he had intellect enough to scrape together two lacs of rupees, which sum occasioned him infinite anxiety. By nature suspicious, he had conceived that no bills could be secure. He therefore determined to take the amount he possessed with him in cash, which was accordingly deposited in eight strong wooden boxes and the freight paid for them. This treasure was sent off from Calcutta in a pilot schooner of the Company's.

Major Webber having asked Captain Bentley to join the dining party at his house, the hoax was to be there carried into effect. Being assembled on the 18th, we at one o'clock sat down to dinner. In the middle of the meal a gentleman came in, who almost immediately told us a melancholy event had occurred in the wreck of the *Warren Hastings*, pilot schooner, which, in going to Kedgeree, had struck upon a sand, instantly overset, and was totally lost, every soul on board perishing, that in an hour not a vestige of her remained, and that the loss was the more serious from her having the packets for the two Indiamen on board.

Captain Bentley upon hearing this turned extremely pale, and with the utmost agitation said his money was on board her. Captain Gore remarked that it was unlucky, but that he could not be a material sufferer, as no doubt the property was insured, to which Bentley in an agony replied, " Oh, no, sir, not a rupee of it. I am undone, ruined, undone for ever," and he burst into tears. Major Webber, who was a humane and benevolent man, was distressed beyond measure when he saw the serious effect of his joke, and instantly said he had no doubt but that the boxes of rupees would be recovered and he would directly send a man on horseback to Calcutta to ascertain the particulars.

Bentley continuing in a state of torpid despair, the Major in a few minutes left the room, and returning immediately said a messenger had arrived to say the account of the loss of the vessel was a mistake, it being a pariah sloop in company to which the accident had happened. Captain Bentley was then congratulated, but the fright had deprived him of the little sense he possessed and he could not rally, sitting weeping like a child. When Major Webber mentioned *the joke*, as he called it, to me, I expressed my disapprobation at it, as being of too serious a nature and likely to produce ill-consequences. The Major thereupon seemed disposed to give it up but was persuaded not by Captain Gore.

CHAPTER XV

ON THE WAY HOME AGAIN

UPON rising to go on board our vessel, I found Captain Bentley had no conveyance but a paunceway, a sort of boat very unequal to go down the river at that season. I therefore offered him a passage in Mr. Lacam's sloop, which he thankfully accepted. At five we got under way with a strong gale from the south, which was in our teeth. Two miles below Mr. Lacam's resided Mr. Playdell, the father of my shipmate, who, with a large party that had dined with him, came to the waterside upon our passing and gave us three cheers, which we returned. That evening we anchored off Budge Budge, where I landed to shake Major Mestayer by the hand.

On the 19th it blew hard ; the vessel we were in nevertheless made considerable progress, being admirably found and well manned. That day we worked down to Kedgeree, there waiting for the ebb tide. During the night the wind increased and we tumbled about dreadfully. The *Southampton* that night lost three anchors. On the 22nd, after a boisterous and very unpleasant passage, we got on board the *Nassau*, then laying in a wild and open sea, surrounded by sands over which the surf broke tremendously in every direction. She was eight miles distant from the nearest land. The first man I beheld on going up the *Nassau's* side was my old *New Shoreham* shipmate, Jerry Griffin, who I found was boatswain, and with whom I renewed my acquaintance.

The 24th, 25th and 26th it blew so hard the pilots dare not move the ships, though we expected our cables would

part every moment, the strain upon them being so immense.

On the 29th the wind being less boisterous, we worked
down a narrow channel about eight miles. The 30th
being still more moderate we made a better progress.
Whilst at anchor this day another schooner joined us, from
which a Sircar of Durgachuru Muckerjee's came, presenting
me with a bond ready filled up for the penal sum of ten
thousand sicca rupees, which he claimed as the amount due
upon balance of account. Although satisfied I did not owe
him two thousand, yet was I absurd enough to execute the
proffered bond and deliver the same to the Sircar, who went
off well pleased with the success of his mission.

The following day being the 1st of May, 1779, the pilot
left us, it then blowing a hard gale from the southward.
We stood to the east-south-east under courses in company
with the *Southampton,* the errantest hog trough that ever
floated on salt water. The orders of Government to the
respective Commanders were upon no account whatsoever
to separate, but always to keep as near to each other as the
weather would permit. As there was not sufficient cargo
ready in Bengal, we were to proceed to Madras and there
fill up with coast goods. Being in the very height of the
south-west monsoon we were consequently obliged to keep
the eastern shore of the bay well on board until we should
reach Acheen Head, when it was intended to stretch across
to the coast of Coromandel.

In the *Nassau* we had only one other passenger,
Lieutenant Grand, of the Artillery, a young man going to
sea for his health. He was brother to the husband of Mr.
Francis's fair friend. Being, though young in years, a man
of observation he at once discovered Bentley to be a sort of
body capable of being made an advantage of, and laid himself out to derive that advantage. Bentley was fond of
cards, conceiving himself a superior player of piquet, an
idea that Grand encouraged. They had frequent contests
at the game for many hours together. In the early part of
the contest Bentley generally rose a winner by three or four

games. As we approached our destination *fortune* changed, and the artilleryman was a gainer of near five thousand rupees by the contest ! The fact was he could and ought to have given Bentley at least twenty points.

The officers of the *Nassau* were Mr. William Greer, chief mate, an abominable sot who kept himself in a state of constant intoxication, as might well be the case from his " grog," as he termed it, being always three-parts spirit ; the second was Mr. John Pascal Larkins, a worthy man and admirable seaman ; Joseph Clarkson, the third ; and John Rogers, the fourth ; John Smith, surgeon ; William Darling, purser. From the time the ship left her moorings at Culpee, Mr. Greer had been confined to his cabin under the plea of indisposition, which Captain Gore asserted was a mere pretence to avoid doing the duty of his station, an opinion that was strengthened by Mr. Larkins declaring the same, and he was not a man to be biassed by prejudice or misrepresentation. Smith, the surgeon, was an absolute maniac. Uncommonly able in his profession, his general conduct was so eccentric as to justify my having pronounced him a maniac. The nickname by which he was generally designated was " Quicksilver Jack."

We had horrid weather for several days after the pilot left us ; an uninterrupted gale with tremendous squalls and incessant rain, accompanied by such peals of thunder and vivid flashes of lightning as are rarely seen or heard. During one of the most boisterous nights (by a little fair management with the man at the helm) we most happily parted from the *Southampton*. At daylight she was not to be seen. Every measure was thereupon adopted to rejoin her, or perhaps I should be nearer the truth in introducing the word *not* before " to rejoin her." Be that as it may, we saw no more of her between Bengal and Madras. We made the Andaman Islands during exceeding tempestuous weather, not a day passing without our carrying away jacks, sheets, or halliards, splitting sails every hour, and altogether being most uncomfortable. During the month of May we only had one observation.

On the 1st of June Captain Gore told me he despaired of ever reaching Madras, and said he must proceed to Malacca to refit and replenish, in the necessity of which all his officers agreeing, we bore up two points, standing direct for the Straits, but four-and-twenty hours afterwards the wind became somewhat more favourable, which induced a renewal of the endeavours to gain our destined port of Madras.

About eleven o'clock in the morning of the 4th the sun broke forth with great brightness, notwithstanding the tempest still raged with unabated fury. This afforded us the important advantage of an observation, whereby we clearly ascertained our latitude. The same afternoon we distinctly saw the northern point of Sumatra and some small islands that lay off it. We also made the Nicobars, of which we had a clear and distinct view, thus ascertaining that the Sombrere Channel was fairly open to us and nothing to obstruct our passage through it. We consequently stood boldly on, all in high spirits in spite of the bad weather, and resolved to do honour to the festival of His Majesty's birthday at our supper.

As the night approached the gale increased so much that we could scarcely bear close-reefed topsails with the wind upon the beam. This did not prevent our filling some bumpers to George the Third's health and being very merry. It drawing towards midnight we were beginning to talk of retiring to our cots, when Mr. Larkins sent a quartermaster to request Captain Gore would come upon deck, a summons that created some alarm amongst us, which was not a little increased by hearing a general uproar immediately afterwards and the people all in confusion. Upon going under the awning, I found land had been discovered close to us, extending from the lee bow to abaft the beam.

Captain Gore, panicstruck, knew not what he was about, giving orders and counter orders in the same breath, and crying out to put the ship about. In the midst of the bustle Mr. Greer crawled from his cabin, desiring that an anchor might be let go, whereupon Mr. Larkins exclaimed, " An anchor, Mr. Greer ! In the name of God what can be

expected from an anchor in such a sea as we are now encountering? Our only chance of escape is by making sail
and endeavouring to clear the land that has so unexpectedly
come in our way." Every person on board competent to
judge felt the force of what Mr. Larkins said, and all were
equally ready to testify to the very extraordinary skill and
exertions of the boatswain, Jerry Griffin, who, when the
men hesitated to perform a requisite duty from the risk
attending it, himself set them an example, going out to the
weather yardarm of the main topsail and succeeding in
handing the sail, the whole time using the most extraordinary
and out-of-the-way expressions. A reef was forthwith let
out of each of the topsails, the courses reefed and set, and
the ship hauled close to the wind. And this she bore admirably, though we had before thought too much sail was
set, and that something was giving way every half-hour.

We perceptibly passed the land rapidly, which when
nearest to us appeared towering above the mastheads, it
seeming that we must inevitably be upon it. The night was
uncommonly dark, with a tremendous sea running, rendering our situation truly alarming, indeed absolutely desperate.

Upon my leaving the cabin, the other gentlemen followed,
when Larkins entreated me to return, as we might be in the
way and could be of no use. We therefore retired to the
round-house, soon after which Captain Bentley entered
with a candle and lantern in his hand. Quite at a loss to
account for this, I asked him the meaning of it, when, with
his usual simplicity, he answered, " As I hear we are likely
to go ashore I should like to see where to land ! " This
strange speech struck all present most forcibly, Darling,
the purser, gravely observing, " I believe, Captain Bentley,
your light will not prove of any use, for in such a sea as is
now running if the ship once strikes, a few moments will
decide our fate by consigning us all to watery graves."

In two hours we had cleared the land sufficiently to consider the danger over, and congratulated each other upon
our miraculous escape. At four in the morning the day
dawned, showing us the land that had caused our danger

within a short distance upon our lee quarter, but as we had no ground with sixty fathoms of line and all clear ahead we had no further apprehensions.

Mr. Larkins then told us that at nine o'clock, when summoned to supper he had for some time been looking steadily at a black spot nearly right ahead which he could no way account for, that he had made the man at the helm keep the ship half a point nearer the wind in consequence. Still the spot seemed fixed. He called the fifth mate, who was upon the watch with him, pointing out the object that engaged his attention, but this officer pronounced it to be a cloud, as did some of the seamen. Larkins, however, still thought it had all the appearance of land; he ordered a cast of the lead directly. The line being accordingly passed forward and hove in a few minutes, was instantly declared to have struck the bottom with only a few fathoms of line out, and this in a part of the ocean where by all the charts we should not have been upon soundings. Mr. Larkins conjectured that at the first cast there was about fifteen fathoms, after which the soundings varied from fourteen fathoms (the least water we had) to thirty-five, hard rocky bottom.

It is a most extraordinary circumstance that in a passage so much frequented as that of the Sombrere Channel was, and had been for a great number of years, by all ships bound from Madras to China, there should be almost in the middle of it an island totally unknown, or, at least, unnoticed, in the charts of those seas. Yet such indubitably was the fact.

Having escaped this danger, our next dread was that in crossing the bay the current should drive us so far to the northward we should not be able to make Madras. Luckily the wind proved favourable, so that we made the coast within three leagues of our port, off which place we anchored on the 11th of June, having been six weeks on the passage, then considered a fair period against the monsoon and when scarcely any of our ships were copper-bottomed.

Upon landing, I found Mr. Hall Plumer waiting to receive

me, who immediately conveyed me to his house in the
fort, where I had a couple of spacious and handsome apartments allotted to my use. Having dined with my friend,
we got into his phaeton and drove to Choultry Plain, where
he likewise had a delightful country residence, and where
he generally slept. In the neighbourhood of this residence
he was building a magnificent mansion, the superintendence
of which was his principal amusement early in the morning
previous to going to town, and again in the evening upon his
return. He at that time had the contract for completing
the works, particularly an entire newly-constructed sea-
line, presenting a truly formidable battery of the heaviest
guns. These works required his daily attendance for several
hours. The much talked of Paul Benfield had been the
original contractor, but he, having acquired an overgrown
fortune, gave up the works to Plumer, who, according to
public report, cleared sixty thousand pounds thereby. Such
was the advantage arising from Government contracts in
those days.

Two days after my arrival at Madras I called upon Captain Gore, who told me he had just received the unpleasant
information that the foremast was discovered to be so badly
sprung as to be wholly unfit to stand, and he feared there
would be extreme difficulty in procuring a new one at
Madras.

We found the inhabitants of the Settlement exceedingly
gay, chiefly owing to the cheerful example given by the
Governor, Sir Thomas Rumbold, and his lady. There
was scarce an evening without some great entertainment,
public or private, a weekly concert of a superior kind, many
of the performers being of a description that would have
created admiration in any part of Europe. My chief
favourite amongst the fair sex was Mrs. Maule, wife of
Major Maule. At her house we had frequently delicious
music. There was also an elegant theatre, where I was
present at the performance of " Love in a Village " in a
style that would not have disgraced the London stage. A
Mr. Lewin of the Civil Service personated Hawthorn ;

Mr. Storey, an architect, young Meadows ; both gentlemen having uncommon fine voices and being proficient in music. The rest of the characters were very respectably filled.

Upon my being presented to Sir Thomas Rumbold, I was agreeably surprized at finding in one of his aides-de-camp an old acquaintance, Count Shippey, whom I had met at Colonel Cooper's at Tilbury Fort when staying with Mr. Cane at Erith. Sir Thomas, I understood, was much attached to him. Shippey, as I have before observed, was a man of very elegant manners, spoke several languages fluently, and was, in every respect, the *homme du monde*. Sir Thomas found him of real use in receiving and talking to the French officers then recently arrived from Pondicherry upon the capture of that fortress by the British. Sir Thomas, although a man of good address and fashionable appearance, spoke not a word of French, which made his situation as Governor rather awkward by having a number of foreign guests at his table with whom he could hold no conversation but through the medium of Shippey, as interpreter.

Upon my introduction I was, according to the etiquette of the place, invited to dinner, at which I was, by Sir Thomas, presented to Lady Rumbold, and to his eldest son, Captain Rumbold, aide-de-camp to Sir Hector Munro, the Commander-in-Chief, and then upon the eve of sailing for England with the official accounts of the taking of Pondicherry. This young man was rather disrespectfully spoken of from being thought deficient in personal bravery. The nature of his station made it requisite for him during the siege frequently to carry orders from Sir Hector Munro to the officers on duty in the trenches, a duty the Captain, from his mode of performing it, was considered as not liking. It soon became a general remark that upon the sound of a shot whizzing by he bobbed his head, to the great entertainment of the private soldiers, amongst whom it at last became a byword upon seeing a comrade flinch or in any way shy, to say, "He tipped him a Rumbold."

There was an immense party in the evening. Lady

Rumbold very courteously asked me whether I was fond of dancing or preferred it to playing cards, to which I replied I rarely did either, begging her permission to walk about and chat. But that she declared could not be, one or the other I must do. As the lesser evil therefore I chose cards, and was placed at her Ladyship's table, she observing loo was their game, and that they played very *low*, only for Fanams *unlimited*, at which *low* rate I, in about two hours, notwithstanding the utmost caution, found myself minus upwards of six hundred pagodas, whereupon as I suddenly rose from table, Lady Rumbold exclaimed, " Oh dear, Mr. Hickey! you cannot think of giving up already. Pray don't leave the party ! " to which I answered in a somewhat peremptory tone, " Your Ladyship must excuse me. I certainly shall stop now, for were I to continue a few hours longer at the same rate, instead of pursuing my purposed voyage to England, I should be compelled to return to Bengal, there to refurnish an empty purse." Her Ladyship bowed and ceased to importune me further, nor did she during the subsequent four months I remained at Madras ever ask me to touch a card, although I was constantly invited, and always went to her parties, where she behaved towards me with the utmost politeness and attention. In short, she was satisfied with my *fine* of near three hundred pounds, which loss gave me the *entrée* to her really elegant and pleasant coterie, where I met all the fashion of the Settlement, and in those days it was a very gay place.

My greatest intimates were Mr. Paul Benfield, Mr. Alexander Davidson, Major Burrowes, Messrs. Welch, Cochrane, Roebuck, Moubray, Kinloch, and Captain Bagot, the last named being one of the best companions I ever met with. His figure, although Herculean, was strikingly elegant. He had the command of one of the finest battalions of Sepoys in the army, the men of which almost adored him. He had behaved upon more than one occasion with the utmost gallantry, yet, unaccountable as it is, subsequent to my leaving Madras this gentleman's corps being engaged with a body of Tippoo's troops he betrayed the utmost pusillanimity, and notwithstanding his favourite Sepoys, who saw the panic, did everything in their power to encourage and rouse him, he finally turned his horse and fled as fast as the animal could carry him. His ruin as a military man naturally followed, but so universally was he loved and respected by all orders of people that no public notice was taken of his misconduct. He returned to the Presidency, where a considerable subscription being raised by his friends (who well knew he had not saved any money) was privately sent to him with a recommendation that he should leave India and get to Europe in a foreign ship. In obedience to which advice he proceeded to Tranquebar, there embarking in a Danish vessel. I understand he died in London some years afterwards in extreme indigence. Never was I acquainted with a man for whose melancholy fate I felt more real concern than poor Bagot's.

Mr. Plumer's neighbours about Choultry Plain were all agreeable men, so that time slipped rapidly away. We also often went to the red hills, distant fourteen miles from Madras, where Mr. Plumer had a comfortable house upon the border of a noble lake on which he had a sailing boat. His table was there plentifully supplied with game of most delicious flavour.

The first night I slept at this house I was awaked by something, as I imagined, running over the bed, which alarmed me a good deal from an apprehension of tigers, jackals, snakes, and other noxious and ferocious animals and reptiles. After remaining more than an hour under considerable anxiety, I dropped asleep, from which I was again disturbed by I knew not what. Instantly starting up I felt happy at finding light appearing. Having completely opened the windows, I saw not less than a dozen prodigious Bandecoot rats performing their antics about the room. Upon taking off a silk net I always wore over my hair when in bed, I found several holes gnawed by these animals, attracted by the powder and pomatum, of which, according to the then fashion, I wore a large quantity. Upon mentioning the circumstance at breakfast, I was told

I had escaped marvellously in not losing the whole of my hair.

When at Madras I frequently mixed with the officers of the Navy, many of whom were accomplished gentlemen, of which description was Mr. Newcome, eldest son of the famous Dr. Newcome, of Hackney, who had educated some of the sons of the best families in England. This Mr. Newcome was then second lieutenant of the *Rippon*, the Admiral's flagship.

There was in the fleet a very old Commander of a quite different description from those I have mentioned. This was Captain Marlow, who doubtless was an errant old woman in every respect, and the laughing-stock of the whole squadron. This gentleman had started in the Navy with Sir Edward Vernon, with whom he had long been a messmate, a strong regard continuing between them through life. Sir Edward, upon being appointed to the command in the East Indies, had influence enough to get his friend Marlow named as one of his Captains, and soon after he arrived at his station gave him the command of the finest frigate of his fleet.

Joe Revell, of whom I have before spoken as a pickleboy at China in the year 1769, belonged to the Madras Civil Service, and being at the Presidency during my stay there, used to play off this weak and ridiculous man, Marlow, with much effect, making him expose his ignorance in various instances. Revell, in spite of his for ever laughing at him, was a great favourite. He always distinguished Marlow by the title of "Old never sweat, and Admiral never sweat," to which he gravely observed, "The mad boy is not far out when he calls me Admiral, as I certainly am of that rank at this day, and ought to have been so long ago had not improper influence kept me back, but never mind, merit does not always meet with its reward." He was the most illiterate, uneducated man I ever met with in the situation of a gentleman. I once heard him upbraiding a boy who was a midshipman of his ship with being too frequently absent from his duty, finishing his lecture in these words :

" Why the hell devil can't you stay on your own deck, which is a damned deal better than Madras sand. I only wish my curs't duty did not keep me dancing attendance after my commanding officer, the Admiral. If he was not in the way of my will, blast me if ever my foot touched the land, for I never am more betterer, nor weller, than when on board my own ship ! "

This stupid old tarpaulin possessed no merit in his profession, being universally pronounced altogether unfit to command a British ship of war. Nevertheless, to hear him speak of himself one would suppose him a Hawke or a Boscawen. Joe Revell pretended to extol his exertions upon all occasions, especially during the siege of Pondicherry. " There, Admiral," said he, " you convinced the enemy what a knowing cock they had to deal with ; you tickled them up nicely. In what a style you handled the Mauritius lads upon their vain attempt to throw supplies into Pondicherry. Why, they had no more chance with you than a cat in hell without claws." " Aye, aye, young chap," replied Marlow. " For sartin I did make them know their Lord God from John Bell. I showed them they had no child's play to expect, having got the wrong sow by the ear." After working him up to the full bent of his absurdity, Joe went on thus, " Well, Admiral, now pray inform us how many prizes you took whilst laying off Pondicherry." " Prizes," repeated Marlow, " why, damme, they knew me too well to come in my way." " I always understood," continued Revell, " that not a single ship appeared of the enemy's." " How the dickens then was I to take them ? " said Marlow.

During my stay at Madras I met with no less than six old London acquaintances, every one of whom had been ruined by boundless extravagance which compelled them to abandon their native shore. The first was O'Hara, a schoolfellow at Westminster. His father, who was an Admiral, purchased a commission in the Guards for him when only seventeen years of age. Upon entering that fashionable corps he began his career, frequently involving himself deeply in debt. His father could no longer afford to extricate him and was driven to the necessity of sending him abroad as a cadet in the East India Company's service, then the last resource of ruined profligates. At the time I thus met him he had been several years in India, having risen to the rank of Captain. He died at Madras some years after.

The two next were, Tomkins and Lee, both also thentofore of the Guards. The former was son to the surgeon of that name in Coventry Street. The latter, Lee, had squandered away a fine fortune which he inherited from his father and an uncle. He had been distinguished in town by the name of "Handsome Lee." Both of them also fell sacrifices to the climate of India. The next was Byde, usually called "Bouquet Byde," from his constantly wearing a large nosegay. I never heard what was his ultimate fate. The next was Williams, a Captain in Elliot or Burgoyne's regiment of Light Dragoons, who exchanged into the other Burgoyne's, went with the regiment to Madras, and thus cheated his creditors in England. He was killed in one of the battles fought in Mysore.

The last was Darby, a true fox-hunter, who when quite a boy came into the possession of a clear five thousand pounds per annum, which he contrived to dissipate before he reached five-and-twenty. He was a good-natured, simple fellow, whom everyone plundered and everyone laughed at. A grievous accident happened to this young man shortly after his arrival at Fort St. George, owing to the inconsiderate conduct of a sportsman named White, the proprietor of several fine horses. Darby having dined with him, they in the evening went to view his stud, when Darby greatly admired a beautiful horse, which he walked towards, asking if he might go up to him. "Oh yes," said White, "pat his neck." Darby did so, the animal permitting it to the utter surprize of his master and servants, who knew that he invariably began to kick and plunge if a white person was within several yards of him. White always had him blindfolded before he attempted to mount, and even then did so with infinite difficulty.

Whilst Mr. White was expressing his surprize at what he saw, the treacherous beast suddenly put down his head, seizing poor Darby by the fleshy part of his thigh on the inside, and, as if conscious of having effected his object, he instantly broke from his keeper, galloping away at full speed with Darby hanging from his teeth, and every now and then violently shaking him, the blood pouring in streams from the victim. The gentlemen and others present, shocked at the scene, did all in their power to release the sufferer, but many minutes elapsed ere they succeeded, and even then it was only done by one of the servants knocking the horse down with a heavy bamboo. Darby was taken up senseless, miserably torn and lacerated, conveyed to bed and there remained for six months. A cure was, however, made which was deemed a wonderful thing. Darby died of a fever long subsequent to his recovery from the accident

CHAPTER XVI

ON BOARD THE "NASSAU"

THE months of June and July having elapsed without any tidings of the *Southampton*, people began to be apprehensive for her safety. Early in August the *Nassau's* foremast being fished and made as complete as possible, was sent off and again put in its proper place. Sir Thomas Rumbold told me he every week expected a large fleet from Europe under Sir Edward Hughes, and that if they arrived in time we should have Sir Edward Vernon in the *Rippon* to convoy us.

On the 6th Captain Gore invited me to dinner to meet my fellow-passengers that were to be. I accordingly went and found Mr. George Smith, his wife, and three lovely children, who were to occupy the round-house, and Colonel Flint and his wife—as worthy a pair as ever lived. These, with the sagacious Bentley and our ship's officers, then on shore, made the party.

Every day now increased the alarm about the *Southampton*. Accounts arrived of the French naval commandant, Trou Jolie, having with his squadron left the bay and sailed for the Mauritius, where it was said another officer waited to relieve him. All hopes of ever seeing the *Southampton* were over when, early in the morning of the 20th of August, a large ship was seen to the northward working up along shore. From her appearance hopes were entertained that it might be the long given-up ship, and so it proved. In the afternoon the *Southampton* came to an anchor in the roads. Captain Lenox landed immediately, Captain Gore and myself going directly to congratulate him upon his arrival. He appeared much surprized when told the *Nassau* had been ten weeks at Madras. Captain Gore, asking him where he could have been for so long a period, he replied in his broad Scotch dialect, " Hoot awa, maun, do not ausk me, ausk that de'il's cheeld, Chareley, who, with aw his coorsed loonor oobservations and his daumned roond-aboot vagaries, haas keept oos at sea saxteen weeks fra the peelot."

The *Chareley* alluded to was his nephew and chief mate, who although an enthusiastic advocate for the then new mode of working the longitude from lunar observations was not sufficiently experienced in it to avoid mistakes, the ill-consequences of which they had experienced.

The day after the *Southampton* arrived, Captains Gore and Lenox each received an official letter from the Secretary to inform them they must respectively receive on board their ships eleven French officers and seventy private soldiers of the garrison of Pondicherry, and convey them to England, pursuant to an article of the capitulation ; and that the officers being upon *parole* were to be treated with respect and considered merely as passengers. I happened to be with Captain Gore when he received this document, and never beheld a man in a greater rage than he was. He swore he would not take a man of them, desiring his purser to answer the Government letter to that effect. The steady Darling, however, knew better than to do so.

I had now reason to rejoice that I had fixed myself in the cuddy, thereby avoiding such a monstrous addition to the residents between decks. In vain did Captain Gore exert all his interest to get the order revoked, Sir Thomas Rumbold telling him they must get rid of the French without losing a day, but that a liberal allowance would be made for taking them. Captain Gore, feeling himself without remedy, had a part of the steerage partitioned off with canvas for the use of the French officers.

The 11th of October being the day fixed for all ships to leave the Roads, from which to the 11th of December insurances ceased along the coast of Coromandel from Point Palmiras to Cape Comorin, the flagstaff of Madras was struck, and I became somewhat uneasy lest bad weather should begin. There were, besides the two very rich Bengal ships, near twenty sail of valuable merchantmen in the Roads, and the whole British squadron of Sir Edward Vernon. Fortunately, it continued mild and fine.

The Governor was very anxious to have convoy for the *Nassau* and *Southampton*, fearing the French would make efforts in every way to intercept them, but as they were detained at a high demurrage he was also desirous they should depart as speedily as possible. He therefore resolved to wait no longer than the 30th, when if Sir Edward Hughes should not arrive he would dispatch the two ships to Trincomalee with the men-of-war, there to stay during the month of November, and in case Sir Edward Hughes did not arrive by that time we were to sail at all risks without convoy.

On the 29th of October the French officers and privates embarked, when a new source of vexation arose to Captain Gore from one of the officers having a wife, for whom no provision had been made. Colonel Flint had half the great cabin and Captain Bentley the remainder, except a common passage taken off to the quarter gallery, a corner of which passage Captain Gore was obliged to partition off for the lady to sleep in. It was so small that there was literally room only for the cot and herself to stand in.

In the morning of the 30th I embarked. I found Captain Gore in a violent rage from the quarter-deck being covered and the passage blocked up by trunks, chests, bandboxes, and packages of every description, belonging to Mrs. Smith, who he swore had sent on board *one hundred and twenty* different parcels, and to increase his perplexity the French officers had made a formal complaint that they had no place to sleep in. To a man naturally irritable this accumulation of untoward circumstances was a severe trial. Perceiving how much he was annoyed, I strove to console him, though rather unsuccessfully, for he continued to curse and swear outrageously at the unreasonable and shameful quantity of baggage with which the Smiths had encumbered the ship, declaring that in case bad weather came on, which might be expected every hour, the whole must and would be thrown overboard.

In the midst of the bustle Mr. Smith and his family came alongside in the Government boat, Captain Gore instantly attacking poor Mr. Smith with uncommon vehemence, for whom I felt great compassion, the poor man being already sufficiently tormented in attending to the complaints of his wife and children. Mrs. Smith was quite as furious as Captain Gore, whom she honoured with the epithets of brute, sea monster, and savage, vowing she would not stay on board the *Nassau*. " As to you, George," said she, turning to her husband, " you may do as you please, stay or go I care not, but for myself, proceed in this abominable pigsty I will not."

Mrs. Smith's intemperate behaviour quite silenced Captain Gore, and Mr. Larkins just then coming forward and endeavouring to pacify the lady, succeeded. Good humour was restored, and Larkins engaged that in a couple of hours everything should be completely arranged to her perfect satisfaction. I remained in the round-house, assisting Mr. Smith in fixing and arranging his baggage. Whilst so employed Captain Marlow entered, who seeing us so hard at work, directly ordered up his boat's crew, a fine active set of fellows, who soon cleeted and lashed everything in a capital style.

Captain Gore spoke not a word of French, nor did one of the passengers except myself. He therefore requested me to tell the officers they must excuse for a few days the confused state of the ship, after which everything should be arranged for their comfort and convenience. No men could behave better than they did, all of them expressing their readiness to submit to sleep upon their chests, or on the deck until the ship was put to rights. They were remarkably quiet and good-humoured. Two of them, Colonel Russelle and Major St. Paulle, spoke a little English.

At two in the afternoon Colonel and Mrs. Flint came on board ; at five the Admiral made the signal to unmoor by loosing his fore-topsail and firing a gun. Towards sunset the horizon became exceedingly black, and there were strong indications of an approaching gale from the north-east. It fell dead calm, which was considered as a bad symptom. Of course we could not stir. At nine at night a torrent of rain poured down, which continued the greater part of the night, when the weather cleared up.

At daybreak, just as I had fallen into a doze, after laying awake from the moment I went to bed, I was roused by the discharge of a gun, when jumping up and looking out I had the pleasure to see a beautiful morning with a pleasant breeze from the northward, and the fleet getting under way. At sunrise the fort saluted the Admiral, which his ship returned. We made sail, soon losing sight of Madras, and had a capital run that day.

On the 2nd of November we entered Trincomalee, one of the most capacious and best harbours in the world, then belonging to Holland. The face of the country in every direction was beautifully romantic; the houses, with the exception of two or three, execrable. Joe Revell being greatly attached to the Smith family, accompanied them to spend the time we were to pass at Ceylon in their society, and a prodigious acquisition he was from his uncommon flow of spirits and convivial qualities. As he spoke German fluently he was of material use in procuring many things for us we otherwise should not have had. Through his interference a miserable residence was obtained for Mr. Smith on shore, also a room for me in the fort, but so dreadfully hot was I and so tormented by mosquitoes in it that I only tried it for one night, after which I always went on board the *Nassau* to sleep.

The day but one after that on which we anchored at Trincomalee, the monsoon shifted, with a severe gale of wind, incessant heavy rain for six-and-thirty hours, and tremendous thunder and lightning. I remained the whole time on board, and had reason to rejoice at being so well sheltered, for upon landing when the weather cleared up, I found the Smiths, with Colonel and Mrs. Flint, to whom they had given a room, in woeful plight, their apartments being deluged, the rain pouring in through apertures innumerable, so that they had not a dry spot in the house, nor a single change of clothes to put on, all being completely soaked. During two entire nights they had been obliged to sit up, the children having thereby all got severe colds. This grievance being forgot, we amused ourselves by fishing, hunting guanas, and making short excursions on the borders of most beautiful groves, also rowing about various inlets and small bays where we found innumerable guanas, an animal of the lizard kind, but very much larger. They make a rich soup; many people think even superior to turtle. The Dutch eat the flesh too, but that I never could bring myself to do. We got plenty of wild hog with which the island abounds : a high-flavoured, delicious meat.

The frequent heavy showers of rain that fell made it very disagreeable, especially to the French officers and soldiers shut up between decks in a confined, close part of the ship, the heat oppressive, and wholly debarring them from all exercise. Day after day passed without bringing any intelligence respecting Sir Edward Hughes, which made Captain Gore miserable from his dread that if we were obliged to sail without convoy the Frenchmen who doubled our number would murder us all and run away with the ship to France. This idea struck me as being as unjust as it was illiberal. The officers were elegant gentlemen, and I firmly believe men of the strictest honour, the privates orderly, quiet, and well behaved as could be, besides which they were not going to Europe as prisoners, but were by an article of the capitulation to be sent to England on *parole*, to be treated the same as any other passengers during the voyage, and on the ship's arrival at home to be dispatched for France at the expence of Government. Captain Gore, however, was of a very different opinion to me, nor did he seem disposed to change it, always appearing uneasy at seeing the officers walking the deck in their uniforms and swords, which they daily did. To such a length did Gore carry his fears that it came to the knowledge of the French officers, who thereupon sent for me to their berths to ex-

press their surprize and mortification at Captain Gore's
doing them such injustice by suspecting them of conduct
derogatory to their characters as officers and gentlemen.
I could only endeavour to console them by assuring them
the idea was confined to the Captain alone, and advising
them to take no notice whatever of it, by which I was
convinced his ridiculous fears would subside. They with
the utmost good nature promised to follow my advice.

On the 16th of the month (November) Captain Bentley
wrote me a note requesting to have a minute's conversation, and wishing to consult me upon a matter of the utmost
importance to himself. I therefore went instantly to his
cabin, where I found him walking up and down in a state
of the utmost agitation. Enquiring what occasioned this,
he in a tremulous voice said he was so unhappy he could
neither eat, drink, nor sleep; that all he possessed in the
world was in that ship at his own risk; that Captain Gore
had told him he apprehended the Frenchmen on board
would seize the ship as soon as we got to sea, besides which
we certainly must fall in with the French fleet, and he cried
bitterly. I assured him there was not the least apprehension of any improper conduct in the French that were
with us; that as to meeting their cruisers that risk was unavoidable, but even should we do so I did not suppose they
would touch his private property. In an agony he replied,
" Oh yes, they will, they surely will."

Bentley then told me he had thoughts of going to Colombo,
and trying to get a passage from thence to Europe in a Dutch
ship. Finding I made no answer, he asked if I approved of
his plan, to which I said, " Certainly not, so far from it that
I consider it the wildest, the most extraordinary and imprudent that ever entered the mind of man; you clearly
have been highly incautious by omitting to insure your
property, but I think that instead of lessening you will
greatly increase the risk by leaving the *Nassau* to go in search
of a Dutch ship."

Bentley returned me his grateful thanks for my opinion,
appearing perfectly satisfied of the reasonableness of what

I offered, yet his natural weakness and indecision soon set him wavering again. He consulted Captain Gore upon the same subject, who abruptly stopped him, swearing he must be either raving mad or the damnedst idiot in existence, desiring he would leave the cabin.

The silly man next spoke to the Dutch Governor, when Mynheer, like a wily Hollander, perceived he might turn the foolish Englishman's fears to his own advantage. He therefore encouraged him in his scheme, declaring it to be the only safe way of getting himself and property from India, and by adopting it he would show alike his prudence and good sense. He further observed to Bentley how fortunate it was he had spoken to him, as he had a very fine vessel with a most valuable cargo just ready to depart for Colombo, in which he and his baggage might have a conveyance ; that he would also furnish him with letters of recommendation to a friend of his high in office at Colombo, who would in consequence thereof obtain a passage for him to Europe in one of their Indiamen, the finest ships in the world.

The credulous blockhead, delighted at this representation, forthwith went again to Captain Gore to demand an order to the commanding officer on board the *Nassau* to deliver up everything belonging to him (Bentley), whereupon Captain Gore, with his usual impetuosity, exclaimed, "Damn me, if you ought not to be shut up in Bedlam. However, I give you notice once for all, if you put your wild plan into execution of leaving my ship, by God, you never set foot in her more, nor would every chest of your rupees induce me to receive you again, so consider ere you damn yourself past redemption." To this uncouth though good advice, Bentley replied that all he required was the order, which Captain Gore immediately wrote and gave him, at the same time sending to Mr. Larkins to desire that the very moment Captain Bentley with his property quitted the ship he would have the bulkhead of his cabin knocked down, and on no pretence whatever suffer Bentley to come on board any more. The apartment he had occupied being thus thrown open made a spacious and airy room, of which possession was given to the French officers who were delighted therewith.

The day after this had occurred Captain Bentley paid a visit to Colonel and Mrs. Flint, where Captain Lenox happened to be, and who directly attacked him, saying, " What the de'il ha' ye been aboot, mon ? I'm tould ye ha' put aw your pelf into the haunds of a rascally Dootchman. Hoot, mon, de'il tak the baubee ye'll e'er see of it maire. Gin they once gat ye fairly into their clootchees they'll cut your wem, tak your pelf, and thraw your carcase into the oceean ; that's what they'll do, you may depand upon it. Ye ha' made a varry bad haund o' it indeed, Maister Bentley, and moreover, Maister Bentley, do ye na ken that the de'il a Europe shap ha' they at Coloombo, nor wal ha' for sax months to come." This ungracious speech set Bentley all agog again, nor was he rendered a bit less uncomfortable when upon enquiry he found what Captain Lenox had said relative to there being no Europe ship at Colombo was too true. He therefore concluded the rest of his assertions would be equally verified.

Taking alarm, Bentley suddenly became as anxious to regain possession of his rupees, which he had delivered to the Dutchman, as he had been to get them out of the *Nassau*. Whilst that was in agitation away he posted to Captain Gore, saying that upon more mature consideration he had determined to remain in the *Nassau*. This was abruptly, coarsely, and peremptorily refused by Captain Gore again swearing violently no consideration upon earth should induce him to receive him. Finding all he could say of no avail, Bentley next called upon Captain Lenox, to whom he complained bitterly of Captain Gore's ungenerous treatment, observing he was sure he (Captain Lenox) would have acted very differently, finishing his remarks by asking Captain Lenox to give him a passage in the *Southampton*. " Why, as to giving a passage, Maister Bentley, I believe we ha' plenty of room, but these are matters I dunna attend to. Gang awa to my purser, who

will tal ye what a cabin ye may have, and at what *prees*."
In short, notwithstanding all Bentley's eloquence, he could
not succeed with Sawney a bit better than with Captain
Gore.

Bentley then applied to me to exert my influence with
Captain Gore to induce him to receive him again, to which
I observed there was no place, his former situation being
given to the French officers. He eagerly said he did not
want a cabin, only sufficient space to hang his cot up, in
the steerage, or anywhere. As I could not help feeling for
the unhappy man, I did speak to Captain Gore, who flew
into a dreadful rage, asking what the devil I could mean
by wishing the ship again to be annoyed by so insufferable
a madman, and positively refusing my petition.

Bentley had nothing left for it but complying with the
demands of Captain Lenox's purser, and actually consented to pay six thousand sicca rupees for a part of the
great cabin, nor did his miseries end there. The Dutch
chief told him his treasure being shipped and entered in the
bill of lading could not be relanded except at Colombo.
This drove Bentley wild; he threatened that he would
complain to the British Admiral, at which Mynheer laughed,
drily saying he would try to get the money out of the
vessel, though his skipper assured him it could not be done.

Bentley, kept in a state of feverish anxiety for several
days, was at last told his money would be restored upon
his consenting to pay half freight and the port charges,
amounting altogether to six hundred and fifty dollars,
which, finding himself without remedy, he submitted to,
thus dearly paying for his wavering disposition.

Being upon the subject of poor Bentley, I had better
finish his history. Upon his arrival in England, he either
really was, or affected to be, disgusted with the manners
of the metropolis, with the climate, and every circumstance
of the country, and resolved to return to the more congenial plains of Hindustan. He therefore engaged a passage
on board the *Hinchinbrook*, Captain Maxwell, one of the
fleet that sailed under convoy of Commodore Johnston,

who had the famous *réncontre* with the French Admiral Suffren at the island of St. Jago, in which short but violent contest the *Hinchinbrook* being one of the outermost ships was roughly handled by the enemy. Bentley, not liking the appearance of things, in an early stage of the business disappeared, nor was it known what had become of him until one of the ladies sent into the bread-room as a place of safety suddenly exclaimed, "My God! here is a man laying at my feet." The unhappy wight being dragged forth proved to be Bentley. Upon the French fleet's retiring and the ladies being released, this circumstance was publicly talked of, in consequence of which Bentley was sent to Coventry, Captain Maxwell making no secret of his intentions to bring him to a court martial for cowardice. It was supposed that this preyed upon Bentley's mind ; he pined and, without any positive malady, died just as the ship reached Bengal.

No hopes remaining of Sir Edward Hughes's arrival, Sir Edward Vernon gave orders for the departure of the two ships, and on the 30th of November we sailed with moderate and pleasant weather. Scarce had we cleared the land ere symptoms of that horrible disease, the scurvy, made its appearance, a circumstance that increased Captain Gore's fears respecting the Frenchmen. The fourth day after we left Ceylon he told me he must take the French officers' side-arms from them for the safety of the ship ; that he intended therefore civilly to ask them to deliver the same into his custody until they reached England, when he would restore them. I without hesitation gave it as my decided opinion he would be very wrong to require such a sacrifice, Colonel Flint and Mr. Smith coinciding with me, telling Captain Gore nothing could justify an act of that sort. His fears, however, predominated, and he sent Mr. Darling, his purser, with a message to the French officers requesting they would deliver up their swords and fire-arms to remain in his custody during the voyage. After a strong remonstrance against such a requisition, the officers who had appeared upon deck to express their

sentiments, finding what they said had no effect upon
Captain Gore, retired for about five minutes, when they
reappeared dressed in full regimentals with their swords on,
Colonel Russelle again expressing his hope that Captain
Gore would not enforce his orders. Upon finding he was
determined to do so, Colonel Russelle went to the gangway
and threw his sword overboard. His example was followed
by the whole party except one, a lieutenant in the army of
most interesting appearance, who said he felt the unmerited insult so wantonly offered by the Commander of
the ship as sensibly as his brother officers possibly could,
but having no substance independent of his profession,
and his sword having been the last gift of a much valued
parent, then no more, he could not bring himself to throw
it away, as his comrades had very properly done. He then
very gracefully presented his sword to Colonel Flint, entreating he would compassionate his acute feelings and
retain the gift of a revered parent until the ungenerous
suspicions of Captain Gore were done away and he thereby
be entitled to demand the restoration of it. Colonel Flint
accepted the sword in a neat and appropriate speech,
lamenting the mistaken caution of Captain Gore requiring
such a sacrifice of feelings, assuring the French officers that
not only himself but every English passenger on board
the *Nassau* entertained the highest respect for them.
Captain Gore felt ashamed of his suspicions, yet had not
candour enough to admit that he did so.

After being at sea three weeks many of the crew were
so seriously attacked by the scurvy as to be rendered incapable of doing duty, our distress being magnified by the
weather becoming very boisterous off the south end of
Madagascar. We, however, proceeded until the 15th of
January, at which time being in the latitude of thirty-nine
and a half south in order to avoid the enemy's ships, a
tremendous gale came on from the west-north-west, as
adverse a wind as could blow. The ship was laid to under
a balance mizen, tumbling about dreadfully. In three days
we lost six of the hands from the scurvy, all of whom died

suddenly, three of them dropping to rise no more whilst at the helm. Within the following twelve days our loss amounted to thirty-three, when we began really and truly to think we never should reach St. Helena or any port.

Captain Gore, terrified beyond measure at the forlorn state we were in, carried his weakness so far that at last he would not receive the sick list from the Doctor, also forbidding any tolling of the bell, as was customary, previous to performing the funeral service upon a corpse being committed to the deep. He shut himself up in his cabin, from which he never stirred except to attend at meals.

In the height of the bad weather, it becoming necessary to hand the fore-topsail (then close-reefed), the few men we had were so reduced and debilitated by illness that they remained two hours upon the yard in fruitless exertions and endeavours to do the duty they had been sent upon. This so enraged Jerry Griffin, the boatswain, that after a volley of the most blasphemous oaths, he dropped upon his knees, raising his hands as if in an act of devotion, and prayed to the Almighty that there might not be enough left living in the ship to bury the dead. Soon after uttering this impious and horrid wish, he observed the poor creatures upon the yard were likely to succeed in furling the sail. He in the instant clapped his hands, exultingly crying out to the men aloft, "That's right, that's right. Well done, messmates, well done, my lads."

The following morning Colonel Flint was talking to an invalid soldier whom he had often seen when serving with the army. As this man appeared to be free from scurvy, the Colonel congratulated him upon preserving his health amidst such general and fatal disease, asking if he had used any particular means to avoid infection, when the fellow bluntly replied, "Grog, your honour, grog is your only. I'll be damned if scurvy or any other malady ever hurts me while I have plenty of grog, which possesses more virtues than all the contents of the Doctor's medicine chest." During the conversation we were summoned to dinner, and accordingly went into the cuddy where we were scarcely seated ere the Doctor was called out, but as that occurred daily nothing was said by any present. In a few minutes he returned, and to our inexpressible surprize and horror, announced that the man whom Colonel Flint had just before been talking with was dead! A shocking exit this.

CHAPTER XVII

A SECOND TIME AT CAPE TOWN

THE great injustice Captain Gore had done our French officers and privates was now made manifest by their voluntarily coming forward and offering their assistance in working the ship, which from that hour they did with the utmost zeal, a few amongst them who had been seamen proving of the greatest use, and there is not a doubt but we owed our preservation entirely to them. Our companion, the *Southampton*, could give us no aid, the crew being all affected by scurvy, though not of so fatal and disastrous a kind as ours. Smith (the surgeon) was grievously distressed at seeing the ravages made by the cruel distemper without having it in his power to prevent or alleviate the misfortune though he made various experiments for that purpose. Wine, sugar, spruce, and every other antiscorbutic procurable were abundantly supplied, without material benefit. The three first men that died Smith opened, hoping to gain some information from the state of certain parts of the inside, but he was disappointed, all the vital parts appearing sound and healthy.

Mr. Greer, our chief mate, pursued his usual practice, being shut up in his cabin five days out of every six, and when he did show himself upon deck he was generally drunk. This produced many unpleasant altercations between him and Captain Gore, the latter always losing his temper, when he abused Greer as a brute and everything base. This abuse Greer returned threefold; the end generally was Gore's ordering him off the deck. I once heard Captain Gore say to him upon the quarter-deck, " You are a drunken good-for-nothing vagabond. Go to your cabin or by God I'll order you into irons," to which Greer replied, "You dare as well be damned, you scoundrel. Suppose I am drunk, what then? Drunk or sober I know my duty, and can do it like a seaman, which I'll be damned if you are capable of." Captain Gore, mad with passion, ran into his cabin for a sword, and I have no doubt would in his rage have put Greer to death, but during his absence the boatswain had taken Greer up in his arms and by main force carried him down to his cabin.

My daily business was endeavouring to console Mrs. Smith and Mrs. Flint during the bad weather, dividing the morning between them. One day when the motion of the ship was extremely violent I went into the round-house to Mrs. Smith. I had taken her eldest child, George, upon my knee as I sat upon the deck, having just advised her to let the rest also come by me, as being safer than where they then were, when a sea broke over the ship that for a time quite overwhelmed her. Down she went upon her beam ends. The shock was so violent and sudden everything yielded to it. Mrs. Smith, who was sitting on her bed with a child on each side, came, cot and all, bodily over to leeward, as did chests, trunks, and every article in the cabin. How George and myself escaped being maimed, if not killed, was marvellous. Although for some moments I actually thought the ship had upset, I could not help smiling at the scene that presented itself, the female servants floundering about in all positions, Mrs. Smith screeching to them to cover their nakedness, whilst she herself was employed in gathering up curls, toupees, and various articles of her toilette she would not upon any consideration have exhibited to profane eyes.

Mr. Smith had just come in from deck, and was comforting his family by telling them the officers thought the fury of the gale was spent, when the ship took the desperate heel I have above mentioned. He was then standing by the side of his wife's cot, when the violence of the jerk made him lose his hold. Finding himself going bodily to leeward, and being apprehensive of falling upon the children, he by an extraordinary exertion stopped himself by laying hold of a cot-hook fixed in one of the beams, but in so doing swung round with such force as to put his shoulder out of joint. The pain attending it was so acute as to occasion his fainting. His namesake, instantly attending, put the arm into its place again before he recovered. These united accidents were the more distressing and serious from Mrs. Smith's being in hourly expectation of laying in. Apprehensions were therefore entertained that the consequences might be fatal to her. Happily, however, no evil attended.

A fine active lad about eighteen years of age, a midshipman, whose name was Smith, was amongst the earliest of those attacked by the scurvy. Being blessed with fine spirits and an uncommon share of fortitude he resisted the fatal malady in an extraordinary manner, declaring he would not yield, but would do his duty as long as he could stand. He kept his resolution nor left the deck until he dropped, as was supposed, dead. Being conveyed to his cot and medicine being administered, he rallied, though not sufficiently to be able to go upon deck again. We all felt extremely interested in this young man. The Doctor's attentions, too, were unremitting. One symptom of the disorder was an extraordinary listlessness and disinclination to move. Being urged to exert himself, he repeatedly jumped out of his cot, but had not strength enough to support himself and generally fainted. Every comfort the ship afforded was given to him.

We had now only sixteen men who could do any duty of the ship's crew. Mr. Larkins therefore considered it high time to take some decisive step, and having spoken to Captain Gore privately without effect, he after dinner on the 30th of January addressed him before us all, described the desperate state the ship was reduced to, being worked entirely by the French, no officer but himself and the fifth able to appear upon deck, the fresh provisions entirely exhausted, and only water for three weeks left; that under such circumstances they ought to make for the nearest port at all risks.

Captain Gore, terrified at Larkins's speech, asked what he would advise, when Larkins instantly replied, "Make for the Cape as fast as possible." Captain Gore then directed him to speak the *Southampton* and say our situation having become desperate we must run for a port. Going as close as the sea would allow to our companion, the communication was made, when Captain Lenox said he thought it absolutely necessary for the preservation of both ships that we should go into the Cape. We accordingly stood direct for the land. The moment this measure was determined on, we went to inform the poor invalid Smith, who lay gasping in his cot, his death being expected every hour. He seemed much gratified by the intelligence, observing in a languid tone that could he hold out to get a mouthful of fruit he was sure he should survive.

The 1st of February, 1780, we struck soundings upon the bank off Cape Lagullas, early the next morning saw the land, and as it was then blowing very strong direct on shore the two Commanders determined to make for False Bay instead of rounding the Cape, as the most likely way to avoid any French cruisers. We accordingly (certainly at considerable risk) went close in under the land, running along shore until four in the afternoon of the 2nd, at which hour we opened False Bay, stood directly in, and at six both ships came to an anchor. Our invalid, Smith, after we made the land, enquired every quarter of an hour with extreme earnestness when we should get in. About noon of the 2nd he gave up all hopes, lay in the most melancholy state, uttering nothing but, " Oh, fruit, fruit, or I die." Soon after we anchored, a boat from the shore brought off a variety of fruits, vegetables, and refreshments. Everybody ran with the utmost anxiety to Smith's cot with fruit of all sorts. The Doctor held a bunch of grapes to him, which the poor fellow (then speechless and entirely exhausted) by an effort raised to his lips, and with a deep groan expired ! His death was sincerely lamented by all on board.

Upon our arrival Mr. Smith proposed a subscription for the French privates, to whose exertions and indefatigable labours we were indebted for our lives. He set the example by giving one hundred guineas, Colonel Flint a like sum, to which I joined my mite of twenty guineas.

The night we got in, and after poor Smith's death, we all went on shore to Mr. Brandt, the Dutch chief, where we experienced a pleasing change from what we had undergone for many weeks. Instead of a scanty table with scarce any fresh provisions, we sat down to most excellent fish, flesh, and fowl, followed by a dessert consisting of the fruits of all quarters of the world, and, what was still better, light and cheerful hearts. Mr. Brandt told us our escape was most fortunate, Monsieur Trou Jolie with two line-of-battle ships and two frigates having been cruising near three weeks expressly for our two ships, his squadron being in sight all the afternoon while we were also seen crawling close in along shore, the French as the evening approached standing off to keep plenty of sea room, as they did every night, and having no suspicion we should put into False Bay at that season. Had we attempted to go round the Cape we must inevitably have been captured. Luckily, the enemy did not see us, nor we them.

On the 3rd we set off for the Cape Town, where I took up my residence at Mrs. Vanrenen's, with whom I lodged on my way to India in the *Seahorse*. She had taken another husband and was now Mrs. VanCahman. The two eldest daughters were become fine young women, especially the senior, an errant coquette, evidently laying herself out to catch some wealthy Englishman in the bonds of matrimony, to which scheme she in about a year after the time I am now speaking of fell a martyr. A man named Hatfield, being passenger on board a Danish Indiaman from Bengal, stopped at the Cape. He lodged at VanCahman's, cutting an amazing figure, displaying a profusion of shawls and rich Eastern stuffs, several of which he presented to the handsome Dutch girl. The report of Hatfield by the Commander of the ship was that he had amassed a large fortune which he was returning home to enjoy. This account made him the object of attack. The damsel set her cap at him, and he, who supposed she would have at least ten thousand from her mother, readily bit. In short, they were married. It proved a mutual take in, the lady not having sixpence in the world, Hatfield precisely the same. He was an impudent, chattering puppy, and had never been in a higher situation of life than purser.

An explanation took place soon after the wedding, when, instead of mutual upbraidings, the couple laughed heartily at the double deception, wisely determining to make the best of a bad bargain. As they were both remarkably well looking and by no means deficient in mother wit, they concluded from their joint *abilities* a livelihood might be gained *somehow or other*.

The night we landed at the Cape Mrs. Smith was delivered of a daughter, two days after which Trou Jolie and his squadron put into Table Bay from his unsuccessful cruise, his ships being all crippled from the tempestuous weather they had encountered. Enraged at finding the two English ships had slipped into False Bay, he the morning of his arrival summoned the officers of his fleet, when he proposed going round in his flagship, the *Brilliant*, and cutting them from their anchors, insisting that a mere saluting battery, which was all there was at False Bay, could not be considered as protection against their seizing an enemy. This proposition coming immediately to the ears of the Dutch Governor, he sent notice to Monsieur Trou Jolie that if such an unjustifiable measure was carried into effect he should deem it tantamount to a declaration of war, and would act accordingly.

Knowing that the French squadron could not sail until repaired, which must occupy some days, the Dutch Governor put ten eighteen-pound guns on board a Dutch vessel and sent them round to False Bay, where they were mounted, an artillery officer and party of men with plenty of ammunition being also stationed at them, with orders to resist any attempt made by the French to molest the English ships.

This well-timed and spirited conduct of the Governor had the desired effect ; Mr. Trou Jolie did not carry his threat into execution. The alarm this had occasioned having subsided, the French officers mixed with us all in perfect harmony, a few of the chattering coxcombs sometimes lamenting their ill-fortune in losing their shares of two such valuable prizes as our ships would have proved to them, arrogantly affecting to console themselves in the certainty they felt that they should still take them ere they reached Europe. Their Commander stationed a frigate at the mouth of the bay to watch our vessels, and had a line-of-battle ship made ready to follow us should we have moved.

We lived a merry life, having dances, concerts, or plays every evening, at which a number of very fine girls were always present.

Towards the end of the month (February) seeing no chance of the *Nassau* getting away and having already been ten months from Bengal, I became anxious to continue my voyage, the committee having requested I would use the greatest possible dispatch. A fleet of Dutch Indiamen being to sail shortly, I consulted my fellow-passengers as to the propriety of my going on in one of them, which they all advised me to do. I therefore applied to the Commodore, Mynheer Paardakoper, to whom I was introduced by Colonel Gordon, respecting a passage. He said he would give me an answer in two days, at the end of which time he called to tell me I might have his state room, being an excellent apartment, for *six hundred pounds* sterling. The enormity of the demand astonished me so much I knew not how to act, and in my turn said I must take time to consider of it. Indeed, I conceived it would be highly improper to yield to such imposition, but upon speaking to Messieurs Smith and Flint they were of opinion that under all the circumstances I ought, even upon such exorbitant terms, to go as the *Nassau* might not sail for several months. I therefore closed with Mr. Paardakoper, paying him his price, and writing to the committee in Calcutta to inform them thereof and the motives that influenced me thereto.

Upon our arrival at the Cape we had learnt that Sir Edward Hughes, with a large fleet, had touched at the port on his way to India, and only left it in the middle of November.

During the last week of my stay at the Cape I was far from well, in consequence of which I left off drinking wine, except a couple of glasses of Constantia.

My fellow-passengers were to be Colonel de Prehn, a German, who had been many years at the Cape, and had risen gradually to the supreme command of the army; he was a well-informed, accomplished man; his wife, a handsome woman, a native of the Cape, from whence she had never been; they both spoke English perfectly; two Dutch gentlemen who had held situations in the Civil Service; Mr. Paterson, whom I mentioned when at this place in 1777 as employed by Lady Strathmore to collect natural curiosities. Her Ladyship, instead of fulfilling her engagements, suffered his bills to be protested and returned, thereby exposing him to great difficulties, and had it not been for the assistance of Colonel de Prehn, who advanced him money to settle with his creditors, he would have been thrown into gaol at the Cape. The cuddy party was therefore, including the Captain, to consist of seven.

I went off to see the accommodation I was to have, which I found very spacious, airy, and comfortable. The Captain informed me it was customary for passengers to breakfast in their own cabins, but if I preferred taking that meal with him in the round-house he should be glad of my company, to which I agreed. After a handsome dinner, we returned on shore in his barge. On the way he gave me a brief sketch of his life. When quite a boy his father, always partial to Great Britain, had sent him to England, there placing him in an academy, where he was taught English, French, and various branches of the mathematics. His parents' chief object being to make him a perfect seaman, naval tactics were most particularly attended to. Assiduous in his attentions, his progress was rapid, so that at the expiration of the third year he had nothing more to learn.

When only fourteen years of age he went on board a line-of-battle ship under the immediate care of the master, an old acquaintance of his father's. Under this gentleman he acted as mate with infinite credit to himself, frequently receiving the public acknowledgments and thanks of the Commander for his conduct. At the end of that period he quitted the British Navy to return to his native country, bearing with him the most unqualified approbation of those he had served under.

Captain Paardakoper's father, delighted at perusing such flattering testimonials of his son's industry and abilities, exerted his influence with people in power at Amsterdam, soon obtaining a situation for him as second officer of an East Indiaman, in which service, after going two voyages, he obtained the command of one. At the time my acquaintance commenced with him he was about sixty years of age, a hale, strong man, and being then the Senior Captain in the Dutch Company's service, carried a broad pennant and had the title of Commodore, a rank of importance in Holland, the officers in the Company's service all receiving their commissions from the States-General and wearing the uniform of their Navy, a blue coat with scarlet facings, richly laced, waistcoat and breeches also of scarlet.

Captain Paardakoper's ship's name was the *Held Woltemade*, i.e. the Brave Woltemade, so called from the following extraordinary circumstance. A homeward-bound ship from Batavia happened to be at anchor in Table Bay when one of those tremendous gales that occur there at certain times of the year came on. The tempest raged with such violence, blowing direct on shore, that no boat could go off to the assistance of the ship then making signals of distress. Her anchors not holding her from the violence of the sea, she drifted and soon struck, immediately falling upon her broadside, the waves breaking over her with the utmost force, sweeping away everything that opposed them. The sight was truly pitiable to those on shore, there being upwards of two hundred souls on board and no prospect of saving any of them, though not more than a quarter of a mile from the beach. She had several female passengers and children, whose cries and lamentations were distinctly heard.

Large rewards were offered by the Governor to any who should suggest a mode of relieving the unfortunate people. Several boats attempted to get off, but were all swamped in the heavy surf and dashed to pieces. One of the spectators at last determined to afford succour or perish in the effort. This person's name was Woltemade. He was possessed of a large tract of land and farms on the sea coast of the Bay, with every foot of which he was well acquainted, being a famous fisher. He had a remarkable fine horse, milk-white, of uncommon strength, and so sagacious he used to observe of it that it could do everything but speak. It struck him that by riding about a mile along the shore to windward he might be able to swim off upon this favourite horse to the wreck, taking with him the end of a small line, the other being made fast on shore. He and his noble animal accordingly plunged into the foaming ocean in the presence of some thousands of spectators, all most anxious beholders of the extraordinary scene. To their utter astonishment he reached the wreck, his line was made fast to a strong rope which was then hauled on shore, and himself and horse returned in safety, bearing with him two fine boys of eight and nine years old.

By the rope from the ship hauled taut to a post on the land thirty persons reached the shore in little more than an hour, when it unfortunately snapped. The miserable people still on the wreck uttered the most piteous and piercing cries on perceiving the accident, whereupon the generous Woltemade resolved to make a second effort for their relief, although the bystanders observed his horse seemed to have exhausted his powers by the former exertions. He accordingly once more plunged into the turbulent element, and once more succeeded in conveying a small cord to the wreck, but in the instant he had so done he and his noble animal were overwhelmed by the sea and sunk to rise no more. The sympathizing crowd uttered a shriek of despair at the fate of the hero and his extraordinary horse.

Seventy more of the people were preserved by the second hawser, when that also gave way. Night then approaching, more than one hundred still remained in the wreck, all of whom perished. At daylight the following morning the ship had gone to pieces.

In commemoration of the persevering intrepidity of this wonderful man the Dutch East India Company caused the ship I came home in to be built, naming her the *Held Wolte-made*, there being a carved representation of the extraordinary occurrence, very well executed, upon her stern, in which Woltemade and his horse are the principal figures in the act of swimming off to the wreck.

About a week before leaving the Cape, one James Adcock, who had saved a sum of fifteen hundred pounds as a petty merchant in Bengal, when he left by the *Southampton*, offered himself to me as a servant, observing he was sure he could be useful to me in a foreign ship, having acted as steward on board a Danish man-of-war. Liking the man's manner, I engaged him, Captain Paardakoper upon my recommendation appointing him steward, and a capital good one he proved.

Besides the unreasonable sum of six hundred pounds I paid for my passage, I sent on board a chest of English claret which I purchased from Mr. Ballandyne, second officer of the *Southampton*, likewise the same quantity of fine old madeira. Shortly prior to embarking, Adcock called at my lodging to ask if I knew anything of Mr. Paterson, as he had applied to him for a loan of four hundred pounds, proposing repayment in London at a favourable exchange from a considerable sum due to him from Lady Strathmore, which amount he was willing to advance provided I thought he might do so with safety. All I could say was I knew Mr. Paterson had a large demand upon her Ladyship, but when it would be recovered I could not tell; that my acquaintance with Mr. Paterson was very slight, but I had a good opinion of him and believed him to be an honest man who would do everything that was correct and proper ; that as to advancing money he (Adcock) must judge for himself. I heard no more of the matter until we had been some time at sea, when Adcock told me he had lent Mr. Paterson four hundred pounds and showed me his promissory note for it.

CHAPTER XVIII

IN HOLLAND

ON the 9th of March, 1780, I took leave of Captains Gore and Lenox, as well as my other *Nassau* companions, and on the morning of the 10th, with my little pet boy, Nabob, went on board the *Held Woltemade*. I felt rejoiced at leaving the Cape in the hope that my health would mend from the pure air at sea. At one o'clock we sat down to an excellent dinner, contrary to my expectation dressed quite in the English style, instead of everything floating in oil, as I had been led to suppose would be the case. There was upon the table three immense dishes of vegetables, one of them being as beautiful colliflowers as I ever beheld with an appearance as if fresh cut from the garden, and this continued daily the whole voyage. The meat being removed was followed by a dessert of pines, grapes, melons, a variety of plums, apples, pears, and the highest flavoured oranges I ever tasted, added to all which was many kinds of dried fruits, which likewise continued every day.

Upon rising the first morning I saw breakfast upon table, a clean cloth and every article as neat as could be. There was coffee, tea, as good rolls as ever were baked on shore, and what was more extraordinary, admirable fresh butter, toast, eggs, ham, sausages, smoked beef rasped, and lastly an immense cheese. The tea and coffee I found were exclusively for me, my messmate not touching either, but eating heartily of the solids, qualifying the same with two or three draughts of cline (small) beer, as the Captain called it, but which was, in fact, as strong as our porter. He finished by chucking down a glass of the favourite liquor

228

gin, then called for his pipe. Indeed, it was scarcely ever out of his mouth except when eating or asleep. I will not venture to say how many *sopekys* he took between breakfast and dinner. It appeared to me that his servant was in perpetual motion with the gin bottle and glass. True, the latter was small, but the repetition rendered the quantity considerable, and yet I never saw him intoxicated.

Everything was very comfortable on board, and Captain Paardakoper's attentions to me most marked. Observing that I was low-spirited, he tried various ways to correct it, and amongst his good-natured endeavours was that of teaching me trick-track, a game I became exceedingly fond of.

The second night of my being on board, I had occasion about an hour after I went to bed to rise and go to the quarter gallery. Passing through the round-house I was greatly alarmed at seeing the Captain fast asleep upon a couch, a pipe in his mouth, the bowl of which was downwards and the contents laying on the deck. I instantly roused and showed him with terror the embers of tobacco upon the boards, when, with the utmost composure, he said, " Oh, no danger, no danger, the tobacco-ash never gives the fire." Notwithstanding this decided opinion I never afterwards felt quite at ease, often getting up in the night-time to take a peep at the situation of the Captain and his pipe.

About a week after we had been at sea, the Captain, after dinner, said to me, " Come, sir, I perceive that I must be your doctor. Follow my advice and you'll be a stout man very soon." I replied that I was ready to do whatever he recommended. " Well then," added the Captain, " as I know you have good claret on board, let you and I take a bottle of it, instead of that vile sweet stuff you daily drink." I acceded, a bottle of claret was produced which we emptied, took a second, and I never slept better than the ensuing night. His prescription proved so congenial to my stomach that I improved under it every day, soon feeling as well as ever I was in my life.

Captain Paardakoper was in every respect a liberal-minded man. He laughed at the old system of navigation pursued by their ships, which although known to be erroneous was persevered in merely because it had been so for more than a hundred years. One of these follies was that of shortening sail (no matter how the weather) in certain latitudes. His mode of conducting the fleet was precisely the same as in our service, and no British Commander could carry sail in a better style than he did. The fleet under his command consisted of five large Indiamen with a beautiful little ship about three hundred tons, which he made act as a frigate. Three of the captains, being well acquainted with the skill and abilities of the Commodore, obeyed his orders with alacrity. The fourth, an obstinate brute of the old school, would adhere rigidly to the Company's instructions. His ship was called the *Venus*, as errant a tub as the *Southampton*, and from the manner in which she was navigated had been a twelvemonth getting from Batavia to the Cape.

The tenth day after we left the Cape at daybreak we found ourselves close to a large cutter under English colours. There being a very light air of wind, a boat came from her, the officer in her telling us she belonged to the East India Company, was commanded by Captain Bendy, and stationed off the Island of St. Helena to look out for any French ships. We also learnt the Island bore right ahead, distant eighteen leagues. The boat then went back to the cutter, returning immediately with Captain Bendy, whom our Commodore invited to dinner. He accordingly remained on board the whole day.

At noon we saw the land, and at sunset were within five miles of it, when Captain Bendy took leave. As he had told me he should put in to report our fleet, I availed myself of that opportunity to write to my Twickenham playfellow, Robartes Carr, then Chaplain to the Settlement. This gentleman, nearly my own age, had, when a boy, resided with his mother at the next house but one to my father's at Twickenham as guests to Mr. Hindley, who succeeded to

Lord Radnor's beautiful seat. Young Carr and I were constantly together, taking many a hard tug at the oar and other amusements.

At daylight the next morning we had run out of sight of the Island, four days after which we made Ascension, the famous place for turtle, passing it at a great distance.

Notwithstanding the repeated threats of the Commodore to use violent measures, the Captain of the *Venus* continued to torment and to delay us. He never would obey any orders, and daily stopped the fleet four or five hours.

Upon making the Azores, or Western Islands, the Commodore told me his orders were to take the fleet north about, that is, to the westward and northward of Ireland and Scotland, an order he was desirous of parrying, if possible, and which he should endeavour to do from the leaky state of the *Venus* and her being short of water. In a few days after, the weather being moderate and fine, he made the signals for all the Commanders of the fleet to come on board the *Woltemade*. Being assembled, he read his instructions to them, after which he said the state of the *Venus*, he conceived, would justify a deviation by going through the English Channel instead of north about, whereby in all probability a month would be saved. The Captains all coincided in the opinion except the *Venus's*. He, after hearing the sentiments of each, declared his dissent to any breach of instructions on account of his ship, which he affirmed to be as capable of keeping the sea as any one of the fleet, and he should protest against her being made a *pretext* for the necessity of avoiding the north passage. The idea was thereupon given up, to my extreme mortification, for Captain Paardakoper had promised to let me get into the first English ship we should meet in the Channel going into port. He said his directions were to land all passengers, without exception, at Amsterdam ; exactly like a bale of goods to be entered at the Custom House, notwithstanding which he would yield to the *claim* of me by any British Commander.

On the 30th of May we made Ireland, running along the

western side, close upon a wind, in order to go round the northern end of it and of Scotland, to touch at Shetland, where a Dutch ship of war would be ready to receive and convoy us through the North Sea into the Texel. The wind continuing to blow from the east-north-east, we necessarily stood on to the northward so far as to the latitude of sixty-three, where, although we had no night, the weather was exceedingly disagreeable, being dreary and cold, thick fogs, gloomy and threatening skies. I often thought from the tremendous blackness of the horizon we were to be blown out of the water, but as these formidable clouds rose it turned to mere drizzling rain with thick fog.

I one morning upon waking asked my boy Nabob as to the state of the weather, when he answered, " No much ee wind, but too much ee smoke." Not at all knowing what he meant, I rose and looking out saw there was so thick a fog one could not see across the ship, which Nabob called " smoke." The 4th the wind suddenly shifted to north-west ; we hauled in, and the next day, the 5th, made Shetland, off which a very fine Dutch frigate, the *Thetis*, of thirty-six guns, joined us. The Commander, a well-looking man who spoke admirable good English, came on board, desiring the Commodore to follow his ship, as he should bring the fleet to an anchor for thirty hours. He then invited the Commodore and his passengers to dine with him, which being accepted he took leave.

At eleven o'clock the fleet anchored off the principal town. Upon my expressing a wish to see the place, the Commodore immediately ordered his barge to be made ready, into which Colonel de Prehn, Mr. Paterson, and myself went, and were rowed to the most wretched town I ever beheld, principally consisting of fishermen's huts with only three or four houses fit for a human creature to inhabit. The inhabitants received us with the utmost good-nature and hospitality. The herrings were the finest I ever tasted, upon which I should have dined but for my engagement to the *Thetis*.

Having gone through every part of the place we went to the frigate, where we were received by an excellent band of music playing on the quarter-deck. At two (Mrs. de Prehn being come) we sat down to a sumptuous dinner of three courses, the first consisting entirely of fish, in which was the largest turbot I ever beheld, but the herrings were so exquisite I ate of nothing else. A very good band played during dinner. When the cloth was removed some charming songs and duets were sung both in Dutch and German, the music plaintive, sweet, and exactly to my taste. (We had a great deal of it, too, on board the *Woltemade* in a capital style, the greater part of the watch frequently joining in chorus with most correct harmony.) After spending a very agreeable day on board the *Thetis* we at midnight returned to our ship. It was a novel scene to us to have broad daylight at that hour. Indeed, there was no night at all, at least no darkness.

Early the following morning it blew fresh from the west-south-west with thick weather and rain at times, notwithstanding which the *Thetis* made the signal for sailing, and by seven o'clock the fleet were under way. The wind and rain continued but did not prevent the Captain of the *Thetis* from coming to dine on board our ship, Captain Paardakoper having invited him so to do. Considering we had been three months from port the fare was not bad, our guest expressing his surprize at seeing so many good dishes after so long a voyage, and also at the handsome manner in which it was served. This was entirely owing to the abilities of Adcock.

The *Thetis* had left Holland three weeks when war with England was daily expected, owing to a strong French party in the Dutch Councils, the public at large being violently against it. The Captain informed us of the universally lamented death of that great man and able navigator, Captain Cook, which event he said was considered by all Europe as an irreparable misfortune. The news had reached Amsterdam the day he left that city.

The weather continued wet and tempestuous the whole of the 6th and 7th, making me bestow some curses upon Scotland, from which the wind blew direct. The first part of the 8th was fair. At noon a fleet of upwards of three hundred sail of small Dutch vessels hove in sight escorted by two frigates, standing to the northward. At 2 p.m. we were in the midst of them, when the wind suddenly flew round to north-north-west, increasing in violence. For us it was quite fair, but adverse as possible for those we met. They were the annual fleet bound to Shetland and the other islands for herrings. These they pickle and sell to the English, upon whose shores the fish were taken, receiving for the same an immense sum of money every year. This large fleet standing in all directions and all positions, reefing and preparing to encounter the gale, was one of the prettiest sights I ever saw.

It blew so fresh that in two hours we ran so far as not even to see the frigates. The 9th the wind increased to a hard gale, with heavy rain. As our convoy's reckoning made us near the Dutch coast and we could not venture to run closer in such weather, the fleet was ordered to lay to. This was a mortifying circumstance to be tumbling about on a turbulent ocean with the wind as fair as it could blow, but such is the nature of the coast of Holland, and so numerous are the rocks and shoals in every direction that it cannot be approached without previously seeing the land-marks, or the buoys. We lay four-and-twenty hours in as unpleasant a state as ever I was in. The 10th the weather moderated—we therefore once more stood for the land, which we saw at eleven in the forenoon, Captain Paarda-koper saying he had never seen a better landfall, the mouth, or entrance, to the Texel being directly before us. At 1 p.m., the fleet being supplied with pilots, we stood on, passing through the Mars Diep in very shallow water. At seven in the evening we came to an anchor off the Island of Texel in perfectly smooth water.

Having consulted Captain Paardakoper as to my pro-ceeding, he recommended me not to leave the ship until next morning, but to start early in a Dutch boat to a town he mentioned about fourteen miles up the Zuyder Zee, where I might land and pursue the rest of the journey in a carriage. He added that if I would wait until ten o'clock he would accompany me quite to Amsterdam, an offer I, as an absolute stranger in a foreign land, was glad to avail myself of. He accordingly bespoke a boat, into which, after eating a hearty breakfast, the Commodore, myself, and Nabob got, the ship's crew giving us three cheers as we quitted her side.

After a brisk run for four hours we reached Inkhausen, a neat, handsome town, distant about thirty-two miles from the Texel. While our carriage was preparing we took some refreshment, then stepped into a conveyance like a phaeton, except for its being driven by a coachman who sat upon a box directly before us, so that the smoke from his pipe (for he smoked the whole way) came directly in our faces. It was drawn by a pair of immense, tall, black horses that, like their driver, seemed to have a will of their own, taking special care not to hurry themselves.

We changed horses four times, passing through a rich fertile country for about thirty-three miles, when we entered the famous city of Amsterdam, driving to a large hotel, where the Commodore, after securing a bed for me, went about his own business, promising to be with me early the next morning. He accordingly came to breakfast, after which he accompanied me to the house of Messieurs Pye, Rich, and Wilkinson, English merchants of respectability, to whom I had a letter of introduction from Colonel Gordon at the Cape. Mr. Rich was in England, but Mr. Wilkinson received me with much politeness, requesting I would consider his house as my home during my stay at Amsterdam. He gave his chief clerk directions to get my baggage cleared from the Custom House as soon as it arrived there, which he said could not be for some days, probably eight or nine, the Commodore promising to expedite it all in his power.

I preferred keeping a chamber at the hotel, but accepted Mr. Wilkinson's invitation to meals. The Commodore and my host then went to their respective employ. I returned to the hotel, and going into the coffee-room, found a number of English assembled, conversing upon the subject of alarming riots that had occurred, and still subsisted, in London, of which the most extraordinary and alarming accounts had just reached them. In the company was a gentleman whose face seemed familiar to me, and who I observed looking earnestly at me. In a few minutes he addressed me, saying, "If not greatly mistaken I am speaking to an old Twickenham acquaintance named William Hickey." I directly recognized him as the youngest Salvador, with whose family mine had been intimate for many years. He told me he was settled at Amsterdam, and should be happy to show me every attention. He immediately introduced me to some of the first people of the city, from whom I received invitations enough to fill up a month had I been able to remain so long in Holland.

I spent the second day with a gay party at Salvador's. Whilst sitting with them after dinner, a servant whispered me to say a gentleman wished to speak to me in private. I instantly went to him, when I was surprized to find it was my shipmate, Mr. Paterson, who seemed greatly agitated and distressed. Upon my asking the occasion of his uneasiness, he showed me a letter he had just received from Colonel de Prehn, written in harsh and positive terms. It stated that having advanced five hundred pounds at the Cape to enable him to settle with his creditors and leave that place, he expected, if not the cash, at least security for it previous to leaving Holland, which he must soon do, intending to fix his residence in Germany. "Now," observed Paterson, "it is as much out of my power to find money here as it was in Africa, being an utter stranger without a single acquaintance except those who came in the *Woltemade*." Feeling greatly for the poor man, I undertook to speak to the Colonel on his behalf. I did so. At the first interview I could effect nothing, but I discovered the gallant German to be an errant Jew. He declared the sum due with interest was of importance to him, and have it he must and would. I left him in anger!

Upon my return to the hotel another annoyance awaited me, for there I found Adcock in sad tribulation. He had heard that De Prehn threatened to put Paterson in prison, " and then," said he, " what is to become of my debt, the loss of which would ruin me ? " I endeavoured to console him by assurances that he was safe, and that although some time might elapse ere he received the cash ultimately he certainly would do so. After repeating his apprehensions over and over again, I with difficulty got rid of him. He left me declaring I was his sole dependence, that upon me he relied to prevent his utter ruin. He continued his visit and complaints to me daily, crying and bewailing lament-ably, begging and beseeching me to give him some writing to say he was secure. This I declined, truly observing I had nothing to do in the transaction, which was his own voluntary act. He, however, tormented me so incessantly that at last, in order to get rid of him, I wrote upon the back of Paterson's note to him these words, " I do hereby under-take to procure payment of the amount due upon the within note for the within named James Adcock. W. Hickey." Finding I could not bring Colonel de Prehn to accede to any-thing short of the uttermost farthing due, principal and interest, I mentioned the matter to Mr. Wilkinson, who, upon my engaging to exert myself to enforce payment of the protested bills from Lady Strathmore, most kindly liquidated De Prehn's demand.

Captain Paardakoper was remarkably attentive and civil ; not a day passed without his calling to ask if he could do anything for me. I went one evening to the theatre with him, a fine building with very capital actors, where I received much entertainment. Mr. Wilkinson attended me over the whole of the Stadt House and every other place worthy of inspection. At his house I met with a Mr. Swains-ton, an eminent merchant of Liverpool, who occasionally went to Holland on his mercantile concerns. Conversing with this gentleman, who was very inquisitive on the subject of India, upon hearing the length of time I had been on the voyage from Bengal, and the important papers I had under charge, urged me not to think of crossing the Channel from Helvoetsluys to Harwich, as that passage was much infested by French privateers, and that it would be a sad finale of a disastrous voyage to be taken by an enemy in the very jaws of home. He said my only secure way would be to go by land through Flanders to Ostend, from whence neutral vessels were passing over to England every day ; that he always pursued that route, and would join me in the travelling charges most willingly by taking post horses instead of the diligence in which he usually went. Mr. Wilkinson thought the plan an eligible one. He, however, said, as I must at any rate go to The Hague I had better make enquiries there and decide according to what I should hear. Mr. Wilkinson daily received letters from London filled with particulars of the horrid riots which had put the whole kingdom in despair. Several families were so alarmed as to embark for Holland and other parts of the Continent.

Having procured my baggage from the Custom House, I prepared for departure. I had a quantity of shawls and rich gold and silver muslins, presents from different friends of Bengal to their relations. These (as well as some of my own) Mr. Wilkinson said I should certainly lose if I attempted to land them at Harwich, and that the conveyance of the heavy trunk they were in from Amsterdam to Ostend would be attended with enormous expense. He therefore offered to manage the business for me by delivering them to a man he knew who would undertake to deliver them where directed upon being paid 10 per cent on the original cost, and if seized he would be responsible for that amount. This plan I consequently adopted.

On the 22nd (June) it was agreed between Mr. Swainston and me to set off the following day, of which I wrote to inform Captain Paardakoper, who thereupon immediately came to the hotel. Upon my returning him thanks for his kind attentions during the voyage, he shook me very cordially by the hand, saying it would have been most ungrateful in him to have done otherwise, as I had liberally paid for every civility in his power to show. With mutual wishes for each other's health and happiness we parted.

The 23rd my companion and I got into a travelling chaise

he purchased for the occasion, he very good-naturedly consenting to Nabob's being inside with us. It was not without regret that I left Amsterdam, having been treated there with extraordinary kindness by many of the inhabitants, and especially by Mr. Wilkinson, with whom I formed a friendly correspondence that continued while I remained in England. Our first stage was to Haarlaem, twelve miles, where we visited the church, in which is a famous organ said to be the largest and finest-toned instrument in the world. Mr. Swainston being acquainted with one of the burghers, through his interest procured the attendance of the organist, who played several beautiful pieces of music. Undoubtedly, it is a wonderful instrument, the tones sweet and melodious beyond everything I ever heard, the number and variety of stops unparalleled. Judging by the ear I should have supposed the sounds produced by a complete and full orchestra of the first musicians.

After spending four hours in this far-famed town, we proceeded along the banks of a large and beautiful new canal, then recently finished, to the equally celebrated town of Leyden, so famous for its University that has sent into the world some of the most learned men and profound scholars that ever lived. Leyden is about eighteen miles from Haarlaem. There we slept, and rising early went to view the colleges, library, observatory, &c., all of which are magnificent and well worthy the attention of strangers. After a day replete with entertainment, we in the evening continued our journey, seventeen miles, to Rotterdam, considered the second city of Holland in point of opulence and extent. Having made an excellent supper, we retired to our chambers for the night.

The next day Mr. Swainston took me to all the public edifices, of which I found none that pleased me so much as the East India House, a superb building, delightfully situated upon the edge of a noble river that runs through the city, upon which were laying at anchor innumerable vessels of all sizes and of every nation in Europe, altogether constituting one of the grandest scenes I ever beheld.

Though in every respect very superior, it brought to my recollection our mild and gentle Thames at Chelsea.

From Rotterdam our next stage was Delft. Stopping only to change horses we went on five miles more to The Hague, an uncommonly pretty village where the Stadtholder has a palace in a beautiful park. Driving to the principal hotel, we there engaged apartments. After which we, according to the etiquette of the place, went to leave our cards at Sir Joseph Yorke's, the British Ambassador.

During our breakfast the next morning. Mr. Maddison, Secretary to the Embassy, was announced. He came in the name of Sir Joseph Yorke to invite us to dinner, also to request that I would call in the course of the morning, the Ambassador being desirous of conversing with me upon the subject of our India affairs. Mr. Maddison seemed an accomplished gentleman. After chatting about an hour, I returned with him to Sir Joseph's, to whom I was introduced and found him a truly elegant man of fashion. He received me with the utmost affability. After asking a variety of questions respecting the general state of our Settlements, especially Bengal, with the internal Government and politics of which he seemed to be well acquainted, and upon which he gave his opinion freely, a pause ensued, which, as I imagined it might be intended as a hint for me to conclude my visit, I rose, whereupon he enquired whether I had any business to do at The Hague in which he could in any way assist me. To this I replied, I rose from an apprehension I was trespassing upon his Excellency's time, that I had no business whatever, my object being to reach England as early as possible. He then said, " Since that is the case, I must beg of you to resume your seat, having still much to say." I obeyed. He asked me if I was acquainted with the Barwell family in Bengal. I told him I was, and had been intimate with Daniel Barwell, who was drowned upon the coast of Holland. " Yes, he was," said Sir Joseph, " and that unhappy accident occasioned me infinite concern and vexation."

Sir Joseph then related the particulars and the uncommon

pains he had taken to satisfy himself, as well as the relatives
of the deceased, that there was not the least foundation for
a report that had gone abroad of his having been murdered
by the people of the ship and robbed of jewels and cash to
a great amount, but had actually fallen a sacrifice to his
reliance upon superior skill in swimming. "And now,
sir," he continued, "I'll leave you to judge whether I have
not reason to complain of the manner in which I have been
treated." He then took from his escritoire a letter, and
gave it to me. Upon perusal I found it was from Miss
Mary Barwell, couched in the coarsest and most scurrilous
terms. After abusing the Ambassador for what she calls
"his shameful negligence and infamous dereliction of his
duty as representative of the British nation," she directly
charges him with conniving at a base murder from interested
motives, nothing short of participating in the plunder, most
impudently concluding her libellous address by requiring
him to declare what his share of the spoil from her cruelly
murdered brother's property amounted to. I was surprized
and shocked at so disgraceful a letter being written to a
man of Sir Joseph Yorke's unblemished character. Returning the strange epistle, I could only observe the writer must
be insane. Sir Joseph with mildness replied, he understood the lady was very eccentric and odd, adding, "I
immediately dispatched to her documents of so indisput-
able a nature as must have satisfied the mind of any unprejudiced person of the folly of crediting for a moment
the injurious report of Mr. Barwell's being murdered. She
nevertheless protested all those papers were forged and
fabricated."

In the midst of this interesting conversation, the steward
came into the room to say it was within a few minutes of
three o'clock, the hour of dining. Sir Joseph thereupon
apologized for having detained me so long. "However,"
continued he, "there can be no occasion for your leaving
the house now, and I will be ready in five minutes." He
then ordered the steward to summon Mr. Maddison to the
study that I might not be alone. Mr. Maddison instantly

entering the apartment, said, " You must have interested
the Ambassador greatly, for he has neglected some matters
of considerable importance which were by his own desire
to have been settled this morning."

At a quarter-past three, a company of twenty were
assembled, amongst whom were my fellow-traveller, Mr.
Swainston, three young men of fashion in their tour of
Europe, Dr. Fisher, the celebrated musician who married
the widow of Powell, the actor, and La Motte, the famous
performer upon the violin. The latter appeared actually
like a corpse, and was evidently in the last stage of a consumption. The rest of the party consisted of some of the
principal Dutchmen of the place and the Ambassador's
family. Sir Joseph desired me to take the chair next to him
upon his left, and did the honours of his table with the
greatest affability and condescension, dividing his attentions
equally amongst all his guests. Having heard of my intention of passing through Flanders, and my reason for so
doing, he assured me it was unnecessary and would considerably protract my arrival in England, besides encountering a fatiguing journey. He therefore advised me
by all means to proceed by Helvoetsluys and cross from
thence[to Harwich in the regular packet, one only of which
had been captured during the war, although they were
passing and repassing three times a week. Under such an
opinion it would have been the extreme of folly not to do
as Sir Joseph recommended. I was not, however, sorry
to hear three days would elapse before a packet sailed, as
Sir Joseph had insisted upon my attending each of those
days at his house.

His Excellency having expressed a wish to see the petition
of which I was the bearer, I presented him with a copy.
After perusal he declared it to be a masterly and elegant
piece of writing. At night he took us into his box at the
theatre, where there were a set of very good French
comedians. From thence we returned to supper, and at half-
past twelve retired to our hotel. The following morning (the
27th) Mr. Maddison called, as he said, by the Ambassador's

desire to conduct me and Mr. Swainston to the Stadt-holder's Palace. We found it superb, both in point of architecture and furniture. It also contained a choice and rare collection of paintings, as well as one of the finest libraries in Europe. The grounds were laid out with taste, the park abounding with game, an extensive menagerie and aviary stocked with the choicest beasts and birds. Viewing these premises occupied us until it was time to dress for dinner.

At a little after three o'clock Mr. Swainston and I again went to the Ambassador's, where we were treated with similar elegance to the preceding day, all the musical talents of The Hague being collected. I was astonished to see how voraciously La Motte eat. He was reduced to a mere skeleton, skin only covering the bones, pale and melancholy countenance, yet notwithstanding all this there was something interesting in his figure and appearance. He was so reduced and weak he could not walk without help. Ill as he was, he led the band (which was capitally good) the first piece, and afterwards played a solo with such pathos and feeling as to draw tears from the eyes of many of the auditors. The tones he drew from the violin were peculiarly sweet and affecting. When he had finished his solo, Sir Joseph Yorke asked me if I had not been much pleased. I replied that I never had been so much gratified by any performer. " Poor man," said Sir Joseph, " I fear his melodious and touching strains are nearly over." These fears were too well founded. We had heard the last notes he was ever to produce ; he expired the following morning, dying without a pang or even a sigh, closing his eyes as if in a pleasant sleep. He was no more than twenty-seven years of age.

The morning of the 28th I spent in a ride to a fishing village called Sceveling, where stood a handsome pavilion commanding an extensive view over the ocean towards the North Sea. Here was served up a collation consisting of at least a dozen different sorts of fish, all fresh caught and admirably dressed. We had besides various dishes of cold meat, ices, fruits, &c. At two o'clock we returned to The Hague to prepare for dinner at a Dutch burgomaster's, who entertained the whole of the Ambassador's party of the preceding day with great sumptuousness. In the evening there was a concert of vocal and instrumental music, but the recent loss of so superior a performer and so fine a young man as La Motte threw a damp upon all present. Everybody seemed dejected, so that in less than an hour, without any order being given, the music ceased, and was supplied by cards and conversation until supper, after which I took a respectful leave of Sir Joseph Yorke and his family, shook my late travelling companion, Mr. Swainston, cordially by the hand, and lay down for a couple of hours.

At three in the morning, taking Nabob with me in a chaise, we left The Hague for Helvoetsluys, distant twenty-four miles. On our road we crossed an inlet of the sea called the Great Maes, which is four miles broad, at ten reached my destination, having thus gone about one hundred and fifty miles through the most beautiful part of Holland. I was very lucky by finding a packet actually getting under way on my arrival, into which with my little Bengally, one large and one small trunk, I immediately got, when setting sail we bent our course towards old England, running at the rate of ten knots an hour. When about two-thirds over we had an alarm from two very suspicious-looking vessels apparently exerting every endeavour to come up with us, but fortunately we being to windward they could not fetch us. Every person on board the packet pronounced them to be French privateers. At eight at night we landed at Harwich.

CHAPTER XIX

"MRS. POTT"

MR. WILKINSON having given me a letter to a friend of his in the Custom House, who he said would have it in his power to expedite the clearance of my trunks, I sent a waiter with it from the Three Cups Inn, and my compliments, inviting him, if disengaged, to sup with me, as I proposed, if possible, proceeding to London by break of day. In less than half an hour he came. I found him a very gentlemanlike man. He thanked me for bringing the letter from Mr. Wilkinson, for whom he expressed a great regard. He said that in consequence of my wish to go on he had sent for one of the office searchers to come to the inn directly, which would prevent my detention till the office opened. Before supper was announced this person came, whereupon I opened my large trunk, at the same time slipping three guineas into his hand. The man bowed low, and, looking at the gentleman, the latter said, "Mr. Hickey tells me he has nothing but what is for his own use. Do not therefore disturb the packing." The man made another profound bow, and shutting the trunk left the room.

Thus, as matters turned out, had the trunk been full of shawls and other India goods, the whole would have been safe, but alarmed at what I had been told in Amsterdam I had with me only one article I cared about. This was a Japanese cloak I had purchased for my father to travel in, being, although of great warmth, lighter than the thinnest cloth. It cost me two hundred and fifty dollars at the Cape of Good Hope.

At ten we sat down to supper, drank a couple bottles of claret, which brought it to midnight, when my guest went to his own house, and I to bed until five in the morning, at which hour I dashed off in a chaise and four for Mistley Thorn, the first stage, from thence to Colchester, where I breakfasted, then to Witham, next to Ingatestone, at which place Nabob complaining of hunger, I stopped that he might appease his craving and, not to be quite unemployed, I took a sandwich.

From Ingatestone I went to Romford and thence to London, driving to the East India House in Leadenhall Street in order to deliver a small packet addressed to the Court of Directors, which I brought from Captains Gore and Lenox. This I gave into the hands of the Secretary at six o'clock in the evening of the 30th of June, 1780. From the India House I proceeded to St. Albans Street, where I found my three sisters, my father being upon his annual summer excursion to Paris and my brother out of town.

As I had not dined, my sister Mary ordered a hot supper to be got ready as quickly as could be. A little before nine Mr. Richard Burke, brother to the great Edmund Burke, came in and stayed to partake of the supper. Being an old admirer of Mrs. Sulivan, wife of Mr. Stephen Sulivan, both of whom I left in Bengal, he made particular enquiries about her, which brought forward many anecdotes and circumstances of former times. This, and the bottle to which we made frequent application, beguiled the time so that Mr. Burke, taking out his watch, exclaimed, " Zounds ! I could not have believed it. Do you know it is past four o'clock ? " We thereupon parted and retired to rest.

Excess in wine and fatigue together operated so that I slept until near noon. After breakfast, taking a coach, I proceeded with the petition and documents to the chambers of Mr. Irvine in the Temple, who, jointly with Mr. Touchet, was appointed agent for managing the business in Parliament. Mr. Irvine was a solicitor of eminence, and Mr. Touchet brother to the gentleman in the Company's civil service in Bengal and just called to the Bar. Mr.

From a mezzotint engraving by Norman Hirst. Copyright Thomas Agnew & Sons.

Miss Hickey

After the portrait by Sir Joshua Reynolds.

by permission of the owner The Rt Hon. Frederick Leverton Harris, M.P.

Touchet being sent for, the packet was opened and the contents examined in my presence. After perusal of the papers, Mr. Irvine observed that in their instructions from the committee they were particularly directed to consult me in every stage of the business, and should therefore take care to give me timely notice of their proceedings. From the Temple I went with Mr. Touchet to his mother's house in Newman Street, having a letter for her from her son in Calcutta. I found her a remarkably cheerful, pleasant old lady, with whom I promised to dine the following day.

My next visit was to Bryanston Street to deliver a parcel to Mrs. Greer, wife of the chief officer of the *Nassau*. She was an uncommonly fine woman, with three beautiful daughters, the eldest of whom some years afterwards married my *Seahorse* shipmate, Arnott.

Upon my return home, my sister informed me of the death of my favourite, Tom Forrest, he having lost his life from a wound received on board Lord Rodney's ship at the first relief of Gibraltar, at which I was greatly concerned. From my sister I also learnt the horrors of the riots that had occurred three weeks prior to my arrival, which from their novelty and violence paralysed the inhabitants of the metropolis from one extremity to the other, and from the consequences of which they had not yet recovered. I saw upon entering the city some of the effects, and large parties of military, both horse and foot, upon duty in different places, especially at the Bank and in St. Paul's Churchyard. These excesses commenced on the 4th of June, the King's birthday, continuing with unabated fury the 5th, 6th, and 7th.

The 2nd (of July), Mr. Touchet and Mr. Irvine paid me the compliment of a visit in St. Albans Street, as did Mr. Paxton, of Buckingham Street, who, although I had never seen him before, I instantly knew from his likeness to his brother in Bengal, William, now Sir William Paxton, about whom he came to enquire. Mr. Archibald Paxton and I soon became intimate, and were afterwards much together.

Enquiring what was become of my old and sincere friend Mr. Cane, I had the mortification to hear he was completely ruined, and as the only means of avoiding being imprisoned by his creditors had left England, settling with his family in the South of France. Stephen Popham, who attended Sir John Day to India, had been the chief instrument of my poor friend's embarrassments, by having prevailed upon him to join in various bonds as his (Popham's) security, which he consented to do under the most positive assurances that these bonds should be taken up and discharged previously to their respectively becoming due, instead of which he absconded, leaving Mr. Cane alone responsible for the whole to an amount of upwards of ten thousand pounds.

At Mrs. Touchet's I met a pleasant party of eight, among whom was Miss Touchet, a clever woman, also two fine lads, Westminsters, named Imhoff, being sons of Mrs. Hastings by her former husband. The old lady treated us most hospitably, her son, two other gentlemen, and myself doing justice to her excellent burgundy and claret. We did not break up until twelve at night.

On returning home I found a smart fellow in livery waiting to deliver a letter, which he said his mistress had sent him with at seven in the evening, ordering him to wait for an answer no matter how long it might be before he obtained one. It was from Emily Warren, saying she had that moment heard of my arrival and entreated I would immediately call upon her. Enclosed in hers was a letter from my friend Bob Pott, to whom I had written from Amsterdam to announce being in that city on my way to England. This was an answer lamenting his being under the necessity of leaving London for Portsmouth, where he was to embark for Bengal in a ship commanded by Captain Collett. He also gave a short account of all that had occurred during his sojourn in Great Britain, dwelling much upon his unbounded love for Emily who had lived with him a year and a half, and who would have accompanied him to India could he have procured a passage for her. This, he said,

he could not by any means effect, although at his sugges-
tion Emily agreed to put on the disguise of boy's clothes,
in which dress he attempted to pass her as his servant, but
Captain Collett's penetration at once saw the deception,
and he told Pott it could not be as it would lose him the
command of the ship and be his ruin. He (Pott) was consequently compelled to leave her behind.

Thus circumstanced, Pott said he relied upon my friendship and regard for him to bring out his darling Emily with
me, which, if I should fail in my endeavours to do by an
English Indiaman, I might easily accomplish on board a
French, Swedish, or Danish ship. He told me he was rendered miserable at being separated from her, nothing saving
him from utter despair but the certainty he felt that I
would not forsake him in his distress and sorrow. He
further said he had left Emily in a handsome, well-furnished
house in Cork Street, the rent of which he had paid fifteen
months in advance, besides abundantly stocking it with all
sorts of wines, coals, candles, and every article of house-
keeping sufficient for the same period, and had likewise left
her a carriage and pair of beautiful horses which he had
himself driven in his phaeton. Pott concluded by entreating me to pass as much of my time as possible with his
dearest girl, whom he had prepared to love me, which he
was sure she would do for his sake, and he referred me to
her for a thousand particulars respecting them both.

I wrote a short answer to Emily merely to say I would
be with her by eleven o'clock the next morning, and then
retired to bed, from which I was roused before eight, my
father's servant saying a lady in a carriage was waiting for
me at the corner of Pall Mall, seeming extremely impatient ;
and that he had objected to disturbing me so soon, whereupon she eagerly said she must see me, putting half a guinea
into his hand.

Hastily putting on my clothes, I went down the street,
where I saw a dashing bright yellow vis-à-vis having Pott's
arms emblazoned thereon, an elegant pair of bright bay
horses, the coachman and footman in smart frocks of blue

faced with yellow and trimmed with a broad silver lace.
But what was all this outside show compared to the lovely
creature within, looking more than mortal ? Never did I
behold so perfect a beauty.

I had seen this divine woman in 1776, then an unripe and
awkward girl, but with features of exquisite beauty. That
experienced old *matron*, Charlotte Hayes, who then kept a
house of celebrity in King's Place, where I often visited, had
just got hold of her as an advantageous prize, and I have
frequently seen the little sylph, Emily, under the tuition of
the ancient dame learning to walk, a qualification Madam
Hayes considered of importance, and in which her pupil
certainly excelled, Emily's movements and air being Grace
personified and attracting universal admiration whenever
she appeared abroad.

Sir Joshua Reynolds, whom all the world allowed to be
a competent judge, had painted Emily's portrait many
times and in different characters. He often declared every
limb of hers perfect in symmetry, and altogether he had
never seen so faultless and finely formed a human figure.

Upon my approaching the carriage I thought she would
have leapt out of it into my arms. Accepting her proffered
hand she eagerly drew me towards her, saying, " Come in,
come in, my dear fellow, for so you who are such a favourite
of my angel Robert's ever must be." Stepping into the
carriage, she almost devoured me with kisses, laughed,
cried, and was nearly in hysterics, to the surprize and entertainment of several persons who were passing at the time.

Recovering a little, Emily ordered the coachman to
drive home. In vain did I remonstrate and say that being
just as I jumped out of bed I must go and dress myself.
Besides, my sisters would wait breakfast. It did not
signify, go with her I positively should, aye, and stay too.
She said I might write, send, do anything except leave her ;
that she had several servants, all of whom should go wherever I required them, and if they were not sufficient she
would hire chairmen ; that if I wanted more sleep I might
go to bed at her house and no one should disturb me. In

short, had I been disposed to resist the importunities of this angelic creature, which I undoubtedly was not, it would not have been in my power.

To Cork Street we drove, where she conducted me into a parlour that was neatness itself. After kissing me again and again with the utmost ardour and affection, she asked whether I really wished for more rest, for if I did a bed-chamber should be ready in five minutes. I assured her nothing could induce me to lay down but her accompanying me, at which she smiled, saying, " Oh, you sad man, would you treat your friend, whose wife I am, so basely ? " and with more gravity added, " *That* must not be yet, whatever we may do hereafter." She then took me over the house, which was as complete a one as ever I saw in every respect, after which she said, " Now, my friend, this house and *all* it contains " (laying a strong emphasis upon the word *all*) "carriages, servants, and everything are at your disposal. You must consider them, and make use of them as your own, for such was our dear Bob's desire, and such is my earnest request."

At nine we sat down to breakfast. While at table another letter arrived from Robert. She left the room for a few minutes and upon her return, putting her arms round my neck, eagerly said, " Oh, my dear, dear friend, you must comply with our Robert's desire and take me to Portsmouth that I may once more embrace him ere he leaves England." She then put his letter into my hands. It was addressed to me as well as to her, as he concluded I should be in London, begging and praying me to get into a chaise and run down with Emily, the wind being west and no appearance of a change.

I was forced to yield, whereupon with impetuosity Emily rang for her servant, whom she ordered to get four horses for the chaise and another for the groom. I then told her it was impossible for me to leave town that day, having business of importance to transact. Most unwillingly she at last consented to wait until the following morning upon condition that I would send my portmanteau and sleep at her house that night that we might set off very early. Finding me solicitous to return home she ordered her vis-à-vis to convey me, bidding the coachman obey me throughout the day, nor would she suffer me to go without her servant behind, observing it would be dangerous for the coachman to leave the box. Thus attended therefore I proceeded to St. Albans Street, where I found my brother just come to town.

Upon quitting Emily she told me, although she had sent a letter to me with the signature of Warren, she had long dropped that name, assuming that of Pott. This appeared to me strange, nor could I then account for it.

My brother, who saw me drive up to the door, after the usual congratulations and greetings, remarked I had lost no time in making an acquaintance with Mrs. Pott, " And faith," said he, " you are in high luck to be already upon such terms with a woman many of the fashionable young men would give their little fingers to procure a bow or acknowledgment of acquaintance from."

Having dressed, paid my devoirs to my sisters and promised to dine with them, I proceeded in *my* vis-à-vis to the India House, where Mr. Holt, Secretary to the Company, received me with great warmth, my brother having once rendered him a considerable service. While sitting with him an old acquaintance came in. This was the Honourable William Elphinstone, who had commanded the *Triton* Indiaman when I went first to Madras and China, and he expressed much satisfaction at the meeting. Mr. Holt told me this gentleman was become a Director.

I had not called at half the places I intended when I saw it was three o'clock. I therefore drove home and dismissed my carriage, writing a note to thank Emily for the use of it, adding that I should come to her house from the Haymarket Theatre, where I was to go at night with my brother. As the hours were more reasonable in those days than at present I found dinner waiting for me, Mr. Richard Burke, sen., and Mr. William Burke being the only guests. The latter was preparing to return to India overland, he having been appointed agent for the Rajah of Travancore.

After a cheerful meal and plentiful dose of claret, I retired to my room to equip myself in one of my gay India coats, being of scarlet with a rich spangled and foil lace, made from one of Sir Thomas Rumbold's, and of which I was not a little vain. Upon my return to the drawing-room my dress was greatly admired, my brother only re-marking he thought it a little too gaudy.

Having taken coffee, we four men went to Foote's, getting seats in the balcony, opposite which I soon descried one of my Streatham chums in the Junior Lovelace, then a Cornet of Dragoons. Observing him look at the box I was in, smile, and quit his seat to come round, I concluded he recognized me as I had him, and upon his entering the box I was in held out my hand. Then it was I found he did not recollect me, whereupon I mentioned my name. He shook hands with much warmth, expressing pleasure at the meeting. "But," said he, "I had no idea of your being an acquaintance. Seeing so unusual a dress brought me round to look nearer at the wearer of it, who I pre-sumed could be no other personage than the *Lord Mayor's trumpeter*." This facetious speech raised a laugh against me from all who heard it, at which I was not a little dis-concerted. It, however, put me so much out of conceit with my finery that I determined not only to get rid of it immediately, but also of upwards of twenty coats equally ornamented and rich that I had brought from Bengal.

Whilst engaged in conversation with Lovelace, Mr. Richard Burke said, "Who can that beautiful woman in yonder side box be nodding and making signs to ? They seem to be directed this way." Scarcely had he said so when the box door opened, and one of the fruit women whis-pered me that Mrs. Pott desired I would come down to her, she having a place kept for me. Casting my eyes across the house, I saw the beauteous Emily in all the splendour of most fashionable dress, looking like an angel, seated in the front row of the side box next but one to the

stage, an elegant-looking woman being on one side of her
and a handsome young man on the other. The moment she
caught my eye, she beckoned and made all sorts of signs for
me to come to her, which I hesitated doing from a disinclination to exhibit my trumpeter's coat in so conspicuous
a part of the theatre and before a crowded audience, but
Lovelace saying aloud, "Why the devil don't you obey
Emily's summons, Hickey? She certainly will be up here
in five minutes if you do not go down to her," I thought
it prudent to comply, and wishing my party a good night
I descended, escorted by the fruit woman, who desired a
box-keeper to open the door of Mrs. Pott's box, upon
entering which I observed there was no seat vacant, when
the gentleman on her right hand instantly rising, politely
said, "This, sir, is your place," and in spite of my remonstrances relinquished it, slightly bowing as he passed out.

If I felt doubtful respecting my dress, I had still more
reason to be abashed at Emily's reception. I thought
she would have embraced me. Taking hold of both my
hands, she said, "Now I have once more got you by my side
I shall take good care not to part with you again." Her
manner towards me drew the attention of the whole house
upon us, which made me entreat her to be less ardent. At
my gravity she laughed heartily, adding she was too happy
to be considerate, and could not help betraying her regard
for *her bashful swain !* I told her what had occurred about
my dress, to which she replied, "Lovelace is an impertinent
coxcomb. It was sheer envy in him, who would give his
ears for a similar coat. It is an elegant and becoming suit,
and I'll venture to assert there is not a better dressed
man in the theatre. Your hair, too, is charming. Pray who
is your operator ? Is it your own servant ? " I told her
it was dressed by one of Courtoy's men, an Italian named
Freskini ; that he was not above ten minutes about it, and
had intimated a wish that I would take him as a servant.
Emily recommended me to secure him forthwith as an abso-
late treasure, and I took her advice.

Enquiring who the handsome young man was that had

so civilly resigned his seat to me, Emily told me it was the handsome Jack St. Leger, sworn friend and companion of the Prince of Wales, " but," added she, " he is lately returned from the West Indies with a dreadful fever which has reduced him, poor fellow, most dreadfully, and he is by no means himself yet." She further told me that he was intimate with my father and sister, attending all the parties in St. Albans Street, and she was sure he would be a prodigious favourite of mine. She then lamented that she had not introduced us to each other.

The play and farce being over, I accompanied Emily to Cork Street, where we supped, after which she showed me to a neat bedchamber which she said was over her own, and saluting, wished me a good night. I observed that this was tantalizing me with a vengeance, whereupon she gave me another hearty kiss, saying, " To-morrow night I hope to have Robert in my arms, but when he, poor fellow, has quitted the kingdom you will be next to my heart, *and then !* " She once more embraced me and ran out of the room.

As I always made a point of being punctual, I was up and equipped for the journey ten minutes before the time fixed for departure, when Emily tapped at my door and immediately entered. She looked, if possible, handsomer than ever, was most becomingly dressed in a green riding-habit, trimmed with gold frogs. For the first time I was the assailer, seizing her in my arms and glueing my mouth to her enchanting lips, nor was she backward in meeting it.

At a quarter before five we were seated by each other in Emily's own post-chaise, which had every convenience for travelling a carriage could, and was in every respect as elegantly finished as her vis-à-vis. Both were the work of the then celebrated Hatchet of Long Acre. We had four excellent post horses. Tearing away at a great rate we reached Kingston, our first stage, in an hour and a quarter. Two grooms, a man of about thirty and a lad of sixteen, set off with us, the boy riding in advance to prepare fresh horses and the man continuing by the chaise to pay the turnpikes.

When leaving Kingston I observed it would not be possible for the servants to keep on at the rate we were going, as they must knock up from fatigue, to which she replied, "Not they indeed, were it ten times the distance. Eighteen months ago they followed me to Holyhead when I was going to Ireland with Warren, who, by the by, I did not treat well, for I left him who was as liberal as man could be, and *adored me*, to go to Robert whom *I adored* and still *do adore !* "

We got to Guildford by half-past seven, breakfasted, and at eight went on to Godalming, then to Liphook and from thence to Petersfield. Whilst changing horses at the latter place Emily alighted, and, during her absence, the landlord said, "A glorious wind, sir, for the fleet." I asked what fleet he meant, to which he replied, "The East and West India, which sailed last night at ten o'clock." I directly mentioned this to Emily, who would not give credit to it. The landlord assured me an express had stopped at his house that morning at seven, going up to the India House with an account of the whole fleet being clear out at sea, with a fine breeze at north-north-east. Still Emily would not believe what she hoped was not true, so on we went to Portsmouth, which we reached at two in the afternoon.

The master of the George Inn coming to the door upon our driving up to it, Emily eagerly asked, "Are the India ships gone ? " To which the host answered, "Yes, ma'am, they sailed last night." Poor Emily burst into tears, and I apprehended would have fainted. I made them carry her into the house and lay her upon a bed. After a long fit of tears, I prevailed on her to drink some warm wine and lie still for a few hours. Like an infant she cried herself to sleep, as I thought, when I walked to the seaside, leaving a female servant to watch by her bedside.

Upon the beach I saw the two servants amusing themselves amongst the boat people, apparently as much at their ease as if they had only taken a morning's airing in Hyde Park. I asked them if they were not tired, when the lad sharply answered, "Tired, sir ! with what ? We have only rode seventy-four miles." "Well, my fine fellow," said I, " and if occasion required it could you set off for London again to-day ? " " Aye surely, sir," said both in a breath. A waiter of the inn that moment came up to say the lady wanted me, whereupon I walked back to the " George," at the door of which stood Emily's chaise with four horses to it, and saddle horses ready for the two servants.

Upon entering the house I met Emily, who entreated me to leave Portsmouth immediately. In vain did I importune her to take some nourishment first. She peremptorily refused and got into the chaise. I then went to the bar to ask what was to pay, and was told the lady had already paid the bill and for the horses to Petersfield. I therefore took my seat by her, and we drove off.

I felt somewhat surprized that, though indifferent about herself, Emily had not showed more attention towards me by at least asking whether I chose to eat or drink previous to leaving Portsmouth, as I had touched nothing since breakfast. I, however, kept my feelings on that score to myself, but remonstrated against her hasty return as likely to affect her health from over-fatigue and anxiety, upon which she assured me she often had travelled six-and-thirty hours without taking any food, and that she could not bring herself to stay at a place where she had received so bitter a disappointment. She told me she had not closed her eyes, and feigned sleep supposing I should then walk out ; that the moment I was gone she rose, paid the trifle that was due and ordered horses. Taking out my purse, I desired to know how much the expence amounted to so far, that I might reimburse her, an offer that greatly offended her, she saying that when she urged me to sacrifice my time and my own plans to accompany her, she had no idea of taxing me also with the expence, nor would she hear of it.

Observing the post-boys drove immoderately fast, I was about to call to them, which Emily begged I would not, and said that being anxious to get back to London, she had promised them a crown each if they went to Petersfield in two hours, which they did (notwithstanding some long and

steep hills) in twenty minutes less than the time stipulated.
We went at such a rate that the servants with difficulty
kept up.

Emily being very low-spirited, I endeavoured to engage
her in conversation by asking why she had not gone to
Portsmouth with Robert, to which she replied, " I would
have given the world to have done so, but one of his sisters,
her husband, and two children going with him made it
impossible " ; she added that they only left him the morning he wrote to beg she and I would come down. " And
now, pray let me ask you, my dear friend, whether you are
of the chameleon kind and can live upon air ? " accompanying her question by pulling out a drawer below the
seat, in which was a nice-looking roast chicken, cold tongue,
sandwiches of ham and beef, a bottle of madeira, with
glasses and all the etceteras. These things the kind girl
had procured at the " George " in the short time I was
absent. Being really very hungry, I eat voraciously, but
could not prevail upon her to touch anything except a
crust of the roll.

At Guildford, while changing horses, I compelled Emily
to drink a dish of strong coffee and take some toast with it,
after which we continued our progress, arriving in Cork
Street about twelve at night, having thus travelled a
distance of one hundred and forty miles in nineteen hours.

I found a note from my brother requesting me to come
immediately home. Fearing something had happened to
my father, I instantly walked to St. Albans Street, where
I had the happiness to learn from the servant that letters
had arrived from him in Paris that morning and that he was
perfectly well. I then went into the dining-room, where
a large party were sitting after supper. This party soon
breaking up, my brother asked whether I was indebted to
any person who was likely to molest me. I assured him I
was not. He then told me a man of very suspicious appearance had been four different times enquiring for me ; that
he (my brother) had said he could do anything that was
necessary on my behalf, but the man replied that would not

do and he must see me. He would not tell what his
business, was and walked away, the last time muttering to
himself, " By God, I'll watch you."

From my brother's description of the person I conceived
it might be Adcock just arrived from Holland, as he was to
leave Amsterdam in a Dutch vessel bound to London four
or five days after I quitted that place, having the rest of my
baggage under his care. My conjecture proved right. The
next morning Adcock was at the door before I had left
Emily's, and sat down in the hall until I came home. Upon
my asking the reason of his being so impertinent and refusing to tell his name or business, he said Mr. Wilkinson
cautioned him not to do so until he had seen me, and as to
being uncivil to my brother he did not know him, and the
boy Nabob told him he was only a clerk. He said everything belonging to me was safe, laying in a boat at Hunger-
ford Stairs, but that getting them over had cost an enormous
deal of money. Upon his producing his account, I found he
had expended altogether forty-six pounds sterling, five-and-
thirty of which Mr. Wilkinson had advanced. I dispatched
my father's servants with a cart, and in an hour afterwards
all my baggage was in the house.

Mr. Wilkinson wrote me that the day after I left him
a Dutch friend of his called at his office to ask if he had
anything he wanted conveyed to England privately, as he
had an opportunity of doing it with security and would
undertake they should be landed in the Thames above
London Bridge ; that he had closed with the person and,
as he conceived, on moderate terms, the whole being under
fifty pounds, whereas had one of the usual smugglers been
employed it would have cost double that sum. Thus was
I enabled to deliver to the Baroness Nolken and many others
the parcels I brought from India for them, and that free of
every expense, as I thought it would not be handsome to
make them pay a proportion of what I expended.

Having unpacked my trunks, I displayed all my fine
clothes to my sisters, but as Lovelace's speech had made
a great impression upon me, and I did not like the thoughts

of being mistaken for a *trumpeter*, I resolved to get rid of the stock. I therefore applied to our old servant, Mary Jones, who had been in the family prior to my birth, desiring she would obtain the best price she could for them. I, however, retained a full suit of beautiful velvet of four colours, which I knew must always be in fashion, and two others of those least ornamented with lace. The rest were carried off the same morning by a Monmouth Street salesman, who paid me forty-seven guineas for what had, I suppose, cost me seven times that sum, and most of them were nearly new.

CHAPTER XX

MORE LONDON DAYS

I NOW wrote to my father, at Paris, to announce my arrival and the business that brought me, upon the subject of which I embellished a little, taking special care also to assure him I came with ample funds for the time I should remain in England. I had just finished and dispatched my letter when Emily sent her vis-à-vis for my use, stepping into which I went to a tailor named Knill, to whom I had been recommended as a fit person to equip me *comme il faut.*

He advised my having a dark green with gold binding, dark brown with the same, a plain blue, and for half dress a Bon de Paris with gold frogs, all which he spoke of as being much worn and of the highest *ton.* I bespoke the four suits accordingly. My next calls were at Rymer's for boots, Wagner for hats, and Williams of Bond Street for leather breeches. In three days I was to come forth a proper " Bond Street lounger," a description of person then just coming into vogue. The rest of the morning was filled up in visits to my friends.

During this round my vis-à-vis was stopped several times by fashionable people who, knowing the carriage and liveries, halload to the coachman, to draw to the side, concluding the much-admired Emily was within, instead of which they found an ugly male stranger. Amongst these disappointed heroes were His Grace of Queensberry, Lord Carlisle, Charles Wyndham, Harry Greville, and Colonel Fitzpatrick, against each of whom my fair friend afterwards had a hearty laugh.

261

Having promised to dine in Cork Street, I drove there and found Nabob already housed and quite at home, Emily having taken a great liking to him. Indeed, he was a little pet with all the ladies, being an interesting-looking handsome boy. I dressed him, too, very smart as a Hussar. As a servant he was not of the least use to me.

There came to dine with Emily, Harriet Powell, an old flame of mine, who had been a contemporary of Emily's at Charlotte Hayes's, and they had continued uninterrupted friends thenceforward. Powell was in high keeping, and drove to the door in an elegant chariot of her own. The fourth of the party was a gentleman dressed in the very extremity of the fashion, having a valuable diamond ring upon one of his fingers. He also arrived in his own carriage, and was introduced to me by the name of "Mount." I afterwards found him to be the only son of the great stationer upon Tower Hill, under the firm of Mount and Page. His father, being immensely rich, allowed this young coxcomb to squander what he pleased. I soon discovered Mr. Mount was no small favourite of Emily's. The dinner and wines being of the best, and Mr. Mount no flincher at the glass, by seven o'clock we had disposed of a tolerable quantity of champagne. We therefore adjourned to the play-house, going in Harriet Powell's carriage and returning in the same to supper.

At a late hour we broke up, and I was preparing to go home when Emily said she must speak to me. Mr. Mount at that moment drew her aside, when a whispering conversation took place between them. He seemed angry. In a few minutes she wished him good night and, coming up to me, said, "I have so much to say to you we must not part yet." She then led me, not to the chamber I had before slept in, but to her own room, where I passed a night that many would have given thousands to do.

Although to look upon Emily was to look upon perfection as far as figure and features went, yet my continued intimate acquaintance with her convinced me that she was totally void of feeling, and was indeed cold as ice,

Notwithstanding this I believe she was sincerely attached to Pott, loving him as much as she was capable of loving anyone. I also believe that her partiality to me rose entirely from her knowing the affectionate regard he entertained for me. Of a common failing of her sex she possessed a large portion, that is, love of admiration and flattery. She was, too, with all her personal accomplishments, vain, weak, extravagant, and ignorant. As to the latter, that is not extraordinary her life and origin considered. Charlotte Hayes met her in the streets of London when not quite twelve years of age leading her father, a blind beggar, about, soliciting charity from every person that passed. Struck with the uncommon beauty of the child's countenance, she set her myrmidons to work and, without difficulty, soon got her into her clutches. The young beggar proved an apt scholar, so far as walking and common address went. She could neither read nor write, though by no means deficient or awkward in conversation, nor do I recollect ever to have heard her make use of a vulgarism or a phrase that could mark her illiterateness. I had been acquainted with her some time before I discovered the deficiency. True, I often observed that upon her receiving a letter or note in my presence she always left the room. I had frequently written to and received answers from her, but never saw a book in her hand or in the house. At last I asked the meaning of this, when she candidly declared her ignorance. Upon expressing my surprize thereat she said she had never had time to attend to learning, nor been connected with any person sufficiently interested about her to induce the acquirements of reading and writing until she went to Bob Pott, who intended to have been her instructor himself on the passage to India, but unfortunately he failed in his endeavours to get her on board ship. This discovery, mortifying as it was to her vanity, was attended with some advantages as, instead of running upon every occasion to her cook, her long-established amanuensis and secretary, I often officiated in reading and answering her *billets-doux*, by which means I discovered her incontinence, and that attachment to her absent love was no bar to her amours. Somewhat hurt at my finding out this infirmity (which, by the by, I had from my first acquaintance suspected) she solemnly protested that whilst living with her dearest Robert she had never once gone astray or known another man, an assertion I very much doubted the truth of.

On the 6th (July) I was engaged to dine in St. Albans Street to meet my favourite, Miss Cecilia Forrest, Mr. and Mrs. Broadhead, the Duke of Hamilton, Sir Watts Horton, and other *tonish* friends of my eldest sister. It being my first meeting with Miss Forrest, she cried much from recollecting her brother Tom's great attachment to me. In the evening she presented me with a lock of his hair, observing it would be a melancholy memento of my deceased friend and companion. I immediately had the hair set in a pair of sleeve buttons with his cypher and have worn them from that time to the present day.

At night Major St. Leger came in, when my sister introduced me to him. Smiling, he observed, " Although not personally acquainted we have met before," alluding to the play-house scene with Emily. My brother could not endure this gentleman from his coxcombry and insolent hauteur, neither of which failings could I ever perceive. In dress he was like every other young man of fashion, and so far from foolish pride that when, as frequently was the case, I have met him walking arm in arm with the Prince of Wales he, notwithstanding the elevated rank of his companion, always saluted and spoke to me with the utmost good humour and affability.

My brother having heard me say I wished to purchase a couple of saddle horses, proposed our going to Fozard's livery stables near Hyde Park Corner, both he and my father having kept their horses there and dealt with him for several years. We accordingly walked up, and he immediately furnished me with two capital horses for which I paid sixty guineas, a sum they were well worth, turning out remarkably well. I had also the use of an Irish mare belonging to my sister, who had left off riding, so that I was tolerably supplied with horseflesh and generally rode two or three hours every day.

On the 8th I dined again in Cork Street. At night Emily conveyed me to Vauxhall, she having heard me say I was fond of that entertainment, meeting several acquaintances there of both sexes. We formed a large party at supper, having French horns and clarionets playing to us until near three in the morning and drinking burnt champagne the whole time. About that hour we drove home.

The following morning after breakfast Emily took me in her carriage to view the various scenes of desolation and enormity committed by the rioters; dreadful and shocking to behold they were. We first drove to the ruins of Langton's distillery in Holborn, then to that of the Fleet prison and Newgate, the toll houses on Blackfriars Bridge, proceeding to the King's Bench in St. George's Fields. The city and suburbs were still filled with the military, regular guards continuing to be mounted daily at the Bank, St. Paul's, the Old Bailey, and several other public buildings. There were several large encampments in and about London; one in St. James's Park, another in Hyde Park, a third in the gardens of the Museum, and a fourth in St. George's Fields. While looking on and expressing my surprize that such excesses could have been committed in the very heart of the metropolis, the coachman, who had witnessed some of the outrages, assured me that at the commencement none were engaged in it but a parcel of the most abandoned women and boys of from ten to fifteen years old, and, he was convinced, twenty resolute men might have dispersed the whole, but everyone seemed helpless and inactive, from which, and the mob finding themselves unopposed, their numbers accumulated, being joined by pickpockets, horse-breakers, and thieves of every description. He told me that at midnight of the 6th of June he counted no less than eleven dreadful conflagrations, all raging with the utmost fury at one and the same time.

This most extraordinary event which struck the inhabitants of London with horror and dismay originated in the fanaticism, or perhaps it would be more candid, and nearer the truth, to say, in the insanity of Lord George Gordon, son to the Duke of Gordon, and with whom I was upon the excursion I have related from Mr. Cane's to France and other parts in the year 1776, at which time he was a reasonable and elegant young man.

On the 10th my brother and self went to dine with the kind-hearted Mr. Holt at Camberwell, where we were received and entertained by him and his good lady with the utmost hospitality. The party consisted of Lord Loughborough, the Chairman and Deputy of the Court of Directors, Sir George Colebrooke, Sir James Cockburn, and other men of rank and consequence in the City. We continued with him until a very late hour, and even then were obliged to steal away so unwilling was he to part with us.

About the middle of the month my father returned from Paris, when I had the happiness to see him looking quite as stout and well as when I left him in 1777. A few days after his return, while walking with him towards Fozard's, I was surprized at meeting Commodore Richardson, whom I left commanding the Bengal Marine. He told me he reached London only the evening before from Plymouth, at which place he had been landed from the ship that brought him home, and he said he was then going in search of me. My father invited him to a family dinner that day, which he accepted with apparent gratification. We talked over many circumstances that had occurred on the banks of the Ganges. From him I learnt that Major Walter Bourke had come home in the same ship with him and was very desirous of seeing me.

The Commodore, in the course of conversation, observed he was at a loss to decide in which country he should settle, England or Ireland, and that he intended visiting the latter soon. He then said to me, " I wish you, who I have so often heard express a desire to see that Island, would accompany me. Since we met this morning I went into a stable-yard, upon the door of which was a printed notification of a nearly new and fashionable post-chaise, with a pair of able horses, to be sold by auction that morning. Five minutes after I entered the lot was knocked down to me at two hundred and fifty guineas, and I was driven to my lodgings in the new purchase. My plan now is to buy a couple of common road horses for myself and servant, and thus to travel leisurely and by easy stages to Holyhead, cross to Dublin, and after passing a month, or at most six weeks, among relations and friends in Ireland, return to London."

This scheme I mightily approved, but was afraid the business of the petition I brought home might interfere ; I said that if that were not in the way I certainly would join him. My father thereupon observed nothing could be done until Parliament met, which would not be earlier than November, and as he approved of my visiting the sister kingdom, where many of his family lived who would rejoice to see me, I accepted the Commodore's offer. We thereupon agreed each to dispatch a trunk of clothes by the waggon, and I ordered my valet, Freskini, to hold himself in readiness to move with my horses. Upon mentioning my intended expedition to Emily, she expressed an earnest desire to be of the party, which I told her I had no doubt my travelling companion would willingly accede to.

A week after this Adcock called to say he heard I was going abroad, and hoped I would previous to so doing settle with him. As I conceived he meant payment for acting as steward of the ship from the Cape, although I knew Captain Paardakoper had liberally rewarded him, I presented him with a bank-note for twenty-five pounds, which he thankfully accepted, but said the settlement he wanted was of Mr. Paterson's money, the sum being of great consequence to him. To this I replied that my father, to whom I had spoken on the subject, had promised to speak to Lady Strathmore and persuade her to pay what was due. Whereupon Adcock departed, as I supposed, perfectly satisfied.

My father having been several times at Lady Strathmore's house without meeting with her, addressed a letter to her, commenting in strong terms upon the injustice of her behaviour towards Paterson, a young man of merit whom she had sent to a distant and savage clime to gratify her desire of collecting rare natural productions, a man who had been most industrious and zealous in her service, but who, instead of rewarding, according to his deserts, she had refused to do common justice to, whereby she had nearly consigned him to a prison in a strange land. To this letter the unworthy woman gave no answer. My father therefore resolved when I returned from Ireland to commence an action against her for breach of contract.

Three days prior to that fixed on for our setting out for Holyhead, I sent off two trunks by the waggon. The day after so doing I called at Mr. Richardson's lodgings in Clarges Street, where I was told he was gone out of town, but had left a letter to be given to me, opening which I found it filled with expressions of concern at being unable to proceed upon the proposed journey, an unexpected event having occurred that required his immediate presence in the north. He, however, hoped I would accompany him to Ireland in the spring. I enquired for his address, but the people either did not know it or were desired not to tell me. They said he had discharged his lodgings, saying he would occupy them again in about three months if then disengaged.

I felt vexed at the disappointment, giving Richardson credit at the same time for the truth of what he stated in his letter, nor had a suspicion to the contrary until calling upon Major Bourke he began to abuse Richardson for his unhandsome behaviour to me, observing he had given his opinion very undisguisedly thereon. Really at a loss to conjecture to what he alluded, I asked an explanation, when he replied, " Surely you must know that he left London the day before yesterday for Ireland, taking with him a little dirty strumpet whom he picked up at the theatre, and became violently attached to. He mentioned the circumstance to me, saying he felt awkward about you, and must make the best excuse he could." My blood boiled with anger upon receiving this information.

Having got Richardson's direction from Major Bourke, I wrote to him to lament I had ever been acquainted with so despicable and deliberate a liar, declaring I would proclaim him such wherever I heard his name mentioned. I had reason to know my letter reached him, yet, notwith standing his bearing a commission as lieutenant in the Royal Navy, and being a commodore of a squadron of fighting ships belonging to the East India Company, he never took the least notice of the language in which I had written to him. I was the more hurt at this duplicity of his from my sister having written to several friends in Ireland to prepare them for my visit.

Emily offered, and indeed pressed me, to set off with her, saying she would answer for it we reached Dublin before my blackguard India friend. Inclination would have led me to comply, but a moment's reflection convinced me of the impropriety of such a step, for how could I appear in the midst of my father's family and connections accompanied by a woman of Emily's character, and that, too, in Dublin, where she was as well known as in London? I therefore put a determined negative upon it. Thus ended my meditated excursion to Ireland, and I have never visited that country.

As I was returning one day from the City in Emily's vis-à-vis I saw my old *Plassey* shipmate, Sam Rogers, in the midst of a crowd collected in Cheapside. I stopped the carriage and called to him, whereupon he came up and was greatly surprized at seeing me whom he supposed to be in Bengal. We were mutually gratified at the meeting, having a sincere regard for each other. He told me he was on his way to Camberwell, where he lived with an uncle, and had stopped in the street to look at a boxing match between a hackney coachman and a carman ; that he had only been in England a fortnight, the Frenchmen that took his ship (the *Osterley*) having detained him a prisoner at the Mauritius, though they released Chatfield, his chief mate, a few days after reaching the Island, because, forsooth, they discovered that he was a freemason ! "And so," continued he, "finding some use in being *a brother*, I resolved when I got home to be *made*, as they call it, and am at this time one of the elect." He then, with his usual oath, swore that having thus unexpectedly met, he would not part so soon, but would bilk the old codgers and their fat ribs of Camberwell by dining with me at some coffee-house. This I could not refuse, though engaged to a pleasure party at Emily's. I therefore ordered the coachman to drive to the Bedford.

From the Bedford I sent the carriage home with a note to inform Emily of what had happened to prevent my coming to her. Sam insisted upon my ordering dinner, and he was sure then of having a good one. I did my best. Whilst waiting for its dressing, I saw Emily drive up to the piazza, and going to her, she said, "Very pretty this, Mr. William. Do you think to deceive me with your old shipmate and your Sam Rogers's ? Believe me it won't pass, so come along this moment, get into the carriage." I urged the impossibility of leaving my friend, and sending for him to the carriage door, I introduced him to Emily, who laughingly said, "I really thought you was deceiving me and was at your tricks, but as that is not the case, you must both come in. I can sit on your knee, William." Rogers, however, could not be persuaded, pleading deshabille, long beard, dirty shirt, &c. Emily, finding him determined, was obliged to leave us to our fate, unwillingly driving away alone.

Rogers informed me that his uncle and other friends had sent in proposals to the Court of Directors to build another ship in the place of the *Osterley*, which had been accepted, and the keel was to be laid immediately. At nine at night he set off for Camberwell and I to Cork Street.

The next day, being in the City, I heard of the ship *General Barker's* arrival, with Sir Thomas Rumbold and his family, also Mr. Strange of the Civil Service, with whom I had been very intimate at Madras. Although a young man, he had filled so lucrative a situation as to acquire a handsome fortune in the small space of six years. The same morning, passing through the Royal Exchange, I there met Mr. James Grant, who had preserved me and Jacob Rider from drowning when overset from a canoe at the Island of Joanna in the year 1769. He told me he had been in England a few months, had resigned the Company's service, and become a West India merchant in partnership with his elder brother, Peter ; that their office and town residence was in Colman Street, and that he had an excellent country house at the retired and pretty village of Drayton, between Uxbridge and Colnbrook, to which he gave me a pressing invitation to go and pass some time ; he said that he generally went down on Friday and remained until Tuesday. A gentleman was in company with him whose face was familiar to me, though I could not recollect when or where I had seen him, nor was I clear whether I ever had been acquainted with him or not. After Grant and I had interchanged civilities, his companion, addressing me, said, "You seem to have forgotten me, Mr. Hickey, although it is only two years since we were much together in Bengal. My name, sir, is Macintosh." I instantly recollected him as formerly a Lieutenant in the military service of the East India Company and afterwards a Captain of his own ship.

Upon entering the drawing-room at my father's, my sisters began to laugh heartily, the cause of which was a visitor who had just called to see me, whom they thus described. Notwithstanding the weather being unusually sultry and oppressive, he was completely enveloped from head to foot in shawls, appeared quite worn down by age and infirmity, dreadfully yellow complexion, more hideously ugly than any human creature they had ever beheld, and so deaf they with the utmost difficulty could make him hear a word. "Then," said I, "his name must be Lacam," which they admitted, producing his card. I certainly should have known him by the description, which was not in the least exaggerated. I had, however, that morning been informed of his arrival and that he had come from Bengal in the same ship with Mr. Francis, Mr. Harwood, and my respected friend, Mr. Tilghman.

Seeing by his card that Mr. Lacam lived in Cecil Street, I directly went to his house, and arrived there before he had recovered from the fatigue of his unsuccessful attempt to see me in St. Albans Street. I found him looking wretchedly ill. He told me he had recently been at death's door, expecting daily to die during the voyage from India ; that at the time the ship arrived off Dover his dissolution was hourly predicted, and he felt sure he owed his existence to the extraordinary attention and unceasing kindness of Mr. Harwood.

After tormenting me for an hour with his hackneyed subject, " New Harbour," Mr. Lacam asked whether Captain Henry Mordaunt, of the Bengal military establishment, who came to Europe in the same ship with him, and who had been making earnest enquiries for me, had yet found me. Before I could answer the question, the very person was announced. He entered the room with his usual scowling countenance, but for a minute smiled and shook me by the hand with apparent cordiality. He then began damning the climate, the brutality of the common people, and the general stupidity of London, cursing his own folly for being such a blockhead, such an inveterate ass as to quit the paradise of Hindustan to visit the sink of everything despicable by comparison, England, a country no man who had ever enjoyed the blessings and comforts of India could feel comfortable in. As I saw that his cynical discontent and snarling annoyed Mr. Lacam I proposed a walk, to which Mordaunt agreed, and we set out to visit Mr. Francis in Upper Harley Street.

Upon getting to Mr. Francis's house, we were shown into the drawing-room, where Mrs. Francis with two fine-looking girls her daughters, were sitting. In a few minutes Mr. Francis came in and was very courteous, making some civil speeches to me. He like Mordaunt, abused the climate as being far inferior to that of Bengal. This I thought extraordinary in him who had been so short a time abroad. He particularly complained of the closeness of the rooms in London, the oppressive heat of which he said almost suffocated him. He invited Mordaunt and myself to dinner, good-humouredly saying he wished me to come that day because Tilghman, whom he knew I had a regard for, was to be with him. I accepted the invitation, and was rejoiced to see my shipmate looking remarkably well. He told me his inducement for visiting England was to endeavour to get into the Company's Civil Service in Bengal, which if he succeeded in doing he should immediately return to India and resume his situation at the Bar of the Supreme Court, as his ultimate object was the appointment of Advocate-General.

At night, Tilghman, Mordaunt, and myself went to Vauxhall, on the way to which they gave me the particulars of the duel that took place a few months before in Bengal between Mr. Hastings, Governor-General, and Mr. Francis, which ended without bloodshed. It originated in party dissensions in Council, those gentlemen always violently opposing and abusing each other.

Wherever I went into public Mordaunt fastened upon and stuck close to me, always grumbling and snarling, and always excessively disagreeable, yet I knew not how to shake him off without absolute rudeness. As his constant theme was the stupidity of England, wishing he had never come near so horrid a country but remained in India, I endeavoured to console him by observing that he would be better pleased and in better humour after he had made some acquaintances with both sexes, as at present he knew scarcely anybody. Besides, London was always thin of company and barren of amusement at that season of the year. I likewise observed that the absence of his brother, Lord Peterborough, who was upon the Continent, was an unfortunate circumstance, as had he been upon the spot he would have introduced him to his numerous friends. To these attempts of mine to put him in good-humour he sulkily damned London and everything appertaining to it, and said that it was impossible anything could ever make him change his opinion respecting it, and was there a ship to sail the following day he would gladly embark on her for Bengal in preference to staying another hour in such a sink of gloom and dullness.

Not having seen Emily for two days, I went to dine there, and in the evening accompanied her to Colman's theatre, where Mordaunt spying me was soon at my side, nor could I get rid of him during the whole play. Indeed, when the entertainment was over he made a bold push to be invited to supper with us, which I was determined he should not be, and whispered Emily not to ask him. I at last prevailed on him to leave us upon a promise that I would next day introduce him at a house of fashionable resort where he would find a choice of beautiful girls and might pass his leisure hours agreeably. I accordingly called upon him at his mother's, Lady Peterborough, in Dean Street, Soho, from whence I took him first to Mrs. Weston's famous receptacle in Berkeley Row, where having introduced him to the *Lady Abbess and her Nuns!* we next visited Mrs. Kelly and her bevy of beauties in Arlington Street. Here even the cynical Mordaunt was obliged to confess the women were lovely, and he made some efforts to say civil things to the girls, but his common address and manner was so morose and so unpleasant that the Cyprian lasses soon distinguished him by the appellation of the "Surly Nabob."

Mr. Strange called in St. Albans Street to inform me of a serious misfortune that had happened. This was the total loss of the ship, *General Barker*, in which he had returned from Madras, an account having just reached the India House of her having been blown from her anchors in the Downs during a heavy gale of wind in which she had drifted over to the coast of Holland, and was there wrecked, going entirely to pieces in two hours after she first struck, many of her crew being drowned, the rest saved by the extraordinary exertions of the Dutch pilots. Mr. Strange told me he had lost everything, his clothes of every sort and a large quantity of shawls, kincobs, and muslins that cost him some thousands of pounds. I consoled him at his having left the ship previous to the accident, which I understood some of the passengers had not done.

My father took a great liking to little Nabob, and, perceiving that he was of no use to me, he proposed sending him to school to be taught reading and writing, which he did, the boy making a rapid progress in both. At the end of a few months he expressed a great desire to become a Christian. I therefore, after he was duly instructed, caused him to be baptized at St. James's Church.

CHAPTER XXI

MARGATE, LONDON, AND DRAYTON

IT now drawing towards the end of the month, London being both hot and dull, my brother asked me to make an excursion with him to one of the watering-places, to which I agreed, observing, however, it could not be until subsequent to the 28th, for which day I had invited a party to dinner at the Royal Hotel in Pall Mall. We accordingly met there, fifteen in number, the company consisting of Major Bourke, Mr. Touchet, Mr. Archibald Paxton, the snarler, Mordaunt, Mr. Strange, his brother, Sir Thomas Strange, afterwards Chief Justice at Madras, Sir Thomas Rumbold, Mr. Elphinstone, the India Director, Mr. Dallas, now Chief Justice of Chester, Mr. Holt, Mr. Wilberforce Bird, Messieurs William and Richard Burke, my brother, and myself. The master of the house furnished an admirable dinner and all the wines were of the best, nor did we spare them, some of the set remaining at the bottle until four in the morning.

My brother and I had arranged everything for going to Margate on the 29th, but the overdose of champagne rendered me totally incapable of moving. I was half dead with headache and sickness at the stomach. This dinner cost me rather more than forty pounds.

On the 30th, being somewhat recovered from my debauch, we set off after breakfast for Margate, which we reached the same evening, driving to Mitchiner's, where we each got an excellent bedchamber and a very good sitting-room commanding a full view of the pier and roads with the shipping passing up and down. As I had previously dispatched

Freskini with my horses, we rode every morning to Dandelion, Ramsgate, Dover, the Reculvers, and all the different charming rides with which the Isle of Thanet abounds. The rest of the morning we passed in lounging from library to library, billiard-table, and public rooms, in the evening the subscription assemblies, coffee-rooms, and theatre, the latter having a very tolerable set of actors, who were constantly repaid for their exertions to please by crowded audiences.

At Margate I first became acquainted with Mr. Metcalfe, then a Captain, or young Major, in the East India Company's service, since become (especially in his own estimation) a prodigious great man, having for several years been a baronet, an M.P., and an India director. There I also first knew a Mr. Anderson, of the Dragoons, a rattling pleasant fellow, and with thes two gentlemen my brother and I spent much of our time.

After we had been at Margate a fortnight, Mr. William Burke arrived, in order to cross from thence to Ostend on his way to India overland. He was accompanied by Mr. Richard Burke, junior, who had come to see the last of his friend on British ground. Hearing we were in the house, they joined us and we agreed to mess together during Mr. Burke's stay, which would only be until a packet sailed for the French coast. Mr. Burke had come from Madras as the agent of the Rajah of Travancore, to endeavour to procure redress of grievances the Rajah suffered under, and, having proved successful, was now returning with the gratifying news to Travancore.

While we were sitting at the window in momentary expectation of dinner being announced, a smart landau with four post-horses, drove up to the door, which Mr. Burke immediately observed contained two lovely girls, with an old woman, and a child of twelve or thirteen, he having seen them changing horses at Canterbury. Upon their alighting, I saw it was my Arlington Street friend, Mrs. Kelly, and two of her nymphs. I therefore ran down to speak to them. Whilst so doing Mr. Burke joined us, and calling me aside he desired I would ask them to dine with us, a desire that somewhat surprized me, as I imagined he would cautiously have avoided introducing such personages to his young friend, Richard, at that time a steady, reserved lad. As, however, I felt that was no business of mine I obeyed his wish and gave the invitation, which the old lady most graciously and willingly accepted.

Upon joining us Mrs. Kelly became very communicative, telling us she was on her way to Ostend to place her daughter (the youngest girl) in a convent there for education, and that the other two ladies had kindly consented to bear her company to France and back again. Upon enquiring of Mitchiner, we learned that an Ostend packet would sail at seven o'clock the following morning, that being the hour of high water. Mr. Burke and the ladies sent instantly to take a passage and secure the best cabins.

At and after dinner our whole party made rather too free with the champagne, the effects of which were particularly conspicuous in my brother, for the wine being in and the wits out he was easily persuaded to consent to escort the ladies across the Channel and back, a piece of gallantry I most positively refused to accede to, protesting a voyage of nearly eighteen months had quite satisfied me, and I certainly would have no more to do with salt water until returning to India. The girls, however, ceased not to importune me, declaring I must and should go, and that they would pull me out of bed and forcibly convey me on board. My brother was so drunk that at ten o'clock we were obliged to have him carried to bed.

Before five o'clock in the morning one of the frail sisters bounced into my room, awakening me out of a sound sleep, crying out that I must rise directly, the rest being nearly ready and my brother quite so. I renewed my assurances that my movement should not extend beyond the pierhead, to which I would go and see then set sail. I accordingly dressed, and going downstairs found my friends over an early breakfast.

My brother had no recollection of the engagement he had

entered into the preceding night, but seemed not unwilling to fulfil it until he found me resolved not to make one, whereupon he likewise declined, joining, however, in the general upbraidings of me for my ill-nature, though he afterwards expressed his satisfaction at my having prevented his taking the cruise. Mr. Burke complained of the wine having heated him. He appeared low and dejected, I believe solely from being so soon to part from his favourite, Richard. At half-past seven they cast off their fastenings to the shore, in a few minutes after which they were fairly out at sea, and in little more than an hour were hull down running at a great rate before a strong southerly wind. Upon their departure Mr. Richard Burke, junior, got into a post-chaise and set off for London.

By noon my new acquaintances, Metcalfe, Anderson, and half a dozen fashionable coxcombs were with my brother and myself, making earnest enquiries after the *divine girls* they understood had arrived the evening before, seeming grievously disappointed when told the objects of their visit were by that time *half seas over* on their way to Ostend. I could not help giving Metcalfe a wipe for this lamentation, observing I should have thought he had enough to attend to *at home*. He at that time was the professed keeper of Mrs. Cuyler, a woman without pretension to manners or beauty of face or person, and only an under-strapper upon the stage of one of the London theatres. With this woman, however, such as she was, Mr. Metcalfe appeared to be deeply enamoured, nightly exhibiting himself by her side in the front row of a balcony box.

In the middle of August a report became current that our outward bound fleet of East and West Indiamen had fallen in with a squadron of French and Spanish ships of war, and that a great number were captured, but it gained no credit, and after two or three days died away.

On the 4th of September my brother and I returned to London, where I had not been six hours before the snarler, Mordaunt, heard of my being in town and came to St. Albans Street, if possible more discontented than ever.

The day after my return I called upon Emily, who declared it was her intention to have set off for Margate the very next morning in search of me, as she began to think I was lost. She told me she had been supremely happy during the three days that it was thought the Indiamen were taken from a hope of seeing Robert, but the account proved unfounded.

The night I came to town there was to be a masquerade at Mrs. Cornelys's rooms in Soho Square, and Emily said I must go with her to it. I therefore sent for a domino, &c., and at ten o'clock she and I drove there. She was in a man's domino, with a smart hat and feather, and looked charmingly, her fine figure and graceful air attracting attention wherever she appeared. She promised me to go home early as I was tired by my journey and little sleep the preceding night, and said that to avoid being importuned to stay by any of her acquaintances she would not unmask. Vanity, however, prevailed over her inclination to oblige me, for, finding herself followed and admired in every direction, she could not resist taking off her mask to let the delighted beholders see that the face corresponded with the figure they had been pursuing from room to room. One mask in particular persevered in following her, and whenever opportunity offered by my talking to any friend, poured abundance of fulsome compliments into her ears. I suspected from her manner she knew who it was, though for some time she assured me that she did not. Upon pressing her on that point, she said it was a fine boy of Robert's acquaintance, named Treves. This young man I knew something of, and had often observed that he bowed to Emily whenever he met her. He was a handsome lad of seventeen, a great admirer and follower of the most celebrated women of the town, but his means being very slender he was forced to content himself with the liberty of bowing to several of them, and seemed happy when his salutation was returned, which always was the case with Emily, she honouring him with a gracious and familiar nod, or kiss of the hand. Some years afterwards this Treves became one of the most dashing bucks of the metropolis and the constant companion of the Prince of Wales, His Royal Highness having long been intimate with his father, a man of convivial habits, who sang an excellent song, and was in every way calculated to please such a dissipated character as the Prince then was.

One of the first persons I saw at Carlisle House (the name Mrs. Cornelys's then went by) was my blackguard friend, Sam Rogers, who, coming to me, said aloud, "Damn my eyes, Bill, but I'm glad I've met with you, for I wanted to tell you that my uncle has met with a man who has a ship just finished, which as he has some pounds to fool away he had rather not command, at least, had rather not leave England so soon as she must. An exchange has therefore taken place. She is to be the *Osterley* and I her commander, he taking what was to have been my ship next year, so stand by, my lad, to be at a launch in five or six weeks." At the same place I likewise met James Grant, who made me promise to accompany him to Drayton the next day. I did so, and was there first made acquainted with his brother, Peter.

James had with him at Drayton a little woman whom he kept, and was fond of supposing he had debauched. She had a good voice, sung prettily, and knew something of music. Her proper name was Brown, she being daughter to an advertising tailor of that name upon Ludgate Hill. She had at least the merit of constantly keeping the interest of her father in view, by recommending all Mr. Grant's friends to employ him in his business. This cost me some pounds, as I was obliged to get three or four suits of clothes made by him, which were so badly executed I never could wear them and they were altered to fit my little Bengally.

I had not been more than an hour at Drayton when Emily's lad (the junior groom) brought me a letter from her, enclosing one written by Robert as a prisoner at Madr:d, in which he said that after the fleet had been three weeks at sea in hourly expectation of making the Island of Madeira they saw four strange sail in different directions, two being upon the lee quarter, and two to windward. In half an hour after seeing the above four, two others were discovered right ahead. A line-of-battle ship that was the convoy thereupon made the signal to prepare for action, in consequence of which a smart post-chaise, a curricle, and gig of his, also some handsome mahogany furniture stowed between decks, were upon the above signal to clear ship all thrown overboard. The man-of-war then hailed the different Indiamen to say he thought the strange vessels were detached frigates belonging to a fleet of the enemy, and, if so, more of them would soon appear, in which case he would hoist a Union flag at the main top-gallant mast-head, and upon seeing that flying every ship must do the best to escape, both East and West Indiamen. Thus they run on until about an hour before sunset, when seeing the Union hoisted they dispersed, his ship carrying a press of sail all night, but at daybreak had the mortification to see two Spanish eighty-gun ships within two miles of them, to one of which they were soon afterwards compelled to strike. While the enemy were taking possession they had the further humiliation of beholding several other of their companions in the like predicament with themselves.

Robert (I think) stated that six East Indiamen and a great number of West Indiamen were captured, the enemy consisting of upwards of twenty sail of large ships, Spaniards and French ; that the ship he was in being prize to a Spaniard he was taken into Cadiz, where all the prisoners, male and female, were treated with the greatest respect and kindness, all being at liberty upon *parole ;* that he availed himself of that opportunity to see more of so famous a part of Europe and, having obtained permission, proceeded to Madrid, where he met with equal attention, especially from the Donnas, who, if they had a fault, it was overwhelming him with love ; that as he found from the liberality of the people there was no want of cash, and that he could get as much as he thought proper for his bills upon England he should be in no hurry to leave so inviting and charming a country, which he must in common justice pronounce a perfect Paradise ! By Emily's letter I could perceive she did not at all like the rapturous style in which Robert spoke of the Spanish ladies.

During my stay at Drayton, a female servant who had the care of the poultry one morning came into the room where we were sitting at breakfast, apparently in great anger. Taking from her apron what I imagined were four fine eggs, she laid them upon the table, violently exclaiming, "If that cursed Juno is suffered to range wherever she pleases there will not be an egg left for the use of the family." While she was speaking I had taken up one of the eggs, which I found to be an empty shell. Upon expressing my surprize what could have occasioned it, there being no crack or mark that I saw, she petulantly said, "What could occasion it ? Why, that cursed brute Juno, to be sure, who sucks them all, and my master there allows of it." To this I replied, "It was impossible a dog could get the contents without injuring the shells, every one of which seemed to be perfect." "Aye, so they are, perfectly empty." This wit of the maid's caused a laugh. Grant then taking up one of the shells showed me at the end a hole so small that I could scarce perceive it, appearing as if made by the point of a pin, but through which, small as it was, the animal, he assured me, had sucked out the contents. I should have observed that Juno was one of the largest greyhounds I ever beheld. This appeared to me so improbable I could not help expressing my belief that some two-legged hounds must be aiding and assisting. Grant assured me it was a fact within his knowledge. "However," said he, "you shall have ocular demonstration." He sent for an egg, which laying upon the carpet, he called Juno, and desired her to take it. The servant thereupon with much wrath said, "Ah, you thief, if you offer to touch it I'll cut your heart out," a threat that had full effect upon Juno, who did not venture near the egg until patted and encouraged by her master, when she squatted down, extending her fore paws, between which she dexterously fixed the egg, and putting her mouth to it in three or four minutes it was as completely emptied of its contents as either of the four the maid brought in. Certainly if I had not been an eye-witness of this fact I could not have thought it possible.

The 7th (of September) I returned to town, being engaged to dine with Major Metcalfe on the 8th at his house in Suffolk Street, Middlesex Hospital. At this party I met Lord Fielding, eldest son to the Earl of Denbigh ; General Smith, of whom I have before spoken relative to *cheese* at the Island of St. Helena ; the General's son, a fine young man in appearance, who had, I know not why, been nicknamed Tippoo ; Mr. Devaynes, the India Director ; Captain Douglas, who commanded the ship *Queen*, and some others whose names I do not recollect. We had a very jolly set, and as I was in those days a great promoter of hilarity I invited all that remained to a late hour at table, being those above specified, to dine with me that day week at the Royal Hotel in Pall Mall. This they agreed to do. I added to the number, Mr. Paxton, the discontented Mordaunt, and my brother, who when the day arrived was so much indisposed that he was unwillingly obliged to give up the pleasure of joining us. We had, as usual, a hard batch at drinking and were very merry, keeping it up until an early hour of the morning.

My brother, who never shunned a jovial set himself, took it into his head to tax me with being the instigator of his committing excess. Under this idea, certainly an unjust one as to me, he, more than once, when we were engaged to great tavern parties, has said to me, " William, this must from some of the names I see in the list, be a sad debauch which in prudence we had better avoid. Let you and I therefore get out of the way of temptation, mount our horses and ride gently to Richmond, Brentford Ait, or any other place within ten miles of London that you prefer, where we might take a quiet dinner, a pint of port each, and jog soberly home in the evening." To so steady a plan, which I really liked, I readily consented. The event, however, never answered ; entirely the reverse. The first excursion of this kind that we made we dined upon the

Island off the town of Brentford, where there is a house famous for dressing pitchcocked eels, and also for stewing the same fish, and got so completely intoxicated we were incapable of mounting our horses and obliged to take a post-chaise to convey us to town. The wine being remarkably good, we ordered bottle after bottle until poor prudence was quite drowned. I thought our inebriation this day might have been purely accidental, but I found the same consequence followed two or three subsequent *quiet* dinners with my brother, and although our pretence was sobriety by avoiding a large drinking party, it never answered the purpose. On the contrary (to use a vulgarism) we fell " out of the frying-pan into the fire." I came to the determination never again to join my brother in those *tête-à-têtes,* but to take my chance in whatever set I might be invited to.

In the latter end of September I had dined with some convivial fellows at the St. Albans tavern, where according to custom, I took my full proportion of wine. My companions proposing to adjourn to King's Place, a wonderful fit of prudence came across me. I declined, declaring as I was close to my home I would for once resist temptation and go to bed. " Aye, no doubt of it," said one of the young men, " with Emily, to whom you are sneaking away." I assured him he was mistaken, as was the fact, for Bob Pott was daily expected to arrive from Spain. I therefore actually proceeded to my father's, distant only four doors from the tavern.

Upon going in, the servant told me my Aunt Boulton, her three daughters, Mr. and Mrs. Broadhead, and others whom he named, were in the parlour sitting after supper. I marched into the room and having scarcely spoken to my aunt and cousins since my arrival from India, I made a number of complimentary flourishing speeches to them, with which they seemed highly gratified, declaring that being tipsy made me vastly agreeable, a pretty broad insinuation that they did not consider me so when sober. I found my elder sister, Mrs. Broadhead, and one or two more were going to a masquerade at the Opera House, and as they recommended my doing the same instead of stupidly going to bed, I at once subscribed to that opinion. Upon my ringing the bell to desire that a domino and mask might be sent for, my sister observed she could supply me with a *suitable character for the state I was in,* and, going up to her own apartment, soon returned with a complete dress of white linen, being the garments worn at a particular convent in Paris.

My female friends could with difficulty equip me from excessive laughter at my hiccupping violently the whole time they were employed about it. Having at last accomplished the business, I got into a chair and was conveyed to the Haymarket. The house was very full, but I soon spied out my sister and her party, to whom I was staggering up, when they darted off and most cautiously avoided me, conceiving it would not tend much to their credit to be acknowledged by a *drunken nun!* undoubtedly not a character often seen. Indeed, the novelty of it attracted universal admiration. I was the cause of much wit and fun. A crowd of both sexes followed me, some putting ridiculous questions, others affecting to be shocked at beholding one of the sisterhood in so unseemly and disgraceful a state, exhorting me to retire to my cell and do penance for my grievous transgression. I reeled about, singing, talking sad nonsense, and jostling every person that came in my way, every now and then tumbling and unable to rise until assisted by the bystanders. Much ashamed of myself did I feel when made acquainted with the follies I had committed.

The 15th being the day of my dinner at the Royal Hotel, about one o'clock I went to take my usual ride in Hyde Park, where, seeing Emily's vis-à-vis, I galloped across the grass for the purpose of speaking to her, when I had the pleasure to find my friend, Robert, in the carriage with her. He had reached town that morning, and expressed most unfeigned joy at our once more meeting. He insisted upon my dismounting and squeezing into the vis-à-vis, protesting he would not part with me for that day at least, but upon my telling him how I was circumstanced, desiring Emily to give him up to me for a few hours and she good-humouredly complying, he promised to join my party in Pall Mall, with every one of whom he was well acquainted. I endeavoured to prevail upon Emily to accompany him, which she would not hear of, observing one woman amongst such a party of riotous men would only be an offensive intruder, nor should she herself like it. I went to Cork Street with them, at Robert's request sending for Freskini and my clothes.

At five o'clock Robert and I drove to St. Albans Street, where, after stopping to take in my brother, we proceeded to the hotel. I made a point of always asking my father to be of my parties, which he declined, observing his race was already run, that though he believed no man ever lived more freely than he had done, both his age and his inclination concurred to make him now avoid excess. He therefore felt he should contribute nothing by his presence amongst such jolly fellows and desired to be excused.

We had in the opinion of all but Robert, an excellent dinner, he alone pronouncing it execrable, saying, " Let me give you a dinner at Le Tellier's, and I'll show you how a table ought to be covered to deserve commendation." All readily consented to indulge him. Five days afterwards we partook of his catering, when certainly there was a more showy and far more expensive, but as I thought, not a bit better dinner as to the materials than mine.

General Smith, Mr. Devaynes, and a few others of the graver sort, having departed, Robert called for pen, ink, and paper, and wrote down the following names : Mr. Roe Yoe (M.P. for Coventry), Lord Fielding, Wilberforce Bird (of Wood Street), Lord Peterborough, Smith (Tippoo), Henry Mordaunt, Joseph Bird, William (now Sir William) Curtis, James Curtis, his brother, Messieurs Marjoribanks and Lovelace, senior, of the Guards, Captain Belford of the Horse Guards, Harvey Coombe (now one of the Members for the City of London), Lovelace, junior, Tom Vaughan (the author), Arthur Shakespear, Captain Sutton, young Horneck (of the Guards), William Hickey, and Robert Pott.

" And now," said he, " let these twenty dine together twice a week during the winter, each person ordering a dinner at which he is to preside, at whatever tavern he pleases within London or Westminster, and, when the whole list has gone through, finally to fix at whatever house a majority of the members should pronounce to have been found the best."

The rules or regulations proposed were simple and few in number, the charge per head for the dinner to be left entirely to the discretion of the master of the house ; the dinner to consist of every article procurable, whether in or out of season ; any member absenting himself from the meetings, no matter what the cause thereof, to forfeit one guinea for each and every time he was so absent ; the President for the day to discharge the bill, and to collect by himself or his own servants the proportion due from each member ; the proprietor of the house to send in his bill by one o'clock of the day next after that of the dinner to the residence of the President.

This plan being unanimously approved, was immediately adopted, and Pott being requested to commence by taking the first chair, I attended him to his favourite place, Le Tellier's, in Dover Street, to order the dinner. He told the landlord the nature of the meeting, concluding thus, " From the experience I have had of your abilities and the superior excellence of your cookery, I have no doubt if you exert yourself we shall finally establish ourselves at your house, and it will, I conceive, be well worth your while to endeavour to attract as constant customers twenty gentlemen who are indifferent about the expence, and being lovers of the bottle will consume a handsome allowance of wine, in which, as I understand, the chief advantage to you tavern keepers arises." The landlord assured Pott he would take special care to have the table supplied with the very best provisions, and, with respect to wines of every sort, he could venture to defy all England to supply better than his cellars were stored with.

Several of the members being about to leave town for

a few days the first dinner was ordered for the 2nd of October, on which day seventeen of us met, the elder Curtis being prevented from attending by illness, Lord Peterborough and Horneck being both upon the Continent. The landlord kept his faith with us, every person present agreeing in opinion that a better dinner could not be, and that all the wines were fair, the claret particularly good. Upon this general approbation, Mordaunt proposed no further trials, and that we should at once establish the club where we had commenced so well. This being put to the vote, a majority were for adhering to the original plan, though it was observed that in all probability several of the members would have the dinner at Le Tellier's. Lord Fielding, requesting leave to be the next president, said he intended to try Hunt of the Star and Garter in Pall Mall, where, if he was not greatly mistaken, we should be as well treated in every respect as on that day. The fact is, any set of gentlemen acting upon the principle we did must be served in the best possible manner, nor could there be any material difference between the taverns of repute.

CHAPTER XXII

THE FIRST MEETING WITH CHARLOTTE BARRY

ADCOCK now became troublesomely importunate respecting his demand upon Mr. Paterson, whom he spoke of as being at hide-and-seek, nor could he discover any fixed place of residence that he had. He said he had twice met him accidentally in the City, at both which times he prevaricated and shuffled in attempting to state his present and future prospects. I own I thought it rather extraordinary, considering the nature and extent of the favours I had conferred upon this said Mr. Paterson, that he should never once have called upon me since his arrival in England, nor written a single line, or in any manner whatever, directly or indirectly, acknowledged a sense of gratitude for the obligations he must have felt he lay under to me, nor has he to the present day ever done so.

This gentleman in a year or two after his return from the Cape of Good Hope got a commission in a new regiment raised by Colonel Fullarton from his own tenants in Scotland, the Colonel having a knowledge of and regard for his (Paterson's) family. With this regiment Paterson went abroad to New South Wales or Botany Bay, as it was then called, where in due course he rose to the rank of major, and subsequently became Lieutenant-Governor of the Settlement, which post, I believe, he still continues to hold, or did so very lately.

I assured Adcock that his money was in no danger, and he would ultimately receive the uttermost farthing with interest to the day of payment, but that he must have patience, Lady Strathmore being then in Scotland and likely to remain there some months longer. Notwithstanding these assurances of mine were sanctioned and supported by my father, who more than once spoke to him upon the subject, and told him no coercive measures could be resorted to until her Ladyship's return, he continued daily tormenting me with his supplications for payment, and I was under the necessity at last of telling him he was impudently intrusive. This, however, had no effect. He persevered in his visits every day ; the last two or three times that I saw him in the hall having another man with him. Upon finding such determined insolence, I gave the servants orders in his and his companion's hearing never in future to allow him to come within the door.

After this I heard no more of him for upwards of a week, when one afternoon just as I was stepping into a coach to go to our club dinner a decent-looking man addressed me, taking off his hat and very respectfully begging to speak to me in private. I answered that being already late I could not then stop, but should be glad to see him at any hour most convenient to himself the following morning. He civilly observed his business was of such a nature it could not be postponed. Surprized at this urgency, or what it could arise from, I returned with him into the hall, when he took from his pocket a paper which he said was a warrant upon a writ issued against me by one James Adcock, and that he had taken the liberty of requesting I would go into the house again in order to avoid executing it in the public street. My father, fortunately for me, being at home instantly undertook to bail the action to the sheriff, which the bailiff being perfectly satisfied with, I was allowed to proceed, presenting the man with a couple of guineas for his marked attention and *politeness*. I then got into the carriage and drove off.

It is rather extraordinary that I who, throughout my life had been beyond measure extravagant and thoughtless, incurring debts to a considerable extent in every direction, should never, except in the above instance, have been arrested, and this once for the debt of another person, in which transaction I had not derived the smallest advantage nor had personally anything to do with it. This reflection was exceedingly mortifying.

Adcock having iniquitously obtained a judgment against me, my father informed me the amount of debt and costs must be paid within a certain period. This I told him I could not do without discounting one of my bills at a great loss. My brother therefore called upon the plaintiff's attorney to ask a month's time, which he without scruple consented to give, but being a pettifogging blackguard he chose afterwards to deny having given any such promise, and the moment he was entitled so to do, issued an execution upon the judgment, Adcock attending the bailiff who had the writ of *Capias ad satisfaciendum*, in order to point me out to him. They went together for the purpose to St. Albans Street, where it was supposed I should be found. Adcock showing the house to the bailiff, he knocked at the door and enquired for me. The servant answered I was out of town he knew not where, nor when I should return.

The bailiff joined his employer to communicate this information, and they thereupon adjourned to an ale house in the neighbourhood, from whence Adcock sent a person to call the servant, who directly obeyed the summons. Being asked where I was, he answered that he did not know, nor when I should be at home. Adcock then offered him a guinea if he would tell where I might be found, which the servant indignantly spurned at, calling him an ungrateful villain whom, if he would engage not to take the law, he would thrash although twice his size and strength. Adcock not choosing to accept the challenge, the servant left him and immediately mentioned what had occurred to his fellow-servants in the kitchen, where Nabob being present and hearing it, without saying a word to anyone, ran over to the public-house to Adcock, to whom he said he knew where I was. "Do you so," answered Adcock, "and pray where is he ? " " With a lady in Seymour Street," said the boy. "If you please I'll go with you and show you the house." "And pray," asked Adcock, "do you know what

I want with your master ? " " Oh, yes," replied he, " Mr.
Gibson (the name of my father's servant) told us all in the
kitchen you would send him to prison because he would not
give you money."

Adcock, ill as he had himself behaved to me, was shocked
at such base and unfeeling conduct in the little urchin,
knowing as he did full well, the extraordinary and uniform
kindness with which he had been treated by me during the
voyage, and which had been continued by every one of
my family since I had reached England. So greatly did he
feel it that he actually gave the boy some smart boxes on
the cheek and kicked him out of the house. Not satisfied
with that, he went in person to my father's, and knocking
at the door, desired to see the housekeeper (Molly Jones),
to whom he related the circumstance, adding, " I declare
to you, Mrs. Jones, that this black rascal's scandalous ingratitude towards such a master as Mr. Hickey has so confounded me that I could not avail myself of his infamous
offer."

Molly Jones instantly dispatched one of the men-servants
to tell me that Adcock, accompanied by a sheriff's officer, had
been looking after me. Upon receiving which information
I immediately went into the City, got the requisite sum,
which a clerk of my father's carried and paid to the plaintiff's attorney, who gave a release to the action. I knew
nothing of Nabob's treachery and baseness until upon the
eve of leaving England, when Molly Jones desired I would
be upon my guard and not place any confidence in Nabob,
and her reasons for giving me the caution. Upon my return
to Bengal I had another strong proof of his total want of
gratitude or attachment to me, which I shall in its proper
place notice.

On the 4th of October I went to the launch of the *Warren
Hastings*, East Indiaman, having received an invitation
thereto from the senior Mr. Larkins, who was principal and
managing owner. She was to be commanded by that
gentleman's third son, my friend and *Nassau* shipmate,
John Pascal Larkins. We had a handsome cold collation

at the dockyard, and a splendid dinner afterwards at the Queen's Arms tavern in St. Paul's Churchyard, followed by a ball and supper for the ladies, the whole being conducted in the most liberal manner.

Soon after the *Warren Hastings* had been consigned to her proper element, I attended another ceremony of the same description—that of the *Osterley's* launch, when Captain Rogers entertained near one hundred and fifty of his friends at Woolwich.

In the early part of the winter a new species of evening's amusement became quite the rage under the name of " The Promenade." Mrs. Cornelys's truly magnificent suite of apartments upon the principal floor were opened every Sunday night at seven o'clock for the reception of company. So much did it take that the first people of the kingdom attended it, as did also the whole beauty of the metropolis from the Duchess of Devonshire down to the little milliner's apprentice from Cranbourn Alley. The crowd from eight to twelve was immense. When in town I never failed attending at it. There I first was in company with Charlotte and Nancy Barry, two sisters then in high vogue and much sought after by the young sprigs of nobility. There was a something about the eldest, Charlotte, though she certainly could not be pronounced a beauty, that pleased me beyond any woman I had ever seen, and I looked at her with admiration. She had hold of the Earl of Tyrconnel's arm, while her sister, Nancy, was escorted by Mr. Van, a dashing ensign in the Guards, who stuck so close to their respective fair companions that I had no opportunity of becoming acquainted with them that night.

About this time we had a tempest of wind, rain, thunder and lightning so tremendous as to alarm everybody. When it commenced I was at dinner at Colonel Byng's, where the ladies of his family were sadly frightened, and certainly not without reason, the appearance being awful and terrific. The severity of it burst over London and the environs to a distance in each direction of about five miles. Hammersmith suffered in a peculiar degree, scarce a house that was not entirely stripped of its tiles or slates, the church was materially injured and every window demolished. Several persons, besides a quantity of cattle, were struck dead by the lightning. Some months afterwards we heard that on the very same day and hour an equally fatal hurricane arose in the West Indies, wherein the *Stirling Castle* and *Thunderer*, two fine seventy-four gun ships, with two large frigates that were in company, went to the bottom and every soul on board all four ships perished.

In the middle of October, Bob Pott proposed that Emily, he, and I should run down to Bath for a fortnight, to which I had no other objection than the possibility of its interfering with the business of the Bengal petition, Parliament being prorogued to the 1st of November. I therefore went to the agents, Messieurs Irvine and Touchet, who said the House would only meet on the 1st to adjourn to a future day, and beyond a doubt no business would be done. Upon this assurance I made one of the Bath party, spending fourteen days very agreeably in that gay city.

Upon returning to town I found several letters, the first I opened being from Alderman Woolridge, containing an invitation for me to become his guest at the approaching feast at Guildhall on the 9th of November, the day upon which the mayoralty of Sir Watkin Lewes commenced, and as the knight was a professed patriot all the members of opposition and liberty champions were to be present. Never having been at one of those entertainments I was glad to avail myself of the opportunity by accepting the alderman's offer.

I likewise found a card from Mr. Paxton, asking me to dine with him on the 3rd of the same month in Buckingham Street. This was the very day I returned from Bath. I accordingly went and met a very jovial party. He treated us with some of the most exquisite burgundy I ever tasted, the flavour of which Sir James Douglas, a veteran admiral, seemed to smack his lips at and enjoy equal to any of the young people. During this dinner our mirth received a check by accounts coming in of the melancholy and lamented death of Major André, a rising and very promising officer

who, having accepted the dangerous office of entering the
enemy's camp in disguise in America, was discovered and
hung as a spy. His conduct was so manly and firm at the
time of his execution as to excite the pity and the tears
even of the Americans themselves who witnessed his last
moments.

My father hearing me talking to my brother about another
party I proposed having at the hotel in Pall Mall, expressed
his surprize that I should unnecessarily incur a heavy
expence by giving dinners at those extravagant houses when
I might have the use of his, with that of his servants, which
would save me two-thirds of the expence, and be at least
as comfortable, if not more so, than a tavern or hotel. " In
making this offer," continued my father, " do not imagine,
young man, that I intend to supply your dissipated companions with my wines ; at least, with claret and madeira
you must furnish yourself." I gladly availed myself of
my father's offer for, independent of the comforts I knew
would attend adopting it, my sister Mary had great taste in
the arrangements of dinners, nor was old Molly Jones at
all inferior. As to wines I could confidently rely upon
Mr. Paxton. All I had to attend to was taking care that my
parties never should clash with those of my sister, of which
she generally had one a week, consisting of what, in the
language of the day, were called "fine people," especially as
to the men.

The first party I had in St. Albans Street proved the justness of my father's remark, for it did not cost me near half
of what I had been charged for a larger company at the
hotel and was beyond comparison better, my guests all
declaring they never had seen a more elegant or a better
dinner, nor better served in every respect. The excellent
quality of the wines too called forth the highest praise and
approbation. For that I was indebted, as I have before
mentioned, to Mr. Paxton, who always made one of my
party. He constantly took as large a share of claret as
anyone at table, and when his head was affected by excess
used to whisper in my ear how much he liked me, that I

Miss Hickey

After the portrait by Sir Joshua Reynolds
by permission of the owner Mrs Malkin.

was a noble fellow and always should have the best wine his cellars afforded, a promise he most strictly kept.

I always was ambitious of sitting out every man at the table where I presided, which by a little management I generally accomplished. By eating sparingly of some one plain dish, avoiding malt liquor, and desiring the servants to take away my glass after a hob-nob the moment I put it down, I was the better enabled to do the duty of president when the cloth was removed, from which moment I never flinched, and contrived to send my guests away quite happy and contented. When, as was sometimes the case, I felt the wine disposed to revolt, chewing two or three French olives without swallowing the pulp would relieve and enable me to get down half a dozen more glasses. By these little fair manoeuvres I established the character of being a capital host.

The 9th being the Lord Mayor's day, I arrayed myself in my full suit of velvet. Alderman Woolridge called at my father's and conveyed me in his chariot to the Guildhall at half-past four o'clock, about an hour after which the procession arrived from Westminster. At six we sat down to a profusion of turtle and venison, followed by all the etceteras of French cookery, with splendid dessert of pines, grapes, and other fruits. I was seated between Mrs. Healy, sister to Wilkes, and Lord Lewisham, eldest son of the Earl of Dartmouth. Mrs. Healy almost enveloped me in her immense hoop, but was vastly attentive to me, whom she perceived to be a stranger, ordering one of her servants to wait upon me, and naming to me the different persons who sat at the same table, amongst whom were most of the great officers of state, the Lord Chancellor, Judges, and Master of the Rolls.

The heat from the crowd assembled and the immense number of lights was disagreeable to all; to many quite oppressive and distressing. The Lord Mayor's table at which I was, and nearly opposite his Lordship, was less so than other parts of the hall from being considerably elevated above the rest.

The wines were excellent and the dinner the same, served too with as much regularity and decorum as if we had been in a private house, but far different was the scene in the body of the hall, where in five minutes after the guests took their stations at the tables the dishes were entirely cleared of their contents, twenty hands seizing the same joint or bird and literally tearing it to pieces. A more determined scramble could not be, the roaring and noise was deafening and hideous, which increased as the liquor operated, bottles and glasses flying across from side to side without intermission. Such a bear garden altogether I never beheld, except my first visit to Wetherby's which it brought very forcibly to my recollection.

This abominable and disgusting scene continued till near ten o'clock, when the Lord Mayor, sheriffs, the nobility, &c., adjourned to the ball and card rooms and the dancing commenced. Here the heat was no way inferior to that of the hall and the crowd so great there was scarce a possibility of moving. Rejoiced therefore was I upon Alderman Woolridge's saying he would take me home whenever I wished it. I eagerly answered, "This moment, if you please." He therefore took me through some private apartments and down a flight of stairs to a door opening into a back lane, where his carriage was ready, into which we stepped without the smallest difficulty or impediment and were driven home. Completely exhausted, I retired to bed, perfectly satisfied with having once partaken of a Lord Mayor of London's feast.

Our club went on well, nothing ever occurring to interrupt the harmony of it except now and then some expressions of displeasure at the unprovoked snarling of the discontented Mordaunt, at which the majority always laughed, which seemed to mortify him more than complaining of or finding fault with his moroseness.

The 17th of November I received notice from Messieurs Irvine and Touchet that the petition was to be presented to the House of Commons on the 23rd, upon which day they requested my attendance and my company to dine with them afterwards at the British coffee-house. I accordingly went on the day appointed to Westminster, Mr. Burke taking me in hand, by which I got a very good place in the gallery and was much entertained for two hours listening to the different speakers. The petition being received and read was ordered to lie on the table, the member who presented it observing he should on a subsequent day move that a committee be appointed to take [it into consideration and report thereon.

In the regular course of business the petition was referred to a committee, General Smith being the chairman of it. Amongst the other members were Mr. Burke, Sir Gilbert Elliot, now Lord Minto, Mr. Long, and (on account of his uncommon parsimony) the much talked-of Mr. Elwes. From the time of their first meeting I was obliged to attend daily in the committee room, and I underwent a very long examination relative to the practice of the Supreme Court of Judicature and the general line adopted by the judges thereof in their official capacities.

Whilst this matter was under investigation Mr. Richard Barwell arrived in England from Bengal, with a fortune, according to common report, of upwards of four hundred thousand pounds sterling. In a very few days after this gentleman reached England he became a candidate for a seat in Parliament. He likewise purchased the extensive and valuable estate of the then late Earl of Halifax situate at Stanstead in the county of Sussex. His first habitation in London was in a house belonging to an old maiden sister, Miss Mary Barwell, of whom I have already spoken, in Great Ormond Street, Bloomsbury.

It having been suggested to the committee that in all probability much important information might be gained by examining Mr. Barwell, especially respecting the impediments that had been thrown in the way of Colonel Watson in the carrying into execution his plan of constructing wet and dry docks in the neighbourhood of Calcutta, by which impediments and interruption the nation, as well as the individual promoter of the work, had sustained a great and irreparable injury, a summons was ordered to be issued requiring Mr. Barwell's attendance before the committee.

The messenger who went to Ormond Street for the purpose of serving the summons, not finding Mr. Barwell at home after calling several times, at last left the summons with his servant, telling him what it was and that he must take care it reached his master as soon as possible. On the day named in the order, Mr. Barwell not making his appearance, nor any answer sent or reason assigned for his not doing so, another summons was issued, but the messenger had no better success. He could not meet with the object of his search, nor would the *valet de chambre* say where his master was, or at what hour he expected him to be at home. The messenger therefore returned to the committee, but was forthwith ordered to go back to Mr. Barwell's house and not leave it until he either saw him or ascertained where he was. A third time the messenger went, when the valet, after much prevarication and impertinent language, said his master was at Bath, and upon being asked how long he had been there and when he would be back, with much insolence swore he knew nothing about the matter and would give no other answer.

Upon this being communicated to the committee, one of the members observed it could not be true that he was at Bath, he having met him at Charing Cross not two hours before. Messengers were thereupon ordered to bring the valet before the committee at the time of their first sitting the following morning. They accordingly did so, when the fellow was very pert and flippant, but being told by one of the committee that the moment they had done with him he should be committed to Newgate, he seemed surprized and became somewhat more respectful in his manner. Being asked where his master, Mr. Barwell, was, he replied he did not know. " Was he in town ? " (After a considerable pause.) He said he believed not. " Was he at Bath ? " (After another pause.) He did not know ! " When had he last seen him ? " As he did not seem disposed to answer this question at all he was threatened with immediate commitment, whereupon he said he had seen his master about an hour before ! " Where ? " At home in his own house, where he was when he left it !

A burst of indignation burst out from the whole committee, and one of the members proposed that the fellow be directly committed to Newgate. The room was thereupon ordered to be cleared, and all strangers to withdraw. We in consequence went into an adjoining apartment, the insolent servant being taken into custody by the messengers. While in this chamber, I asked him what could have induced him so far to forget himself as to behave in so disrespectful and unwarrantable a manner to a committee of the House of Commons, by which he had got himself into a most serious scrape, and would be very severely punished. The man looked very foolish, simply replying, " It was hard upon him who was no way in fault, having only obeyed his master's orders who had directed him to give such answers."

In about an hour we were readmitted, when we found the clerk making out a fresh summons for Mr. Barwell, which was delivered to a messenger with orders to take a sufficient number of persons with him to search every room in the house, and upon discovering Mr. Barwell, without permitting a moment's delay, bring him before them. In a little more than an hour the messenger returned with the object of his search. Upon being brought into the committee, one of the gentlemen asked him whether or not he had received any summons from that House. He answered he had. " How many ? " Altogether three ! and his reason for not obeying them was . . . Here he was prevented from proceeding by the chairman's hastily saying, " Stop ! not a word more, but withdraw." The room was again cleared, and we kept out half an hour, during which we could hear the voices of the members in loud debate.

The doors being once more opened, Mr. Barwell was placed at the end of the table, when the chairman (General Smith) addressed him to the following effect : " Mr. Richard

Barwell, you have behaved in a manner that calls for the highest degree of reprehension ! Your daring to treat a committee of the House of Commons with contumely reflects disgrace upon the person so acting, and it is the more extraordinary that you should presume to do so at the very time you are yourself a candidate for becoming a member of that House you are thus indecently insulting. This committee feel with the utmost surprize and indignation your ungentlemanlike conduct, a conduct that imperiously demands the severest censure, and I am directed to inform you that nothing prevents the committee from representing your contemptuous and disgraceful behaviour towards them to the House, but an unwillingness to break in upon the very serious and important avocations in which they know that House to be now engaged. I am further directed to tell you that the uncommon insolence and shameless prevarication of your servant has not passed unobserved by this committee, an insolence that should not remain unpunished did not the committee feel convinced that no man in the low station that person is would have dared to betray the impertinence he has unless he had been encouraged and instructed so to do by his master. Withdraw."

The humbled and mortified nabob began a speech with, " I beg leave to assure this honourable committee . . ." " Withdraw ! " haughtily said the chairman. " Not a word more. Withdraw ! " accompanying his imperious order with a contemptuous motion of his hand towards the door, whereupon the messengers and attendants forced Barwell out of the room. Never was a purse-proud, haughty man so mortified as Mr. Barwell upon this occasion. Wealth did not operate ! The culprit, although of unbounded riches, was treated with no more distinction than would have been the lowest plebeian under similar circumstances.

What rendered the above reprimand the more severe and humiliating was the channel through which it was pronounced being General Smith who, though of inferior rank and influence in India, had always violently opposed the measures of Mr. Barwell, and they were sworn enemies.

The mortification of the nabob did not end with the reprimand, for after being kept three hours waiting in the ante-
chamber, he was dismissed with an order, delivered to him
by a messenger, on his peril not to fail attending the next
morning at ten o'clock, and thus was he treated for three
succeeding days.

When at last called into the committee room to be
examined, Mr. Barwell seemed disposed, like his servant, to
be saucy and give himself airs, affecting not to understand
the questions put to him, and when repeated, sometimes
more than once, giving evasive answers. Mr. Burke, who
had undertaken the examination, with perfect coolness
though blended with a commanding countenance and
manner, said, " What your object is in such conduct,
Mr. Barwell, I acknowledge myself quite at a loss to say.
Probably you scarcely know it yourself. I, however, take
the liberty of assuring you it will not answer your purpose
whatever that may be. If you expect to weary me or ex-
haust my patience or that of the honourable members
constituting this committee, I can with confidence assert
you will fail and have egregiously mistaken the characters
of those you are now before, and likewise *that you know me
not !* (With strong and marked emphasis.) Answers !
intelligible and direct answers to such questions as I deem
necessary and proper to put, I must and will have ere I have
done with you. I therefore conceive it will tend to your
own ease, and that it will be prudent in you to drop the
puerile and silly behaviour (to use no harsher epithets) you
have hitherto adopted." Mr. Barwell felt the full force
of the rebuke, followed Mr. Burke's advice, and from that
moment gave his evidence distinctly and without hesitation or evasion.

A few days after this scene had occurred to the nabob,
I accompanied Mordaunt to dinner in Ormond Street, where
I met with the highest degree of ostentatious parade.
Dinner being announced ready we proceeded to the dining
parlour, wherein stood a table sumptuously filled with every
kind of rarity in food, and eighteen covers laid, although

the party consisted of no more than six. We had three regular courses besides dessert, the whole served upon plate. We were attended by two men out of, and four in, livery, everything else being correspondent. This I understood was the daily custom without any special order being given. For so expensive and unusual a practice Mr. Barwell was pleased to give the following reason to me : " I have two brothers who are authorized to consider this house as their own. They therefore not only come themselves to dinner whenever it suits their convenience or pleasure, but frequently bring with them three or four guests. I, too," said he, " sometimes in my morning rambles pick up a friend or two who are kind enough to accept of a short invitation and come home with me. Thus our parties varying almost every day, I considered it the best plan to order a table constantly to be arranged for eighteen."

CHAPTER XXIII

WITH BOB POTT AND OTHERS

ON the approach of Christmas, Parliament adjourned over the holidays. I therefore took that opportunity to visit Mrs. Forrest, the Admiral's widow, at her beautiful seat at Binfield in Berkshire. Upon my reaching the place I was concerned to see that it was fast falling into decay from want of timely and trifling repairs, the poor woman's means being too scanty to allow of her paying bricklayers and carpenters. Mrs. Forrest's mode of life was precisely the same as when I had last seen her. Whimsical in every respect in the extreme, she seemed to make it a rule always to act unlike everybody else. Thus she reversed the ordinary custom by sitting up the whole of the night and laying in bed during the day.

Our meeting was, as I expected it would be, very distressing to us both, the sight of me bringing most forcibly to Mrs. Forrest's memory her then recently deceased and lamented son, Thomas, who died of the wound he received at the first relief of Gibraltar. She wept bitterly—nor did she recover her spirits the whole of the day. Arthur, the eldest son, having involved himself deeply in debt, had been obliged to sell his commission and secrete himself to avoid arrest, after which some friends of the family procured for him a cadetship in the Corps of Engineers belonging to the East India Company and he had sailed for Fort St. George a short time before I arrived in England, leaving his wife, a Greek whom he had married when serving with his regiment in the garrison of Gibraltar, and one child, a boy, to be a burden upon and increase the difficulties of his already deeply embarrassed and inconsiderate mother. Her daughters continued to be the same charming and interesting young women I had ever known them. After spending three days at Binfield, on each of which Mrs. Forrest paid me the extraordinary compliment to make her appearance at three o'clock in the afternoon instead of eight at night, her usual hour, I took my leave of the unfortunate family and returned to town.

In January, 1781, meeting Mr. Barwell at the opera, he told me our volatile friend, Pott, had promised to let him have his company for a few days at Stanstead, in order to give his opinion and advice respecting alterations and additions he intended making to the house, he (Mr. Barwell) having much confidence in his judgment and taste ; that he should feel happy if I would join the party, a seat in his post-coach being entirely at my service. Having no way of passing my time more pleasantly, I accepted the invitation.

After breakfasting in Great Ormond Street, Mr. Barwell, his second brother, Pott, and myself on the 3rd of the month set off post for Stanstead. The house was an immense pile of buildings, the greatest part very old-fashioned, one wing alone, which had been erected by the last Lord Halifax, being in the modern style. It was altogether a straggling, irregular structure, on the outside by no means pleasing to the eye, but it contained many noble apartments and was richly furnished. The garden, pleasure grounds, and park were extensive and could not be exceeded in natural and acquired beauties. Attached to this estate was a parliamentary borough returning two members, likewise two livings in the church, one of a thousand pounds a year, the other seven hundred ; timber fit for cutting to the amount of seventy thousand pounds, with game of every sort in profusion.

The estate had long been in the possession of the Halifax family, but the last Earl, by his unbounded extravagance, having materially injured his fortune, his embarrassments became so serious that he endeavoured to dispose of this part of his property. It was accordingly advertised for sale, but no more than one hundred and forty thousand pounds being bid, a sum considered far below its value, it was bought in. Upon the Earl's death his debts were so great and the creditors so clamorous that the executors to his Lordship's will made another attempt to dispose of the Stanstead estate by public auction, when only one hundred and ten thousand pounds being offered it was again bought in. A year, the period allowed by law for the executors to arrange all matters on account of the testator, having elapsed and the creditors being extremely importunate, they came to a determination, after consulting the most eminent lawyers upon the situation they were placed in, of letting the property go to the highest bidder. It was therefore advertised for sale a third time, the notices announcing that the sale was to be an actual and peremptory one. Mr. Barwell became the purchaser at ninety thousand pounds, and it was universally thought to be the cheapest bargain that ever was known, but the purchase money being, by one of the conditions, to be paid within three months after the day of sale, and few persons having command of money sufficient to enable them to pay down so large a sum, occasioned Mr. Barwell to obtain it considerably under its real value.

It being promulgated to the neighbourhood that the new proprietor was arrived at the mansion house of the estate, the Corporation of Chichester, which town is only a few miles distant from Stanstead, waited upon Mr. Barwell the morning after our arrival with a complimentary address upon his coming into the neighbourhood, which address was spoken fluently and gracefully enough by the Mayor, ending with a polite request that he and his family would honour them with his and their company (on a day specified) to a dinner and ball at the Town Hall.

This mark of respectful attention, so politely offered, was received in an awkward and cold manner by the pompous East Indian. He, however, did accept the invitation, and we naturally concluded he intended to keep the engagement, nothing passing to lead us to suspect the contrary.

On the day appointed his coach-and-six and chaise-and-four
came to the door at three o'clock, when he desired us, that
is, his brother, Pott, and myself, to get into the former,
which we did, concluding he meant to follow alone in the
post-chaise. We drove to the Town Hall of Chichester,
where the whole Corporation and all the principal people of
the place were in waiting to receive us. Surprized at not
seeing Mr. Barwell, the Mayor made a civil enquiry respecting him, to which the brother answered he would follow
immediately. An hour elapsed without any tidings of
him, when young Barwell went downstairs and sent off a
servant to see what detained his brother. The man being
admirably mounted, returned in little more than half an
hour, saying his master was not well and did not intend
coming at all, but this he had only learnt from the steward,
Mr. Barwell saying he had no message to send back.

The brother, confounded at such deliberate rudeness,
made the best apology he could, and we sat down to a
sumptuous entertainment, at which I felt ashamed of
being considered the friend of a man who had acted in so
insolent and unpardonable a way. The dinner and evening
ball went on with the utmost harmony and good-humour,
no reference, after the first surprize, being made to the
great man's strange behaviour. The wanton insult was,
however, felt and resented not only by the Mayor and
Corporation of Chichester, but by the whole county, every
individual thereof with one consent sending the insolent
nabob to Coventry ; not a single gentleman visited or took
the least notice of him upon casual meetings.

Not content with insulting the men of Chichester,
Mr. Barwell made it his study, as it should seem, to render
himself obnoxious to persons of all ranks, shutting up gates
and paths through his parks that had, as an indulgence,
always been open to the public, preventing the poor from
supplying themselves with water from a spring they had
long been used to frequent ; in short, doing everything that
was illiberal, offensive, and ill-natured. His very name
from this conduct soon was held in such detestation that

men, women, and children hissed and hooted at him as he passed, with all his Oriental state, through the villages.

After persevering in this offensive line of conduct about six months Mr. Barwell began to think that being completely shut out from society, except what he had from London, and those mostly East Indians, was not pleasant. He therefore began to relax by not only opening the former paths, roads, &c., but making additional ones, likewise extending every indulgence ever granted by Lord Halifax. He even condescended so far as to humble himself to the Mayor and Corporation of Chichester for his rudeness, thereby making his peace with them, which having effected, he invited them and all the principal families round the neighbourhood to a magnificent dinner, ball, and supper. Some few of the gentry had spirit enough to spurn his attempt to be acquainted, and declined being present at his fête, but still there were always people enough who, although they despised the man, could not resist the temptation his splendid dinners and excellent wines afforded.

Parliament being to reassemble on the 8th, Pott and I returned to town that I might resume my attendance upon the committee, the chairman having desired me to do so.

A few nights after I came to town, being at the Opera House, I saw Mordaunt standing in Fops' Alley with his brother, Lord Peterborough. I thought he looked less surly than usual. He soon after came up and shook me by the hand with much cordiality. I congratulated him upon the favourable change, remarking that he was in better spirits than when I left London, and I conjectured was not in such a violent hurry as he had been to revisit Bengal, *the only part of the world fit for a man to live with comfort in !* (his own language), whereupon he hastily exclaimed, " Oh, damn the place, don't mention it. I should be devilish glad never to be obliged to see it again so long as I live." Upon reminding him of my having predicted that when his brother returned to England and introduced him to his numerous connections he would be better pleased with

London and everything attached to it, he admitted I was quite right, for he felt as happy and contented as man could be.

A curious circumstance now occurred. I had dined with a jovial set at Wilberforce Bird's in Wood Street, Cheapside, where we drank a large quantity of wine. Soon after midnight, the company breaking up, someone proposed finishing the night at Malby's. A hackney coach being sent for, six of us crammed ourselves into it : Bob Pott, Coombe, Shakespear, Lord Fielding, Vaughan, and myself. We had got as far as Ludgate Hill on our way to Covent Garden, when Pott, thinking the coachman did not drive fast enough, damned his blood and bid him move on. Coachie made a gruff answer, which offended Master Bob, who thereupon poked at him through the front window with the hilt of his sword, a salutation John Bull not approving he instantly returned the compliment by the butt end of his whip. Pott, in a violent rage, crept through the window and began pummelling the fellow with all his might. After a sharp but short conflict they tumbled together off the box into the street. A mob collecting, the horses were stopped and we all got out to the assistance of our associate. A kind of general engagement ensued, chiefly between us and the watchmen who had come to support the rights of the brother of the whip. The battle ended as might be expected it would by three of us, that is, Vaughan, Pott, and myself, being violently seized and dragged to the watchhouse in Fleet market, Lord Fielding, Shakespear, and Coombe having very prudently made good their retreat, thereby avoiding being taken prisoners by the enemy.

The constable of the night, a respectable-looking person, upon seeing three full-dressed men brought in, all abominably intoxicated, upon the coachman's making his complaint, with great good-nature said, " Come, come, young gentlemen, this is, I perceive, a drunken frolic. You must therefore pay for your folly and go quietly home to sleep off the effects of too much wine."

While the constable was speaking, a good, fat-looking

body, who declared himself to be a peaceable citizen and pastry-cook in Fleet Street, came up, the blood streaming from his nose, protesting against the unjustifiable conduct and violence of our party, who had assailed and maltreated him merely because he had stepped forward and exerted himself to rescue them out of the hands of an offended mob, rendered more angry by the appearance of and the story told by the coachman, who certainly had sustained some injury in the affray.

Although my head was by no means clear, I nevertheless felt the full force of the kind constable's very sensible advice, and putting my hand into my pocket was about to make a pecuniary recompense for our transgression when Pott, who was in one of his wicked and facetious fits, and resolved to have some fun before he paid, cried out, "No. No! I protest against the doling out of cash, so, proceed, sir, to do your duty. Observe, I am a profound lawyer, deeply read in the statutes since the establishment of Englishman's pride and glory, Magna Charta, so stand by, my old cock, and let me see that I do not catch you tripping, for blood and hounds! if I do I'll circumfloborate you and all your base understrappers." The constable looked with some symptoms of surprize at Pott, and after hemming once or twice, said, "I think, young gentleman, that after the experience of thirty years I do pretty well know my duty. I will convince you that I do know it by clapping you for the remainder of the night into the black hole, young gentleman, do you see, and I have no doubt but the air of that *agreeable* apartment will restore your senses."

"Black hole!" repeated Pott. "Take care, old Dogberry, you are upon the edge of a precipice into which if you fall the devil himself will not be able to relieve you, though I can. Proceed therefore with caution. You talk of black holes without a trial! Come, proceed. Ascend your magisterial chair and take down depositions, otherwise you will be all at sea and cast away upon the rocks of error and ignorance. Proceed, I say."

"Very well! very well, young sir, I believe you may be

right in this notion and I will act conformably." While preparing to take his seat, Pott slipped behind him and occupied it, to the great entertainment of the bystanders. Again the black hole was alluded to. Bob therefore relinquished the chair, which the humble representative of justice immediately filled, and, taking up his pen, prepared his book ; Bob in the meantime got behind him and twirled his wig round, putting the back part in front. Again a burst of laughter broke forth, and again the black hole was threatened.

The constable then demanded to know his name. "George," answered Pott. "That's not true," observed the constable, "for I just now heard that gentleman (pointing to me) call you ' Bob.' " "That gentleman," said Bob, "is too drunk to tell his own name, and I am sure cannot distinguish any other person's, so get on, most upright judge, you second Daniel." "Well, sir," asked the constable, "who are you ? " "A son of the King's," said Bob. The man stared, and in a hesitating voice said, "I do not exactly understand what you are at, young sir. I wish you would act like a reasonable creature." "Proceed, thou mirror of all that's just, or by the mighty Jupiter, I'll jumble you to mincemeat."

The constable losing his temper at being made a laughing-stock, ordered the door of the black hole to be opened, whereupon Vaughan, with vast solemnity, addressed him, saying, "I have hitherto, sir, been a quiet spectator of all that has passed, and although wrongfully brought and detained here as a prisoner, have not uttered a syllable, but when I hear you talk of more rigorous confinement of my friend, I consider it right to caution you as to your proceedings, for which, if wrong, depend upon it you shall be made responsible, and give me leave further to inform you that I am the more competent to caution you as to your measures from myself having the honour to be in His Majesty's Commission of the Peace for the County of Middlesex. I therefore once more recommend you to take care what you are about."

" I am sorry to hear you are yourself a magistrate, sir,"
said the constable, " because if that be the case you ought
to know better than to commit a breach of the peace by
kicking up a broil and riot in the streets at midnight. However, sir, that matter you shall settle before the sitting
alderman in the morning."

Growing tired of the scene, I took one of the constables
aside, to whom I observed I thought my young companion
had sufficiently amused himself, and that I should be
obliged to him if he would settle the business, and let us get
home. This he very good-naturedly undertook, and after
talking apart with the coachman, returned, saying the
coachman at first demanded five guineas, but had finally
consented to take two. The disinterested pastry - cook
declined receiving any pecuniary recompense, very considerately saying the personal injury he had sustained was
trifling, and although he at first felt much offended at the
treatment he had received, he was now convinced it arose
entirely from a drunken frolic, the gentlemen not intending
or wishing to injure anyone. I therefore paid the coachman two guineas, gave two more to the people of the watch,
and we departed, cheered by the hearty huzzas of all present,
the spectators declaring we acted like gentlemen ; that they
were sure if the *fair one* (meaning Pott) was not a son of
His Majesty's he must be nearly allied to the Royal Family
from his likeness to them. But at any rate, be he whom he
might, he had that night proved he was a very comical, and
certainly was a very fine-looking, handsome fellow.

In the beginning of February Pott told me he had agreed
for the whole of the round-house and half the great cabin
of the ship *Lord Mulgrave*, commanded by Captain Urmston,
which ship would sail for India in six or seven weeks ; that in
consideration of a large sum of money the Captain had consented to receive Emily on board, and they both (Emily
and Pott) flattered themselves that I would join the party
by occupying the half of the great cabin, which he (Pott)
had taken in the hope that I would do so. To this I answered
that it was impossible for me to leave England until some-

thing decisive was done respecting the petition I had
brought home. Pott thereupon laughingly said, "Psha!
nonsense, Bill. Why don't you speak honestly and say,
as the truth is, that your money not being yet expended
you have no inclination to leave this paradise, nor do I
wonder at it. Emily's vanity made her think you would
sacrifice much to have her society during the voyage, while
I had too good an opinion of your taste to suppose you would
quit England until compelled by dire necessity. I only
lament that my finances will not allow of my waiting
another year for you, as by that time I fancy your stock
will be pretty well exhausted. However," continued he,
" under these circumstances you must be with us as much
as possible until our departure," a desire I had real satisfaction in agreeing to.

Being at a masquerade with Pott and Emily at Cornelys's,
I there again met with Charlotte Barry, hanging upon the
arm of my cynical friend Mordaunt, who, after introducing
me, whispered that he had taken her into keeping. Pott
being seized with a violent headache, Emily and he went
home before twelve o'clock, whereupon I joined Mordaunt
and his new favourite. He being fond of running about the
rooms to speak to every acquaintance he saw, frequently
left Charlotte under my care, and we soon became mutually
attached, so much so that from that evening our love ended
only with the dear girl's life.

Our club continued to meet twice a week, ultimately
fixing entirely at Le Tellier's, I believe more from the name
and central situation than any superior merit. The house
I pitched upon and gave my dinner at, or rather presided at,
was the St. Albans, where, though one or two general
snarlers found fault with the dinner, all admitted the wines
to be exquisitely good, the champagne especially. The
taverns we had tried were : The Star and Garter, Pall Mall,
unanimously approved ; the St. Albans, as I have above
mentioned ; Thatched House, St. James's Street, tolerable ,
Crown and Anchor, Strand, dinner capital, wines abominably bad ; Devil, Fleet Street, the dinner indifferent and

wines the same, with the exception of port, which being remarkably good, nothing else was drank ; Queen's Arms, St. Paul's Churchyard, dinner and wines in general pronounced passable, and the London, Bishopsgate Street, which in my opinion far surpassed every other tavern we went to. The dinner was allowed to be excellent and served in a style of magnificence peculiar to that house, wines all of the best. Here everybody was so well pleased that several of us remained at table until seven o'clock in the morning. Had our original plan been strictly adhered to, doubtless the club would have settled at the London, but a considerable number of the members residing at the west end of the town objected to the *horrid bore* of going so far as Bishopsgate Street to dine. Le Tellier's therefore was decided to be the *best house !*

About once a month I gave a dinner at my father's, my friends always doing me the honour to say neither Le Tellier's, the London, or any tavern in the metropolis could surpass me in the excellence of the viands and liquors.

We had another very good sociable meeting occasionally, twelve or fifteen of us, attended by some of the most fashionable women of the time, going to March's, the Windmill, at Salt Hill, where we spent three or four days together in all sorts of frolic and fancy.

We usually went on Friday, staying till Tuesday, except that on Sunday evening, Mordaunt, Charlotte Barry, and myself would after dinner get into a post-chaise and four, and dash up to Cornelys's promenade, where after strolling round the rooms, chatting to acquaintances, we returned in the same manner to Salt Hill to sleep, but generally found some of the party up, engaged at hazard, to which several were greatly addicted, especially Major George Russell, who, about four years before, had returned from Bengal with a fortune of upwards of forty thousand pounds, the whole of which he had squandered away or lost at the gaming table, he at the period I became acquainted with him not having five hundred pounds left. He lost at one sitting near ten thousand pounds to the Duke de Chartres, afterwards Duke of Orleans, who fell a martyr to that dreadful revolution which he was very instrumental in bringing about, dying under the guillotine, unpitied and unlamented, the mob who attended him in his last moments stopping the cart in which they were leading him to execution opposite his own palace, and there bestowing all sorts of abuse and opprobrious epithets upon him.

Major Russell used to say that the night after losing the above large sum he met the Duke at Ranelagh, and bowed, but His Grace neither returned his salutation nor took the least notice of him, a rudeness that greatly offended Russell. He was, however, most likely mistaken upon the occasion, and probably the Duke who was uncommonly near-sighted, did not see his bow, for if he had doubtless he would have returned it, being universally allowed to be one of the most affable and best bred men in Europe.

My Sunday night excursions from Salt Hill to Soho Square cost me a coat each time, for Mordaunt, like my friend Bob Pott, always falling fast asleep in a carriage, Charlotte and I, during his naps, kissed and fondled like a pair of turtle-doves, and as the women then wore large quantities of pomatum and powder, and Charlotte had a profusion of hair, I was constantly covered with them. When Mordaunt observed this he would say to me in his usual rough snarl, " What the devil have you been about to make such a figure of your clothes ? " to which Charlotte without hesitation replied, " I followed your bad example and went to sleep with my head upon his shoulder." " Did you, by God ! " said Mordaunt, " the more fool he for permitting it. I'll be damned if you ever shall spoil my clothes so." " Never fear, there is not the least danger of my attempting it," contemptuously said Charlotte.

Riding in Hyde Park, I there met my Fleet Market watch-house companion, Thomas Vaughan, Esq. After talking together some time upon common topics he said, " I frequently see you in Suffolk Street, and yet, although so near and that you have often promised to give me an opportunity of introducing you to Mrs. Vaughan and a house full

of daughters, you have never done me the honour of calling." I made some commonplace apology, and the subject
dropped. After riding some time, we left the Park together, and his horses standing at Fozard's, we dismounted
and walked up Piccadilly, during which he took out his
watch, observing, " It is, I see, only three o'clock. Suppose
therefore, as you will afterwards have ample time to dress
for dinner, that you come home with me now and let me
make you acquainted with my family." As I knew not how
to parry this proposal I went with him.

Upon getting to his house we found the street door open.
Mr. Vaughan therefore desired me to follow him upstairs,
where, without any announcing, he opened the drawing-
room door. Upon entering the room, I found six very nice-
looking girls at high romps, and all in dishabille. The two
eldest were just rising into womanhood, extremely elegant
figures. They appeared distressed beyond measure at a
stranger's thus unexpectedly coming upon them, exclaiming, " Fie, papa, how could you bring a gentleman in
without affording us an opportunity of retiring ? " Nor did
the father lessen their embarrassment by saying in an
audible whisper to me, " There they are, Hickey, a complete half-dozen, all good-looking girls. Damn me, if I
know what is to become of them, or how I shall be able
to provide for them as they grow up." Mrs. Vaughan was
not at home, but I had been introduced to her a few evenings before at a great party given by a Mrs. Treves. She was
an uncommon clever woman and had written several things
of extraordinary merit, which were published under the
name and as the production of her husband, though he was
in no way equal to composing one of the kind, being a weak,
empty coxcomb. They were both particularly attached to
the drama, constant attendants upon the theatres, criticising
in the public newspapers all new pieces and new actors.
Mr. Sheridan was said to have had this couple in view when
he wrote the characters of Mr. and Mrs. Dangle in his celebrated work of " The Critic."

Mrs. Vaughan brought her husband a fortune of ten

thousand pounds ; he held a sinecure place under Government of about six hundred a year, but being not only extravagant but a bad manager he was always involved, finding it difficult to support with decency a numerous family. Indeed, he would have proved wholly unequal to do so had he not received material aid from the writings of Mrs. Vaughan, which becoming fashionable were read by everybody, consequently had a great sale. Three of this gentleman's daughters some years after my awkward visit went to India, where they all married. The mother has been dead a long time, and Vaughan himself, as I am informed, a prisoner in the King's Bench for debt.

CHAPTER XXIV

CHARLOTTE AND MORDAUNT

TOWARDS the end of February the committee to which the petition from Bengal had been referred made their first report to the House of Commons, which rendered any further attendance on my part unnecessary, a circumstance I was not sorry for, having just received an intimation from Charlotte Barry that Mordaunt was making a party to go hunting and shooting in Oxfordshire, requesting that I would be one amongst them. This I could not do, having promised Emily and Pott to accompany them to Portsmouth and see them embark, an order to do which they were in daily expectation of receiving. From this promise, however, I was relieved by Robert calling one morning upon me and saying that he, upon consideration, felt that such a jaunt upon such an occasion must be far from pleasant to me and would undoubtedly be most distressing to him as well as to his dear girl when we should come to the final leavetaking, a ceremony he knew we mutually abhorred. Pott thought it would be better to waive the Portsmouth engagement, and proposed in lieu of it that I should go with them to Salt Hill, to which place he must pay a visit in order to see his brother, Joseph Holden Pott, then at Eton School ; he said that he and Emily would stay there until summoned away, and I, after passing one or more days, as I pleased, with them might slip off *sans cérémonie* and proceed to join the Oxfordshire party. Thus it was arranged and executed. After spending three days at March's, all low in spirits, I rose at break of day on the fourth morning, and leaving Pott and his lovely companion in bed, stepped

319

into a post-chaise for Reading on my way to Chapel House near Chipping Norton to join the sportsmen, and so avoided the formal adieus of my greatly esteemed friend, Pott, and his beautiful Emily.

Upon our arrival at Chapel House, Charlotte greeted me with extraordinary warmth, while her jade of a sister, Nancy Barry (as wicked a little devil as ever existed), cried out, "Now's your time, Hickey! That beast Mordaunt was called away this morning by his Earl of a brother, who is on a visit at Lord Hilsborough's, somewhere in the county, to whom he wants to introduce the nabob, so that you will have a couple of days' enjoyment together, and I have no doubt you'll make the most of them." The males of the party had not yet returned from the chase. From the women I learnt that it consisted of Joe Bird, Harvey Coombe, Wilberforce Bird, Van, Lord Semple, Lord Field-ing, and Ulysses Browne, the last-named having just then quitted the Horse Guards, in which he was an old Captain, but was obliged to quit from having lived rather too fast for his income.

By five o'clock the chasseurs being all assembled at the inn, we sat down to dinner, were exceedingly merry, and kept it up until midnight when we separated. Notwithstanding the fair opportunity and the mutual regard for each other between Charlotte and me, we had both our scruples of conscience, from her then living exclusively with Mordaunt, whose intimate friend I was considered to be. She also assured me she never had been unfaithful to any man with whom she lived, that from her soul she detested her present keeper, Mordaunt, and would get rid of him very soon, but while under his immediate protection she wished to act with propriety. Neither could I forget Emily's speech to me when in something of a similar situation.

At ten we breakfasted, then mounted our horses, Charlotte being one of the best horsewomen I ever saw. We took a long ride towards Birmingham, during which we were once very near falling in with the hounds and obliged to turn short, galloping off as fast as our steeds could carry

us in order to get out of their track, my fair companion
having no more relish for the sports of the field than myself.

At Chapel House I spent four as pleasant days as ever
I experienced, in the enjoyment of women, wine, and admirable society. When at table the men often remarked
that although I shunned the chase, over the bottle I was
as keen a sportsman as the best of them.

On the fourth evening Mordaunt returned, and as he
seemed more savage and looked surlier than ever, I bid the
party adieu ; ordering a chaise-and-four I set off for London,
giving Captain Browne a passage.

Upon reaching St. Albans Street I found a letter from
Mr. Pott, Robert's father, most earnestly requesting to see
me immediately upon a business in which his happiness was
materially concerned as well as the future welfare or irre-
trievable ruin of his son, my friend Robert. This letter I
was concerned to see dated the morning upon which I had
left town. I, however, thought it right to wait upon him,
and directly went to his house in Hanover Square, telling
him I had only that hour received his letter. He was much
distressed upon first seeing me, and expressed his grateful
sense of my kind attention towards him. Almost in tears,
he said that knowing the great influence I possessed over
that inconsiderate boy, Robert, he had taken the liberty
of sending for me to beg my interference and exertions to
preserve him from absolute destruction by preventing his
committing an act pregnant with every possible evil, but
which he feared was then past remedy, adding in an agony,
" For, do you know, Mr. Hickey, the unthinking boy has
taken that infamous and notoriously abandoned woman,
Emily, who has already involved him deeply as to pecuniary
matters, with him to India, a step that must not only shut
him out of all proper society, but prevent his being employed in any situation of respect or emolument. I have
nevertheless the melancholy consolation of feeling that I
have strictly performed my duty as a parent towards him
and done all in my power to save him from disgrace and
ruin, and if I have failed in accomplishing an object I had

so much at heart no blame surely can be ascribed to me ; his folly be upon his own head, *mais ses vues sont courtes.*"

I received the same day a long epistle from Robert, telling me that after an ineffectual attempt to get to sea they had returned, and still lay wind-bound at the Mother Bank (Portsmouth) ; that he was extremely uneasy at the detention, as the old buck (meaning his father) was stirring heaven and earth to defeat his wish of keeping his dear woman with him. " Nay," adds he, " do you know, Bill, he has carried it so far as to apply to the Court of Directors, and the stupid soap-boilers in consequence directed their addle-pated secretary to address a letter ' *upon the service,*' to Captain Urmston, admonishing him against so unpardonable a fault as permitting a common prostitute to find her way to India on board his ship. But it's all in vain, my dear Will, go she must, and go she shall by all the powers of heaven and hell. Poor Urmston is in a woeful panic, saying it may be the means of his losing the command of his ship, and the service altogether. But I know better ; the worst the cheese-mongering varlets of Leadenhall Street can do is to mulct him a few hundred pounds, which I, of course, shall pay." He then again pressed me to join them, observing he had a noble cabin quite complete and ready to receive me, with a set of passengers I should like. I, however, felt no inclination to avail myself of this friendly offer, having too many attachments to England to quit it until dire necessity should make me do so.

Two days after this, I believe about the 6th of March, taking my usual exercise on horseback in Hyde Park, Mordaunt rode up to tell me he had the evening before brought Mrs. Barry to town, apprehending her to be dangerously ill ; that the physicians, however, consoled him by saying that was by no means the case, and, although she might be confined for some time, would ultimately do very well, but that perfect quiet was indispensably necessary, and that nothing should disturb or agitate her for a week or ten days.

" For my part, Hickey," continued Mordaunt, " I begin

to suspect she is in love with you. She is so damned ill-natured and out of spirits except when you are present, and when you are she is all life. The hour you left us at Chapel House she became as cross as the devil, and I could get no good out of her. Damn her, I won't talk any more about her, but leave her to her infernal apothecaries' bolusses, draughts, and dark chambers. How horridly stupid London is, nothing going forward worth notice. I wish you was not so wedded to it and would dash off somewhere for a week or so."

I told him I was ready and willing, having no particular inducements just then in London, but where should we go to ? "To Portsmouth," said Mordaunt. "I was told an hour ago that the grand Channel fleet are at an anchor there, affording to the people on shore a glorious spectacle. Let's get into a chaise and be off directly."

That I told him I could not do, being most particularly engaged for the rest of that day, but would accompany him on the following morning at as early an hour as he chose. He growled sadly at this *delay*, as he called it, pressing me to give up my engagements and set off, but as I positively refused it was settled that I should breakfast with him the next morning at eight o'clock at his mother's house in Dean Street, Soho, from whence we should start on our expedition.

Upon my arrival at Lady Peterborough's I saw standing at the door a smart travelling post-chaise, having the family coat-of-arms and coronet handsomely painted upon the panels. Having finished our breakfast, we stepped into the carriage and set off in high style. Upon enquiring how Mrs. Barry was that morning, he replied, "Oh, curse me if I know anything about her, as from the infernal doctor's prohibition I am not allowed to touch her. I slept last night at my mother's, nor have I seen her since I brought her to town and left her at her lodgings the night before last. I have no doubt, Hickey, but you could cure her much sooner than the whole college of medical men."

When Mordaunt and I left London the weather was, as it

had been for a fortnight before, serene and beautifully fine, but before we had gone twenty miles it became dull and overcast, and when we reached Petersfield there was every indication of a complete change. The Forty-second Regiment was marching into that town at the time we entered it, on their way to Portsmouth, where they were to embark for India. The officers had engaged almost all the horses in the place, and before we could procure four, without which Mordaunt would never stir, it became dusk and began to snow. I therefore proposed staying where we were comfortably housed until the next morning, to which my companion agreed readily enough. We eat our dinner and supper in one, drank a bottle of claret each and went to bed. Upon getting up the next morning I saw the whole country covered by a thick body of snow, the sky overcast and dull. We met at breakfast, Mordaunt looking as gloomy as the weather. While taking our coffee I remarked that the object we set out upon being entirely defeated by the unfavourable change in the weather, I thought the most prudent thing we could do would be to bend our course back from whence we came. Whereupon Mordaunt angrily said I might do as I pleased, but as he left town for the purpose of going to Portsmouth most assuredly he should proceed.

"For what purpose?" asked I. "Do you conceive it possible to see the fleet or, indeed, any object at the distance of one hundred yards in such weather as the present?"

"That may be," growled my chum, "but by God I'll go on. I perfectly understand why you are in such haste to return. It is that you may ingratiate yourself," and he muttered something more to himself. Though I could not distinguish what he said I knew he alluded to Charlotte, but having determined not to be put out of temper by his moroseness, I mildly replied he was mistaken; that I had proposed relinquishing the rest of the scheme we had set out upon merely from seeing so unfavourable a change in the weather, nevertheless if he thought it advisable to go on I was ready to attend him.

Without a word more Mordaunt told the waiter who had come into the room to take away the breakfast-things, and bring the chaise to the door as soon as possible. In a few minutes it was announced ready. We got in, but before we reached Portsmouth the snow recommenced, falling so fast and so thick that when we got out at the George Inn we literally could not distinguish the houses on the opposite side of the street. As it began to freeze before we left Petersfield the roads were so slippery the horses could not keep their feet, and we were full four hours going the stage to Portsmouth.

Mordaunt, more sulky than ever, would not speak when I wished to consult him about dinner. I therefore desired the landlord to furnish the best his larder afforded. At five we sat down to an excellent dinner. A few glasses of madeira restoring my misanthropic companion to somewhat better temper, we chatted over the bottle until after coffee was served, then played piquet until bedtime.

The next morning the weather had not in the least mended, we nevertheless so far set the snow at defiance as to walk to the coffee-room upon the Parade, from whence in clear weather there is a fine prospect of Spithead and the Isle of Wight, but in the state we had it we could not see twenty yards from the windows. Here we met a number of naval officers and entered into conversation with several. We also had a very good match at billiards, thus beguiling the hours until towards four o'clock, when two smart young lieutenants accepted an invitation we gave them to partake of our dinner at the George. We gave as much madeira and claret as they could carry away, and at midnight they departed in high spirits, well pleased with their entertainment.

A second day and evening went off vastly well. The third morning a tremendous snow continued falling with severe frost. We repeated our visit to the coffee-room and played billiards, but there being a court martial that drew away all the officers we could not procure a single guest to join us at dinner, so that the snarler and I had a *tête-à-tête.* I perceived he was much out of humour from his determined silence during the meal and his frequent application to the bottle. Having drank our coffee, I called for cards, beating him seven games, not at all improving his manners. A little before eleven I looked at my watch to see the hour, whereupon with great violence he dashed down his cards upon the table and looking fiercely at me the following dialogue ensued :—

Mordaunt : " Pray, may I venture, without giving offence, to ask how long you propose staying in this attracting town of Portsmouth ? "

Hickey : "I cannot consider that otherwise than an insulting question, and most extraordinary to come from you, Mordaunt. Had I put such a one to you it would have been more appropriate and reasonable."

Mordaunt : "For the soul of me I can't see why. Be that as it may, and let your object in continuing at Portsmouth be ever so good, I am satisfied, quite satisfied, by God. I have had enough of Portsmouth, the enviable, delightful spot, and will leave it this instant."

Hickey : "Not in such a night as this is, I imagine, for that would be too wild a measure for even the very eccentric Captain Mordaunt to adopt."

Mordaunt : " The eccentric Captain Mordaunt, however, certainly will not stay another hour in this infernal town, sir."

Hickey : "Probably you are not aware that travelling in such tremendously bad weather as the present, and through such a hilly country, must be attended with considerable personal danger. That, I fancy, will influence you, Captain Mordaunt, though prudential motives may lose their effect."

Mordaunt : " Again you are mistaken. No motives whatsoever shall keep me here," and he pulled violently at the bell. A waiter obeying the furious summons, he ordered a bill immediately, and four horses to be put to his carriage to take him the first stage to London. The man stared and looked frightened, but did not move, upon which Mordaunt began to curse and swear, and walking towards the waiter he made a precipitate retreat.

In a few seconds Bolton, the landlord, made his appearance, saying, "The waiter, gentlemen, tells me you propose setting off for London." (I interrupted him to assure him I had no thoughts of that kind, not being absolutely insane.) He bowed to me and, addressing Mordaunt, proceeded to observe the weather was more dreadful than he ever had known it, so uncommonly bad that he should feel averse to sending his horses and post-boys abroad in it; that the roads from the immense fall of snow and severity of the frost must, he imagined, be rendered impassable or, at any rate, exceedingly dangerous. If, however, his (Mordaunt's) determination was to commence his journey at so inclement a season he could have no chance of succeeding except by Gosport, the Petersfield hill being impracticable to ascend in such weather. Mordaunt answered it was a matter of indifference to him by what road they took him, but go he would. The landlord withdrawing to order the horses might be put to, I resumed the conversation with Mordaunt by saying, "Surely, Mordaunt, this is an excessive wild scheme of yours?"

Mordaunt: "I cannot help your thoughts. Mine happen to the very opposite, and I know no reason why yours are to bind me."

Hickey: "Yet anyone except a madman would agree as to the propriety of my advice upon this occasion. One advantage I shall derive from your obstinacy—it will prevent my ever going upon an expedition with a madman in future."

Mordaunt: "You are becoming amazingly rude."

Hickey: "If I am, your strange conduct, your want of temper, and your absurdity, to use no harsher phrases justify me."

Mordaunt: "I cannot conceive upon what principle of civility or good breeding I am bound to shut myself up in an inn at Portsmouth when it is disagreeable to me to continue there."

328 MEMOIRS OF WILLIAM HICKEY

Hickey : " Give me leave to ask what brought us here but your unaccountable perverseness and obstinacy. Did I not when at Petersfield strongly remonstrate against continuing the journey from seeing so total a change in the weather had taken place, and observe to you that the purpose for which we set out being so completely defeated the best thing we could do would be to return to London ? Did you not most pertinaciously and mulishly insist upon going on in spite of frost, snow, and all I could say to induce you to abandon your intention ? "

Mordaunt : " Perhaps I did persevere in wishing to accomplish my object. Perhaps, too, the *mulishness* you speak of influenced me. Certain it is the same *mulishness* and not knowing or feeling myself your slave now determines me to pursue my own inclination, which leads me to leave Portsmouth, but surely that need not influence you."

Hickey : " Most indisputably it shall not, nor will I make such an ass of myself as to stir from hence without at least the benefit of daylight."

Mordaunt : " My resolution is unalterable."

Hickey : " I am ready to give you full credit for possessing a greater degree of obstinacy than ever fell to the lot of one man. I shall nevertheless take the liberty of once more repeating that I should not have been here but to indulge your capricious whim ; that nothing could be more disgusting to me than remaining here in your society three tedious days, yet that having occurred I do not see the necessity of beginning a journey at midnight in such dreadful weather as now prevails. We arrived here together, let us return like reasonable men together. Stay till the morning and I will accompany you."

Mordaunt : " Damn me, if I stay a single hour."

Hickey : " Then go and be damned."

At that moment Bolton brought the bill and announced the chaise being at the door, but again very strongly recommended Mordaunt not to stir until daylight. His advice was thrown away. Mordaunt then took from his purse a banknote, which he threw upon the table, saying, " There's

CHAPTER XXV

INFATUATED WITH CHARLOTTE

THE club broke up at the end of March. The two last months of its existence I had scarcely been once at it, my whole time being given up to my new favourite, Charlotte, in attending her to masquerades, theatres, The Pantheon, and every other public place that was open, to no one of which would she ever consent to go unless I made one, and although Mordaunt was exceedingly jealous of her avowed partiality towards me, he often entreated me to let them have as much of my company as I could, observing that Charlotte was not at all the same person when I was absent, being then dejected and so damned ill-tempered he could make nothing of her. " Nay," said he, " she has even gone so far as to tell me to my face that her object and intention is to give herself up entirely to you." After a pause in which I could see he had worked himself into a rage, he with extreme vehemence added, " but that, by God, she never shall do, to you or any other man breathing, so long as I live." As I felt awkward upon the subject I made no answer, and besides, I had given my solemn promise to Charlotte that I would avoid quarrelling with Mordaunt, and leave the bringing about a separation entirely to her.

In April, Ranelagh, to which I always had been partial opened, and we were constant attendants thrice a week on Monday, Wednesday, and Friday evenings. Even the general grumbler, Mordaunt, acknowledged he found that entertainment more pleasing than any other of the public places. He one morning took me to look at a famous travelling-coach building for his brother in Long Acre. In

333

size it was nearly, if not full as large as the Lord Mayor of London's state carriage. It accommodated three persons on each side with superabundant room. In the centre there drew up from the bottom, by springs, a table, sufficiently large to dine six persons comfortably. Under the floor were all the requisite apparatus of saucepans, gridiron, &c., for cooking, likewise knives, forks, plates, dishes, and other articles of a sideboard. Beneath the seats complete bedding for four persons was stowed, which, when wanted for use, were taken out and placed upon a frame, crossways, four capital beds being made ready in five minutes. In a projection from the back of the body of the carriage and the same forward was ample stowage for wines, and all sorts of liquors, handsome cut glass bottles of various sizes being secured in fixed frames, so that no motion, short of an absolute upset, could injure or derange them. In short, this stupendous vehicle was a moving house, having in and about it every convenience appertaining to a mansion. It was finished in point of workmanship and decorations in the highest manner, the Peterborough arms and heraldic ornaments being painted in a style of taste and with a delicacy that did the artist infinite credit.

The young Earl's object in building so uncommon a vehicle was to ensure for himself every common comfort when travelling upon the Continent, especially through Italy, where by woeful experience he knew the inns were execrable, abounding in dirt and filth, the beds swarming with bugs, fleas, and vermin of every description. The greatest objection to this carriage was its extreme ponderosity, which when I first saw it struck me so forcibly that I asked the coachmaker whether he did not apprehend its extraordinary weight might prove so serious as to render it useless, to which the mechanic candidly replied, "Undoubtedly it will, sir. Its weight is an insuperable impediment to its ever being of any real use, much less that for which it is intended, for no number of horses that could be attached together in harness would ever be able to drag it along the dreadful roads of Italy, Germany, and many parts of France, and so I have taken the liberty of telling his Lordship over and over again since this carriage has been in hand, and although I am convinced his own good sense satisfied him of the truth of what I said, he insisted upon my completing the work. Such crowds of people came daily to look at it while it remained in the front shop as greatly to impede and interrupt my workmen, the evil increasing to such a degree that I was at last obliged to remove it to this private warehouse, and refuse entrance to all persons applying to see it."

While Mordaunt and I were engaged in this conversation with the coachmaker, Lord Peterborough came in, and upon his brother's repeating to him the purport of what had just been said respecting the carriage, he readily admitted the justness of the opinion, saying he had no idea he should ever be able to use it in the way he intended. " However, that don't much signify," said his Lordship, " and it certainly has been a source of much amusement to me and my friends whilst building. Besides, Henry (addressing Mordaunt), if I am disappointed of its uses, it will serve you and your sultanas admirably well in your excursions about the country, and as you will neither require the bedding, nor any of the stores, when all those are taken out the draught will be easy enough for four horses, and I am convinced it will prove a most comfortable carriage to travel in." Mordaunt replied, " Very well, Peterborough, I certainly shall make the trial ere long."

On the 1st of May, at the particular request of Mordaunt, and the desire of Charlotte expressed to me privately, I accompanied them from London to take possession of the house at Drayton. Mr. Grant waited there to receive and entertain us, leaving us the next morning. I continued there two days, when the sulkiness of Mordaunt became so offensive, he from morning to night abusing Charlotte and scowling at me, and declining everything like conversation, that I could no longer submit to it, and, bidding her adieu, I mounted my horse and rode to town. In the evening of the same day Mordaunt, in great agitation, came to me at

my father's, begging and entreating that I would return with
him to Drayton, Charlotte being suddenly seized with an
illness of so alarming a nature he was quite miserable about
her. I told him his conduct was so unbecoming towards
her as a woman that I was astonished any consideration
on earth could induce her to remain another day with him ;
that as to myself, his behaviour had been so strange and so
rude during my last visit I should not voluntarily subject
myself to a repetition of it : he must therefore excuse
my declining any more being a guest of his. He begged
so hard, however, and expressed so much sorrow and contrition for the violence he had been guilty of, ascribing it
to a natural infirmity which he was resolved to correct in
future, that I relented and consented to return with him to
Drayton. He then told me that James Grant and Mrs. Grant
would be of our party, and all should be good-humour and
hilarity.

The following morning we four went down together in a
post-coach. Although only a distance of sixteen miles, and
notwithstanding all Mordaunt's fair promises, the devil
burst forth from him twice or thrice during our short journey,
for which Mrs. Grant, who possessed a great command of
words, and could, when she pleased, be excessively severe,
rated him unmercifully. She concluded a most bitter
lecture, declaring her astonishment that so mild and sweet
a girl as Charlotte Barry was could ever have consented
to be an inmate of the same house with him or, having inadvertently done so, that she should continue to submit to
the caprices and ill-humour of so insufferable a brute. This
attack from the lady was renewed after dinner at Drayton,
when she repeated all she had said in the coach. This she
was led to do from his short and surly answers to Charlotte,
notwithstanding he had represented her as being dangerously
ill. He stood the attack with apparent composure for some
time, but at last flew into a terrible rage, calling Mrs. Grant
a dirty little drab, an impudent and most abandoned
strumpet, whereupon Grant jumped up from his chair, and
putting his fist close to Mordaunt's face, told him his own

house alone protected him from that chastisement he was disposed to give him, and which his insolence and vulgarity so richly deserved. Poor Charlotte, dreadfully frightened, was thrown into hysterics by the scene, and whilst I and the servants were attending to and using means to recover her, Grant took his lady by the hand, walked to the inn, where they got into a chaise and went off for London.

It was upwards of an hour before Charlotte recovered. The moment she was herself Mordaunt began to bewail the misery constantly attendant upon his yielding to the momentary impulses he felt, and, turning to me, he said, "Hickey, you can have no idea of my sufferings. My whole soul is wrapped up in that woman (pointing to Charlotte), who by her neglect and contemptuous treatment drives me almost mad, so that I know not what I say or do. I fear she loathes and detests me in return for adoring her, and her only pleasure is involving me in disputes and quarrels upon her account. Into what a dilemma has she now brought me. In my frenzy I have shamefully ill-treated James Grant, who has upon several occasions shown himself my zealous friend. I must and will pacify him. There is no submission, no apology, that I will refuse to make." I reminded him that the state Charlotte was in was ill calculated to bear further noise or alarms, and recommended his being more temperate. To this he acceded, saying he would leave me to console his dearest girl, while he followed and endeavoured to make his peace with Grant. We soon after retired to our respective chambers, Charlotte pleading her illness in order to be left alone for the night, which Mordaunt, though ungraciously, was obliged to consent to.

The following morning while Mordaunt and I were at breakfast, for Charlotte did not leave her room, he told me he was going to London to apologize to Grant and persuade him to return with him to Drayton, requesting I would take care of Charlotte during his absence. He said he would, if possible, be back to dinner, but desired I would not wait beyond the usual hour. He then called for his horse and

set off at full speed, followed by his groom. The moment
he was gone Charlotte joined me, and we hugged ourselves
in the thoughts of enjoying a few hours uninterrupted by
his brutality. Time passed rapidly away.

The time of dinner coming without Mordaunt's appearing, we sat down together and had a comfortable meal. In
the evening we strolled about the grounds, which were very
pretty. Agreeably disappointed at Mordaunt's continued
absence, we took our coffee, tea and, at ten o'clock, supper.
I then *good-naturedly* began to hope, either that he had
broken his neck or that Grant had blown out his brains.
At eleven we determined to go to bed. My room was the
next to Charlotte's, and as all the servants were in my
interest they were ready enough to do everything to accommodate and please me. Upon Charlotte's retiring, the
butler, with great civility, begged my pardon for what
he was going to say, but as he and his fellow-servants were
sensible of my goodness to them upon all occasions, and the
same respecting their worthy mistress, they had desired
him to assure me that their master should not take me by
surprise, for in case he arrived in the night they would take
care to keep him long enough at the gate, and make sufficient noise to apprise me of his approach. Besides which,
his lady's maid would sit up. Thus secured against accident, I with confidence usurped the tyrant's place.

We rose at an early hour in the morning, breakfasted
at ten, the customary time, and after it mounted our
horses, bending our course towards the great western road.
When about two miles on the London side of Colnbrook
we met Mordaunt with Mr. and Mrs. Grant, going at a
furious rate to Drayton. After exchanging a few words they
proceeded, and we turned back. Upon getting home we
learnt that Mordaunt on his reaching town had directly
gone in search of Grant, but after running about for several
hours without success, resolved to wait patiently at
Mrs. Grant's for his coming, which he did at one in the
morning, when Mordaunt, though with considerable difficulty, made his peace, getting from him a consent to

accompany him to Drayton again at eleven o'clock in the morning, before which time Mordaunt was at their door with a post-chaise and four.

Soon after we got to Drayton, Mordaunt and Grant went to the stable to look at the horses, the two women and I strolling about the garden, when the character of the master of the house was very freely discussed, Mrs. Grant avowing that although James had thought proper to forgive his unexampled impertinence she was far from having done so, and was determined in some way or other to be revenged for the infamous epithet he had bestowed upon her.

Mordaunt in addition to his various eccentricities had several antipathies. Himself beyond a doubt in some measure insane, nothing occasioned him so much terror as encountering any unfortunate maniac. It therefore became an object with these two wicked and mischievous girls, wherever they were, and Mordaunt one of the party, to bring into the room some person labouring under that heavy affliction, a female if procurable, whom they taught suddenly and unexpectedly to seize Mordaunt round the neck and embrace him. From a trick of this sort I was once witness to, I actually thought he would have died from the fright he was thrown into. Another of his violent dislikes was to frogs, the sight of which animal would put him into a cold sweat, and the same with respect to cats. Great pains were therefore taken to put in his way frogs and cats.

At dinner the day the Grants returned Mordaunt was in tolerable good-humour until offended by the incessant mirth of the two women, at which he grew crabbed, asking what the devil they were giggling at. From their significant nods and signs to each other, I conjectured some mischief was on foot, though I knew not what, not having been let into the secret. The meat being removed, pastry succeeded. Mrs. Grant, drawing a dish to her, said to Mordaunt who sat next to her, " Captain Mordaunt, will you allow me to help you to a bit of this tart ? " He gruffly answered, " No, ma'am," to which she, with a broad grin, replied, " Dear ! now that's very ill-natured, for you like cherry tart and always eat it, and these are, I understand, the first of the season." He then said he could help himself, pulling the dish from before her, and began to cut it. The moment he took off a piece of the upper crust, out jumped an immense large frog, followed by two or three of lesser size in succession as fast as could be. Mordaunt instantly fell back in his chair as if he had been shot. Recovering, however, in a few moments he seized a carving knife that lay before him, and had not Grant, who sat on the other side of him, arrested his raised-up arm I have not a doubt but he would have stabbed Mrs. Grant. His face was of a livid hue and countenance horrible. Both women, excessively terrified, screeched and ran out of the room, the servants gathering up and carrying off the offensive animals.

It certainly was as malicious as imprudent a prank, near producing an awful consequence, yet I could scarcely pity the savage man who suffered so materially under it. Although he did Grant and me the justice to say he did not suspect either of us of being privy to the circumstance, we had the utmost difficulty in pacifying him, nor do I believe we should have succeeded had not Charlotte come to our aid and by her caresses soon brought him about. She certainly had great influence over him, and he was dotingly fond of her. He professed to have pardoned Mrs. Grant, but took infinite pains to discover which of the servants had assisted in the infamous trick (as he termed it). None of the domestics would betray the actual persons. Mordaunt was therefore reduced to vent his spleen upon a poor undergardener, because, he said, the damned animals must have been supplied by him, notwithstanding his protestations of innocence, and he dismissed him from his service.

On the 18th we all went to London and the following day to Epsom races in Lord Peterborough's famous coach, which I have already described, being the first exhibition of it upon the road. We got on inimitably well with six horses and three postilions. Mrs. Grant, Charlotte, and myself sat on one side, Mordaunt and Grant on the other. We had previously engaged private lodgings at Epsom, or, rather, in the neighbourhood, being half a mile distant from the town, for the race week. Each day upon making our appearance on the Downs, the novelty of our vehicle drew the attention of all bystanders, a mob constantly collecting round us, with open mouths staring at the extraordinary machine and criticising every part of it. It certainly was the easiest and most comfortable carriage I ever sat in.

The races being finished we left Epsom for London, Mordaunt's natural vile temper not being at all improved by being three hundred pounds minus by the week's speculation, and that entirely owing to his obstinacy and self-opinion, which made him back a particular horse, notwithstanding Grant, who knew much more of the matter than he did, told him that several of the knowing ones had cautioned him against laying upon the favourite, as he had not a chance of winning. He spurned the advice, lost his money, and the sulk consequently increased.

Charlotte and I kept a man and horse in full exercise galloping backwards and forwards between Drayton and London, for whenever Mordaunt was likely to be absent six or eight hours she instantly dispatched the man with a line to give me notice, in consequence of which I was with her as speedily as four horses could convey me.

Mordaunt having invited me one day to take a seat with him in a gig his brother had lent him, which, like all the Earl's carriages, was uncommonly elegant and, of course, bearing the arms, coronet, &c., I accepted the offer. We set off from Park Lane and drove through Hyde Park. In turning out of the Park one of the stage-coaches with a number of outside passengers, huzzaing and hallooing, frightened our horse. He began to plunge and kick, finally running us against a post of a new Sunday turnpike then erecting, whereby both shafts of the gig were snapped short off and Mordaunt thrown out, but not materially hurt by the fall. He then sent his groom on to Kensington to procure a post-chaise to carry us on the rest of our way. The carriage arriving in a few minutes, the gig was given to the charge of the ostler with directions to take it to a coachmaker's to be repaired, and he (Mordaunt) would call for it on his return from the country. We then proceeded to Drayton without further disaster.

The following morning Charlotte, Mordaunt, and myself, during our ride on horseback, met Sir George Metham, a debilitated but high-spirited old debauchee. He was quite of the *vieille Cour*, elegant and well bred. In the years 1770–1773 I had often been upon drunken parties with him. He instantly recognized me and bowed. Being also slightly acquainted with Mordaunt, he joined us. In the course of conversation discovering that we were at Drayton, he observed he was only a few miles distant from that place, having a cottage upon Coleshill, to which he requested our company at dinner the next day, and, addressing me in particular, said, " You, Mr. Hickey, will find an old friend there, who I am sure will be very happy to see you." Mordaunt, with more suavity than was usual, said he would wait upon Sir George with pleasure, provided he would go home with us and spend the rest of the day at Drayton. This Sir George consented to do. Upon our getting there he dispatched his horses and servant to say he should dine out and to order his carriage to take him home at night, observing he was too old to venture on horseback in the dark and with wine in his head. Sir George still enjoying the bottle, we drank freely, so much so that Mordaunt got extremely intoxicated, and we were obliged to send him off to bed. Sir George remained with Charlotte and me until midnight, when he wished us good night and departed.

The next day Mordaunt was totally incapable of moving, and so ill that he begged I would escort Charlotte and make his apologies to Sir George. I accordingly did so. Upon our arrival at Coleshill I was much gratified at being greeted by a very old female friend, Mrs. Carter, with whom I had thentofore been engaged in many a jovial scene, she, in those days, being known by the name of Bet Pye. She appeared equally happy at the renewal of our acquaintance and talking over matters long past. Sir George had merely told her a gentleman she had formerly known was coming to dine with her. The rest of the party consisted of a young man, natural son of Sir George's, Lord Spencer Hamilton of the Guards, and an elderly gentleman of the neighbourhood whose name I have forgot.

We had a delightful day in every respect. So gay and cheerful were we all that the hours fled imperceptibly, until Charlotte, casually looking at her watch, exclaimed with surprize, "Is it possible that my watch can be right ? If it is, time has indeed flown upon wings, for it is past two." And so it undoubtedly was. I therefore rang to order the carriage, but Sir George, like an old sportsman, insisted upon our taking the *Dukkin Dorreege* (I know not whether I spell it correctly. It means the parting glass, or glass at the door, in the Irish language),[1] and he produced some burgundy which, if not quite equal to Mr. Paxton's, was of a very superior quality to what was generally met with. At three we drove off, and having sixteen miles to go it was near five ere we reached Drayton. We found Mordaunt, early as it was, already up, stalking up and down the walk under the wall of the garden, in high dudgeon at our long stay, the cause of which he asked with great acrimony. He then said he supposed *we had not slept in the carriage*, with peculiar sullenness. However, whether we had or not, madam would not have many hours of it then, as he had received a letter which made his presence in town necessary by eleven o'clock, where he should be detained upon business some days. Charlotte and I, who were in those days both full of health and vigour, declared our readiness, if he wished it, to set off immediately, neither of us feeling a want of sleep. This put him into good-humour. He condescended to say it was very kind in us, and as he was anxious to see his lawyer he would avail himself of it. Breakfast being ordered to be made ready as soon as possible, by a quarter-past six we got it, directly after which we got into a post-chaise and departed for London.

[1] Evidently Hickey is referring to the Scotch custom of the " wee Deoch an Doris."—ED.

My brother and I went that day to dine with the useful, if not respectable, Madam Kelly, in Arlington Street. In the evening we attended three of her *chickens*, in the old beldam's coach, to Turnham Green, to drink tea at the Pack Horse and treat the misses to a swing, there being a capital one fixed up in the garden. We had only been a few minutes engaged at the swing, when into the garden walked Mordaunt with my dear Charlotte hanging upon his arm. She looked very much displeased and would scarcely deign to speak to me. After a very short stay they returned into the house and I saw no more of them that evening, but upon getting home some hours afterwards, I found a letter from Charlotte wherein she in strong terms upbraided me for degrading myself so far as to appear at a public inn with such companions as she had seen, concluding with an earnest desire, if I valued her advice, to avoid all connection with such females as I had spent that day with, alluding to two remarkably fine girls, though certainly rather notorious, who were distinguished by the nicknames of the Duchess of Portland and the Duchess of Devonshire, from a likeness they were respectively thought to bear to those elevated personages.

In June Mordaunt made a party for Drayton, of which I was one, and he proposed our going down together, saying he had received information that his brother's gig was repaired, and if I had no objection we should ride to Kensington and there get into it, letting our servants lead the horses on. This mode was accordingly adopted. We found Mr. and Mrs. Grant, with Captain Macintosh just arrived before us, and soon after Sir George Metham and Mrs. Carter drove to the door.

Before the hour of dinner Lord Semple, Captain Addington, of the Dragoons, Van, and Nancy Barry, all arrived. We consequently sat down a jovial party, doing due honour to Mordaunt's wines, which were all of the best. Soon after the cloth was taken away, Mordaunt complained of sudde indisposition. He therefore requested I would do him the favour to preside, and he left the room. We all thought it was a pretence in order to avoid drinking, in which we did him injustice, for he was dreadfully sick and continued so several hours. As his locum tenens I did due honour to the chair, nor quitted it until every one of the guests positively declined having any more wine. The next morning we all rose at six o'clock in order to be present at Guildford races, for which place we set off, eight of us in Lord Peterborough's famous coach, Lord Semple and Captain Addington in a post-chaise. The races being concluded we went to an inn to dine, and late at night all returned to sleep at Mordaunt's.

Charlotte Barry and I now became almost inseparable, and I was very frequently at Mordaunt's at Drayton. If he left that place but for a single day either with Lord Peterborough or any of his Lordship's friends, I received immediate notice thereof, and away I went to console my favourite and pass some hours in her society uninterrupted by the brutality and ill-temper of Mordaunt. For the sake of her company I gave occasional entertainments at Richmond and other places in the vicinity of London, and we constantly went twice a week to extravagant suppers at Vauxhall, which sort of life ran away with a great deal of my money.

In July I hired one of Roberts's eight-oared barges, and a smaller boat to attend with horns and clarionets, having previously invited a party to dine with me at the Castle at Richmond. At ten in the morning my darling Charlotte, her sister Nancy, Mrs. Grant, and a sweet pretty little girl of about sixteen she brought, Mordaunt, Grant, the junior Lovelace, and myself embarked at Whitehall stairs and proceeded to Richmond. The plan we had arranged was, after having dined, &c., to take wine on board our boat and row gently down to Vauxhall and there sup. Mordaunt from the moment we started was more than usually sulky and cynical, so much so as to throw a considerable damp upon the spirits of the party. At dinner he got exceedingly drunk without its at all mending his temper.

At nine at night we re-embarked, and Mordaunt was so troublesome I protested if he did not cease he should be turned out of the boat. At this he became outrageous, and I actually ordered the helmsman to go to the bank just below Brentford, where I bid three or four of the watermen bundle him out. Finding me thus resolute, he said he would go without force, but that I should answer for my ill-treatment of him. When quitting the boat he wanted to take Charlotte with him, which I would not permit. Again he was outrageous, but I made the people push off, leaving him to vent his fury by himself.

We proceeded to Vauxhall, had a cheerful supper, and were just preparing to depart when the ferocious gentleman made his appearance in the gardens. He had hired a carriage at Brentford, in which on his way to town he slept off the fumes of the wine. Finding himself tolerably sober he drove to Vauxhall, but neither drunkenness nor sobriety made any difference in him. Invariably a brute, nothing could change him. Without taking the least notice of anybody except Charlotte, he began upbraiding her violently for not accompanying him upon his leaving the boat, and laying hold of her arm was about to force her away, whereupon I once more interfered, observed she was my guest for the day, and, unless by her own desire, she should not leave the party. Mordaunt talked big, was very free with threats of what he would do, but upon my making Charlotte take hold of my arm and assuring her she might rely upon my protecting her against all personal violence, he left us, vowing vengeance upon me. After setting Charlotte down at her lodgings, where I offered to remain but she would not permit it, I went home to St. Albans Street.

In August Mordaunt's resources began to fail. His chief supplies of cash had been from his mother (Lady Peterborough) and Mrs. Brown, a widow of good fortune, sister to her Ladyship, but his applications to those ladies became so frequent and to such an extent they were at last, though reluctantly, obliged to tell him they could no longer furnish cash to support him in his extravagancies. Driven to great distress he asked a loan of the Earl, without success, the noble peer being as hard drove as himself for money.

After failing in every quarter, Mordaunt had the meanness to write me a begging letter, wherein, after stating the predicament he was reduced to, he besought me to assist him with a couple of hundred pounds, which if he did not obtain in two days he certainly should be arrested and conveyed to a spunging house. Notwithstanding I very much disliked the man, I felt unwilling to refuse, and having the amount by me I immediately sent it to him, for which he expressed in person the highest degree of gratitude, and said that he never should be unmindful of the kindness. He also made the most sacred promise to repay me within six weeks, a promise he failed to perform, nor did I receive a guinea from him until two years afterwards in India. This sum was of consequence to me, as at the time I advanced it I began to have some fears for myself, the style I lived in running away with the cash so fast that the sum I brought home with me was nearly exhausted, but as I resolved to return to India at the end of the year, I flattered myself the salary allowed by the Bengal Committee would be sufficient to bear me through.

CHAPTER XXVI

CHARLOTTE BECOMES "MRS. HICKEY"

MAJOR WALTER BOURKE, whom I have already spoken of, had often mentioned his intention of giving me and my brother what he termed a snug little dinner, at his chambers in the Temple. "Not," said he, "that I can attempt to entertain *en Prince* as you do. All I will be bold enough to say is that with respect to wine I shall at least rival you : better, London does not produce, and I will treat you to a bottle of such madeira as is rarely to be met with. I have myself had it a dozen years, it having been imported by Mr. Verelst when Governor of Bengal. For dinner you must for once be content with a good dish of fish, and a plain roast or boiled joint of meat." After repeating these sort of speeches whenever we met, he at last proposed a day whereon we were to partake of his promised fare. My brother and I accordingly went at the hour fixed to his apartments up three pair of stairs in Brick Court in the Temple. Upon entering the outer room, we found a tall, meagre old Swiss servant in a threadbare uniform scarlet coat of his master's, turning a string to the end of which was suspended a small bit of a miserably thin, ill-looking neck of mutton, the whole appearance of the room and its contents bespeaking the utmost poverty and wretchedness. The Swiss, with the natural civility and politeness of his country, showed us into what he called "the best chamber," saying his master was not yet returned from the City, but he expected his arrival every moment, the hour at which the dinner was ordered to be ready being already past.

During our conversation with the Swiss, a very gentlemanlike-looking man, apparently rather above fifty years of age, knocked at the door and was admitted, he also being an invited guest. Shortly after our arrival the Swiss brought into " the best chamber " a crazy kind of card table, which he placed in the middle of the room, spreading over it a cloth of such scanty dimensions as merely to cover the surface. Upon this he put four plates, with knives, forks, &c., leaving a very small space indeed for viands, so that we began to doubt the possibility of putting more than a single dish upon the table.

In about half an hour our host came in, apologizing for being so late by urgent business detaining him in the City. He directly called vociferously for dinner in French, speaking nothing else to his servant. In another half-hour the Swiss entered with a small punch-bowl, which having placed upon the table, the Major desired us to take our seats. The next thing was, "Did we choose soup ? " All answered, " Yes," and he proceeded to serve out, not soup, but the most abominable, washy, tasteless broth that ever wretched cook produced. The stranger, myself and brother, made each an attempt to swallow a few spoonfuls, whilst our host baled up two plates of it as if it had been most delicious stuff.

Our next dish was about a pound and a half of scrag of mutton taken out of the punch-bowl, and which had produced the ocean of broth. Whilst pulling the vile morsel to pieces he proposed a *general* glass of wine. I certainly expected the delicious Verelst madeira, instead of which I sipped at some rot gut Lisbon, which with much ceremony he himself took from a cellaret that stood in the corner of the room, the bottle not being half full.

As the Major could not help perceiving we did not seem to relish his wine, he commenced an harangue upon the abuses of Custom House officers, by whose infamous tricks he was disappointed in the pleasure he intended of treating us with his famous East India madeira. "However," said he, " I hope to recompense you by my port, which is deemed excellent by all my friends." I directly proposed tasting it.

He ordered his Swiss to bring the " Vin rouge." The man going to the cellaret brought forth a bottle containing just three glasses, one of which being offered to me I angrily said I was not in the habit of drinking stale bottoms of bottles, and refused to take it, my brother following my example. The Major thereupon began to abuse the poor Swiss who, shrugging his shoulders, simply observed he only *obeyed orders*. In a few minutes a fresh bottle of common tolerable port was brought, of which I took half a glass, for not having had anything to eat I felt no inclination to drink, and waited the approach of the string-twirled bit of mutton which in due time came forward, and of which I got a single bone.

In the midst of this extraordinary scene of meanness and penury our host seemed perfectly satisfied, nor made the least apology either for the scantiness or quality of his meal. A piece of mild Gloucester cheese being brought, through its aid I was enabled to drink another glass of port. The bottle from the industry of the master being nearly emptied, he loudly called, " Du Vin," but after repeated similar calls no " Vin " appearing he rung a little hand-bell that stood by him on the table. The ever-ready Swiss obeying the summons, was desired to bring more wine, when, after a pause and doubtful look, he whispered his master, who immediately exclaimed aloud, " Your neglect, sir, is unpardonable," at the same time pulling his purse from his pocket and taking therefrom half a crown which he gave the man, observing to me he always purchased his port *fresh and fresh* from the Devil tavern, because it was near his chambers and they always sent the best of wines.

This systematic meanness was more than I could bear. I bounced up, seized my hat, and saying it was out of my power to wait the arrival of a *second bottle*, departed, my brother and the other gentleman immediately following my example. Even the love of money that prevailed over every other consideration with Major Bourke did not quite reconcile him to our abrupt and sudden secession from his *entertainment,* and I had subsequently reason to know that he sincerely repented his scurvy treatment of us.

This dinner became the subject of general conversation, occasioning much wit and some ridiculous paragraphs in the newspapers, the women, too, getting hold of it. Whenever Major Bourke appeared in public a buzz went round of "That's the mutton broth Bengal Major," "The scrag Major," "The famous madeira Major," and other phrases of a similar nature which greatly mortified him.

Upon leaving Major Bourke's chambers, I proposed adjourning to a tavern in order to get some dinner, which being agreed to by my fellow-sufferers we walked to the Devil in Fleet Street, where we speedily sat down to an admirable soup, a dish of fine fresh fish, and high-flavoured venison, washing the whole down with a plentiful allowance of very tolerable claret, more than once drinking to the amendment of our late host's table for the benefit of any future unfortunate guests he might have.

In September Mordaunt took Charlotte to Brighton, and I consequently once more occupied my rooms at my father's in St. Albans Street. Returning from a tavern dinner about two o'clock in the morning, I found one of my sister's large and elegant parties just breaking up, and was then introduced to the Duke of Hamilton, Sir Watts Horton, Mr. Loraine Smith, and Mr. Macpherson, the last of whom was upon the eve of going out to Bengal in the Supreme Council, he afterwards becoming Governor-General and a Baronet. Previous to retiring to my chamber, my sister particularly requested that I would dine at home the next day, as Major St. Leger was to be of the party and she much wished me to meet him. Having previously promised my brother that I would go and dine with him at Richmond that day, I made an apology for not keeping my engagement and mentioned the reason, upon which my brother also determined to dine at home. He had taken a great dislike to St. Leger, which he marked by sulkiness and ill-humour, scarcely uttering a word except to answer the questions directly addressed to him. The company consisted of

Major St. Leger, Mr. Campell, now Lord Cawdor, and Harry Greville. Notwithstanding my brother's sulky fit we spent a pleasant day and were very merry.

On Mordaunt's return from Brighton Charlotte sent for me to say she was resolved to leave Mordaunt, and requested I would take her under my protection. This I with pleasure acceded to. She then begged I would not say anything about it until our return to Drayton, when she would communicate her intention to Mordaunt and come back to London with me. Upon our arrival at Drayton he was, if possible, more surly than ever, continuing so the whole day. After supper Charlotte abruptly told him she intended leaving him the next morning and no longer to submit to his brutality. This made him outrageous. Seizing a knife from the table, he swore with the most horrible oaths that rather than permit her to quit his house he would bury it in her heart, and from his action and manner I really expected him to put his threat in execution. I therefore instantly placed myself between him and Charlotte, reminding him that even insanity would not prevent his being hanged should he commit murder. He abused me in the grossest terms, insisting upon my leaving his house. Having armed myself with a poker I set him at defiance, spoke my sentiments of him with great freedom, and told him I would not stir unless Mrs. Barry accompanied me. The perspiration ran down his face in streams from rage, and I actually thought he must have died with passion.

At Charlotte's most earnest entreaty I consented to leave the house that night and wait at Uxbridge until I heard from her. I accordingly, after again cautioning Mordaunt, declaring I would make him responsible to the law for any act of violence, left Drayton and went to an inn at Uxbridge. The next day about noon, just as I was dispatching a messenger to her with a letter, I received a note from her, saying Lord Peterborough had called with another gentleman to take Mordaunt to Windsor ; that previous to going he had with a drawn sword at her breast compelled her to swear she would not leave the house during his absence, but that she could not consider a promise so obtained at all binding upon her, therefore requested I would send a post-chaise for her. Ordering one immediately, I went myself in it to Drayton, took her in and drove to London, carrying her at her own desire to her sister Nancy at Mr. Van's in Park Lane. After a short consultation with her sister, we three sallied forth (Van being upon duty at the Tower) in search of lodgings, as Charlotte was determined no more to enter those in Queen Ann Street, they having been taken by Mordaunt. After looking at several, we fixed upon an excellent first floor in Upper Seymour Street, Portman Square, where Charlotte and I, after getting her trunks from Queen Ann Street, took up our abode and slept that night unmolested.

The next evening being that on which Vauxhall closed, Charlotte and I drove there about nine o'clock. One of the persons we saw upon entering the gardens was Mordaunt, in company with Lord Peterborough and a large party of young men of fashion. To our utter amazement he took not the least notice of either of us during the whole time we continued there, which was until near one, when we returned home. Between three and four I was awakened by loud and repeated knocking at the street door, and before I could get on my clothes one of the servants had opened the door, when I heard the voices of several persons, especially Mordaunt's and the servants', the latter strongly remonstrating against their going upstairs. By Mordaunt's language I knew he was drunk.

Charlotte, much terrified, entreated I would not go out of the room. As, however, I felt that would encourage the party I instantly unlocked the bed-chamber door, when I met Mordaunt, Lord Semple, and two other young men in the regimentals of the Guards upon the stairs. Addressing the strangers, I desired to know the meaning of such an outrage upon a gentleman's private apartments. Mordaunt instantly replied, " Oh, damn him, never mind him ; he has got my woman away from me and, by God ! he shall now give her up." Lord Semple interrupted him, saying,

" For shame, Captain Mordaunt, you have deceived us and thereby led us to the commission of an unpardonable offence." And, turning to me, his Lordship made the handsomest apology for the intrusion of himself and two friends, which they had been led into from Captain Mordaunt's telling them the house belonged to a female friend of his who had plenty of girls with her. To this I observed the more his Lordship knew of Mr. Mordaunt the more occasion he would find to blush for him and to feel ashamed of his conduct. The three gentlemen then by main force compelled Mordaunt to go downstairs and leave the house, he cursing and swearing that he would put me to death.

As whenever Mordaunt committed excess, which was frequently the case, he always visited Seymour Street, making a noise and riot at the house door, I considered it necessary to put a stop to it, and therefore determined upon his next attack to get a constable to carry him before a magistrate.

A few nights after Mordaunt's violent attack in Seymour Street, Charlotte having asked Mr. and Mrs. Grant to dine with us, we four went to the opening for the season of Covent Garden Theatre. We had not been long seated in one of the green boxes when Mordaunt entered. Being more than half drunk, he was as usual exceedingly abusive, offensive, and troublesome, whereupon I, with the utmost composure, assured him that if he did not desist and instantly leave the box I would break every bone in his body. Grant, too, at the same time loudly execrating his behaviour, he retired, but at the door of the box he called out, " Hickey, although you have treated me scandalously ill, by God ! I cannot bear to see you the dupe of that double-faced Scotch pedlar Jemmy Grant, who, after benefiting by your generosity in various ways and partaking of your hospitality for upwards of a twelvemonth, has now ordered his servants to refuse you admittance whenever you call at his house, and, not content with this, he abuses you wherever he goes as a thoughtless, extravagant spendthrift."

Neither Grant nor myself made any comment upon this

speech at the time. It, however, struck me very forcibly, for I thought I had lately observed a change in Grant's manner towards me. It also brought to my recollection having called several times in Colman Street without ever finding Grant there, which had never before occurred. Determined at once to ascertain whether there was any foundation for what Mordaunt had said at the play-house or not, I went the following morning to Grant's. Upon knocking at the door the servant, who knew me perfectly well, said his master was out. I remarked that Mr. Grant was not in the habit of leaving home so early, but that as such was the case, and I wanted much to see him, I would wait his return, and I immediately opened the parlour door, where to the utter confusion of Mr. James Grant, he and his brother were sitting quietly at their breakfast. Addressing Mr. Peter Grant, I apologized for my unseasonable intrusion, shortly giving my reason for it, adding that I was sorry to find there was but too much foundation for what Captain Mordaunt had said, and that his brother James had acted towards me with a duplicity and meanness inconsistent with the character of a gentleman.

James Grant seemed confounded and quite at a loss how to act. After a very awkward pause he, in a hesitating, ungracious manner, said, " It was evident to everybody that knew me that I was living in a style it was impossible I could support ; that he had been credibly informed I had already applied to several persons with whom I had only a slight acquaintance to borrow money from them ; that his situation in life as a merchant, a West India agent, and citizen of London, of course everything depending upon his moral character and conduct in life, made it extremely indecorous for him to be seen constantly in public places with a set of dissipated and extravagant young men, nor could he afford to advance to me, or any other who lived beyond their means, cash to support a system of inconsiderate folly; that for these reasons he was free to acknowledge he was desirous of dropping the intimacy that had subsisted between us, although he should never cease to entertain the most sincere regard for me as an old and esteemed friend."

Extremely mortified at such an avowal from a man who had been my constant companion and, as Mordaunt truly observed, a participator in all my absurd and ill-bestowed hospitality, I spoke my sentiments respecting his conduct and what he had just declared in pointed and contemptuous terms, and lamenting that it had ever fallen to my lot to have any intercourse with so despicable a being as I considered him, walked out of his parlour and house. Finding his servant waiting in the passage, I said, "You have been under the necessity of telling several falsehoods lately ; though relieved from anything of that sort in future on my account, I fear in the service of such a man as your master you will always be liable to similar culpability." The man civilly bowed, but made no answer.

This unhandsome behaviour of Grant's had the good effect of making me turn my thoughts to the actual state of my finances, upon examining which I found I had only remaining in my banker's hands about two hundred pounds, and three hundred and fifty odd from the Bengal agents, the balance of salary due to me. Besides this I had a claim upon them for the extra expence I had incurred by proceeding from the Cape of Good Hope in a Dutch ship, which measure I had adopted solely with a view to expedite the object they had sent me to Europe upon, this expence amounting to upwards of eight hundred pounds.

These united sums I flattered myself would prove sufficient to send me and my darling Charlotte off to India in the month of December, the dear girl having declared that her very existence depended upon my consenting to take her out with me. I immediately wrote to the agents, saying that as my further attendance upon the business of the petition was unnecessary, I requested they would settle my account, which I enclosed, as I proposed embarking for India by the first ship of the season. After a lapse of several days they wrote me to say that as the committee in Bengal had not furnished them with any instructions or authority to defray any charges relative to my voyage to Europe, and having a very small sum remaining in their hands, they could not venture to take upon themselves the paying me the eight hundred pounds I demanded, without a previous reference to Calcutta.

This was a thunderstroke to me, for having entered into no written engagement with the committee, nor having any possible means of enforcing payment from Messieurs Irvine and Touchet, I felt myself remediless. I therefore told Charlotte my situation, and the absolute necessity there was for our retrenching every kind of expense forthwith. I can safely and conscientiously affirm that from that day the dear girl never expended an unnecessary guinea upon her own account and, as far as lay in her power, prevented my incurring any expense that could be avoided.

Having prior to my unpleasant explanation with Messieurs Irvine and Touchet respecting money matters engaged to go upon a party into Oxford with Van, Nancy Barry, Harvey Coombe, and a few others, we, in the month of October, set out upon it, and after spending ten days very cheerfully at Chapel House and stopping at Oxford two days to visit the different colleges, and see all the curiosities of that seat of learning, returned to London and began directly to make preparations for our departure to Bengal.

Upon going to the India House to make enquiries about a passage, and afterwards for the same purpose to the Jerusalem coffee house, I had the mortification to find that as three of His Majesty's regiments were that season going out for the further security of the Company's possessions the whole accommodation of their ships was exclusively kept for the officers belonging to those regiments, and that it would consequently be impossible for me to obtain a passage. Notwithstanding this unfavourable circumstance I deemed it right to make every effort, and therefore applied to several commanders with whom I was acquainted, saying I would submit to any inconvenience to get out. All expressed their inclination to oblige me, but declared the impracticability of accommodating a lady. Captain Thomson,

of the *Calcutta*, with whom I had been intimate, said
he had given up his own cabin to the Major of one of the
regiments for himself, wife, and daughter ; that he understood the lady to be in so precarious a state of health as to
make it doubtful whether she would be able to proceed
on the voyage, and if she did not he promised me the apartment, observing that her going or not must be decided in
ten days.

The morning after returning from Oxfordshire, taking
a ride in Hyde Park with Charlotte, we there met Mordaunt,
who directly turned his horse and followed us up and down
as long as we stayed, but did not offer to speak. At night
we went to the play, where we again found Mordaunt, and
being intoxicated he became violently noisy, abusing both
Charlotte and me in the most blackguard manner. He at
last became so troublesome that three or four gentlemen,
offended by the interruption to their entertainment, forced
him out of the box. We saw no more of him at the theatre.

Returning home we supped and retired to rest. About
three o'clock in the morning I was roused from sleep by
a tremendous noise at our room door, and I soon heard
Mordaunt calling me by name with all sorts of opprobrious
epithets. I immediately opened the door that went into the
drawing-room, which I had scarcely entered when he made
a blow at me with a thick stick he had brought with him.
Luckily, he missed my head which he aimed at, but severely
bruised my shoulder and arm. I instantly grappled him, got
him down and belaboured him with his own stick until he
roared for mercy, screeching. out, "Murder ! Murder ! "
This brought up the master of the house, who summoned
the watch, and Mordaunt was carried off to the round-house.

I then learnt that Mordaunt had made his servant ring
the street door bell until Freskini got up to see what was
the matter. The fellow said he had brought a letter from
Captain Thomson, of the *Calcutta* Indiaman, for me, which
was of the utmost consequence and required an immediate
answer. Freskini thereupon called up one of the maids to
strike a light, which being done he opened the street door.

when Mordaunt rushed in, knocked the poor Italian down flat in the passage and ran upstairs, followed by the maid with the light, she crying out, "Thieves!"

In the morning I went to the Watch House and found Mordaunt had procured bail and was gone home, but so maimed and hurt they were obliged to carry him in their arms to the sedan chair that conveyed him away. I heard nothing more about the *gentleman* for four days afterwards when Captain Grey, of the Dragoons, called upon me, as he said, at the request of Captain Mordaunt, who was still confined to his chamber from the ill-treatment he had received from me, and for which he required me to name time, place, and weapons, to give him satisfaction. I told Captain Grey I was ready to comply with his desire if after hearing my statement he, as a gentleman, would say I ought to do so. I then related all that had occurred on the night of Mordaunt's brutal attack upon me at my own lodgings, at which Captain Grey was quite confounded, declared I had done no more than such infamous conduct deserved, and that I should have been completely justified in the opinions of all mankind had I put him to death at the moment. He then expressed his sorrow at having given me the trouble of an explanation, which he had been led to by the gross and ungentlemanlike misrepresentation of Captain Mordaunt, whose acquaintance he should drop in consequence, after telling him the discovery he had made of his falsehood.

A week after this visit of Captain Grey's, Mr Van called in Seymour Street to say that Mordaunt had suddenly disappeared, no person knowing whither he was gone to, though many to their cost knew he had left debts to a large amount unpaid. The general opinion seemed to be that he had got on board an American vessel, but upon further enquiry I discovered that he had gone as fast as four post-horses could convey him to Margate, at which place he hired a small smuggling cutter to carry him over to Ostend, where he engaged a passage to India in a Danish ship that had touched at that port for the purpose of receiving him and other English passengers. I am free to confess I felt happy at thus getting rid of a man who had been a great grievance to me, and who never failed to annoy me some way or other when his spirit was raised by excess in wine.

Soon after the opera opened for the winter. I accompanied Charlotte to it, and in the pit recognized my quondam acquaintance, Commodore Richardson, who behaved so shabbily relative to our proposed journey to Ireland. He was dressed in his full Bengal marine uniform, which from its gaudiness, being covered with lace, and two immense rich bullion epaulettes, at that time not used in the British Navy, drew all eyes upon him. Upon seeing me he had the assurance to come up and address me with the utmost familiarity, presenting his hand. I mustered the most contemptuous look in my power, and without making any answer or taking the least notice of his proffered hand, turned my back upon him, to the infinite entertainment of several young coxcombs that witnessed the scene.

Captain Thomson now wrote me a letter, expressing his concern that it would not be in his power to give me and Mrs. Hickey(for Charlotte had dropped the name of Barry and assumed mine) a passage to India, the Major he had before alluded to, with his family, having determined to embark on board the *Calcutta*. He very civilly assured me that could he have anyhow contrived it he should have felt much pleasure in having us as shipmates, but it was unpracticable.

I now began to feel seriously alarmed lest I should lose the season altogether, and was thereby rendered very miserable. In the midst of my anxiety I one day dined at Mr. Plumer, senior's, where, mentioning the extreme difficulty I found about a passage and my apprehension that I should ultimately fail in procuring one, Mr. Plumer said under such circumstances he would advise me to go to Lisbon, from which place I might find frequent opportunities of proceeding to India in as fine ships as any in the world, and have spacious cabins. He further observed that he had many esteemed friends in Portugal to whom he would give me letters of introduction, and he was certain I should in every respect find it an eligible way of getting to India. I at once determined to adopt that mode. He likewise told me that the end of the year would be the proper time for me to proceed to Lisbon, the earliest Portuguese ships sailing between the 15th and 31st of January. Charlotte was delighted with this arrangement.

We spent the short period we had to remain in London as gaily as possible, attending the theatres, and every other public place of entertainment.

Mr. Plumer gave me the warmest letters of recommendation to Messieurs Horne and Sill, De Visme and Penry, Sir John Hort, the Consul-General, and Messieurs Mayne and Company. From other friends I obtained letters to the Honourable Mr. Walpole, the British Ambassador, Mr. Paisley, Mr. Koster, and several other respectable mercantile houses at Lisbon.

As I found Mr. Plumer, in some of his letters, had mentioned me as a married man, I told my Charlotte thenceforward we must pass everywhere for man and wife, and having had most convincing proofs of her sincere attachment to me, of her uncommon sweetness of temper and many estimable qualities, I proposed making her really so by going through the marriage ceremony. But this she peremptorily refused, observing that she was already as happy as woman could be ; that should she avail herself of my generous offer and I at any future period repent of what I had done, it undoubtedly would break her heart. She therefore begged that she might still depend upon my disinterested love, which she felt confident she never should by any act of hers deservedly forfeit. From that hour I considered myself as much her husband as the strictest forms and ceremonies of the Church could have made me.

Towards the end of the month of December one thousand seven hundred and eighty-one, upon another review of my private affairs, I found only a few pounds remained in my banker's hands. I therefore once more applied to the agents, Messieurs Irvine and Touchet, on the subject of my disbursements in getting home from the Cape of Good

Hope, but I had no better success than on the former occa-sion. The agents, however, who admitted they thought me hardly dealt by, of their own accord offered to advance me the sum of one hundred pounds upon my own security, which they accordingly did, and I granted my promissory note for the repayment thereof within three months after my return to Calcutta.

Although this one hundred pounds furnished me with the means of paying off several small demands, I well knew how inadequate it was to clearing me from all debts and enabling me to prosecute my Lisbon scheme. I therefore stated my unpleasant situation to Mr. Thomas Plumer, son of the gentleman I have above mentioned, and brother to my Madras friend, Mr. Hall Plumer. This Mr. Thomas Plumer is now, and has been for upwards of four years, His Majesty's Solicitor-General. Upon receipt of my letter he also advanced me one hundred pounds upon my bond, payable in Bengal.

Although the much-loved original was to accompany me to India, yet I was desirous of possessing a good portrait of my dearest Charlotte. She had presented me with one painted by Engleheart, which I thought did not do her justice, besides being a stiff, formal picture. This made me wish to have one by Cosway, then in high reputation as an artist, and very deservedly so. I therefore called to ask if he could oblige me by taking a miniature likeness in the course of a few days, I being upon the eve of leaving England. He replied that he never had been so deeply engaged in business, or so much teased by persons pressing for their pictures as at that period, nevertheless, as he really wished to oblige me, and saw a peculiar character of countenance in Mrs. Barry of which he was sure he should succeed in making a superior picture, he would for once in his life act a deceitful part by shutting himself up and refusing admittance to anybody under the plea of illness, until he had completed the work. He requested she would come and sit to him the following morning. I accordingly accompanied her, and was much amused by observing the progress of the picture, soon perceiving that he would make a beautiful thing of it. Freskini who, since Charlotte and I came together, always dressed her hair, did so upon this occasion in the most fashionable and elegant style, so much so as to draw from Cosway the remark that he never had seen a finer head of hair.

After Charlotte had sat twice we, one morning upon our return from riding, called at Cosway's in Berkeley Row, not with any idea of her then sitting again, she being in her riding-habit, but merely to see the progress he had made during the preceding day. The weather being uncommonly clear and fine for the time of year, we had taken so long a ride as to put her quite in a glow, and she looked remarkably well. Some of her curls having blown loose, she had taken off her hat and was standing before a glass arranging them when Cosway entered the room. He gave a start of surprize, exclaiming, " Good God ! what an alteration for the better. I declare on my honour I should not know you for the same woman. Come here, come along with me this moment, just as you are. No more dressed head, powder, or pomatum. I never saw such a change, so now is the time to show you off to advantage." Then presenting his hand he led her into his painting room, rubbed out the elegantly arranged hair, and drew her exactly as she then sat before me, making as he had truly predicted one of the most beautiful pictures I ever beheld, the likeness being inimitable. After sitting full three hours, I saw evidently that he was greatly delighted with it himself. With some difficulty I prevailed upon him not to touch it any more, feeling satisfied it could not be improved and might be hurt by attempting at a higher finishing. I would willingly have carried it away at that time, but that he would not hear of, saying he must touch the drapery a little, besides which he was too proud of his performance not to be desirous of showing it to a few persons who were real connoisseurs. A week afterwards I received it from Cosway, and it has ever since been my inseparable companion.

CHAPTER XXVII

TO LISBON WITH CHARLOTTE

IT now became necessary that I should leave England. I therefore fixed upon the 1st of January, 1782, for my departure for Falmouth, being to embark at that place for Lisbon, and arranged my matters accordingly. As no one of my family, except my brother, knew of the attachment that subsisted between Charlotte and me, consequently could have no idea of my intending to take her out with me to India, I was the more solicitous to keep that secret, which required some management. After consulting with Charlotte, it was agreed that I should proceed to Exeter without her, but wait her joining me at that city.

Being rather short of ready cash, an indispensable requisite for travelling, I was under the disagreeable necessity of leaving Mr. Cosway and a few other creditors unpaid, my unsettled debts not exceeding altogether one hundred and fifty pounds, the whole of which I discharged with interest in a few months after I reached Calcutta.

As I always had a particular dislike to formal leave-taking (which I believe I have already observed), instead of waiting to breakfast in St. Albans Street the morning of the 2nd, as I told my sisters I should do, I ordered a post-chaise at midnight of the 1st, into which I and Nabob got. Thus, at the time my family imagined me to be fast asleep in my own room, I was dashing away at the rate of nine miles an hour towards the western extremity of our sea-girt island. For stealing off in this manner I had, by letters, many severe reproaches from my sisters. But my father and brother admitted they thought me right in avoiding

364

a distressing and unpleasant scene, always better shunned than courted. Through life, at least since I became to a certain extent my own master, I have made it a rule to quit those persons I loved, when doomed to separate, without announcing the precise hour of departure.

Poor Freskini, who had no doubt but that he should accompany me to India, was thrown into sad grief upon my telling him it could not be. The fact was that having received intimation of the enormous expense attending a residence in Lisbon, I was compelled to reduce my establishment, an additional servant being a matter of serious importance. Previous to my leaving London, however, I took him to old Captain Larkins, father of the then Commander of the *Warren Hastings*, and who had always been very kind to me, and this worthy man promised me to procure a passage for him on board one of the Company's ships the following autumn.

About nine o'clock in the morning of the 2nd I breakfasted at Whitchurch in Buckinghamshire, fifty-seven miles from London, proceeded that day to Bridport in Dorsetshire, where I slept, and the following morning arrived at Exeter, one hundred and seventy-three miles from the capital. I took up my abode at the new *hotel !* a term then little known in England, though now in general use, every little dirty coffee-house in London being dignified with the name of *hotel !*

Having ordered a chicken and steak for my solitary dinner, whilst it was preparing I sallied forth in quest of Doctor Carrington, the Dean of the Cathedral, for whom I had a letter of introduction from a nephew of his, who was an old associate of mine, and one of the senior clerks in the Secretary of State's office. I found the Reverend Dean at home in an excellent mansion, who received me very kindly, pressing me much to stay to dinner, which I declined, expecting to see my dear girl every hour, but I promised to wait upon him the next day.

Whilst prosing over a newspaper without knowing one word I read, about eight o'clock in the evening my Charlotte arrived, greatly fatigued, not having taken any refreshment or stopped, but to change horses, the whole journey. She was attended by a favourite female servant who had lived with her three years. She was one of the most beautiful creatures I ever beheld, accomplished far beyond her station, and, as Charlotte assured me, strictly virtuous, of a delicate form, with a little constant cough that I thought bespoke consumption, and so it unfortunately proved. Had her life been spared she would, I am convinced, have been soon advantageously married in India.

That night was one of the happiest of my life, having the quiet, undisputed possession of the woman I almost adored, who had proved the warmth of her affection for me by sacrificing country and friends to bear me company to a burning and unhealthy climate.

Whilst sitting at breakfast with my amiable partner the next morning, I received a very polite note from Dean Carrington, saying he had that moment heard of Mrs. Hickey's arrival and entreating her company also at dinner. Before I could write an answer, the Dean and his lady were announced, politely coming to visit us, and thus did my Charlotte for the first time appear in a character nature as well as education intended her for, and which during the remainder of her short life she filled with credit to herself and me, becoming the admiration of everyone who knew her for her sweetness of temper and elegantly easy manners.

At the hour appointed we went to the Dean's, who introduced us to three grown-up daughters, all good, fine young women. They, as well as their mother, were delighted with Mrs. Hickey, and before they parted that night urged her most kindly to endeavour to prevail upon me to leave the hotel and reside with them during our stay. The Dean informed me that the post of that morning had brought intelligence of four packets having all sailed together from Falmouth in the afternoon of the 2nd ; that it was therefore certain no other would be dispatched for six weeks to come, and as Falmouth was at all times a very disagreeable place for a stranger to reside in we had better remain for a month, at least, at Exeter, which he hoped to render pleasanter to us than the former town could be, as he was sure his wife and daughters would do everything in their power to make it so. Upon joining the ladies they attacked me with entreaties to continue at their house, but as I conceived I ought not to accede I declined, saying, however, I felt the kindness of the offer and that for our own sakes they should have as much of our company as they could desire.

In consequence of what the Dean had told me I determined to follow his advice by remaining where I was, but in order to avoid all risk of disappointment limited my stay to half the period he had mentioned, that is, three weeks.

The Dean and his family showed us as much kindness as if we had been friends of long standing. Every day some new amusement was adopted, and we were introduced to several charming families between whom and the Dean's mutual hospitalities were exchanged. Thus time glided away imperceptibly until the day of our departure arrived, to the mutual regret of all parties. On the 24th of January a melancholy crying scene took place between the ladies, from which I tore my Charlotte away, placing her in a post-coach and four, and we drove off. I certainly never felt so sincere a regard for a family with whom I had so short an acquaintance as I did for the Dean's.

I hoped and intended to reach Falmouth the same night, but found the roads so extremely rough and bad my progress was slow. The days, too, being very short, I thought it most advisable to stop at Saint Michael's, eighteen miles short of our destination. There we slept in the most wretched of hovels, though by the sign before the door announced to be an *inn* and to afford *entertainment* for man and horse.

Having no inducement to stay in so poverty-stricken a house, we left it early in the morning, by ten o'clock arriving at Falmouth. This is a corporate town, and I will be bold to say the most despicable one in His Majesty's dominions. The post-boys, being left to make their own selection, drove us to the King's Arms, which they asserted to be the best house in the place. All I can say is that if

such was the case, bad indeed was the best. Neither victuals
nor drink, except of a kind that would have disgraced the
lowest ale house, could I procure, yet in one point they undoubtedly supported the name of an inn, I mean the ex-
orbitance of charges.

Mr. Holt, of the India House, having given me a letter to
the Company's agent, in the afternoon of the day of my
arrival, having ascertained where he lived, I went to deliver
it. His name was Bell. Upon reading the letter I gave him,
he expressed the highest respect and regard for Mr. Holt,
to whom he said he lay under great personal obligation ;
that it would therefore afford him much satisfaction to
show every attention to any friend of his, and he begged I
would command his best services. Upon my mentioning
the circumstance of having slept the preceding night at
St. Michael's, he observed that it was unlucky that I had
done so, a packet having sailed for Lisbon at eight o'clock
that morning. This I thought an unfortunate commencement of my journey and future voyage, but repining at
what could not be remedied being useless, I did not mention
it to Mrs. Hickey.

In my conversation with Mr. Bell I complained of the
inn I was lodged at, whereupon he recommended me to
go into private lodgings, by which I should secure comfortable apartments for sitting in and sleeping, though not
mend the eating part, as I should be obliged to get my supplies from the inn, the townspeople and innkeepers having
such an understanding that no private person or tradesman
would ever allow a lodger to have anything dressed at home.
Mr. Bell then very politely attended me to an exceedingly
neat and well-furnished first floor at a turner's shop directly
opposite the King's Arms, of which I took immediate possession.

Mr. Bell, being a married man, invited us to spend the
following day with him, where we were handsomely entertained. The party were delighted with my Charlotte's
singing, an accomplishment she excelled in, her voice being
both sweet and melodious. At this dinner I met Captain

Smith, an old post-captain of the Royal Navy, distinguished by the nickname of "*Boolwaggey*" from a ridiculous song he frequently sang in which that word was often repeated, and with peculiar drollery.

At Mr. Bell's I was likewise introduced to Captain Todd, Commander of the *Hanover*, a Lisbon packet which, being next in rotation we, of course, should embark in. Captain Todd told me he had no doubt of sailing in ten days or a fortnight at furthest.

On the 30th of the month, I was agreeably surprized at being addressed by a tall, well-looking young man, who introduced himself to me as an old and intimate friend, but as I had no recollection of him he told me his name was Daniel Hoissard, and that we were schoolfellows at Streatham. I then recognized him as one of my favourites at that Academy, though grown quite out of my knowledge. He had just arrived from London on his way to Lisbon, where he was established in business, being a junior partner in Paisley and Company's firm. As he was remarkably fond of music and himself a proficient he was excessively pleased with Mrs. Hickey's powers in that way, and except at the hours of rest was never away from us. Independent of his musical talents, he proved a great acquisition to us, possessing a fund of good-humour with great vivacity.

The weather being favourable we made excursions about the neighbouring country, our first being to the romantic and beautiful residence of Sir John St. Aubyn at Mount's Bay. It is erected upon a high rock surrounded by the sea, except at nearly low water when it might be approached over a hard sandbank for full half a mile. The tide being in when we visited it we were conveyed across in a commodious boat. The house is splendidly furnished, and the views in every direction uncommonly grand. Upon the summit of the rock, projecting over an abyss of several hundred feet, a rude seat without front or back is cut. The person who attends to show the place tells the visitors that whoever sits in that seat, if a lady and unmarried, will always have the command over her future husband, and the same of a bachelor and his wife. No one of our party chose to take the seat. Indeed, it is awful and tremendous to look at, and in my opinion extremely dangerous to effect.

Our next jaunts were to Truro, Penryn, and Redruth. At the latter little village we got as nice and comfortable a dinner as ever I sat down to, which we all three did complete justice to. Lastly, we went to the Land's End, which being upwards of thirty miles from Falmouth we started at seven in the morning and had a very pleasant day. We dined at the small village of Trevascan upon delicious fish.

During my sojourn at Falmouth a packet arrived from the West Indies, in which came young Georges, a smart boy, at that time a midshipman belonging to the Admiral's ship on the Jamaica station, he having been obliged to return to Europe from bad health. His father was brother-in-law to Sir Ralph Payne, and his family were upon the most intimate terms with mine. Hearing there was a Mr. Hickey in the town, he called at my lodgings and was rejoiced to find in me an acquaintance. Being short of cash, I supplied him with sufficient to procure a seat in the stage for London, which his father repaid me with many thanks while I was at Lisbon.

On the 10th of February, having received notice that we should sail the next day, I immediately sent off our baggage to the *Hanover*. Early in the morning of the 11th we embarked, Mr. Hoissard accompanying us. The wind dying away, it was night before we got clear of the harbour. About eight a strong gale sprung up, which drove us at so quick a rate that at daylight in the morning of the 15th we made the Rock of Lisbon, passed over the bar at the entrance of the Tagus by noon, anchoring in a couple of hours afterwards close to the city. Our passage from Falmouth was said to be one of the shortest that had ever been known.

Lisbon forms one of the grandest spectacles imaginable from the river, and must strike a stranger with astonishment by its grandeur. It stands upon seven different hills, constituting a sublime and romantic scene.

Mr. Hoissard proved of material service to us by his local knowledge, procuring far superior accommodations for us than we should have been able to get for ourselves. Going on shore in the first boat that came alongside the packet, he returned in little more than an hour to say he had engaged apartments that he hoped we should approve. Taking us on shore, he conducted us to a noble mansion standing upon the point of a lofty hill called Buenos Ayres. It commanded a full view of the city itself, of the river and vessels innumerable sailing in every direction, with a distant view of the bar and ships out at sea. The house was kept by an old Irish widow, named Williams, and admirably well calculated she was for the situation, filling it with equal advantage and credit to herself and satisfaction to her guests. I had a suite of spacious rooms leading from one to another, consisting of a capital dining hall, a handsome apartment for breakfasting, and superb drawing-room to receive company in, besides two lesser ones, an excellent bed-chamber, with dressing-room and all other requisites, the servants' chambers being over ours and communicating thereto by a private staircase. Nothing could be more commodious or elegant than the whole of the establishment, but the expence was enormous, and considerably increased by the necessity of keeping our own table, it not being customary for ladies to join the general mess.

Our fellow-passengers in the packet were a Portuguese gentleman, Mr. Hoissard, and a Miss Nancy Spottiswoode, a clever, intelligent girl, daughter or niece, I forget which, of an eminent attorney in London. Her father being apprehensive she had symptoms of decline, sent her off to a milder climate, which was recommended by the faculty as the most likely to prevent a serious attack.

Mrs. Hickey suffered a good deal from sea-sickness, though not so much as she expected. Having a strong gale the whole way, right aft, with a very rough sea, the motion of the vessel was extremely violent, but we ran at a prodigious rate.

On the sixteenth I delivered my letters, and was very

kindly received by all those to whom I carried introductions, but more especially so by the lovely Mrs. Walpole, wife of the British Ambassador, the two Miss Sills, sisters of a partner in Horne's mercantile house, and the amiable family of Wardens.

The second day after our arrival we received at least a dozen invitations to dinners in succession, commencing with a sumptuous one at His Excellency the Honourable Mr. Walpole's. The next was an equally splendid one at Sir John Hort's, then at Mr. Mayne's, Mr. Horne's, Mr. Sills', Mr. Warden's, Mr. Koster's, Mr. Paisley's, Mr. Penry's, &c. At Sir John Hort's we had some excellent music, both vocal and instrumental. Sir John sang with great taste, and entertained us highly, singing some charming duets with a Miss Cole, though when they first struck up I could hardly preserve my gravity, Sir John being a man of six feet two inches, very thin, and upright as an arrow, Miss Cole a diminutive little creature of about four feet and a half. The piece they commenced with was, " Drink to me only with thine eyes and I'll pledge thee with mine." Nothing could be executed in a more masterly style, but the contrast in the figures, Sir John towering some feet above his fair companion, upon whom he literally looked down most languishingly, was superlatively ridiculous, constantly exciting risibility from the auditors.

At Mrs. Williams's hotel at the time of our arrival were lodged the Earl of Winchelsea, to the astonishment of all who knew and had seen him during his illness, just recovered from what the physicians had pronounced a lost case, a confirmed and immovable decline, or consumption as generally called. In the next suite of apartments to mine was Mr. Mundy, Member of Parliament for Derby, his lady, a sister of hers, Miss Mesnil, and Mrs. Mesnil, their mother, with two children of Mr. Mundy's. This was a very amiable family with whom we spent many happy days. They had visited Portugal in the hope of benefiting Mrs. Mundy's health, who, though without any acknowledged disease, was in a delicate state. Whilst we remained at Lisbon she certainly improved in health, but I was sorry to hear afterwards relapsed and died the ensuing winter in the South of France.

There were also several other male invalids, all of whom assembled every morning in the coffee-room, a noble apartment sixty-five feet long by thirty-six wide, commanding in two different directions the grandest prospects in the world. Here I usually employed an hour or two daily in reading English and other newspapers and admiring the beautiful scenery from the windows. It was, however, a great drawback to my amusement to observe several of the invalids daily sinking into the grave, yet notwithstanding this was too evident to every person who looked at them, the victims themselves seemed unconscious of their danger.

I could not help feeling extremely interested for one very elegant young man who stood in this class. His name was Richardson, only two-and-twenty years of age and in possession of a large estate in Devonshire. His patriotic zeal had induced him to take an active part in training a newly raised corps of Militia, in the performance of which duty he exposed himself to more hardships than he had strength of constitution to bear, sleeping in a tent in damp and swampy situations, which produced first cold and cough, then tendency to consumption. The physicians, pursuing the customary routine, began their operations at his own house, then ordered him to Bristol hot wells, and finally to Lisbon, where he had been two months when we arrived. He grew gradually weaker and weaker, so much so that at last he with difficulty could crawl from his bed-chamber to the coffee-room assisted by the arm of his servant, yet, although reduced to that miserably languid state, and having become an absolute skeleton, he thought not of death. On the contrary, he talked with confidence of future plans that he intended carrying into effect, remarking that as he did not think he had derived any material benefit from the climate of Lisbon he would return home for the summer months, and if it proved necessary that he again should move he would try Italy, and this he said at a time when I used to look at him with the most anxious alarm from actually expecting every moment to behold him fall from his chair a corpse. When we had been at the hotel about a month, his servant, entering his room to open the window shutters one morning, found him laying half out of bed, his head on the floor, quite dead, and he must have been so some hours, the body being cold and stiff.

Mr. Hoissard telling me a carriage was an indispensable requisite at Lisbon, I hired one by the month. In form it was like an English one-horse chaise, had a hood with curtains to draw close in front, two wheels, and a pair of horses which were driven by a coachman who sat upon a small box just above their rumps. Altogether it is an easy and pleasant enough conveyance. Contrary to the rule observed as to driving with us, the Portuguese always keep the right-hand side of the street or road, the reason for which I never could learn.

The first time that Charlotte and I went abroad in this vehicle the driver, upon turning out of a narrow lane into a handsome square, suddenly stopped, and drew our curtains quite close. He then quickly descended from the box, falling upon his knees in the midst of the mud and dirt. At that instant we heard a loud singing, when peeping through a round glass about the size of a crown-piece I perceived a procession of priests, one of whom bore aloft a figure of our Saviour upon the Cross. Each priest had a lighted wax candle in his hand and all joined in a solemn dirge. I observed every passenger knelt down whilst the procession passed, devoutly crossing themselves. Carriages of every description likewise stopped. When gone by to a distance of about one hundred yards, our coachman opened the curtains, resumed his seat, and, crossing his breast with his finger, drove on.

I afterwards learnt that this was called the elevation of the host, a ceremony frequently occurring in Catholic towns, and that all persons, no matter how high his rank, are bound to stop and kneel as the procession passes. I was further told that had any of the fanatical priests or even the common people seen, or supposed, we were within the carriage we should have been compelled to get out and kneel like the rest, and probably have been insulted for not having done so of our own accords, and this was the reason the coachman had shut us up, that his carriage might be imagined empty.

At the time we reached Lisbon everybody was complaining of the weather being uncommonly cold, and, indeed, we felt it so owing to the spaciousness of the apartments, with immense large windows and doors, and no chimneys, as it very rarely happens that the want of a fire is felt. Upon getting out of bed in the morning of the 19th (of February) and looking out of window, I was greatly surprized to see the ground and tops of buildings covered thickly with snow, a circumstance Mrs. Williams said that had not occurred for forty years before. The Catholic clergy, with their usual bigotry, declared this phenomenon portended some dire calamity to the kingdom, to avert which and appease the wrath of an offended God every church in the city was immediately opened and prayers offered for pardon and for mercy.

In consequence of my complaining of the sharpness of a keen northerly wind, our considerate landlady directed her servants forthwith to fix in our sitting-room a stove exactly similar to those used in the cuddies of East India ships during the winter. The funnel passed through one of the panes of glass in a window, but as it failed in performing its function the smoke beat back, soon filling the room and almost suffocating us. This obliged us to open a window, making our alternative to be either perished with cold or smoke-dried and choked.

On the 17th, Mr. Nathaniel Bateman, a member of the Board of Trade in Bengal, arrived. His object in visiting Portugal was, like mine, to obtain a passage from thence to the East. Having had a slight acquaintance with him in Calcutta in the year 1778, we now renewed it, and agreed, if possible, to proceed on board the same ship. Upon making enquiries upon the subject, we had the mortification to learn that no Indiaman would sail at the soonest in less than three months, sad news for me whose cash ran very low. Being without remedy I endeavoured to make the best of the matter that Charlotte might not discover my cause of uneasiness. We therefore spent our time gaily, the mornings in viewing the curiosities of the city, contemplating the numerous mementoes that still remained of the horrid devastations made by the fatal earthquake in 1755, and the remainder of the day in pleasant society. We also went upon parties formed by Mrs. Walpole or Mrs. Warden to the different Royal palaces and principal noblemen's castles, especially those of Cintra and other beautiful spots within twenty miles of the capital, these excursions being made in carriages, on horseback, and donkeys (asses), the latter animals being exclusively for the ladies' use.

One of the greatest attractions for strangers, and which we went to view, is the famous and stupendous aqueduct of Alcantara, which conveys a fine stream of excellent spring water through two lofty mountains and over a wide and deep bottom of a valley to the heart of Lisbon. The height and width of the centre arch over the said valley is said to be such as to admit the largest ship in the British Navy completely rigged, and with every sail set, to pass under it. This magnificent work struck me with surprize and pleasure, while the dreadful havoc committed by the earthquake above alluded to created only melancholy reflections.

The churches in Lisbon are all magnificent and more splendidly decorated than those of any other country I have ever been in. We frequently went to hear high Mass at the church where the King, Queen, and all branches of the Royal Family were present, sitting within a few feet of them. Their Majesties appeared wrapped up in their devotions, but not so the Prince and junior branches, who seemed to be much more engaged in looking at the strangers and making observations to each other than by their prayers.

At the commencement of Lent the theatres, opera house, and every other place of public entertainment were closely shut, nay, with such rigidness was that religious season observed that not even a private dance at the houses of any English resident, or other foreigner, was permitted. After saying this it will hardly be credited, though strictly true, that under the idea of a sacred representation a kind of puppet show was countenanced and supported by the Court and churchmen, which abounded with scenes of the most offensive ribaldry if not absolute blasphemy. The story represented was the destruction of the world by the flood, with the history and proceedings of Noah, that personage appearing in *propria persona* on the stage, and there entering into terms of contract with the chief carpenter of the Royal dockyard to build the ark, in which Master Noah betrays a strong inclination to make a hard bargain with the mechanic. The dialogue throughout abounded with indecencies and the errantest balderdash stuff that ever was uttered. How so inconsistent a thing could be allowed I never was able to discover, nor the origin of it. The strange and incongruous performance concluded by the Virgin Mary, bedizened with jewels and a profusion of gold and silver ornaments, dancing a fandango with our Saviour, his head being covered with an immense full-bottomed periwig well powdered !

We had several very pleasant parties with Mr. De Visme, at a beautiful seat of his a few miles from Lisbon, where he entertained in a manner never surpassed and seldom equalled. The establishment was in every respect princely, the house a perfect cabinet, the grounds laid out with peculiar taste, having in them all the rarest plants of the European world and some even from Asia and America, but what delighted me was the songs of nightingales innumerable pouring out their sweet notes in broad daylight. Mr. De Visme told us he had been at great expense in enticing them by various stratagems to his woods, but had at last so completely succeeded as to have their music for full eight months in the year. This gentleman was brother to the supercargo at China, of whom I have already spoken.

CHAPTER XXVIII

DETENTION AT LISBON AND THE START FOR INDIA

ON the 20th of the month the *Phœbe* frigate, commanded by Sir William Burnaby, arrived in the Tagus with Commodore Johnston on board on his return from the Cape of Good Hope, after his successful attack upon and capture of a number of Dutch ships that had sought to shelter themselves in Saldanha Bay, in which he gained more credit than by his disgraceful battle with the French squadron under Admiral Suffren in Port Praya Bay, and which occurred on his way out. The Commodore left the fleet that had been under his command to proceed to England with the prizes, whilst he, striking his pennant in the line-of-battle ship, hoisted it on board the *Phœbe* and ran into Lisbon for the purpose of marrying Miss Charlotte Dee, a fine woman, but rather masculine both in person and mind.

It was considered very extraordinary that Commodore Johnston should select Sir William Burnaby's ship for such a duty, it being generally known throughout the fleet that they were not upon terms, so far otherwise that the Commodore had more than once threatened to bring Sir William to a court martial for disrespectful and contemptuous treatment of him as his superior officer whilst upon actual service. On the other hand, Sir William denied the charge in pointed terms, avowing, however, without any sort of reservation, his contempt for the Commodore, and that he was determined the moment he ceased to be his commanding officer to call him to a personal account for his tyranny and ungentlemanlike behaviour towards him upon several occasions.

The day after the Commodore arrived he did me the honour of a visit, telling me my father was one of his oldest friends. He brought with him Mr. Henry Warre, who was second mate of the *Seahorse* Indiaman when I went out in her in the year 1777, but was then first lieutenant of the flagship, and had the Commodore's promise to get him made a post-captain on their return to England, and he kept his word, Mr. Warre now being an Admiral.

After sitting an hour with Mrs. Hickey and me, Warre whispered the Commodore, who thereupon looked at his watch, saying, " You are right, Harry, and I thank you for reminding me, for I have been so well entertained here that I forgot what ought to be uppermost in my mind." He then took his leave, going, as I afterwards found, from my lodgings to the English Ambassador's chapel, where he was immediately joined in wedlock to the dashing Charlotte Dee.

The same morning Sir William Burnaby, to whom I had been introduced by my brother some years before, called to see me. Upon my mentioning the visitor who had preceded him, he gave me a long and minute account of his quarrels with Commodore Johnston, whom he abused in the most violent terms, declaring his determination to spit in his face when out of commission, which must happen upon his reaching England, Captain Sutton, who commanded a ship of his fleet, being resolved to bring him to trial for cowardice or something worse in the action with Suffren. " But," continued Sir William, " I shall take good care to chastise him properly before Sutton's attack. I'll make the scoundrel fight me, for want of personal courage is not amongst his faults."

The wedding dinner was given at Mr. Walpole's, all the principal English of the factory being invited by the Ambassador. Mrs. Walpole had let my Charlotte into the secret, but I knew nothing of the occasion of the entertainment until I saw the happy pair there. Soon after the cloth was removed, the Commodore, addressing himself to Sir William Burnaby, said, "If your ship could be ready and it would suit your own convenience, Sir William, I should wish to sail early to-morrow morning." To which Sir William with great formality replied, "The *Phœbe*, sir, is always ready to perform the public duty. She can sail, if such be your order, in an hour, and waits only your directions as commanding officer."

Mrs. Johnston, who was present at this short conversation, directly said she could not leave Lisbon for some days, and therefore Sir William Burnaby need not hurry himself to prepare his ship. Whereupon the Commodore with considerable warmth said, "We must, my dear Mrs. Johnston, embark to-night and sail at daybreak to-morrow." "My dear Mr. Johnston," retorted the new-made bride, "I beg leave to assure you that I will neither embark to-night nor sail at daybreak, or at any other time to-morrow." "By God, madam," said the Commodore, "but you must and shall. His Majesty's ship must not be detained at the caprice of any woman." "By God, sir," replied the high-mettled damsel, "I cannot and, what's more, I will not stir from Lisbon until it is my will and pleasure so to do. As to His Majesty's ship and its being detained or dispatched, I neither know nor care one straw about the matter. Everything relative to her, I presume, depends upon you at present. She is your ship, but be pleased to recollect, sir, that I *am your wife!*" speaking the last sentence in a very sarcastic manner, intending, no doubt, to reproach him for his base treatment of a very respectable, accomplished, and worthy woman whom he had debauched when quite a child, who had borne him two sons, and conducted herself in the most irreproachable manner, being also an exemplary mother. It was notoriously known that he had over and over again promised to marry her. Even when setting out upon the expedition to the Cape of Good Hope he gave her his sacred word of honour to make her his wife upon his return. His squadron touching at Lisbon outward bound he there saw Miss Charlotte Dee, became desperately enamoured, proposed, was accepted conditionally, that is, if he came to complete his offer on his way back from the Cape. He did so, as I have already

related, uniting himself to a bold girl young enough to be his
granddaughter, thus to his eternal shame and disgrace for-
feiting the solemn promise to the much injured mother of his
children, a circumstance with which Miss Dee was said to
be well acquainted. By this infamous conduct, however,
he condemned himself to misery for the remainder of his life,
his Portuguese bride proving as errant a termagant and
tyrant as ever unhappy husband was tied to, and no human
creature pitying him. They sailed for England in the
frigate on the 24th of the month.

About ten days after this unjust connection was effected,
the expedition packet came in from Falmouth. She was
commanded by Captain Brathwaite, a rough seaman of
Herculean form, an old and intimate friend of Mrs. Williams
who had for many years made it a rule upon his arrival at
Lisbon each voyage to give her a hearty kiss, and the
same on his departure for England. I happened to be
present when he entered the house. Walking up to the
jolly hostess, he took her into his arms, giving her a warm
embrace. The salutations being over, she cried out with
great indignation, " Would you believe it possible, my dear
Brathwaite, that old vagabond rascal, that good-for-
nothing Johnston, has married the tartar, Charlotte Dee,
your favourite for the last twenty years, and has just carried
her off with him to England ? " " Has he, by God ! "
replied Brathwaite. " Why, then, I sincerely hope, and
make no doubt, ere long his forehead will be ornamented
with as many antlers as there are piles," pointing down to
an embankment for a wharf that was preparing on the
beach at the foot of the hill on which the hotel stood.

In March I was introduced to Mr. Luis Barretto, a man
endowed by nature with extraordinary talents and elegant
address, though under the unfavourable circumstance of
an extremely dark skin, indeed nearly black. He was the
descendant of a Portuguese race that had for upwards of a
century been settled with much credit upon the coast of
Malabar in the East Indies, and were all opulent. Mr. Luis
Barretto was born under the British Government, being a

native of Bombay, at which place he was brought up by his
father. Being early initiated in trade, and being active
and diligent in commercial pursuits, he, whilst yet a stripling,
amassed considerable wealth, as had likewise an elder
brother, Mr. Joseph Barretto, by similar means, with the
highest reputation for integrity, at Calcutta, in Bengal,
where he had established himself. The spirit of enterprize
that had always predominated in Luis Barretto, induced
him to engage in a speculation of vast magnitude. It was
that of carrying on an exchange of produce from every part
of Europe with India through the medium of Portugal,
and under the flag of that nation, then at peace with all the
world. But being well aware how jealous the French were,
and the rigidness with which that rival of England scrutinized
the traffic conducted by neutral powers, he determined to
use every possible precaution in order to avoid either seizure
or suspicion. In the latter end of the year 1781 he purchased
a ship called the *Hornby*, constructed and built at Bombay
under the immediate eye of the then Governor, who honoured
it with his own name. A stronger or more complete vessel in
every respect never was launched in any country in the world.
Her burthen was upwards of eleven hundred tons. When he
made the purchase she was nearly new, having been off the
stocks only a few months. He afterwards changed the name
of his ship to that of *The Raynha De Portugal*, in compliment
to the Queen.

Mr. Barretto one morning took me on board the *Raynha
De Portugal*, and a most commodious and beautiful ship
I found her. In this visit we were accompanied by a
Mr. Moore, an English gentleman who had recently been at
the head of the Company's marine at Bombay, in which situation he had established his character as a first-rate seaman.
After this visit to the ship I spoke to Mr. Barretto respecting
his letting me accommodation for myself, Mrs. Hickey, and
two servants, to India, which he said I might have, but that
he should not sail for at least three months to come.

I had now the misery to see the health of my darling
Charlotte in a declining state, and that, too, without any

apparent cause, having no particular malady, yet she gradually fell away, entirely lost her appetite and spirits, and felt it unpleasant to move even from one room to another. I consulted Dr. Hare, the principal physician of the British factory, who had the reputation of being very skilful in his profession. After attending her twice a day for some time, trying a variety of medicines, though without advantage, he recommended me to change the air by taking her away from Lisbon. Mr. De Visme, who happened to be visiting me when Dr. Hare gave this advice, immediately offered a country house of his about eighteen miles from the city, in, he said, as healthy a spot as any in Portugal. I accepted his polite offer. Two days after he sent us thither in one of his carriages with a confidential servant, who had orders to supply all our wants. We found it a romantic and beautiful situation, upon a small rise from the sea, from which it was not quite a mile distant. Charlotte was delighted with everything about it, finding material benefit in four-and-twenty hours. She continued mending so rapidly that in ten days her health was perfectly restored. We therefore returned to Lisbon.

Mr. Hoissard having heard of our return, came to invite us to two religious ceremonies which he said were well worth our attention. The first was on Maundy Thursday, when we saw the Queen, in commemoration of the humility of our Lord and Saviour, wash the feet of a number of poor persons, afterwards waiting upon them and supplying their wants during a dinner given to them in a large hall of the palace.

The other spectacle was by far the grandest I ever beheld. It was a celebration of the Resurrection of our Saviour on Easter Day performed in the richest church of Lisbon. About eight o'clock in the morning of Easter Day Mr. Hoissard conducted us to the church, where we were placed in a gallery that commanded the whole interior of the building. During Lent every place of public worship is hung with black cloth, but the church we were in was peculiarly magnificent, the different altars and recesses being hid from the sight by very full curtains of black velvet, daylight being totally excluded by similar curtains, and the church faintly illuminated by large wax candles in immense massy gold and silver stands.

After the performance of a solemn High Mass, at the instant the Resurrection is supposed to take place, a small shrill bell rung amidst the most profound silence, no other sound being heard, when quick as thought, like the best executed change of scene in a pantomime, the whole of the mourning furniture was drawn down, the curtains thrown open, a blaze of light from brilliant sunshine burst in upon us, and at the same moment an admirable band of music, consisting of full four hundred performers, instrumental and vocal, struck up a grand and sublime anthem. The effect is far beyond my powers of description ; it actually made my blood thrill, seeming to electrify the whole audience. Many burst into tears involuntarily, while several ladies fainted. My Charlotte escaped with a good fit of crying, afterwards telling me she never could have had an idea of anything so awfully grand and affecting. I certainly never shall forget the impression it made upon me.

On the 2nd of April two English frigates came in from Gibraltar : the *Cerberus*, commanded by Captain Mann, and the *Apollo*, Captain Hamilton. In the latter I found a former playmate and brother Westminster, a son of the famous Lady Ann Hamilton. He expressed sincere joy at the meeting and renewal of our acquaintance. In the course of conversation I learnt that he had brought with him another esteemed friend of mine, Captain William Cuppage of the Royal Artillery, whom I had known from his early infancy as an élève and protégé of Mr. Burke's. My satisfaction in thus unexpectedly meeting Cuppage was considerably damped at seeing him a cripple, incapable of moving except by the aid of crutches. It arose from the explosion of a shell whilst he was upon duty in the garrison of Gibraltar, which carried away the fleshy part of his thigh, dreadfully injuring his leg also, so that the latter was contracted and drawn up into a position nearly horizontal. All the surgeons that had attended him pronounced him lame for life, the use of that leg being irrecoverably and for ever gone.

In this lamentable state Cuppage was going home with the forlorn prospect of being invalided. He was, however, more fortunate. The medical men of London did not deem it a desperate case. He was put under a course of fumigations and vapour baths, which had the desired effect. Within a twelvemonth he got the foot to the ground, and before the expiration of a second year regained the complete use of the leg. It was, however, considered as a wonderful cure. He has since been upon much active service, is now risen to the rank of Major-General, and walks as well as any man in England, without the least degree of lameness.

Captains Hamilton and Mann, as well as Cuppage, were constantly with us, and with the addition of the lively Nancy Spottiswoode, who had perfectly recovered her health, we made a pleasant little party daily in our apartments, clouded only by my dear girl's again beginning to droop. The surgeon of the *Apollo*, a clever man, said he was convinced nothing would do her so much service as a trip to sea, whereupon Captain Hamilton very kindly offered us his cabin if we would go to England. I had a great inclination to accept the offer, but she would not hear of it, apprehensive that it might interfere with the India voyage, upon which she knew my future welfare depended. In a fortnight afterwards the two frigates sailed.

Mrs. Hickey continuing to decline, Dr. Hare told me confidentially he was convinced the climate of Lisbon was so hostile to her that she would fall a sacrifice if she remained there. He also said, from what he had already seen, he feared the heat of India would never suit her constitution. This was grievous information to me, but upon receiving it I, without hesitation, resolved that she should not accompany me to Bengal, and I broke to her the necessity there was for our separation. As I expected would be the case, she was at first extremely hurt, declaring my refusing to let her go with me would prove more fatal than any climate, that all she desired was to expire in my arms or under my protection. By argument and mild persuasion I at last prevailed on her, and she consented to do whatever I required. For this acquiescence I was in a great measure obliged to the friendly interference of Dr. Hare, Mrs. Walpole and other of our acquaintances at Lisbon, who all exerted themselves to convince Mrs. Hickey of the necessity there was for our separation, at least for a time. I immediately engaged a passage for her and her servant on board the *King George* packet, commanded by Captain Wauchope, who treated her during the voyage like a fond parent. Nothing could exceed his kindness.

Upon our arrival at Lisbon one of our first visitors was Mr. Thomas Hickey, a portrait painter, with whom my family had been acquainted and done him some service in his profession, but I had never before seen or heard of him. After introducing himself and mentioning the obligations he lay under to my father and brother, he told me that he had been taken prisoner by the combined fleets of France and Spain on board an outward bound East Indiaman, in which he had embarked with an intention to follow his business in the Company's settlements; that having obtained permission from the Spanish Government to return to England, he had gone from Cadiz to Lisbon by land, in order to proceed from the latter place in a packet, but on his reaching Lisbon he had so much employment that he had remained there to very good account, had painted most of the English ladies and gentlemen, and was then engaged upon the portraits of several Portuguese of rank. He occupied four handsome rooms on the ground floor of Mrs. Williams's hotel.

When Dr. Hare pronounced the necessity of my Charlotte's leaving me, I applied to my namesake to paint her picture for me in oil colours. He made a good likeness, though strongly marked with the melancholy depicted in her countenance, at the time she sat, from the thoughts of parting. As she insisted upon having my portrait to take with her, I sat, he making an admirable representation of me. Having promised my sister to send her my portrait from India, I thought the meeting with Hickey afforded a good opportunity of being better than my word. I therefore got him to copy from Charlotte's another of myself, and forwarded it also to my sister by her.

On the 5th of May I took a melancholy and, as I really feared, a last farewell of her I loved more than anything upon earth. To attempt to describe the parting would be as impossible as useless. We were in agonies, our mutual friends at last carrying her away in a state of insensibility. I then locked the room door, and sitting myself down at the window fronting the water, watched first the progress of the boat that was conveying my adored girl to the packet, next the packet itself under sail bearing her rapidly away from me. So deep was my grief, and so lost was I in despair, that I attended not to repeated knocks at my door and summonses to dinner. I had no inclination to eat, all appetite was gone with the packet whose progress engaged my sole attention until, passing over the bar and hauling to the northward, she disappeared altogether. I then surveyed with the deepest interest every inanimate object that had ever engaged my Charlotte's attention. Involuntarily, as it were, I threw myself upon the couch on which she used to recline, and not an article of the furniture but became invaluable to me. At a late hour of the night I retired to my desolate, gloomy bedchamber. Oh, what a difference to what I had been used to feel on going to rest ! What a wretched, sleepless night did I pass !

At five in the morning I rose, fatigued, nay, exhausted, with a dry skin and feverish heat that I conceived must produce a severe illness, but which was averted by the unremitting attentions of Dr. Hare and the solacing exertions of a number of friends, especially Mr. Hoissard, who, in a manner, forced me abroad, taking me to Mr. De Visme's, Mr. Paisley's, and other houses. By slow degrees I became more reconciled to what was not to be remedied, but never enjoyed myself in society as thentofore. I derived the greatest consolation from passing two or three hours in a morning with Charlotte's favourite, Nancy Spottiswoode, until, all on a sudden, I thought I perceived a change in her reception, which became formal, cold almost to rudeness, and she seemed anxious to leave me. Unwilling, in spite of appearances, to believe this possible, I mentioned my fears and my surprize to Mrs. Walpole, who instantly exclaimed, " I wonder you have been so long discovering the baseness of the selfish, ungrateful hussy, who almost from the day of Mrs. Hickey's departure began to speak disrespectfully of her, for which I, who knew how kindly and generously she had been always treated by that absent friend, and the number of valuable presents she had received from her, upbraided her for her shameful ingratitude, her want of every honourable sentiment in endeavouring to injure the character of a person who had done nothing but load her with favours and kindnesses. The detestable, unfeeling little wretch is beneath your notice, and certainly shall never more enter my house."

Thunderstruck at what I heard, and at a loss to account for her acting such a part, I immediately went to Nancy and asked what she could mean by it. She had the further meanness and audacity to assert she had never uttered a word to the prejudice of Mrs. Hickey, for whom she felt the utmost affection. I told her she was an infamous liar, in addition to her other vices, and cautioning her against exercising her malignant talents in future upon Mrs. Hickey, lest I should make a severe example of her, I left her weeping, more, I believe, from concern at being discovered in her infamy than from contrition for her fault. From that time I had done with the imp, never taking the smallest notice when we met.

On the 21st of May I had the supreme felicity of receiving a letter from my dearest girl, dated at Falmouth, which she reached after a pleasant passage in eight days. She assured me the voyage had restored her to health. She should therefore look out for the first ship that should sail for India, and embark in it to join me, without whom she did not consider life worth holding.

At the end of the month I finally settled with Mr. Barretto for a passage on board the *Raynha De Portugal* by taking the state-room, a spacious and excellent apartment opening into the great cabin, and having two ports and two large scuttles in it. Mr. Bateman also took a cabin in the steerage of the same ship. That gentleman and myself, at Mr. Barretto's particular request, made a written application to the Portuguese Minister in the Marine Department for his permission to proceed to Goa on board that ship, and we received a ready and polite acquiescence, also in writing. In a day or two afterwards Mr. Barretto brought two young men to my rooms to introduce to me as fellow-passengers, they having been recommended to his attentions by his valuable friend, Mr. Holmes. One of them was Mr. Kemp, going out as a mere adventurer, the other, Mr. Brown, appointed a cadet in the Company's army on the Bombay establishment. Mr. Barretto, when he made these gentlemen known to me, said he should reject all other applications, being resolved not to take any more passengers.

On the 4th of June, while dressing to dine at the Ambassador's, it being our King's birthday, I observed a vessel running up the river from sea with a Union Jack flying at her main-topgallant masthead, by which I knew it to be a packet. I therefore set out for Mr. Walpole's in high spirits, hoping to get a letter from my darling. During dinner the dispatches were brought us, and with them a single letter. Mr. Walpole, looking at the direction, said to his lady, " This is for you, my dear," sending it round to her. Mrs. Walpole, after opening and reading it, made an apology for leaving her company for a few minutes and went out of the room. Upon her return, addressing the party, she said a much-esteemed friend of hers was just arrived from England in the packet, and she had been giving directions for a carriage to go immediately to the hotel and bring her to her. Soon after this the ladies left the table.

After we had been at the bottle about an hour, a servant came to the back of my chair and whispering me, said his mistress requested to speak to me. Astonished at such a summons I followed the man out. At the bottom of the stairs Mrs. Walpole's own female attendant received and conducted me up to her lady's dressing-room, opening the door of which what was my amazement and agitation at my loved Charlotte's rushing into my arms, bursting into tears, and the next moment insensible in a fainting fit. Mrs. Walpole, considerately aware of some distressing incident from the unexpected meeting, had been secretly watching us, and, upon seeing Mrs. Hickey faint, appeared with hartshorn and all the usual remedies administered in such cases. By the application of these medicines she soon recovered and was restored to composure.

Charlotte then briefly informed me that after she left Lisbon she had found herself so miserable that she resolved, no matter how fatal the consequences might prove to herself, once more to rejoin and accompany me to Bengal, adding these words that are indelibly fixed in my memory : " My dearest William, if I am doomed to die an early death, oh, do at least, I beseech you, let me have the consolation of knowing that I shall draw my last breath and heave my last sad sigh in your loved arms. Without you I cannot exist. Besides, my William, I can confidently assure you that my health is entirely restored ; I am as well as ever I was in my life." I felt too happy, too much rejoiced, at once more being able to press her in my bosom to utter a syllable of reproach at her imprudent return, for such it certainly was, and although I kept my fears to myself I could not but feel alarmed for her life.

After Charlotte's recovery from the fainting fit, Mrs. Walpole left us alone for near an hour, when she again entered the room, kindly saying, " Come, come, my friends, I have allowed your *tête-à-tête* to continue long enough. I shall now insist upon your both joining our party at supper and drinking a bumper of burgundy to the health of our Gracious Sovereign, after which we must all join in the merry dance." Taking a hand of each she led us to the room in which the company were assembled. All showed the most pleasing attention to my dear girl, and after a gay, cheerful evening we returned to our hotel in the Ambassador's chariot.

The following morning Charlotte introduced me to Mr. and Mrs. Pawson, who had come out in the packet with her, with a view to get a passage in a Portuguese Indiaman to Bengal, where they were going to reside with a brother of Mr. Pawson's who was in the Company's Civil Service there. She likewise introduced me to Mrs. Aldus and a wild Irish brother-in-law, the lady being on her way to Madeira where her husband was a merchant. Charlotte told me that all these four had behaved to her during the voyage with the utmost kindness, a sufficient inducement to me to treat them with every mark of civility and gratitude in my power. My Charlotte had met Mrs. Aldus at the house of a mutual friend in London, where they agreed to travel together to Falmouth, and did so to their equal gratification.

I found my darling looking remarkably well, and she said she felt perfectly so, but expressed considerable anxiety and fears about her faithful servant, Harriet, whose cough was greatly increased, as was the languor and weakness, and she had a hectic flush in her cheeks, with a brilliancy of eye that I thought augured ill. Doctor Hare, whom I consulted, thought so too, but observed nothing could afford her so fair a chance of getting over the disease as a long voyage. He, however, acknowledged the chances of recovery were much against her.

Upon mentioning to Mr. Barretto Mrs. Hickey's unex-pected return, and that she and her servant would accompany me to India, he directly gave me a small additional cabin adjoining my own for Harriet to sleep in, which would also answer the purpose of a dressing-room for Mrs. Hickey.

The weather now became as oppressively hot as I ever felt it in either East or West Indies, yet it did not prevent our excursions. We had a number of agreeable parties about the country in the vicinity of Lisbon, particularly to Mr. Walpole's country villa, Mr. De Visme's, Sir John Hort's, and other equally charming seats.

In the middle of June Mr. Barretto gave me notice that we

must embark on the 22nd, as he undoubtedly should sail at daylight of the 23rd. My expences at Lisbon had been great ; I was obliged to borrow eight hundred pounds, procured for me by Mr. Hoissard, for the repayment of which I granted bonds, bearing an interest of ten per cent, payable in Bengal.

Upon Mr. Bateman's taking his passage on the *Raynha De Portugal* he proposed to me to join our stock and mess together. Mr. Barretto had previously informed us that the custom of the Portuguese service made it necessary for him to preside at the table of the Captain and officers. With pleasure I embraced Mr. Bateman's offer. He being a bustling, active man, which I, alas, never was, undertook the management and providing of every requisite. Each of us advanced two hundred pounds, for, with the natural liberality of an Orientalist, he spurned at my calculation of paying in proportion to the number of four which my family consisted of, insisting upon the propriety of the table being between us. This sentiment according with my own, and feeling that our situations reversed I should have acted in like manner, I yielded.

Upon Mrs. Hickey's return to Lisbon the second time that unprincipled little jade, Nancy Spottiswoode, had the insolent boldness to call at our apartments, having previously ascertained that I was absent. Finding my Charlotte at home, she had the effrontery to address her as if no duplicity, no ingratitude, had been shown upon her part, and my gentle and sweet girl, notwithstanding I had cautioned her against the arts of the insincere hussy, could not reject her proffered civilities and her friendly professions. She therefore met her avowals of unceasing regard with as much warmth as if they had come from the heart. Unluckily for the hypocrite, I arrived, when indignantly asking how she dared enter my doors after what had passed, she stammered out she had called to see her friend to whom she felt herself obliged. I replied she only rendered herself the more despicable in my eyes, and I had taken care to place her in a just light to Mrs. Hickey. She then departed.

From that day we saw no more of her, though we heard if she was invited to any party at which we were to be she always sent an excuse.

The last ten days of our residence at Lisbon were spent in a round of entertainments given by our hospitable friends. Mrs. Aldus and her brother-in-law had, principally through the intercession of myself and Mr. Bateman with Mr. Barretto, obtained a passage to Madeira in the *Raynha De Portugal*, Mr. Barretto's objection to receiving them solely arising from the possibility of his not touching at the Island if the weather proved boisterous, but the lady being willing to run that risk and we offering them our table, he consented.

We had agreed to dine on board the 22nd, but this was strenuously and successfully opposed by Mrs. Walpole, who insisted upon the whole party spending the last day with her. Mr. and Mrs. Pawson had made every effort to get on board our ship, but Mr. Barretto resisted them all, wishing to preserve his great cabin exclusively for Mr. Bateman, Mrs. Hickey, and myself. They therefore applied for and obtained accommodation in another ship, and sailed for India eight days prior to our departure.

On the 22nd, having finally settled all my accounts, I sent Harriet, who continued in a declining state, with Nabob and our baggage, on board, Charlotte and myself going to dinner at the Ambassador's, where we found most of the principal English inhabitants assembled to bid us adieu. We had a splendid meal, followed by a concert and ball in the evening, at which the beautiful Mrs. Walpole kindly gave me her hand as a partner, and though dancing had never been a favourite amusement of mine so accompanied it proved delightful, and I entered into the full spirit of it. This lovely woman, then in the prime of life and vigour of health, very shortly after we left Lisbon, from neglecting what was at first only a slight cold, fell into a rapid decline that baffled the skill of the most eminent physicians of Portugal and England, within a twelvemonth terminating in her death.

From Mr. Walpole's we went direct to the waterside, where his barge was in waiting to convey us to the ship. At two o'clock in the morning we got on board and took possession of our cabin, where, notwithstanding the greatness of the change, Charlotte and myself slept sound until awakened at seven in the morning by the Padre and ship's crew chanting their matins at the altar which was close to the bulkhead of our apartment. The sound was grand and awful, occasioning in us both very pleasing sensations. Some of the voices were remarkably melodious. We had these prayers four times in the course of each day.

Upon rising and going up on deck, I saw an elegant-looking man walking up and down, who politely bowed to me, Mr. Barretto soon after telling me he was a French gentleman to whom he had given a passage at the particular request of the Marquis de Pombal. Upon entering into conversation with him, I found he had resided many years in the East Indies, having been an officer of rank in the military service of different native Princes. He appeared to be perfectly acquainted with Asiatic politics, possessing a strong natural understanding which had been highly cultivated. Upon further acquaintance I discovered he had encountered many grievous misfortunes, and had been cruelly treated by those who, if honour or conscience had bound them, must have acted very differently towards him. Various instances of the basest ingratitude had in some measure soured his temper, rendering him at times morose or peevish, nevertheless the scholar and well-bred man were always distinguishable in his conduct and behaviour. He was returning to Hindostan powerfully recommended by the Portuguese Government, and with a hope of obtaining restitution from some of those persons who had defrauded him of his just rights. I am sorry to say his name has totally escaped my recollection.

On Sunday, the 23rd of June, 1782, we unmoored at ten o'clock in the morning, dropping down the Tagus until three in the afternoon, when the flood tide coming in and a fresh wind having been blowing all day direct from sea, we were compelled to bring to a few miles below the Castle of Balaam. At five the wind suddenly shifting and becoming favourable, got up our anchor and made sail ; at six passed the bar, soon after which we took a last view of the magnificent capital of Portugal, a city I left with considerable regret, having been received and treated there with the utmost hospitality and kindness by many estimable persons, by some with an affectionate regard I never can forget.

INDEX

and also in the frankest mood of self-revelation. One is charmed to follow him in his adventures. He was a keen observer of men and things, a shrewd judge of character : he associated with many people of worth and note and with few who had not some points of human interest."

Westminster Gazette.—" A remarkably frank and vivid picture of eighteenth-century life in London and abroad. A second volume which has made its appearance is no less interesting than the first."

Daily Chronicle.—" A genuine eighteenth century vignette, a human portrait of a man of fashion. He is perfectly frank about everything. His sprees, his amours, his debts are all entered and you learn to love him for his very failings."

Scotsman.—" Brings before one in a human document of uncommon frankness the figure of a roystering, buckish, fashionable, elegant and fast young man of the period of Smollett's novels ; his book must always remain one of interest and importance for a student of the English social atmosphere of the eighteenth century."

Manchester Guardian.—" A second instalment of a zestful book which has already caused critics to find analogies in Pepys, Fielding, Smollett, Defoe and Barry Lyndon : it is a lively performance."

Daily News.—" One of the happiest discoveries of recent years. Hickey's autobiography has been compared to Smollett and indeed in its breeziness and variety it deserves the comparison."

Sunday Evening Telegram.—" The first volume was rightly acclaimed as one of the biggest literary finds of modern days. The second volume is every bit as interesting as its predecessor. There is not a dull page, and the light shown on life in fashionable circles in the middle of the eighteenth century is as good as anything we have had since the great novelists of the period."

Yorkshire Post.—" About as lively as anything to be found in Fielding and Tobias Smollett. His adventures are related with droll humour."

Sunday Times.—" The second volume has as marvellous a resemblance to a Smollett romance as its predecessor—records irregular love intrigues a Peregrine Pickle never bettered, and has a wonderful study of almost insane jealousy."

Sheffield Telegraph.—" He has written so intimate a picture of the life of 1775 onward that his book will live in literature with some of the greatest autobiographies."

Sportsman.—" In writing these memoirs he did the world a service he can hardly have foreseen. They rank with the best extant, not only Pepys but Benvenuto Cellini's."

Country Life.—" The picture of London in the middle years of the reign of George III is inimitable."

Outlook.—" He is interested in everything and his interest makes every page interesting also."

The Tatler.—" This new volume is equally as delightful, as amusing, as interesting and (whisper it low) as indiscreet as the first volume."

Land and Water.—" As good reading as the first volume. Every line he writes has an interest : it is human and full of life, and much is of historical value. These fascinating memoirs."